das

Lillian Fuller
The author of the family
from a runner-up —
Harriet A. Gaul
Pittsburgh Pa.
1941.

JOHN ALFRED BRASHEAR

PENNSYLVANIA LIVES

(Volumes previously published)

JOHN WHITE GEARY
Soldier-Statesman
1819–1873
By
Harry Marlin Tinkcom

JOHN and WILLIAM BARTRAM
Botanists and Explorers
1699–1777   1739–1823
By
Ernest Earnest

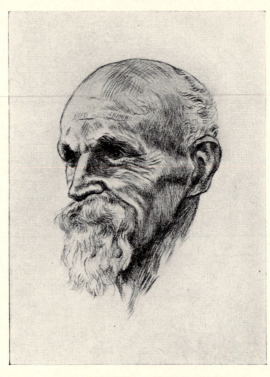

JOHN ALFRED BRASHEAR

JOHN ALFRED BRASHEAR

Scientist and Humanitarian

1840–1920

By

HARRIET A. GAUL and RUBY EISEMAN

UNIVERSITY OF PENNSYLVANIA PRESS

PHILADELPHIA

1940

FOREWORD

Scientists, educators, and school children of western Pennsylvania are equally familiar with the name of "Uncle John" Brashear, who was voted the "most distinguished citizen of Pennsylvania."

This young millwright, who worked so enthusiastically during his leisure hours to become a lens maker, eventually achieved world-wide recognition for his instruments of precision. To appraise the part his ingenious talent played in the scientific pioneering of his time, one should recall the handicaps which impeded progress of research in the new science of astrophysics sixty years ago. Then, equipment of the necessary high degree of accuracy was not immediately available. Instruments were devised and constructed as the need for them arose, and there was a dearth of technicians to supply them. Some scientists had to send to Europe for sensitive instruments which lost much of their value in transport. Others had to make their own apparatus with inadequate tools and materials. All of which involved a very costly expenditure of the time and services of the foremost astrophysicists of the century.

Brashear was early imbued with the desire to disseminate a knowledge of the heavens through a more general use of the telescope. In this ambition he was encouraged and materially aided by his wife, Phoebe. Together they completed their first lens in 1876, and his hobby then became his life work. In the course of his experiments he developed the famous Brashear Process for silvering the front surface of mirrors which is in general use at the present time.

His contract to silver the heliostat mirror for Langley's Mt. Whitney Expedition in 1881 marked the advent of John A. Brashear, the optician and toolmaker, to the scientific world. He was the first man to succeed in producing rock-salt prisms in America. His instruments were soon to be found in every important observatory in the world. Characteristic of the man and the artisan is a letter to Langley, dated 1886, in which he writes, "My humble desire is to give a good account of my 'stewardship' . . . . I may and do make mistakes of judgment but I hope I shall never have the charge of mistakes of carelessness." The record of his stewardship is written in the scientific achievements of those who used his instruments. Langley, Keeler, Young, Campbell, Michelson, and Rowland were among those who availed themselves of his prisms, lenses, mirrors, and plane surfaces for use in their original research. His most valuable contribution to astronomical science is the thirty-inch Thaw Photographic Refractor, the finest and best instrument of its kind in existence today. With this telescope the Allegheny Observatory leads the world in the determination of stellar parallaxes.

Contemporaries honored him with medals, fellowships in scientific societies, and several honorary degrees. But the dream of Dr. Brashear's youth was realized in the dedication of the new Allegheny Observatory equipped with a public telescope and a lecture hall free to the people.

FRANK C. JORDAN

Allegheny Observatory, Pittsburgh
October 1940

CONTENTS

JOHN ALFRED BRASHEAR *Frontispiece*
  Etching by Louise Boyer

                                                    Page
FOREWORD   v
  By Frank C. Jordan

Chapter
    I AN ILL WIND   1

   II THE THREE RIVERS   5

  III AS THE TWIG IS BENT   12

   IV SO IS THE TREE INCLINED   20

    V THE HOUSE ON HOLT STREET   30

   VI THE FIRST LENS   39

  VII MOLTEN SILVER   51

 VIII "WHEN THE MORNING STARS SANG TO-
         GETHER"   61

   IX THE TELESCOPE FINDS AN ANGEL IN THE SKIES   71

    X WINGS OVER ALLEGHENY   82

   XI THE GODS OF THE MILLS   93

  XII THE GODS OF THE MOUNTAINS   101

 XIII "INNOCENTS ABROAD"   108

Chapter   *Page*
   XIV   STEEL KINGS AND ASTRONOMERS ROYAL   117

    XV   "MEET DR. BRASHEAR"   124

   XVI   THE CREST OF THE HILL   133

  XVII   "SUN, MOON, AND STARS FORGOT"   142

 XVIII   THE DEMISE OF "WUP"   149

   XIX   SUMMONS FROM MUSKOKA   159

    XX   BAGPIPES AT SKIBO   170

   XXI   "OVER A ROUGH ROAD TO THE STARS"   178

  XXII   HENCHMAN TO THE SKIES   188

 XXIII   "SWIFTER THAN A WEAVER'S SHUTTLE"   198

BIBLIOGRAPHICAL NOTE   211

INDEX   215

I

AN ILL WIND

THERE was a high wind from the northwest bearing down on the forks of the Three Rivers, that April day in 1845, when a washerwoman started the great Pittsburgh fire.

The wind rocked the gaily painted side-wheelers drawn up by the wharf below the Monongahela House, setting their glass chandeliers to tinkling while their captains clinked glasses with their clients, the coal barons and southern planters, at the famous bar just above. It tossed the ferries crossing the Ohio below the Point, and made long chains of flatboats swerve from their course coming down the Allegheny. The greening trees before the ironmasters' mansions on lower Liberty Avenue tossed in the welcome spring breeze, and from open windows in the cluttered millworkers district the Scotch-Irish leaned to air their linen and German hausfraus shook out their feather beds.

The wind had driven all the fog out of the "Smoky City" and was about to make the spring cleaning thorough by finishing up with fire. Many a housewife, since, has been almost willing to burn down the city if thereby she could get her man's overalls clean and the grit out of the graying sheets.

There was nothing exceptional in a woman's taking advantage of the first sunshine after the "smog" of winter to heap up her outside fire near the common pump and set her boiler on a makeshift stove-top over ill-balanced bricks. To wash out-of-doors was an instinct left from the days and the countries from which these settlers had recently migrated, where all women gather at the side of the stream and pound their clothes clean on the stones. Nor was it exceptional that such a washerwoman with her world-old instinct for gossip should wander away to her neighbor's yard while the water was heating.

What was unusual was the wind, which fanned the unguarded flames against a near-by icehouse. But the ice was also packed with sawdust. While the washerwoman's back was turned not only her water boiled but sparks leaped to the wooden shanties and fences which hemmed in the little back yard on Ferry Street, and jumped to the Globe Cotton Factory on Second Avenue, where nemesis really began. The city, which had long cried to Heaven for a good washing, was licking its face like a cat, to get clean, and licking it with flames.

There was a great gong-ringing and wagon-tire beating to summon the volunteer fire department, and a fast scurrying for uniforms and helmets as rival organizations ran down the narrow streets dragging their hose, and vaulting the pigs wallowing in their way. Clubs who fought each other vigorously at each city election and spent their lighter moments at firemen's balls for the benefit of their brass-trimmed engines, discarded rivalry in a common opportunity for adventure. But the only reservoir they could draw on was choked with mud from the last flood, and their new hand-pumps brought forth only a sandy trickle. The wind roared on up Second and Third Avenues to Market Street, and while crowds of onlookers drew back gasping in the smoke, the red flames rushed on unchecked toward Smithfield and Grant. Only the partisan efforts of the crack Eagle company saved the Third Presbyterian church, but the Bank of Pittsburgh, which had the temerity to lock its doors and rely on its advertisement of being fireproof, was gutted to its vaults.

Thousands of Pittsburgh's pioneer citizens gathered to watch, and to loot when no one else was watching. Men dragged furniture to the streets, but there were no drays available to take it further and what was salvaged by day was stolen by night. Only two lives were lost, but householders later found themselves stripped of what to most Scotchmen is dearer than life itself, their possessions.

Twenty squares and a thousand buildings were reduced to ashes before nightfall when the red glare smoldered out on the bare slopes beyond Pipetown. The new Monongahela House, proud purveyor to the river-boat trade, had nothing left but some wet, red velvet carpeting; the gas works was gone, the

Scotch Hill Market House, whatever was burnable in several iron foundries on the river front, and most important to our story, two glass works, one of which was the pioneer Bakewell Company, famous for its flint glass.

Among the curious who poured into the city to see the wreck of the fire was a Squire Wampler from McKeesport. The news of the conflagration, and even the sight and sound and smell of it, had swept up and down the river towns, and many had hurried from the "sous-side" over the Smithfield Bridge, before it, too, sprang into flames. Crowds straggled in from Allegheny, also, and from its "lower city," called Manchester. They came up the Ohio from Wheeling, down the Allegheny River from the lumber camps, down the Monongahela from the forks of the Youghiogheny. They put out in flatboats or rowboats or followed the covered-wagon trails that all converged at Pittsburgh.

So he was only following natural events when this wandering squire, who was a "lover of astronomy," decided the moment had come for the furthering of a certain enterprise he had long kept in mind. He looked at the glare in the April sky that blotted out his beloved moon, and wished for the hundredth time that he had a telescope which could pierce the smoky atmosphere. But he could not afford to buy a telescope; there were only a few in the whole of America at that time. He decided to do something about it.

For Squire Wampler had already acquired a fine piece of French plate glass that he was saving for a lens, but he had no hard flint glass with which to combine it. He thought of this as his team jogged down the corduroy road toward Pittsburgh. Another thought took shape as he crossed the river by ferry, finding the bridge down. As he stood idly at dusk, watching the stray cats slink through the débris of the fire, he felt impelled to join them. Stealthily as a beachcomber (for he was an honorable and well-known gentleman with no vice except that of being an amateur astronomer, which was to say being considered a lunatic or crank), he poked about in the ruins of the

Bakewell Company for the treasure most dear to his heart, and suddenly stooping, thrust something craftily into his coat-tail pocket and hurried away with his find.

As early as 1818, the Bakewell and Page Company, who were making a great name for themselves, designed a set of flint glass for the table of President Monroe, "each piece engraved with the arms of the United States." But famous as that service had been, it was not to become as famous as one of the pieces of broken glass picked out of the ashes of the Great Fire by Squire Wampler of McKeesport. For with that bit of fire-hardened flint glass, combined with his own French crown glass, he made the lens for his telescope, the first on this side the Alleghenies. And with that telescope he toured the river towns and for five cents a look showed the wonders of the heavens to the residents of the Three Rivers.

McKeesport lies up the winding Monongahela River halfway between Pittsburgh and Brownsville. And in Brownsville was a lad of nine who was taken by his grandfather Smith to look through this itinerant telescope. What he saw through the lens was Saturn and all its rings, a sight he never forgot. But what he saw with his mind's eyes was a vision of all the stars of the firmament accessible to any small boy who cared to look at them—free. To this he dedicated his life. His name was John Brashear.

II

THE THREE RIVERS

THE old brick inn built by John Brashear's grandfather still stands halfway up the hill on Market Street in Brownsville. Halfway up, that is, if you have arrived over the Monongahela Bridge from Pittsburgh. But in the days when it was new, before 1800, it was halfway down the hill, on the road from Virginia, and therefore a natural stopping place for the great overland stages.

A solid oak door set in a wide portal opens to a huge hall, with public rooms on either side and kitchens to the rear, and up the broad staircase a windowed hallway is lined with high-ceilinged bedrooms. Foursquare and strong, it has stood its ground for a hundred and fifty years and, although crowded at present between encroaching buildings, still retains its dignity.

Rows of other two-story brick dwellings line the road climbing the heights, rising tier on tier as they do in all the river towns, flush with the street, their gardens sheltered behind, with here and there an alleyway granting a vista of flowers and a back gallery. A nostalgic quiet haunts the hill that formerly echoed to the rattle of wagon wheels, the toot of the driver's horn, and the answering deep-throated hoot of the river boats waiting for passengers and Potomac freight at the foot of the cobbled street. For Brownsville was long a way-station from the settlements in Virginia to the forks of the Ohio at Pittsburgh, and as the Ohio country beyond Pennsylvania was considered a part of the old Virginia colony at the time this inn was flourishing, it caught the westbound trade.

Basil Brashear, who built it, was the son of Otho Brashear who migrated from Maryland with the famous brothers Brown, Thomas and Basil, founders of the town of Brownsville. Otho further cemented the link by marrying into the founders' family, taking to wife a sister of the Thomas Brown who purchased the land on which the town was laid out. Brownsville was not incorporated until 1815, at which time Basil Brashear, the inn-keeper, is recorded as a member of the first council, and his name is on the vestry of the old Episcopal church in whose fenced-in churchyard he now lies; which makes him one of the first citizens of the first families. This was no milltown in the early days, with dour Scotch-Irish influence tempered with polyglot miners ruthlessly brought from Central Europe. The Church of England was established by settlers from the colony of Virginia, and with them came a liberal Catholic element straight from Queen Mary's Land.

The Brashear family had been French Huguenots who mi-grated from France in 1658 to the James River settlements whence they soon moved on to Calvert County, Maryland. The name was then Brasseuir, changed in 1700 by some dissident descendants to Brashier, and a few years later further anglicized to Brashear.

The Brashears and Browns, however, were not the first to try their fortunes on the Monongahela. There had been a stock-ade and trading post at the mouth of Redstone Creek as early as 1753 which developed into Redstone Old Fort, well known on the Virginia-Ohio route. This was followed by Fort Burd, and in 1774 a Tomahawk Claim was established by Captain Mi-chael Cresap from Old Town, Maryland. By the time the Brashears arrived in 1785 one had to buy his land from previous settlers. The deed for the strip on the hillside where Basil Brashear built his inn was recorded in 1795 as "12 pounds sterling annual ground rent five shillings every Christmas day forever, also one fifth of all good and silver found," the latter being the fee to the king continued in the old leases.

In 1800 Brownsville was so much larger than the struggling town at Fort Pitt, beginning to be called Pittsburgh, that the Cavaliers who settled there said that no great city would ever be formed at that traders' village below them, for it was too near. Simultaneously with Pittsburgh, Brownsville built shipyards and launched her own river boats and commenced to mine coal and iron. All the traffic went by river, and great trains of wagons carrying produce converged at Brownsville for shipment to the forks at Pittsburgh, and so on down the Ohio to Louisville and the Mississippi.

The wharves were piled high with goods from both directions, and in the spring hundreds of migrating families waited there, camping in their covered wagons until the ice melted and let them proceed by flatboat on down the great routes to the west. The Conestoga wagons were so named from the town in eastern Pennsylvania from which they started out. The prairie schooners were supposed to have looked like ships on the western plains with their billowing canvas tops, but long before they disembarked on the further shore of the Mississippi they were like schooners on the rivers, for their wheels were taken off at Brownsville and stored, and the base of the wagon rested on a flatboat that drew little water and was abandoned or sold at the end of the journey. They went down river with their canvas tops still sheltering their families, with grandma sitting knitting in the stern, dogs barking, and one of the boys playing the flute on the driver's seat, now become the lookout.

The inn of Basil Brashear must have prospered, and its cobbled court must have echoed to the shouts of hilarious arrivals after the long trek over the rough mountain roads. It is said that barrels of rum always stood in the hall, and when Lafayette was entertained there in his memorable visit of 1826, French champagne had been brought up by river from New Orleans.

John Brashear's mother never forgot that celebration. She was a little girl of six whose father, Nathaniel Smith, lived near-by on the Albany road. It was Nathaniel who first showed John the stars through Squire Wampler's telescope, and by so doing showed him his destiny.

Not so much is recorded of the Smith ancestry as of the Brashear side of the house, but more is known of them as individuals. Nathaniel came from Massachusetts, a practical New England influence for his grandson, and his wife from Phoenixville, an even more practical Pennsylvania German.

They lived in Allegheny at least part of their married lives, for one of the family stories is that their daughter Julia, John's mother, in her childish play fell into the old aqueduct and was barely saved from drowning.

This would have been about 1835, for the aqueduct was the final flourish of the Pennsylvania canal system, constructed like a water-bridge over a river to bring the towboats across the Allegheny to their basin on Liberty Avenue. The success of steam trains, however, put an end to all such enterprises before the canal was even paid for, and the same men who promoted it financed the new Pennsylvania Railroad.

Low water on the Monongahela, which had only the inadequate beginnings of its present system of dams and locks, had somewhat discouraged river traffic as early as 1825. The new National Pike built across the southern part of the state touched at Brownsville, as now, and at "Little Washington," and terminated at Wheeling. This was a federal project, hotly contested in the state legislature, to give wagon trains the opportunity of transferring their overland freight to high water on the Ohio, and avoid the Point at Pittsburgh. For a while it looked as if Pittsburgh was going to be sidetracked, and there was a panic in 1827. The canal was hurried to completion on the Altoona portage route from Harrisburg, only to be superseded in a few years by the trains which shortly came puffing over the mountains. Brownsville, however, still caught the covered-wagon trade. Merchandise worth $2,000,000 was shipped through this junction in 1845, while only $185,000 worth used the new contraption on the tracks.

Modes of transportation changed rapidly in those days, and so did the passengers. There was a constant shuttling between river towns. Perhaps it was the sight and sound of the gaily painted packets, the roaring excitement on the docks, the singing darky stevedores, which tempted city folks up the gangplank. Nathaniel Smith seems to have divided his time all his life between Brownsville and Pittsburgh.

His daughter Julia must have remembered Lafayette's visit

at the flower-strewn inn as part of a happier childhood when she found herself employed in the Blackstone Cotton Factory in Allegheny. Another illustrious name was on that pay-roll later, Andrew Carnegie, bobbin-boy. He says the time shift was from dark to dark for a dollar and twenty cents a week. Girls earned twice that—and struck, ungratefully, when the ten-hour law was passed by the state and the millowners said they couldn't pay them so much for so few hours and asked them to take a cut. This was the first great strike of women in the United States, in 1843. But by that time Julia had become a school teacher under her father's tutelage, and was back in Brownsville and married.

Nathaniel Smith was a jack of many trades and master of them all. As a master-mender, he set the hours striking with the precision of the Brownsville town crier, and on his trek back and forth to Pittsburgh mended the German settlers' cuckoos and made the moons rise again in the tall "Dutch" clocks. As a master-mechanic he made some of the first gyroscopes in western Pennsylvania, built an electric engine, adapted a machine for the new Morse telegraph, and constructed an apparatus for photography. As a musician he not only could play the piano and organ, the flute, the flageolet, and the violin, but he made musical instruments. He made his beloved grandson, John, an E flat clarinet. And all of these instruments he could and did repair, tuning the few pianos on his route down the river and replacing a G string on many a mountaineer's fiddle. As a lecturer he was in demand on more rostrums than at the general store cracker barrel. No social gathering at church, no camp-meeting was complete without an address by Nathaniel Smith. What dismayed his audience and gave him the reputation of a seer was that he mixed his theology with discourses on the stars (as his grandson did after him) hoping that God's Heaven, with such help, would come closer.

It is as an astronomer that he most deeply influenced his wide-eyed grandson, John. He told him stories of the great comet of 1843, and of the meteoric display ten years before which had made all men sky-conscious. His hobby was a dog-eared copy of Dr. Dick's *Celestial Scenery*, over which he burnt much midnight oil when fog prevented a more personal survey. And as he followed Dr. Dick, who at first had been a school teacher, through his dedication to astronomy and later to religion, he came to consider his book, *The Christian Philosopher*, as another gospel. All of these works he kept on a special shelf, and as soon as small John could reach them he made their contents his own.

Julia's father, the above scientist, was considered to make a good living when he earned twenty-five dollars a week, but part of his income was always deflected toward his experiments. Julia, one of the six children, had to teach school both before and after she was married. Her husband, "Brown" Brashear, was one of the fourteen sons and daughters of the prosperous innkeeper Basil, and became a saddler by profession, a logical and at first a lucrative calling for anyone dwelling on a national turnpike. But he was not robust enough to cope with changing conditions. His disposition was affable (he was the leader of the town band), and all his ways were honorable (he would not press anyone for a bill but trusted them to pay when they came back from the west), yet he never made any success of his various undertakings. There was no leaning on him for a boy of John's temperament; the tree embraced the vine. So it was well for the child that he had the loyal support in his youth of that grandfather whose quizzical eyes turned always to the stars, and that besides the patriarchal influence, he had on his mother's side of the house the practical watchmaker who gave him the use of his hands.

From his grandfather, Basil Brashear, he inherited his aristocratic features and mode of thought, a noblesse oblige that made it imperative for him to give accounting of his stewardship of talent to those thousands who were to call him "Uncle John." From the Brashears, also, he inherited his genius for fellowship, his tendency to turn his own home into an inn, his joy in feeding all and sundry whether he could afford to or not, and his ability, when the time came, to take his place as an equal at the table of princes.

But without Grandfather Smith it is doubtful if his gifts would have matured. Nathaniel Smith was the one who understood this stripling with the direct gaze and piercing eyes, which, from childhood to old age, looked straight into the sky and unequivocally returned the gaze of Heaven.

III

AS THE TWIG IS BENT

JOHN was the oldest child of Julia and Brown Brashear, born November 24, 1840.

What stars stood watch in the firmament that night, when a little boy who lived only to understand them opened his eyes on a bleak Brownsville hill?

The years brought six brothers and sisters, Ella, William, Charles, Frank, George, and Mary. One of them, Charles, died very young, yet John would always say of them, "We are seven." His devotion to his family was one of the fundamentals of his life.

Under Julia's thrifty care and their father's easy geniality they grew up as naturally as the flowers in the garden of their hillside home, a tiny two-room cottage on Huron Avenue, whose front yard was so steep a child could have slid quite down to the Monongahela River winding its way below them.

From here they could listen for the river boats' whistles at the wharf, see the log rafts floating past on the high spring waters and watch the camping caravans of overland "schooners" waiting for their transfer to the flatboats with the melting ice. The sound of far-off confusion was tempered by the song of birds. Without leaving their own small domain, the panorama of the settling of the west was unrolled before them. Daily, John looked out on a fair sheet of water shadowed by high cliffs. His eye fell downward to its blue ribbon, and lifting, encompassed the hills.

And above the hills, the stars. From this high vantage point they seemed to touch the facing mountain, where often the moon rested for a moment before she disappeared.

John Brashear was early conditioned for just such a way of living, and for no other. Years later, when he chose a site for his own home in Pittsburgh, he hunted until he found a replica of his father's hillside. His house on Holt Street, on the South

Side, stands in the same relation to the Monongahela as does his early boyhood home in Brownsville. Always must he look down on the feverish river, always raise his eyes to the cool hills, and above them to the eternal loneliness of the stars.

John may have been one of seven, but his dependence on his grandfather Smith was that of an only child, as if Nathaniel were his father instead of his grandfather. Nathaniel was the one who showed him the constellations and taught him the magical names of the stars, explained the ways of the moon and tides and helped him watch for planets in their appointed place and season. Often after the older children were safely in bed, their bewildered mother would look for her oldest and find him flat on his back on the sloping bank below the house, gazing up at the sky, oblivious to the night in relation to time, aware only of its relation to space.

What should a woman do with a boy who wouldn't sleep if there was a full moon shining? Who wouldn't even come into the house as long as the stars were out. Who spent his play hours listening to the birds, yes, and talking to them, too! Who learned to imitate their calls so well that often his friends would look up from their blackberrying expecting to see the yellow wing of a wild canary, or the blue flash of a jay, and find only Johnny.

A born ventriloquist, he could have earned a living at mystifying the simple river folk much more easily than by the course laid out by his grandfather. To the end of his life he loved to amuse children with this delightful gift. But on the hills of Brownsville his ability set him apart from his fellows—a sort of St. Francis, communing with the birds.

He was only five when he planted the feathers of a hen in the hope that a Plymouth Rock would arise. From that time his mother decided he was called to the ministry. Surely a boy who believed so implicitly in the resurrection, even of a chicken, was marked for Heaven. Was he not always turning his eyes in that direction?

Julia was by inheritance a Puritan, by conviction a fundamentalist, and by conversion a Methodist. Her husband was by inheritance an Episcopalian, and no convictions or conversions disturbed him further. However, since Methodism in America stemmed from the Church of England, as did the Episcopal church, there was no religious conflict in the family. "Wesleyanism" was sweeping the South in the early 1800's, and only the atheistic followers of Thomas Paine escaped its contagion. Presbyterianism flourished where the Scotch-Irish ruled the mill towns such as Pittsburgh, but throughout the rural districts the circuit riders crusaded with their saddlebags packed with Bibles and temperance tracts, apostles of the new religion.

When John was a boy, huge revivals enlivened the river towns, and an epidemic of hymn tunes stilled the voices of the minstrel men who up to this time had monopolized amusement on the showboats. "My Old Kentucky Home," written by that Pittsburgh boy down the river, gave way to "When the roll is called up yonder I'll be there," and it was not long before Stephen Foster's genius was commandeered for camp meetings.

With everyone taking up Methodism it seemed to John's mother that her son's peculiar gifts would lead far. It was necessary to have some schooling, that is true, but she was thankful that Methodist ministers were not obliged to graduate from any college. They relied on oratory to keep their congregations spellbound. And certainly John was a born preacher. Was he not often found down in the pasture at dusk, leading the bossies not back to the barn, but up the sawdust trail? For anyone could see him walking up and down, gesticulating, practising his preaching on the cows!

But if anyone had come close enough to hear what John was saying when he thought he was alone, derision might have turned to surprise. He always began with "Let the stars of the twilight therefore be dark," and however he wandered from his text it always ended, "When the morning stars sang together and all the sons of God shouted for joy." John may have been apprenticed to Wesley, but he was a follower of Job.

So they let him go to school for a few months each winter, three to be exact, and with the other boys and girls he marched up the stairs of the market hall on Jeffries Common, to the two upper rooms presided over by Joshua Gibbons and George Wilkinson. The pupils furnished their own chairs, so anything from a rush-bottom to a ladder-back was drawn up before the long wooden shelf that served for common desk. If a growing boy became restive under these cramped conditions he could always stand at the blackboard and practise writing in round Spencerian hand, "Pizarro conquered the Aztecs of Peru," until he rested his back. John was good in mathematics, but what he laid most stress on in his schooldays was the time he became sick at recess on a "Lady-Finger" cigar. Kentucky tobacco, brought up on the keelboats, cured him more quickly of smoking than all the admonitions of his mother.

For desk-companion he had Richard Knox, brother of the better known Philander of the United States Senate, who was also a Brownsville boy. And out of hours he haunted the wharves with his pals, Tom and John Walsh, and fished off the ferry with Will Sheets, who later married his sister Ella. These names he never forgot, nor the name of his only teacher, the erudite and patient Wilkinson.

The boys played ball with a makeshift made by unwinding yarn from their knitted stockings and rolling it up around a piece of leather cut from an old boot. For bat they used a flat paddle which John's ingenuity was called upon to whittle into shape. And the shouting was just as loud over their game of "corner ball" as it would be today on the same commons.

The shipyards are gone now, where John used to watch the building of the packets. The very names of the river boats are nostalgic—the *Gallatin* for the great man who owned the landing up the river, the *Franklyn* for the patriot of Philadelphia, the *Fayette*, the same name as the county, the *Telegrapher*, which would be as new to them as if we named a ship the *Television*.

When the captain was busy casting off, the boys would sometimes have a chance to stow away in the cargo going downstream, and considered the long walk home over the hills part
of the experience when they were relentlessly put ashore at the
next landing.

Once in a while they would have a passage paid to Pittsburgh,
perhaps to have a tooth pulled by an expert barber-surgeon,
never for pleasure in those stringent days. Their suits were
made by their mothers, mostly from materials woven on their
looms, but sometimes of heavy woolens sold by Scotch peddlers.
Dressed in his brief coat and long pants, with his hair trimmed
under a bowl before he started, his lunch in a "poke" (a newspaper cost twenty-five cents and was not to be wasted), his
cobbler-made shoes cramping his overgrown feet, a boy would
embark for the nine-hour journey to the city. One of the reasons the trip took so long was that anywhere a captain sighted
a customer waving a sheet on the bank, he turned his nose to
the shallows, and with stern wheel churning, threw a plank
ashore. Cows, mules, and children were equally welcome, and
on the return trip the chanting Negroes piled high the decks
with bales of cotton from the South.

The arrival of a packet was announced by the town crier
who stumped up and down the hill announcing the news on the
river front and highway. When the town crier shouted that a
wagon train was arriving over the National Pike the boys ran
out on the road to see what they could salvage. For it was the
law that anything falling off the back of a jolting wagon could
not be retrieved on a government highway, but belonged to
anyone who found it, and many a chicken coop and bedstead
changed hands on the Brownsville hill.

Of especial interest to Johnny was his grandfather Smith's
workshop. Any such collection of tools always fascinated him,
for the intricacies of lathe and pulley, crank and buzz saw, were
no mystery to such a boy, but the road to achievement. Here,
in the shadows smelling of shavings, with sunlight slanting
through open shutters, he could lose himself in the wonders of

mechanics. He learned more useful things under Nathaniel's eye than were ever dreamed of in the tightly closed schoolhouse.

For recreation in the winter months there was the singing school presided over by his mother. Julia reveled in hymn tunes, and pumped the melodeon with her feet while one free hand beckoned and hushed the untutored voices. She taught Johnny to read music. Her husband went further than this— Brown organized a band when trade was slack, and taught his son to play the drum.

On one occasion he took him along in the high bandwagon with its hilarious crew bound down the pike for Canonsburg to give a concert at Jefferson College. Johnny enjoyed the drive, the dinner, and the excitement, but there was a wistful look on the lad's face as he climbed back up again behind the bedecked horses to return home over the mountains. He was saying farewell to the only college campus he had ever seen, and he took it for granted he would never be back there. For fifty years this was true. By the time half a century had gone past, Jefferson College had combined with the one at Washington, Pennsylvania, and the wistful drummer boy returned by urgent invitation to receive an honorary LL.D.

The only education offered him was when he was fifteen, and his grandfather Smith, having secured a position in the Pittsburgh mills, took him along and paid his tuition at Duff's Mercantile College, the earliest business school west of the Alleghenies.

This proved a well-meant mistake, for the boy from Brownsville, while good at mathematics, was very homesick adding up figures with the Scotch, and spent most of his time helping Nathaniel at the more congenial task of packing spikes for the firm of Lewis, Oliver, and Phillips. The course, however, required only a few months, and was finished painfully, with credit, and soon John returned to his beloved river town to try his expert double-entry system on a grocery store. For this he proved over, instead of under-educated.

The *Brownsville Clipper* then took him on its staff, and he gives no reason for leaving that newspaper presided over by the famous editor, Seth Hurd, except that he could not stand being called a "printer's devil." One wonders if his mother was behind this decision, too. Perhaps the objectionable word was so taboo in her vocabulary that she preferred to let him starve rather than have at her table a son suffering under such a misnomer. Perhaps it was because, in those days, all boys turned quickly from one job to another, without the fear they have today of ending by having none.

The country was young, and it was expected that any youth could easily become president of whatever firm he cared to enter if only he had pluck. Success required merely the right toe-hold. Another wrong start for John was a brief experience with an auctioneer, who disillusioned him by offering defective goods at high prices. John's sympathies were always with the buyer rather than the seller. He had not the makings of a merchant prince. Finally he came to rest in the engine works of John Snowden and Sons, on the flats by the river below his home, and his hold on the ladder had begun.

This apprenticeship as pattern-maker for boat engines was his father's idea; so, after all, the paternal influence was more congenial than his mother's stubborn dream for the ministry. However, she kept him reading the prescribed books all this time and did not give up until the final cataclysm.

At Snowden's Mills John assisted at making drawings and sometimes used his Duff's Mercantile education by aiding the owner's son, Nelson, on the payroll. He learned to install the completed engine, and credit must be given his grandfather Smith for his success in finally mastering his tools. The work was difficult and demanded great ingenuity, for he had to bend his long back under the deck above to bore a hole fifteen inches deep with an inch-and-a-half auger in a space of less than a yard, and hit the stringpiece below not over ten inches wide. Three years of this sort of thing and he was equipped for any emergency in the Pittsburgh mills.

In 1859 he set off for Louisville at the falls of the Ohio. In an age when every public utility had yet to be built, a young mechanic was not long seeking work, and he arrived in Kentucky in time to help construct the engines the Dennis Long Company were installing for the new waterworks. He was also fortunate in being able to make his home with old friends from Brownsville, Jack Nieman and his wife. Many a warm evening under a southern moon the three young people sat out by the river while John played on his flute.

These were his last peaceful days. His earnings had been taxed by sending money home and he had saved nothing in two years of employment when the Civil War broke out, and all work on public improvements was suspended. He was so stranded in the general upheaval that he could only think of turning his skill at woodwork into making blacking boxes and trying to sell them. This introduced him to an undertaker who had need for bigger and better boxes, and for a few months John lived by designing coffins.

As soon as he could accrue the wherewithal for passage he visited Brownsville briefly but, as he feared, there was nothing for him here. The little river town was in the doldrums, hardly knowing which side of the war it was on, half of its sympathies being with the South, from which its old settlers came, and half with the North whence it was deriving its trade. None of his brothers or sisters were old enough to be earning anything, and all looked at him with hungry eyes. His father had lost his saddlery business with the South and did not know how to become a war profiteer with the North. He solved the situation for himself by enlisting in the army.

But John enlisted in the equally great army of men who fought the war from the Pittsburgh mills, as they did the World War later. He turned away from Brownsville, and as the little German band on the deck of the boat struck up "Oh! Susanna, don't you cry for me," he did not know that he was looking on its sprawling hills for the last time, as home.

When he reached Pittsburgh, a new steam calliope on a boat at the dock was screaming out "John Brown's Body."

IV

SO IS THE TREE INCLINED

IN April of 1861 Fort Sumter was fired on. In July of the same year John Brashear was hired as a mechanic in the Zug and Painter rolling mills, which stood on the narrow strip along the Ohio below Mt. Washington, then called "Coal Hill."

Pittsburgh was vastly disturbed by the emergency of the war, but not John Brashear. Just as education was denied him because of family finances, so was it impossible for him at this period to indulge in the adventure of soldiering. He did not belong to any gentlemen's military club, such as the Pittsburgh Grays. He was one of those thousands who, in any such upheaval, must keep their minds on their work and earn a living for the family of another.

The question of owning slaves had been solved in this section long ago by freeing the few there were. This was partly because there was no need for them in its type of industry, but also because the laws of the Quaker State, while permitting bond servants in the East, soon ruled against the sale of human beings. At the junction of the rivers colored people were mostly known through the Underground Railway, that secret system of bringing them across the Ohio from the South and concealing them until they could be hurried off north to Lake Erie, and shipped to Canada. Very respectable citizens hid slaves in the lofts of their barns and buried them under the straw in the backs of their wagons while driving them on to the next "station." John was a boy in Brownsville while this was going on, but the custom was universal in the border cities, and early he would have listened to the impassioned speeches of the abolitionists with sympathy for the Negro. All his life he not only favored them, but it is said he literally saw no difference between blacks and whites.

The first uprising in Pittsburgh was when an order came from

Secretary John Flood, before the war broke out, for one hundred guns to be shipped from the arsenal in Lawrenceville to two forts on the Gulf of Mexico. The citizens decided this was putting ammunition right into the hands of the enemy, and crowds gathered in the streets to intercept delivery and threatened to sink any boat that was so loaded. The order was countermanded by President Buchanan. This was the same Allegheny Arsenal that was blown up later, by accident, killing seventy-five boys and girls employed there. The girls had only recently been hired because it was feared the boys might be careless and cause an explosion.

When Lincoln passed through the city on the way to his inauguration, the cheering thousands who gathered before the old Monongahela House moved him deeply. "Where is this state of Allegheny?" he asked, when heavy returns from the district helped elect him. Now his war orders were pouring in, and Pittsburgh bent its back to supplying coal and iron, and all things made from iron; locomotives and freight cars, small ammunition and fifty-ton cannon. River and ocean war boats were built here, wagons, horses and their fodder were shipped, clothing for soldiers and tents for them to sleep in, almost anything but men. Ten volunteer companies, including Negley's Zouaves, marched off with fife and drum, but were enlisted for such short periods that they were hardly missed. The draft that came later found everyone much too busy to lay aside necessary war work, and it became the usual thing for a business man to pay for a substitute to serve for him. The streets were more full of buff trousers and beaver hats than they were of uniforms. The wives of cotton manufacturers sat down in the middle of their voluminous hoopskirts and begun scraping lint for bandages.

Pittsburgh was generous with the wealth she came by during these chaotic years. Just before the close of the war she raised $320,000 during the eighteen days of her great Sanitary Fair, managed by the women and patronized by the men, and what was left over from this fund, because there was not time to

spend it, was used as a foundation for the Western Pennsylvania Hospital—a new need.

The fighting never came near enough the city to disturb its
tempo. There was one scare when Morgan's men were raiding
along the Ohio, and another when they feared Stewart's cavalry
would sweep their way when the Southern army was as near as
Chambersburg. That was when the mill men gave their workmen
a day off, with pay, and supplied them with picks and shovels
to dig the embankments which still remain on the hills. But
Gettysburg put an end to fears in Pennsylvania, as well as to
a great many lives. When the war was over Pittsburgh celebrated
in its own colossal fashion. Cannon thundered from the arsenal,
mill sirens shrieked, and drunken crowds marched up and down
Fifth Avenue singing war songs and revival hymns while dodg-
ing the nightly fireworks. Even in Brownsville the boat whistle
on the dock blasted out for a week.

All this noise became the thunderous undertone of a dirge
at the news of Lincoln's assassination. It seemed to the mill men
of Pittsburgh that he was not only a sacrifice to the nation, but
peculiarly their own sacrifice to Tubal Cain, God of the forges
they had built to win the war. Their profits seared their fingers,
ashes as hot as those of the slag heaps of their furnaces. The
newspapers came out with black borders and they shut down
the mills. John Brashear went home from Zug and Painter's and
wept.

A western junction had turned into a metropolis without
knowing it, with its future attention centered on quelling the
riots hard times brought, after the war, to the gigantic mills
which war needs had created. John worked in the same plant
on the Ohio flats until 1867, and in those six years much happened to him as well as to the city where his stars had led.

Grandfather Smith was employed in the Manchester mills
when John secured his first place across the river. From this
snug little town with its narrow streets flanked by tight rows of
brick houses, below the heights of Allegheny, he could ferry
back and forth to his work. There was no double span of bridges

over the Point. The South Side was reached from Smithfield Street by the new suspension bridge across the Monongahela, finished in 1861 by John Roebling, fifteen years after the old covered one had been burnt down in the Great Fire.

Over the Allegheny there were four bridges, but over the Ohio, which was John's shortest route to the mills, there was still need for the steam ferry which ran from Chartiers Street to the foot of Saw Mill Run. Formerly there had been a one-man affair operated by ropes and pulleys from Ferry Lane. This had given way to an engine-run cable, which in turn was abandoned as early as 1832 when growing river traffic prohibited such an obstacle. Ice in the winter, and sandbars in the summer, always made travel over the ferries hazardous, and slow-moving strings of coal barges pushed by stern-wheelers often blocked the way. It was this difficulty that soon drove John to leave his grandfather's congenial society in favor of dwelling on the south side of the Ohio near his work.

He became acquainted with Phoebe Stewart, the girl he married, almost immediately on arriving in Pittsburgh. She was teaching in the Sunday school of a Methodist church near the mills, and he was the choir director.

The pretty girl's father, Thomas Stewart, was not at all impressed with the young man of twenty-one who wanted to marry his nineteen-year-old daughter. The fact that John was earning only ten dollars a week, part of which he had to send back to Brownsville, and part use for board to the Stewart family (where he had come to live while courting Phoebe), doubtless had much to do with parental opposition. The Stewarts were of Scotch descent and loth to lose their daughter and their boarder at the same time.

Phoebe stole out of the house on a September night with the aid of her brother Morgan and his wife, and fleeing to the home of another brother, William, married her John in the wedding dress of her sister-in-law. Thus the formalities were observed, and the only ones who did not understand the situation were the old folks, who caught them kissing in the kitchen next morning, where Phoebe was making an apple pie for the wedding breakfast. The anger of the dour Scotch father drove them back across the river to the protecting arms of Nathaniel Smith.

This was a worthy beginning for a great romance which became an enduring marriage, the epic of John's life. Reading between the lines of the simple record we can only imagine how his heart leaped when he saw this beautiful girl for the first time, whose portrait, done from a daguerreotype soon after their marriage, now hangs in the Phoebe Brashear tea-room in the South Side. Her dark hair is parted in the center and falls in waves to a knot behind, tied with long velvet ribbons. Large oval-shaped earrings show beneath it. Her wide eyes look guilelessly pleasant and her dimpled chin is firm. Her mouth droops slightly at the corners as if she would speak soon and to some point. Her short nose interrogates the world from her pouting lips. Her dress, with its low round bodice and full skirt, is of flowered silk, the sleeves laced with ribbons. She wears a brooch, and a long chain is wound around her short throat. One elbow rests on the arm of the chair, for she is sitting, and her hands are in her lap. These were the hands, it is said, which made John's work possible; gifted hands that never rested from their labor on the lenses.

A matching picture of John, of the same period, shows a lanky young man with a shock of long black hair swept back from his high forehead. Deep-set eyes with heavy brows, straight nose and generous mouth, with neck lost in a too large, standing white collar. Probably his suit of black broadcloth was borrowed, for it is too large for him, also, and there is a rakish black ribbon dangling down his stiff shirt. He looks like a composite of young Lincoln and Edgar Allan Poe.

There is an hysteria in any wartime which leads to quick marriages. Tempers are high, nerves are strung taut; to live for the day seems enough, with night so soon to follow. Many such marriages rush to their doom before any peace is signed, but the union of John and Phoebe Brashear was forever. We can estimate the strength and rightness of its beginning by the fact that it endured to the end.

As if it pleased him, and proved that their love was mutual, he says in his own memoirs that she "set her cap for him" the first time she saw him in the choir loft. What sort of intuition was given such an inexperienced girl, that made her so sure of herself, and of him, and life? She knew immediately, without writing any letters for advice to whatever Dorothy Dix was of her period, what she wanted and how to get it. We can learn much from Phoebe. Her influence became supreme in shaping her husband's character, beginning at the place and time where Grandfather Smith left off. Day by day, hand in hand, they went on together far into the next century.

They had no children except two whom they adopted, and one of these, the boy, died before he reached maturity. But they filled their house, later, with the descendants of the little girl. No children? Like Mr. Chips, the English schoolmaster, they had hundreds of children who came to their door continually and were never turned away; children who came to examine John's workshop and look through his telescope and listen to his stories of the stars. Father of none, John became "Uncle" to a whole city.

His elopement had brought him back again to the wrong side of the river. As he could not afford the ferry fare he borrowed a skiff to row back and forth, but the ferryboat would not permit this competition and accidentally smashed into his borrowed boat one windy night when they were each off their courses. The little fund that Phoebe had begun for a telescope was immediately depleted, for every week they had to pay out money to the owner of the defunct skiff.

Their poverty must have made life exhausting, but John did not complain. Like any other lover, he claims that these days were some of the happiest of his life. Phoebe shared his concept of communion with the stars, and no one studying the heavens as they did could have much interest in war. While Pittsburgh guns boomed south of the Mason and Dixon Line they made their plans for the future.

Shortly after he was married he was asked by the manager of Zug and Painter's to put a tooth in a large spur-wheel. As he accomplished this difficult feat in a few hours, instead of the usual twenty-four, his pay was raised from ten to twenty-five dollars a week. There was rejoicing all the way to Brownsville.

Another bit of luck came to Phoebe through her youthful husband's skill. Having made such a success of mending the wheel, John was called upon again when the "squeezer" broke down, which ordinarily necessitated closing the mill for several days. This was a great machine for pressing the slag and air bubbles out of the hot, liquid metal in the process of puddling iron. Because John set the mill in operation again in two days, Mr. Painter told him to choose what he would like for a present. He did not hesitate. He chose a silk dress for the girl who married him in a borrowed gown, and in those days the yardage of a woman's hoop skirt made it cost the donor fifty dollars.

Doubtless they bought the green silk at Mr. Boggs's emporium over on Allegheny Commons, for that was the most likely place for importations. Perhaps it is the very dress Phoebe wore when her daguerreotype was made, as otherwise her elegance in that picture is inexplicable. And it may be that Nathaniel Smith, John's grandfather, who was an expert in these lines, made the daguerreotype for a belated wedding present, as soon as the dress was done.

When John's wages were raised they crossed the Ohio once more and rented an old house near the rolling mills. This district was called "Temperanceville" because its founder had stipulated that no liquor be sold there. However, by the time John and Phoebe had arrived all such rules were forgotten, and the only signs of temperance were in the societies of that name, founded by such church people as themselves.

John shoveled the cinders out of the yard, wheeled in hundreds of loads of earth, and started a vegetable garden. Grandfather Smith would join them on Sunday, and Phoebe would cook for him and cut his hair and make the old gentleman comfortable. Precious as this companionship was, it could not last forever. Nathaniel Smith died in Brownsville a year or two later, and John's everlasting regret was that he had not lived to see the stars, which he had been so instrumental in pointing out to him, through a lens of his grandson's making.

Perhaps it was sheer loneliness after Grandfather Smith had gone away that prompted them to adopt a baby whom they named Effie Afton, from the song. And a song she always was to them, something to love and cuddle in spite of poverty, a blithe little girl who became such a real child of their own that John would never permit anyone to remind him of the contrary. It was at this time, too, that they refused to content themselves with their house on the flats, but must put more money into a field on the top of Coal Hill behind them. Phoebe wanted it so she could extend her garden, and was surprised that John, perfectly willing to climb the cliff like a goat, after his day's work was over, did not make a success as a farmer. But to him the lot was always a success. What he wanted it for was to have a quiet place where he could lie on his back and look at the sky.

Living in the center of piles of pig iron, with coal dumps and railroad tracks all about him, did not prevent John from making astronomical observations. He would take his star map out on the river bank and by candle light locate the positions. When the smoke of the mills had abated on Saturday night and the skies were more clear, he would row out to a sandbar and get a longer look back up over the hills on the south of the Ohio.

John's conflict during the war was not whether he should enlist, but whether he should become a preacher. He had heavy financial responsibilities, both for his own and for his father's family; and for contrast with his days in the rolling mills he had his nights on the hill; and for conflict with astronomy he had still to make up his mind about going into the ministry. For although many of his friends advised against it, after seeing his absorption in science, literally tripping on him of a dark night if they chanced to take the upper path from the mills, yet there remained the old allegiance to his mother's dream which came to haunt the dreams of his own making.

Before he had left Brownsville he had managed to read the books prescribed by the Methodist Conference and had passed the examination to become a local preacher. He had waded through Wesley's *Sermons*, learned Watson's *Institutes*, compared Butler's *Analogy*, and penciled the margin of Whatley's *Logic*, which he preferred to them all. As early as when he was located in Louisville he had assisted at the river-front missions, where the keelboat men were induced to sign the pledge, and Kentucky mountaineers ended up their spree in the city by a whole-hearted repentance on the mourner's bench. Now both he and Phoebe were helping with the choir and Sunday school in the Bingham Street Methodist Church on the South Side.

The pastor, the Reverend John C. High, asked John to supply for him in the pulpit while he went out of town. A well-known fundamentalist himself, he had not bothered to look into John Brashear's background, much less make himself acquainted with his mind. He took it for granted that a boy from Brownsville had been brought up on narrow paths and that the congregation would be safe in his hands. But the pastor made the mistake of not leaving the city as he had intended, and of being right there in the church to harass John, when he preached the sermon that eventuated in a crisis.

John had taken his text from Genesis, and gave a discourse on "Creation," from the first four chapters. Unfortunately he undertook a scientist's point of view, backing up his arguments by Dana's *Cosmogony of the Bible* which, though in complete accord with the sacred text, made his listeners squirm in their seats and stare at the young man with mounting suspicion. Watching their reaction he grew cold. He had put all the sincerity and poetry of his being into this thoughtfully prepared sermon, and he had the courage to stumble on to the end. The final hymn was sung, the last prayers were said. The congregation filed out in silence while John waited in vain for a single encouraging word. Then it came. The outraged parson complimented him with faint praise, and ended with a ringing rebuke which alienated him forever from the ministry.

"I do not think," said the Reverend Mr. High, "a knowledge of creation is necessary to the believer or seeker of truth, for the Bible teaches us if we believe we shall be saved, and if we believe not, we shall be damned, and this is the sum and substance of the whole matter."

The sum and substance of the whole matter to John Brashear was that he was through. What he had to offer was not wanted. Totally surprised by the rebuff, with his heart almost broken by having disappointed and disgraced his mother, and particularly chagrined because he had failed in his precious subject, he gave up all idea of becoming a preacher. His wife and various kindly members of the little church tried to gloss the incident over, but he knew too well exactly what it meant. He decided to serve God more directly by opening up the kingdom of the heavens to the blind kingdoms of earth.

Two score years and the world was more ready to understand him, for at the turn of the century he was speaking in every sort of church and chapel, Jewish, Protestant, and Catholic, colored and white. And he was always asked to speak about whatever he pleased, which turned out to be the stars.

V

THE HOUSE ON HOLT STREET

AFTER the Civil War, as after the World War of 1914, the Pittsburgh mills continued to run full blast on momentum. It was not until ten years later that hard times came, through the failure of bankers to realize that they could not lend money indefinitely to all would-be expansionists because they were boyhood friends. Few were as successful as "Andy" Carnegie.

But at this time the workmen, many of whom had been coaxed from Europe with wild promises of riches and induced to live in box cars temporarily, were beginning to wonder why none of the Midas gold around them came their way. In 1867 there was a puddlers' strike at Zug and Painter's bar mill, and John Brashear found himself locked out.

He had never been what is called a "puddler's pup." That apprenticeship had been spared him because of unusual ability. He had been promoted to millwright after three months' service, and was now one of the most trusted men in the plant. When the strike was called he took time to put the machinery in perfect order before the men walked out, a precaution never followed since. His salary was payable by the year, but he could not collect when the mills were not running. Casting around for means of livelihood he entered the employ of the McKnight-Duncan Company, another iron mill on the same side of the river, and moved to Thirteenth Street in Birmingham.

It is commonly said that John Brashear used to work in the old Carnegie mills, because later in life he became a personal friend of the great promoter. But the facts do not bear out the tradition. Carnegie was only five years older than Brashear, but was well on his way to fortune at this time. He had been in the telegraphic and railway business before the war, and during that upheaval did important service in transporting troops. Before the great merger of 1892 into one Carnegie Steel Company, he was interested in such mills as the Cyclops Iron Works, the Keystone Bridge Co., the Union, the Edgar Thompson at Braddock, and the new Homestead steel plant. In none of these did the maker of lenses ever work. Nor was "Charlie" Schwab a boon companion of his millhand days. Schwab was twenty-two years younger than John. It is Schwab, and not John, who was one of "Carnegie's boys," for he began his career at the Edgar Thompson plant. Greatly influenced by Brashear in his youth, at the height of his own career he gave him such a tribute at a banquet in Pittsburgh that his listeners assumed they had worked side by side. He said he rated John Brashear as "the most successful man of my acquaintance." In one thing these friends were alike. Success, to Schwab, was evidently no more a matter of having millions than it was to the star-gazer.

Many years before John located on the South Side part of it sloping down to the river had been the Homestead Farms of John Ormsby, who had come over the mountains with General Forbes. Several of the streets of Birmingham bear the names of the girls in this family. And just as the city fathers named new streets for their daughters, Jane, or Sara, and river captains named their boats for their sweethearts, *Myrtle*, or the *Bessie B*, so did the ironmasters come to designate their gigantic furnaces the Lucy, or the Isabella.

Below the Smithfield Bridge toward the Point, where iron mills were founded because of the proximity of ore in near-by cliffs, the district was called Sligo. Here was erected the first Monongahela Incline in 1867, an elevator on cables large enough to lift the citizens up to the top of Mt. Washington while sitting in their carriages. This was one of the developments of the Pittsburgh steel cable also used in the first suspension bridges and cablecars.

One would have to give a long look backward to visualize the South Side as it was in John Brashear's day. But the little old brick houses with their prim shutters and white steps would be about the same and the people in them hardly any different. The Germans moved in to work in the glass factories and they have never moved away. Their culture brought a certain dignity to the neighborhood which made it a pleasant place for the young Brashears to live. There were the Maennerchors, societies of men who sang the Bach chorals, and the Gesangvereins, mixed choruses, and in every little parlor on Sara Street could be heard the scraping of a violin as someone practised for the Saturday night quartet.

John and Phoebe enjoyed the social life of these few years before the seventies. He still led the choir of the Methodist church where he had preached his ruinous sermon, but fortunately the theology of a choirmaster is seldom questioned. He founded a cantata society for the singing of sacred works, and drew all the church choirs of the district together for the rendition of *Queen Esther*. He taught himself the thorough-bass system, with aid of such books as Tindel's *Thorough-Bass without a Master*, and studied Wolfhart's *Composition of Melodies*, of which he essayed a few. Phoebe had a good soprano voice and he sang tenor, and as he was one of the few young men of Birmingham who could read notes, their company was welcome. He taught singing classes from the bare rudiments he had improved upon since his old teacher in Brownsville, George Wilkinson, had initiated him and the rest of the boys into the intricacies of the Tonic Sol Fa system.

Largely because of its German influence there was as much music in Birmingham of the sixties as there was across the river in the city. Pittsburgh already had the Gounod Club, but the famous Mozart Society, often referred to as its first musical association, was not formed till ten years later. The Art Society, the first to import concert artists, was founded in Allegheny in 1873.

Four years of this happiness, and the bar mill caught fire one early December morning in 1871, resulting in John's being obliged to spend the entire winter in superintending its rehabilitation. As it was well covered by insurance and had long needed overhauling, Mr. McKnight was glad to give him leeway in its reconstruction.

"Watch and pray," he said to John, "but don't take both jobs! You do the watching and I'll do the praying."

In the following May, using modern methods of driving by belts, and eliminating the square shafting, the mill was ready to reopen. The partners were so pleased with its improvements that they raised John's wages three hundred dollars a year and dated the new salary back to the first of January. This enabled him to take the only vacation with his wife that he ever afforded, a wedding trip ten years after their marriage.

Taking little Effie Afton along, the child they had adopted the first year they were married, they set off on the dangerous train journey to Cleveland, for never having left the river valleys before, they longed to see Lake Erie. Nor did they know that a boarding house on the edge of the Lake could be so hot and uncomfortable as it proved. Undaunted, leaving their nine-year-old Effie with the landlady for safekeeping, they embarked on an excursion boat for Put-In-Bay. How proud they were of this adventure is shown by John's remarking that neither of them was seasick. He did not know that before he died he would cross both the Atlantic and the Pacific.

They had purchased two twenty-foot lots on the cliff behind Twenty-second Street in Birmingham, and fortified by the raise in his salary as soon as they returned from Ohio began to plan the little house at No. 3 Holt Street, where John was to spend the most constructive years of his life.

His brothers were grown up and working, and the pressure behind him was relieved. William and Frank Brashear, who was fifteen years younger, followed John in the Brownsville mill and then followed him to Pittsburgh. Charles, talented in much the same way as John, had died at the age of seventeen. George became a trusted employee of the shipping department of the Jones and Laughlin steel mills and worked there for thirty-four years. His sister Ella was comfortably situated with her able husband, Will Sheets, one of the organizers of the mechanical firm of Best, Fox and Co. Mary married James Stevens, an engineer, and went out to California with him where she raised

a family of children. His father was, at this time, working as
gate-keeper in the mills John had recently equipped for the
McKnight-Duncan Co., and he planned as soon as he had a
home to have his father and mother living with him, which
they did for a few years.

The location of his well-known house on Holt Street is the
one which duplicates John's boyhood home in Brownsville. For
ten years he had been shifting around in various rented places,
and now that he was able to have a home of his own he intended
to have it where he wanted it. He must have searched the hill-
sides to find what he was long determined to possess. It is not
quite at the top of the hill, for behind the house as well as before, the terrain is so steep that a long flight of steps is necessary
to reach it. In his day there was no such aid, and he and his
young wife climbed back and forth on paths that nearly pitched
them headlong as their nimble feet gathered speed, or made
them pause for breath on their way home. Yet, though we
wonder they had the temerity to choose this situation, and how
they managed to get the material there to build it, we do not
wonder that they loved it.

From their doorstep the whole Monongahela valley could be
seen. Across from them the buildings of Pittsburgh flanked the
river beneath its hazy hills. The water route was crowded with
side-wheelers and stern-wheelers, with flat coal boats from up-
river and passenger packets from the Mississippi, and, so close
below them they could not see it, a line of tracks paralleled
their own cliffs. Birmingham, a city of red tin roofs, nestled
under the bank in diminutive perspective. The iron works and
the glass works were far to either side, and if there was any
sky visible through the smoke rising from their hundreds of
chimneys, here was the right place to enjoy it. The murky sun
went down in its curtain of red fog behind the Point on their
left, and rose through veils of purple on their right. The moon
soared over the river. From this high vantage point a mystic
could lean out of his upper window and pick up a handful of
stars in his bare hands.

They were anxious to get their little home finished before winter, and aided by the "boys" from the plant they had an old-fashioned house-raising. The mill hands made short work of digging a cistern, and Phoebe made one of them sick with her bountiful dinner featuring oyster stew. They cut down an oak tree on the lot for the posts on which the house rested, for although its back could settle comfortably on the hill, its front had to be balanced in mid-air. Without attempting its completion, when it still lacked floors and the stairway was purely imaginary, they moved in. The lowly joys of Birmingham were abandoned for the higher joy of a hillside home.

The plans called for four downstairs rooms opening, as a child would draw them, on either side of a central hall, with entrance both front and back. Two tall chimneys gave open fireplaces, one in each room. Much later a half-story was added above with three gables, the larger one making a flat-faced point above the door. The house was ornamented with wide cornices, and open scrollwork bridged the gable over a pointed window which balanced the broad doorway topped with a transom. The narrow entrance porch had no roof, doubtless a concession to star-gazing. The whole architecture was of the period known as "steamboat Gothic." Many such houses with their pointed roofs and windows and ornamental cornices adorned the banks of the rivers, taking their style from the ornate passenger boats, for they were designed by the same builders. Just as in New England coastal towns the houses were built by able ship carpenters, so along inland waters one could go to a shipyard and have all the lumber cut for a river-front house.

They had barely been in the new home a year, and were still living in three rooms lined with paper-plastering, when the great cloudburst of the early seventies tore it right off the walls. The wind was so high that it shifted the house five inches out of plumb, getting under the floor from the open piles and lifting it bodily, only to let it fall with a sickening rock that must have made little Effie think they had put out to sea.

This was no ordinary spring flood of the tormented river valley. It was an unusual blight, a thunderstorm so severe that not only their house but hundreds of others were threatened, and many of them tossed into the river where they knocked the boats from their moorings. Squaw Run in Allegheny, Saw Mill Run in the West End, Beck's Run up at Homestead, all turned into cascades and waterfalls, and many river dwellers were drowned. John Brashear's house must have been exceptionally well built to withstand such a storm. Quickly repaired with the help of his father, and finally finished, it stands today as it stood in 1872, and where John Brashear lived in it for fifteen years.

As soon as they moved into the house, and long before work on it was done, they bought a coal-shed from a neighbor, moved it to the rear of the hillside lot and set up a "shop." Everyone in those days had a "shop" on the place, even a doctor or lawyer had a separate little office built out in his own side yard. But John's was for a very special purpose, one so erratic he didn't like to talk about it—another reason for building in such an isolated place. It was for making a telescope. And from its inception, the plan was to make it possible for any child, such as he had been when he looked through the traveling glass of Squire Wampler, to be able to see the stars at will, and see them free.

Always he builded and planned for children as if adults would never care for what he had to offer; as if they had passed that time when wonder was a part of their days. His experience with his sermon had made him sensitive to possible hostility. He did not know any other scientists; he worked alone, as if no one before him had ever built a telescope, as if each detail of its perfection must be worked out from the very beginning. That is why no one afterward had more to teach him, why he himself became the authority.

During these first ten years of his marriage John had been studying the stars with the naked eye. Now he had a place of his own he determined to make a lens. But even on Holt Street he was interrupted, for although it was exactly the right location for his nightly labors it was hardly convenient for his day's work. He was a master millwright, which means he was responsible for all machinery in the plant. When things went well, his was the final word; when wrong, he became the last resort. The hours were from six to six, sometimes longer. And even if he were safe in bed, at six sharp toots of a certain whistle he would have to rush back to see what had broken down at the mill. Each important man had his call, and he recognized it as quickly as does a farmer listening for his ring on a party line. When John heard his, he hurried, putting on his clothes as he ran down the hill.

While the rafters in his house were still exposed he suspended two shelves by wire to the beams of his bedroom where he could reach up and take down a book after Phoebe was fast asleep beside him. If the whistle blew six, he simply marked the place and came back to it perhaps two days later. He began a scientific library, buying a book every pay day, until Phoebe never knew whether he would arrive home with the Saturday corned beef or a tome on planets. "All right," she would say gently, "but remember we can't afford another one this week."

His first enthusiasm had been discouraged by a Pittsburgh optician on whom he had called for advice, and asked the cost of an object glass. "If you do buy it," this man had replied, "you wouldn't know how to mount it, or how to use it!"

Cruel words and true. John Brashear promptly secured the address of a firm in New York who were importers for English makers, the Chance Brothers (ominous name!) and wrote for a pair of five-inch glasses which he would cut himself. Then he borrowed a two-inch telescope from a German acquaintance and began to experiment. One evening, Bolivar, the cat, ran out over his shoulder while he was setting up the little tripod and upset the tube and bent it. John had to take it to be repaired before daring to return it, and in this way began his life-long friendship with Mr. Steiren, an able optician, who helped him in many ways.

While waiting for his own glass to arrive he outfitted his laboratory. He constructed a bench for a small second-hand lathe, designed an engine and installed a little boiler. Phoebe always had the shed in immaculate order when he climbed up the hill from work, the lamps lit and their frugal dinner ready, after which he would concentrate until midnight. The only problem was whether to spend the evening finishing the house, which she might have preferred but was too generous to insist upon, or to complete his preparations in the shop, the mainspring of their whole endeavor. The shop must have won, for he says they began work on their first telescope in 1872, which is the year they moved into No. 3 Holt Street.

There is an inscription on the door of this house which reads, in his own words, "Somewhere under the stars is work which you alone were meant to do. Never rest until you have found it."

VI

THE FIRST LENS

The Pittsburgh panic of 1873 upset all calculations. And not only among financiers, but spreading like a plague it reached across the river to the South Hills and devastated the plans of John Brashear.

After the failure of Jay Cooke in New York, bank after bank in the "golden triangle" closed its doors, and soon the Mc-Knight-Duncan mills, where John was employed, could not keep theirs open. Even the gate-keeper, John's father, was not wanted, which left him after a year in his new home with five people to support, as well as an unborn telescope.

No smoke rose from the chimneys of the rolling mills, etched like a series of organ pipes against the length of the river. When no soot falls in Pittsburgh the people starve. As he stood looking down on the too quiet valley, John wondered if the glass works were similarly affected. Their red tin roofs had an air of German thrift. Perhaps they were not making stemmed wine glasses now, but certainly they would still be making beer bottles. Slowly he scrambled down the hill, and quickly rushed back again to disconsolate Phoebe. He had been engaged by the Adams Company to turn plungers in their mold shop.

This work was quite new to him, but he learned the use of the lathe and accurate fitting of the matrix, knowledge that was invaluable when he came to making his own lenses. And none too soon, for he was only with them a few months. Christopher Zug, who had formerly been one of the firm of Zug and Painter, had started the Sable Iron Works in Bayardstown on the Allegheny, leaving old Painter's Mills to fend for themselves on the banks of the Ohio. Hearing that his former millwright, who had been forced out of their plant a few years back because of a strike, was wasting his valuable skill on something as transient as glass, he drove over the bridge and urged him to go back with him.

Mill-master Zug was a well-known character of German descent, a judge of horses, raised on a Pennsylvania Dutch farm, who drove a fast team to his mills in the broad-brimmed felt hat and long black coat of the Mennonites. Because of this, and because he would have nothing to do with war (except to expand his business), he was considered a Quaker. This type of man, bluff and sincere, always favored John. There was never a mill owner he worked for but asked him to his house.

Here was a real dilemma. If John accepted the offer he would have more pay with which to buy tools and materials for telescope making, but he would have no time. The Sable Iron Works stood over in that section which is now called the Strip, then called Bayardstown, a seething district between the Allegheny River and the railroad tracks beneath Herron Hill. It would be a long journey by horse car which would only take him part of the way. He must descend his own hill, find his way to the Smithfield Bridge, and bisect the city, before he would arrive at work. Phoebe, ever undaunted, advised him to accept. If she had known as much about that section as is known today she might not have been so willing.

Bayardstown had first been called the Northern Liberties because outside the city no rules held, and they were permitted to build slaughter houses. Once the stench was established, tanneries and breweries followed, and the Bayardstown Irish learned to mix their whisky with German beer. When the mills came along with their thousands of thirsty workers this resulted in a specialty of Pittsburgh, the Puddler's Cocktail. The Pittsburgh Stogie, a long, thin, lightly rolled cheroot, popular with the mill men, was named for the drivers of the Conestoga wagons.

Phoebe, however, did not know she was sending her husband into the most riotous part of the city. And although John worked there for ten years, he was so absorbed during the noon hour giving lectures on the stars to his fellow workers that he never knew it either.

When in doubt, compromise. John compromised with his dilemma by doing both, taking the job and getting up at dark in order to arrive before the whistle blew. But when he climbed the hill again he came up faster than he went down, for there was the light in the shop, waiting, and there was dear Phoebe, ready to begin. Her determination was the only puddler's cocktail he needed, although he frequently met himself getting in and out of bed.

He found the machinery in the new Zug plant vastly improved from the days when he had worked with that eccentric gentleman before. There was no more square-shafting, no flywheels with wooden arms always getting out of condition, no timbers that had to be laboriously replaced under the engines. Yet, as master millwright, when a break did occur, he could not return home until he had repaired it. Men would be thrown out of work and, what was worse to "Chris" Zug, good iron-melts wasted, if the machines lay idle. Often John waved good-bye to Phoebe on a Thursday and didn't come back until Saturday night.

They worked on the first five-inch lens for two years.

After the square glass had arrived from New York it had to be cut into circular form, and it was necessary to compute the curves. This they somehow managed to do without knowing anything about the index of refraction or dispersion of the glass. He fastened the disk to the bench with pieces of wood to hold it in place and ground off the corners with a band of hoop iron. This took four weeks.

Phoebe would separate the coarse sludge from the fine because the emery must be used over and over again. A jelly glass filled with water stood on the window-sill so it could be sprinkled on at intervals. And during the course of this unaccustomed work Phoebe developed a rare feeling for "fining," the working of the dampened emery over the surface to bring it up to the polishing point. This is considered a great gift, and without either of them knowing it, John had in his wife a partner of unusual ability. So markedly successful was she in this part of the work that she continued it as long as they had the shop on

Holt Street. Her extremely delicate touch was instantly able to locate foreign grit and separate the emery, particle by particle, a great advantage to them both, and the envy of all scientists who came to know them later.

Yet they had great difficulty in grinding and polishing and testing. Just as they would approach a time when the surface was ready for the final finishing off, a scratch would appear, and it would all have to be done over. The nights ran into months and the months into years. Finally, one evening when they thought their preparations were complete, and one of the five-inch disks was ready for polishing, John lifted it to the light and in his eagerness let it slip.

It fell to the floor with an almost imperceptible tinkle, quivered on one edge and failed to roll. Each made a quick move to retrieve it, stopped, and stood immobile, not daring to look in the other's eyes. Phoebe shuddered as John turned to her, mutely. He had broken the crown lens in two pieces.

There it lay in half, and it seemed to him that half his life had broken with it. This lens had been his life for a long, long time. Twenty-five months of labor had only brought him to the place where he must labor for more months, and on what? The lens was gone.

He thought of the mills, and the long way to the mills, and the way home, and the homeward path up the hill, and suddenly he felt very tired. He could see himself climbing up and up, to this moment, to the stars . . . The stars? Why yes, the stars would still be there. He blew out the lamp, and putting his arm around his wife, drew her over to the doorway, where they stood looking out together.

A sympathetic English friend offered to send for another glass, and in the months they waited for its arrival across the ocean they finished the second one still left in their possession. Then the work began all over on the new glass from England.

Another stretch of arduous devotion and the difficulty of cutting it to circular form and grinding the curves had been accomplished, and finally the double disks were ready for mounting. They started to make a six-foot tube, and John's brother-in-law, Will Sheets, a pattern maker, volunteered to help him with the carpentry work. But soon they found their glass required something even longer, and extended the tube three feet more. It grew so long the shop could not contain it and they moved it over to the hallway of the house. John finished the brass parts, after they had been cast, by turning them on his lathe until they were right for adjusting the draw-tube and mounting the lenses.

Their triumph came in 1875 after three years of hope and despair. Lifting the telescope carefully, together, they pointed its nine-foot nose out of their high bedroom window. It was ready now for the purpose for which it had been built.

Which one of them looked through it first, Phoebe or John? Perhaps it was Will Sheets, who had helped them, or John's father, or his mother or even little Effie Afton who would be twelve now and quite at an age to be jumping up and down with excitement. But the first view that John disclosed is known to be Saturn, that same majestic planet with all its luminous rings, which he had seen from the hills of Brownsville through the telescope of old Squire Wampler. Saturn had been waiting there for him for twenty-five years.

This was the moment when his heart cried out for his grand-father who had taken him, a lad of nine, to see the constellations and had always held their grandeur before him. But Nathaniel Smith had long since gone to that place in the stars prepared for him, and all John could hope was that he was looking down on the little house in Holt Street.

John rushed out of the door to gather in the neighbors. Never from the beginning had he envisaged this moment for himself alone. His entire concept was to give eyes to the world, to his own world of working people. Phoebe stood in wonder, gazing at the new stars visible which hitherto had been unim-agined, and which it seemed they must suddenly have created.

John's days of solitude were over. For this culmination had

he lived, but it was difficult to live through it. People poured in from mill, church, and grocery store, to find out what that curious thing was sticking out of the window up the hill. He found a disused column at a near-by works and made the equatorial parts with his own tools, but even before he had the mounting done, and the telescope properly erected on a platform in the second story where he had ruthlessly cut a hole through the roof, the house overflowed with visitors.

One of his neighbors, a skeptic up to the time he put his eye to the lens and peered incredulously into the sparkling sky, turned back to him with the highest praise he could bestow. "Mein Gott!" he exclaimed, as if thereby he pronounced the whole venture a complete success, "we have them same stars in Germany!"

During the identical years that John Brashear was struggling to perfect a telescope single-handed, over on the other side of the rivers an astronomical society was springing up. It was not because John did not know this that he held aloof, but because of modesty. Many a night, lying on his slag heap beside the river after the smoke had cleared, he had looked longingly across to where he knew these few seers were gathered together for the same important purpose. He had often climbed Coal Hill to gaze entranced on the dome of the new observatory that was rising on the east of the Ohio, but made no effort to make himself known to the men who could afford to build it. Probably he felt he must have something tangible to offer, some excuse for arriving, before he knocked on their door and humbly asked to be allowed to look through their new telescope. And also, he had heard rumors about the director of the Telescope Association, that strange Professor Philotus Dean, who guarded it so closely that he not only refused to permit anyone to look through it, but had a shotgun on hand to keep people away.

The meetings of the Allegheny group who studied stars had begun before the war. They gathered, sociably, in one another's homes, and when they first decided to buy a telescope they intended to erect it on a house-top in Federal Street. Later, as others joined the association, land was donated for a real observatory, and through the generosity of Mr. William Thaw, instead of buying an eight-inch lens which had been their modest plan, they ordered one of thirteen inches from Fitz of New York, who had completed a similar instrument for Albany. There were at this time only half a dozen observatories in the country.

Professor Philotus Dean was proud to accept the honorary position of director, which he held from 1862 to 1867. But although serving without salary except the rental of his house, he took his charge so seriously that the use of the telescope was practically prohibited. He became obsessed with the idea that the lens was so precious that someone would steal it, and, aptly enough, someone did. He had divinations, and had predicted this would happen in a poem whose words came to him fully clothed in imagery beyond his powers of conception. This was when John Brashear lived near the mills on the Ohio. Certainly he would have heard the story, but nothing that he heard could have induced him to cross the river up to the time the lens was stolen, and then it was too late.

In 1867, having incurred a large indebtedness, the trustees decided to deed their troubles to the Western University of Pennsylvania, which was also one of their projects. The various stockholders donated their previous gifts, and what was more to the point raised a fund which covered the present deficiency and started an endowment. William Thaw, always the most interested man on the board, contributed another $100,000. The first plan had been that the director of the observatory should also teach astronomy at the university, but Thaw stipulated that the two positions should be distinct. Samuel Pierpont Langley, formerly on the staff at Harvard, was made the new director.

And it was not until Professor Langley arrived and took a turn at playing intermediary that the missing lens was recovered. He had insisted that the thief should be punished, for the lens had evidently been kidnaped for ransom, rather than done away with. But when Langley finally met the culprit on a wooded path near the observatory, where he walked up and down with him affably discussing the matter, the thief remarked, "You are a gentleman, and I am a gentleman, we must trust one another." So the lens was returned and restored to its place, without payment and without revenge. One cannot help but wonder which one of the gentlemen of Allegheny it was who had been inspired by the fanatical Philotus Dean to attempt a burglary of anything so hard to dispose of as a thirteen-inch lens.

John was thirty-five when he finished his first telescope. After the excitement had subsided he was critical enough to be dissatisfied, and decided to write to Professor Langley for an interview. No one knew better than he that his glass needed further correction, and now he had come to the moment when, lens in hand, he dared go across the river to the observatory whose dome he had often stared down on from the heights.

No street cars ran out Perrysville Avenue. Such cars as there were jerked along narrow tracks behind a team of horses, and long waits occurred while "Joe" changed the team at the car barns. Straw lay thick on the floor so that passengers could shuffle their feet in it to keep warm, in case the stove in the corner ran out of cordwood, and at the end of the run the ashes and straw were raked out with the tobacco tins and apple cores. What the cars lacked in elegance was made up by the courtesy of Joe, the driver. He not only would "Whoa" anywhere he was hailed, but would wait obligingly while a passenger ran back home to get his umbrella. And if John Brashear was asleep, or immersed in a book, Joe would sling his reins around the brake-handle and come back and shake him by the shoulder. One could not travel more than two miles without the familiar "All Off! Change Cars! End of the Line!"

There were horse cars across both the Monongahela and Allegheny bridges, but after John had passed Boggs and Buhl's store he was faced with a two-mile walk. He carried his lens in his pocket wrapped up in his bandanna, and kept his hand upon it.

The houses thinned out and the wagon road led through a wood. To the left, below him, were glimpses of the Ohio through budding maples, and the feathery wild cherry and flat-faced dogwood were white against the pale willow. Low along the banks, pink mountain laurel tempted him to pause and take some home to Phoebe. The hills were not so softly green on his side of the river, they were barren cliffs, devoid of flowers, scarred with coal mines. The mills lined the river bottoms; the owners lived above the smoke, in Allegheny. And near their mansions they had built their observatory.

Now he had come to it, a long, low, brick building half-covered with ivy, where the Director lived at one side behind wide, shuttered windows. The center was an octagon, topped with the dome he had seen from across the river. The slit for the telescope was open. Evening had fallen while John found his way after many mistaken turnings. He wondered if Professor Langley would keep him long enough to see the stars through his thirteen-inch lens, or brusquely let him depart. He raised the knocker and was surprised to see a stooped figure peering out at him with hand shading his eyes, a man unpretentious, and about his own age. As soon as he had made his errand clear, the door swung wide. Together they stepped into Langley's study and John handed him the lens.

What a long time he was, turning it this way and that under the light! The man who had spent three years making it could wait no longer. Was it good? Or would it be better to let it fall, as the other had, and be done with a vain dream? Why had he, a millwright, raised his eyes so high? He trembled at what one man's decision might mean to him and Phoebe.

"You have done very well, Mr. Brazier!"

He doesn't know the name, thought John, but he does know lenses! There couldn't be so much the matter with it, after all.

The chief matter, he discovered, was that he should never

have attempted this sort of lens. He should have made a "re-flecting telescope," in which the image is reflected back to the beholder through the use of a silvered mirror. This would have only one glass surface to correct and would not require such costly optical glass. And although John Brashear had not the faintest idea how this silvering was to be accomplished, he agreed with Langley that it would be better to give up trying to improve his five-inch "object glass" and commence anew on the type suggested. This seemed very easy as they stood discussing the matter while Langley confided his own trials in making telescopes with his brother, back in New Eng-land. He explained how much simpler the work would have been for John if he had followed the general principles laid down by Alvan Clark (whom John had never heard of), the foremost maker of optical surfaces of that day. He asked him what book he had read on telescope building, and when John answered "None," hurriedly concealed his surprise by offering him his precious volume of Draper's *Construction of a Silvered Telescope and Its Use in Celestial Photography.* As John de-murred, he added that of course he expected him to bring it back.

John had been painstakingly buying books of a sort, but he did not know what was best to order. Several private libraries in Pittsburgh had once tried to combine in rooms they called Library Hall, but lack of finances had put an end to the ven-ture before this time. Nor could he qualify for the Anderson Library in Allegheny, where "Andy" Carnegie, as a boy, had difficulty of entrance. This was strictly for "youthful appren-tices." It was because Carnegie recognized this tremendous lack that later he established his own great system. But even if there had been a place in Pittsburgh to borrow books it is doubtful if John would have found anything about astronomical physics on the shelves.

Samuel Pierpont Langley had come from Boston and had the Bostonians' reputation for reserve. He was never very well un-derstood in Pittsburgh, where the millionaire ironmongers called each other by their first names. He had been trained as an engineer before going abroad to study art, but had returned convinced that his vocation lay in astronomy. He spent three years learning the uses of a telescope and studying astronomy in Boston libraries, and no one was more surprised than he when Harvard offered him an assistant professorship. After two years teaching at Cambridge and one at Annapolis, he was asked to come to Allegheny and was astonished when he found out what the city was like. When an enthusiast like John approached him he was baffled both by his open manner and his untutored ability. John could not guess that his readiness to help him proved how much he was impressed, for he had never met a man like Langley. Nor had Langley ever met a man like John, nor would he again.

Professor Langley had already made his observatory renowned by giving accurate time to the railroads, setting the hours by the infallible movement of the stellar bodies, and making it possible for trains to cross the Pennsylvania mountains on schedule. The various clock towers en route were each precise but differed so widely according to location that it was difficult to set the switch for the "ten-fifteen." This gave rise in middlewest towns to "sun time" versus "railroad" time, and the latter came to be the more respected. The city that was first to build locomotives, bridges, sleeping cars, and iron and steel rails, was first to offer a regulation for their dangerous use.

But if John had hoped they would discuss this matter he was mistaken. Nor could he know that later he was to help Langley on his invention of the bolometer, a delicate instrument for measuring heat-waves, or that before and after Langley had left for Washington, the experiments he had begun for mobile craft propelled by wind would be carried on in John's shop in Allegheny. Neither of them was trying to divine the future; one was an astronomer, and the other a maker of lenses that were to push forward the frontiers of science. Soon came the anticipated moment when he was invited to look through the observatory telescope before he returned home, discouraged.

They went up the little iron stairs into the dome, swung the telescope to position, tilted the tube, and again—Saturn!

This was the third time John had seen that same stupendous body at epochal moments, the first through Squire Wampler's telescope, the second through his own, the third through the thirteen-inch lens of the Allegheny Observatory. From the beginning to the end it seemed to focus all his endeavor. He was not thinking of its grandeur now. With that he was familiar. He was thinking how, after seeing it through this telescope, he would never again care to see it through his own. Before it was perfected he had outgrown the five-inch lens.

A better working team of scientists could hardly be devised than these two. John Brashear was lucky in finding Samuel Langley in Allegheny at a time when he needed instruction in astronomy. Langley was fortunate in having an expert near at hand who could devise any sort of delicate instrument required for his research. The old Allegheny Observatory had, by chance, brought together two men of genius, who between them gave it a place in the sky.

VII

MOLTEN SILVER

THE Philadelphia Exposition opened in 1876, the spring that John made his visit to the Allegheny Observatory, and having gone that far from home he decided to go farther. He had heard there were some remarkable telescopes on view.

He was familiar with expositions, for Pittsburgh had started one of her own the year before, down the Ohio on Kilbuck Island, and the new Chamber of Commerce was planning great things for future exhibitions of Pittsburgh machinery. Perhaps he thought that by the time the projected buildings were erected at the Point he would have a telescope ready to place on view beside the Pullman cars and pickles. After examining Professor Langley's thirteen-inch lens he was ambitious to produce another, and never having seen one before, now determined to investigate all there were. Nor did he particularly want to return to Allegheny for further instruction. He felt he might be more welcome in Philadelphia.

His resources, however, were not equal to such a long trip across the state, and he hardly knew how he could purchase the glass and silver for a large telescope mirror even if he succeeded in learning how to construct one. At this time he was not even able to buy a whole suit of clothes at once. His equipment, too, was inadequate. There was no gas in his house or shop, and for water in his cistern in the winter he melted snow which he tried to shovel in before the soot fell.

One night when he was sitting at his supper table, there was a knock on the door, and supposing it was someone who had arrived, as usual, to see the five-inch lens, he let in a stranger dressed like a preacher. This man said he had just been released from a four-year term in the penitentiary across the river, and had returned to find his family scattered and no way to feed himself until he secured work. Would John please give him credit at Freeman's grocery store on the corner? John agreed, and a few days later found the man had run up a bill of twenty-eight dollars, more than Phoebe spent in a month. The grocer became suspicious and followed "the reverend" to a saloon where he caught him exchanging a basket of potatoes for a pint of Kentucky Bourbon. He reported the matter to John.

"He's living a whole lot better than you are," said Mr. Freeman, "and at your expense." To which he received the very unsatisfactory answer, "I'd rather be beaten by fifty beggars than turn down one hungry man whom the Lord directed to my door." Freeman canceled the bill and closed the account.

John summoned courage in the late spring to ask for a week's vacation that had somehow been neglected in the three years he had been employed by Christopher Zug, and which the iron-master did not see why he needed. Had he ever taken an "off," himself? While the favor was in abeyance Phoebe decided to visit the mills where he worked and take along their little boy, Harry, a child not yet two, but who offered excuse for seeing the men make nails.

After the five-inch lens had been built John felt he had justified his existence, but not so Phoebe—not quite. If a telescope was to her husband like a new child born, to her it was a reminder that no matter what they achieved in creating lenses her life as a woman was not fulfilled. They had adopted their little girl the first year they were married. Now, in the first flush of success over their achievement she insisted that they adopt a little boy. And the fact that Effie Afton was thirteen was all the more reason for hurrying. Phoebe's hands might be gifted when it came to "fining" lenses but her arms yearned for another baby's soft, round head to cuddle on her motherly shoulder.

So this pleasant May morning John was expecting them both at the plant, and would have a father's pride in showing off his new son to the men, at the noon hour. While waiting their arrival the head roller in the mush-mill called his attention to a foreplate that needed correction, and he went to get the proper pattern for adjustment and carried it into his little workshop forty feet away.

Just as he was fastening it to a vise a terrific explosion occurred. So shocked was he by the concussion that it was as if he were blinded. Hurrying out, he discerned through the clouds of rising dust that the roof of the mill had been torn off. Forced on by reflex action he tried to find the key to the fire alarm but was too stunned to locate it. The first thing he recognized was the body of the workman with whom he had been talking. The boiler in the nail-mill had blown up.

Where were his wife and child? John had been in many accidents in the mills but never in one that so completely demoralized all initiative. He rushed through the mounting flames, half-crazed, finding other mutilated bodies in the wreckage, but never a woman, never Phoebe, and no sign of a tow-headed child. It was not until hours later that he found they had been delayed. They had not taken the street car on which he had expected them. They were on the Tenth Street Bridge when they heard the explosion over in the city and supposed the arsenal had blown up.

John was so unnerved that he was of no help to the hundreds who gathered to search the ruins. Christopher Zug decided that while they were adjusting the insurance his millwright might as well take that vacation he had begged for and spend the interval at the fair. The Mennonite was also unnerved by what he considered an act of Providence. Shamed by the loss of so many of his workmen, he gave up driving his fine team of thoroughbreds and appeared at the mills behind an old mule, singed from the fire.

But John was unhappy in Philadelphia. This was not the carefree time he had anticipated. He saw the big telescopes, marveled at the instruments of precision, tried to understand the Corliss engine, but jumped whenever he heard a sharp sound behind him, and keeping Phoebe firmly by the hand hurried from exhibit to exhibit and hurried home again.

However, this glimpse of mechanical wonders had given him fresh impetus. While he labored on the difficult task of rebuilding the Sable Iron Works he had an antidote in the lens-making which went on simultaneously at No. 3 Holt Street. For the reconditioning of the Zug mills after the explosion was harder than that he had accomplished at the old McKnight-Duncan mill, after their fire. John never knew when they lifted a piece of wrecked machinery but that it might disclose the mangled body of a friend.

The book on telescope making that Professor Langley had lent to John Brashear became both primer and graduate course. Every night he studied it, making its contents his own, and when he did not understand some problem wrote to its author, Dr. Henry Draper, for first-hand information and was grateful that his letters were answered. Dr. Draper was one of the first successful photographers of the stars, and carried on his experiments in his own observatory on the Hudson. From 1860 to 1882 he was professor of natural science at New York University, where he had graduated in the medical department, and where he also became dean. After his death in the eighties, his widow gave his star catalogue, called the "Draper Classification," to Harvard Observatory, as a memorial. His letters to John Brashear are examples of that rapport so often sought between pupil and teacher, and so seldom found. Many years later, when John visited the old observatory at Hastings-on-Hudson, after Draper had died, and had the opportunity of looking through the telescope with which he had made his first lunar photographs, he could see nothing for the tears in his eyes.

Having decided that twelve inches in diameter was the limit to any mirror he could handle, John sent for the glass to Heroy and Marrener in New York, and ordered two pieces at the same time, in case one should be broken as before. Then the work of cutting the squares to a round, and polishing and "fining," began again. To help Phoebe further with her marvelous touch they tried a new experiment, modeled on the "Foucault Test" recommended in Dr. Draper's book. This was to make an imitation star, by punching a hole with a needle in the tin shade of a kerosene lamp and letting a tiny ray fall on the glass that was being polished. Irregular rays could be cut off with a sharp knife until the image was perfect, and in the clear spotlight errors could be detected in the glass that could not be discerned in any other way. These Phoebe would rub down with a well-rouged thumb.

The shop was too small to contain all the apparatus, and they had to carry on their work in the open space under the house, where the front part projected over the slant of the hill. Later, this was properly inclosed for a cellar, but at this time it was open to the four winds that swept down from the heights and up from the river. As the temperature of the glass must remain the same they labored under a difficulty, enhanced by the fact that their interval of labor was so short, always being done at night. They would not use their Sundays. Phoebe still taught Sunday school and John still led the choir. Consequently he never had time to wait for the result of increased temperature caused by the friction of polishing. A raised mark, due to the touch of a finger, would be leveled, only to result in a depression when the glass cooled. It was a year before the twelve-inch disk for the reflector was ready for its coat of silver.

A ten-foot focus had been decided on, and a young friend, Edward Klages, a carpenter, made the long tube. John ordered a casting from a pattern he had cut, and designed a light equatorial mounting. This had to be set upon an outdoor brick foundation with a platform built around it to command whatever sky was not obstructed by the southward hill. The mirror was tried on the moon before silvering, and although only one-eighth as powerful as afterward, promised success.

But John was no chemist, and neither was the furniture man he consulted as an authority—who could tell him how to silver the back of a wall mirror but not the mirror of a telescope. He tried the process recommended in Dr. Draper's book, and wrote him again and again, but the result was always unsatisfactory. Finally, the same English friend in the Adams glass works who had helped him replace his broken five-inch lens, called his attention to an article in the *English Mechanic and World of Science*, and borrowing a few back copies for perusal, John decided to use a method it described that required heat.

Silver was expensive and they had wasted plenty of it, but this was to be the last time. They went to the shop right after supper and warmed the water in a containing vessel over steam heat, to insure cleanliness, and poured in the silver solution with its reducer to change it to metallic form. Their elation was complete when they saw a beautiful deposit of liquid silver spread over the twelve-inch glass.

Then a crack. The sound was so faint they saw the result before they heard it. The reflector had split in half.

This was the second time this had happened to them and to John it was the end. He shut up the shop and went home and would not speak. All night he tossed on his bed wondering what had caused it—unequal heating of the glass? But this had been done so carefully! A draft coming in through a crack in the wall? But the doors and windows were shut and there were no cracks. No matter how his tortured mind reviewed it, the result was the same, some part of the glass was cooler than its component part and it had broken.

Phoebe, distressed by his terrific disappointment which she well understood, but which did not worry her so much in itself as the reaction on John, got up out of bed and went to the kitchen and prepared food, always her solace to the weary spirit. But the only one who could eat it was little Effie Afton, who stole out from her room, wide-eyed, to see what was going on. She thought she heard an impossible thing—a man crying.

"It's only the baby," said Phoebe quickly. For young Harry, disturbed by the unwonted noise in the house, by the lights, footsteps and voices, had awakened to add his small misfortunes to the unending night.

John stuffed the pillow in his ears. "He sounds like a small dog howling at the moon," he thought. "He knows there's a death in the family."

Phoebe walked the floor. John lay stubbornly in bed staring at the back of Dr. Draper's book. Sleepless, he rose next morning to drag tired footsteps down the hill. He did not tell Phoebe what conclusion he had come to; he did not speak to her at all.

"I can't take you all the way," said the street-car driver. "There's a strike on and I don't want to get no rock throwed at the team. Wonder you want to go that way, yourself. Nobody's workin', the militia is called out."

John knew all about this strike. The men in the Pennsylvania railroad yards had started riots on Saturday because eastbound freight had been run as double-headers, to save expense, and brakemen had lost their jobs. Crowds had stood around the streets when John came out of the mills at four o'clock, but he had hurried home to use his extra hours for work on his adventure. He had been too absorbed that night and the next to notice the glare in the sky across the hills. Now he found that dreadful things had also happened in the city.

Infuriated by the arrival of troops from Philadelphia, brought on because the Pittsburgh militia refused to act, the mob had attacked the soldiers in the roundhouse they had tried to barricade. On Saturday night they ran ignited oil-cars down upon them, and on Sunday chased them all the way to the arsenal in Lawrenceville. They looted the box cars standing on the tracks and set fire to everything that would burn, including the old Union Station. A grain elevator on the Monongahela caught fire by accident when the conflagration spread that way, and the rioters ended where they had begun, by tearing down the roundhouses and burning them up too. All the district below Twenty-eighth Street under the hill along the railroad tracks was a shambles.

John picked his way through the sullen crowds watching the soldiers, and went to work in the Sable Iron Mills. It would take more than a railroad riot for Christopher Zug to close his gate. Some of his men were still off duty, because of repairs being undertaken after his own accidental explosion of the year before. "What am I here for?" wondered John. "What part have I in all this violence?" And then a more sickening thought came to him as he realized that he had just decided to throw in his lot with the mills forever. There would be no respite from now on. For better or worse—and things seemed unaccountably worse this July morning—this was his life, and this was to be the whole of it.

He hurried by the men in the mill who tried to stop him and talk about the strike. The struggle that he was immersed in was within. He argued that he must give up making telescopes, and then wondered dully at the sense of loss, instead of peace, which that decision brought him. It was not only that he had been content while working on the telescope, but that all the thought he had expended on its construction had been like a glowing backlog to whatever else occupied his days. Now he must no longer even think about such things, because they were quite over, and he missed the company of his dreams. Like a man who had decided to give up playing the violin, or painting, his life had become empty of its purpose. He went through the routine of the hours half-dazed. Whenever he forgot his misery through sheer exhaustion, he said, "What is it I have forgotten?" And then it all came back to him. Suddenly in his trance-like state, he heard a voice, apparently his, saying words he had not expected to say. He states the message was so clear that anyone who had been with him could have heard it.

"What a fool you are to worry this way! This worry will never mend that broken glass."

John did not consider himself a believer in telepathy, but from the moment he received this communication he felt things were going well at home. He could not imagine what had changed there, where he well knew all was lost, but the relief was immediate, certain, and lasting. This was at four o'clock. At six, with light step, he went back up the hill.

Phoebe had the steam up in the shop, the engine oiled, the extra disk in the lathe ready to have its edge turned. When he showed ashamed surprise she ignored it. "Why not?" was her attitude.

"But we have been through all this before," he said, "we broke the first lens, too."

"Broke it? It is because we made another lens after we did break it, that I know we can make this mirror."

"They cost too much to break."

"What did we buy an extra one for, then?" she demanded.

There was not a little of the Scotch in Phoebe Stewart. One would have thought that not to have used the duplicate glass they had purchased for such an emergency was wasteful; that she would have been disappointed if their expenditure were unjustified.

John would never have begun again if it had not been for Phoebe. He acknowledged that in every breath of a life-long devotion.

Now he tried out various processes without wasting a good glass on them, and commencing with modifications he says were suggested by Burton in the *Scientific American*, he invented his own formula.

In 1878 the twelve-inch reflector was finished. A bright coat of silver was safely deposited over the surface of the large glass, and also on the little diagonal mirror for reflecting the beams from the central cone to the side of the tube as required in the Newtonian type of telescope.

So elated was he with his success that, after he had tried the new process long enough to be sure it was infallible, he sent it to the *English Mechanic and World of Science*, that famous old weekly from which he had taken the disastrous information on silvering that caused him to shatter his former glass. That part of the story he politely omits to mention, for his article that revolutionized silvering for all time is on record in the issue of June 11, 1880, signed "Brashear, Pittsburgh, Penn., U.S.A."

Having noticed several inquiries in reference to silvering specula, particularly the inquiry of "Vega," I thought I might make myself useful to my fellow workers by giving some hints on the subject that have been valuable to me, and I indulge the hope that they may be useful to others.

His hints were, indeed, so useful they were copied in every scientific journal in the world. Present-day instrument makers are baffled to know how he achieved such sure results from such uncertain beginnings, for his method was, as he went on to say, "so simple as to be easily carried out by almost anyone."

His article of two thousand words tells exactly what sort of glass to use, how to prepare it, what kind of dish to put the silver solution in—"tin, cleaned with ordinary roofing-pitch," a coal-tar product which he states is easily procurable in America. He advises the novice to make plenty of the reducing solution, for which he also gives the formula, as "the longer we keep it the better it gets." The letter is illustrated with a design he drew for a vise to hold the mirror while silvering it. Nothing was withheld, forgotten, or omitted.

"Well I must close now," he finished, "as I have already written too long a letter, but let me ask any of your readers who try the above silvering process to say how they like it."

How they liked it is proved by the fact that the method used today is his. On publication, and with no attempt to patent or even keep the new process for his own work, his method was adopted by everyone. Without knowing it, an uneducated mechanic of Pittsburgh had become one of the great scientists of his day.

Since then, aluminum coating has been perfected, but the silvering of mirrors still has important usage, and has been done continuously for over sixty years by the method evolved by John Brashear in 1878.

VIII

"WHEN THE MORNING STARS SANG TOGETHER"

THE twelve-inch telescope in John Brashear's hands was like a key with which he might unlock the secrets of the sky.

"Beware the dreams of youth," says an Arab proverb, "lest later they come true." Now, at last, did the morning stars sing together, and "all the sons of God shouted for joy," for the silver glass brought the great nebula in the constellation of Andromeda nearer, disclosed the amazing star clusters of Perseus, and revealed a marvel John had only imagined as existing beyond the fog—the double star, Albireo.

There was less light absorption in his reflector than in the refracting telescope he had envied at the Allegheny Observatory, and the colors of the twin star appeared to him for the first time in their natural tints, a golden yellow and blue. His joy was so uncontrollable that he broke out in the words of the prophets he had studied when he was a boy practising his preaching from metaphysical texts: "Which maketh Arcturus, Orion, and Pleiades, and the chambers of the south." That last phrase had seemingly been put in the Bible for his own guidance on the "South Hills."

It had been a long climb to this success, speechless with anxiety most of the way. Now he could sing with Job. For two dark years he had worked on his first five-inch lens, only to break it on completion. He worked another year only to be disappointed when he compared his new effort with the larger lens he found in Allegheny. For two years more he struggled with inadequate silver formulas only to crack his first twelve-inch glass. Phoebe insisted on going on. Still another year went by before he had in his hands, and made by them, the sort of telescope that could penetrate the skies and disclose the imagined glories of "the chambers of the south."

If dozens of people had come to look through the five-inch

telescope which thrust its sharp nose through his humble roof, hundreds now arrived to gaze through the great twelve-inch instrument mounted on its outdoor platform.

His home still retained its unfinished simplicity, but strangers were all made welcome in Phoebe's kitchen where she left the coffee pot on the stove. They never had the luxury of a dining room. Four fireplaces, burning great lumps of soft coal, heated the square rooms, and the friendly back door opening to the shop on the hill was used more often than the front. John designed glass shades, mounted in bronze, for the large oil lamps hanging from the high ceilings, and their simple lines retain a modern spirit. The plastered walls were finally papered, and the floors painted. The casements, door frames, and mantel shelves are almost Georgian in their dignity. His own and Phoebe's room was downstairs at the back, with the front room used for the children and on the other side of the wide hall a parlor and kitchen. This is the sort of house that was visited by the great and the near-great, scientists, teachers, students, and mill workers. Not that they noticed anything but the kitchen. They came to see John Brashear's stars, and stayed to know Phoebe's hospitality.

Chautauqua classes were coming into vogue at this period, 1880. Beginning with the inspiration of the parent resort in New York State, itself the outcome of a Methodist camp-meeting ground, teachers and students were taking their first mail-order or home-study courses during the winter, following their summer vacations spent on the Chautauqua grounds. Finding astronomy rather obscure without any telescope, they applied to John for permission to see through the great new reflector. One at a time, or in hesitant groups of two or three, these seekers after light climbed the hill to Holt Street.

Professor Andrew Burt, author of *Burt's Grammar*, and a well-known pedagogue of Pittsburgh, arrived one night, and with him brought a group of earnest school teachers. Brashear had never had any education except those few winter months each year under Wilkinson in Brownsville, and he realized the

importance of the individual teacher. He knew that the majority of young people were unable to attend college and
could not take advantage of such courses in astronomy as were
now being offered in the Western University of Pennsylvania.
However, as they attended common schools, he felt the teachers of these grade schools should be more efficient, a theory
he passed on twenty-five years later to Henry Clay Frick, who
was able to do something about it. But long before he met any
philanthropist, and afterward, John Brashear was a teacher
of teachers.

Professor E. E. Barnard, the astronomer associated with both
the Lick and the Yerkes observatories, arrived by train one
early morning and searched all over the South Side trying
to find John's address. As no one could tell him where Holt
Street was he finally stopped a workman coming down the
hill with his lunch pail in his hand. He also denied knowing,
but when Barnard asked for John Brashear a light came into his
puzzled eyes.

"Right over there is where Uncle John lives," he said,
pointing to a near-by house.

This was the first time, Barnard wrote John long afterward in a letter celebrating his seventy-fifth anniversary, that
he ever knew a man to be better known than his street and
number. Perhaps he had always lived in level, geometrical
cities. Even today if you were looking for No. 3, it would be
wiser to ask for John Brashear's house than for Holt Street.
It is not properly a street at all, but a horizontal driveway following the side of a steep hill between two perpendicular
roads; its houses on the upper side only, connected with
wooden sidewalks whose steps surmount various levels. A car
could not pass there, for it resembled a mountain deer run.
Pittsburgh takes no exception to such "streets." In the day-
time, looking up at the cliffs, you would perhaps think them
uninhabited, but stand across the Monongahela at night and
see the street lights twinkling tier on tier on the opposite side,
and you will sense a city rising above a city.

Another point that Professor Barnard emphasizes in his congratulatory letter is that Phoebe surprised him with her ample breakfast of ham and eggs, coffee, and hot biscuit. But neither would that surprise a native of the South Side. In fact he would be surprised if he called on anyone in, say New England, and was not offered breakfast. At the junction of the three rivers they feed anyone who comes along at any hour.

John used his telescope, when others were not using it for him, to examine, among other things, the surface of Jupiter and the craters of the moon. When he found the cooling slag at the iron mills formed little craters of their own he studied them intently. Here was a volcano in miniature, the hot molten bed underneath forcing the hardening crust above into cones and pyramids that broke down suddenly to let out the gaseous fluid.

Professor Draper, of New York University, whose book had helped him and with whom he was in close touch, was taking the first lunar photographs, but John Brashear noted that the slag from the rolling mills made replicas of the formations he had seen through his own telescope. At a much later date, Professor W. H. Pickering, of the Harvard Observatory, made a complete survey of volcanic formations on the earth, discovering that the live craters of Hawaii duplicated those found on the moon. He had heard of John Brashear's study of the slag craters and considered them so valuable he came to Pittsburgh. The mills were using the Bessemer process by that time and it was difficult for John to find the same result for Pickering to investigate, but he had encased one of the formations in plaster-of-paris and this was cut in half and photographed to illustrate a chapter in Pickering's book on the moon.

At the noon hour John would gather the mill men around him and show them his little replicas of volcanoes and tell them wonderful stories of the skies. He was their H. G. Wells. He invited them to come up to Holt Street and look through his telescope, and one by one they did. The entire office force arrived in a body, headed by stout Chris Zug, who came panting up to the platform fanning himself with his broad-brimmed felt hat. From other mills also came young men attracted by the unusual peep-show and not afraid to ask questions of one of their fellows. In this way John soon made the acquaintance of "Charlie" Schwab, a youngster of twenty in 1882, employed as stake driver at the seven-year-old Carnegie mills up the river at Braddock, named for Edgar Thompson, president of the Pennsylvania Railroad.

"He that hath eyes let him see." Schwab not only saw the stars for the first time, but saw he was in the presence of a very great man, a conviction that grew when he served on the same board with him in the founding of the Carnegie Technical Schools twenty years later.

This became one of those strange friendships John had with all the millionaire mill-masters. Strange, that is, because he was always humble and forever poor, but not at all inexplicable in the light of their own origins, which naturally they never forgot but relived in his inspiring presence, as if he were their younger selves, retaining forever an innocence which they had traded, inadvertently, and somehow lost. It was their common beginnings that made them understand each other.

Charles Schwab had been born in Loretto, son of a farmer who ran a stage, and when working for a grocer in Braddock, as a lad, came to know "Captain Jones," superintendent of the Edgar Thompson works. Seven years after he had been employed as stake driver for a dollar a day, he was made head of the engineering department for the whole Carnegie interests. After they bought out the Homestead Works, a mile from the foot of John's hill, in 1881, it was Schwab who planned their remodeling. He became, in turn, superintendent of the Edgar Thompson and the Homestead mills, and president of the Carnegie Steel Company when Frick resigned in 1899. He founded the Bethlehem Steel Company and it is said at one time refused $50,000,000 for his stock in it. In 1939 he died poor, and not because he had planned to give his fortune away as Carnegie had, but due to reverses in the "depression" of the early thirties. Yet to the end of his life he frankly took John Brashear as his standard.

Finding that untutored persons were willing to listen to his stories of the constellations, John began writing for the local newspapers. He preferred to have his articles published on weekdays rather than on Sundays, he said, because he had more two-cent than ten-cent friends. As fast as he discovered anything—and the whole science of astronomy was new to America at that time—he was eager to share it.

In the early 1800's, all that was popularly known about the heavens was through the makers of almanacs who followed Benjamin Franklin. The Reverend John Taylor, first rector of Trinity Episcopal Church in Pittsburgh, had lectured to night classes in the Pittsburgh Academy, guaranteeing the accomplishment of "reading the stars" to his students, for he wrote the weather forecasts followed by farmers in Cramer's yearly almanac, the authority of Western Pennsylvania. In 1833 a great meteoric display, and in 1847 a new comet, turned all eyes to the skies, including John's grandfather's. Alvan Clark began to make telescopes in New England which were put into half a dozen of the early universities, and, encouraged by the popular lectures of Professor Mitchel in the observatory down the river at Cincinnati, the "gentlemen of Allegheny" finally ordered one for private use to examine Donati's comet of 1858. When they put Samuel Pierpont Langley in charge of their new observatory ten years later, astronomy began to make important strides at the Three Rivers. But Professor Langley was too involved with his time machine for the railroad and his experiments on the radiation of the sun to popularize star-gazing. He was best known to other astronomers in the east and to his board of trustees.

Before 1880 John had contributed to the *Evening Chronicle*, the *Ledger, Dispatch, Commercial Gazette,* and the *Alleghenian*. His prestige began to roll down the hill from his shop to the river like a great snowball, gathering momentum with every turnover. These articles he was writing out of enthusiasm and with no pay brought his name before a different class of people. They began to wonder who this man was, over on the South Side, said to be a mill worker, but who taught thousands of Pittsburghers more about the stars than they ever learned in any other way.

To the boys of his neighborhood he was a hero and a friend whom they defended from each other. They rallied around his shop that was always left wide open, and not only never stole anything but kept watch, long before the days of Boy Scouts, over his sacred instruments.

He was not content merely to allow anyone to intrude on his precious evenings of work, he felt he should help them further. With this in mind he inserted a single advertisement in the *Scientific American:*

> Silver glass specula, diagonals and eye-pieces
> Made for amateurs desiring to construct their own telescopes,
> Address John Brashear,
> No. 3 Holt Street,
> South Side, Pittsburgh, Pa.

Letters of inquiry immediately began to overburden the postman climbing to his door. He had no secretary, no typewriter, no stamps, no time to answer, for he was working in the mills from six to six. Of course he had not capital to invest in materials. On Christmas of 1880 he made this note,—

Shipped the three mirrors I had made by Adams Express today. One to Hunt, C.O.D. $59.50. One to Hesse, $23.50. One to Bishop, $35. These are my first actual shipments and I do hope they turn out good.

We hope he was paid for them; nothing is said about that.

Not only money matters harassed him from the outset, but his health was overtaxed by double duty, day and night. He was forty years old now, and had found the good way of life delineated by his grandfather Smith, but something had gone wrong. Doubtless he had more than average resistance and strength, that extra pound of effort all artists put into creative work, but although he became a maker of delicate instruments for others he had taken no care of that delicate instrument which was himself. His mode of working accelerated the brain tissues and sapped his physical energy. Like a car driven a long distance without using up its generated electricity, he was surcharged. The batteries were not going dead for lack of stimulus but were being burnt out.

There was a well-known and beloved doctor in Allegheny, by the name of William Herron, who used to call on John every Saturday night. He also possessed a little telescope, and the two men were warm and congenial friends. Finding John sick in bed in the spring of 1881 he issued an ultimatum to the effect that he would have to give up his work in the rolling mills or give up his night work in the shop. This caused John to have a relapse. He could not afford to lose his income and he would not relinquish his telescope. He and Phoebe talked all one night about what they should or could do.

It now seemed fortunate that Effie had married the year before, when she was only seventeen, and brought her young husband home to live. For James McDowell, the adopted daughter's husband, who was employed at the glass works of the Bryce Company down on the flats, had a natural gift for mechanics that John had begun to appreciate, and was willing to help. He would continue to earn his part of the family living by day, and assist in the shop at night. John would give all his time to the business of making astronomical instruments, and they would combine their incomes. His twenty years of work in the mills, from 1861 to 1881, were over.

In the summer of that year Professor Langley sent for John to silver his heliostat mirror. He was about to make an important trip to Mount Whitney, the highest peak of the Sierra Nevadas, to make a study of the selective absorption of the earth's atmosphere, and also to see the solar corona, if possible, without waiting for the time of an eclipse. He wanted the

observing telescope he was carrying with him in perfect condition. The mirror had been made at Clark's, well known eastern manufacturers, but instead of sending it back to them he
entrusted it to John. Evidently he was more impressed with
his ability than the modest workman knew. For although there
had been a few friendly visits back and forth, this was the first
direct commission Langley had given him, and the first opportunity for the new shop. It was to John in the nature of a test
case, and he took great care that there should not be the slightest microscopic scratch on the silver surface.

After he had finished the resilvering, with which he was
now very accurate, he wrapped up the precious mirror in ab-
sorbent cotton and carried it back to Allegheny. It had been
a dark day in Pittsburgh. There was no wind to blow the
smoke out of the valleys and soot hung over the sun like a
black gauze, so that one could look it straight in the face at
noon and see it riding red and round, while one walked below
in gloom instead of sunlight. It was there, in full sight, but it
would not give out any radiance. This made the whole city
swelter. Gas lamps had been lit in all the offices, and people
who had nothing except lamps gave up whatever they were
trying to do because of darkness within doors.

At evening, as John walked the miles through the Allegheny
woods, the light between the trees ahead of him showed crimson, as if the sky were an open hearth and he was approaching
melted iron. No clouds drew various colors across the horizon.
Seering the far hills of the Ohio, the red disk sank fast into its
own metallic brightness, angry with the kind of city which
caused such effect. It would be hotter tomorrow. At four there
had been a sudden thunderstorm which did nothing toward
cooling off the streets. The rain evaporated immediately from
the steaming roofs, and on each doorstep John had passed in
the lower city women sat holding their babies, waiting for the
west wind to rise. The kind of day, as the people in Allegheny
would say, when the Germans buy rope.

John wanted to tell them that it would be better soon, when

the stars came out, but he was not sure they would appear. He felt a little ashamed to be carrying this expensive silvered mirror to someone able to leave the city with it and seek the clear heights of western mountains. Had his sort of work anything to do with reality, after all, or was it, as he thought, the ultimate reality, and all the rest of the city's life delusion? He saw that he had inadvertently incurred a debt to those left behind or beneath, by being this small space removed from his former struggle, for he felt guilty to have left the mills and forsaken the lot of the many.

And because he was very tired, he wondered if, after all, he had been a fool to leave the low road and take the high. Perhaps this visit would tell. For with no margin of capital he might easily be forced to abandon lens-making before he was fairly launched. So far, all that had happened financially was that he could not pay his grocery bill. At least the men in the mills had bread, even if buttered with soot.

As he turned up the observatory hill he looked over his left shoulder to the white crescent of the new moon rising above the city behind him. "That's lucky," he said.

IX

THE TELESCOPE FINDS AN ANGEL IN THE SKIES

SAMUEL PIERPONT LANGLEY was sitting on the old observatory steps talking in the dusk with a stranger. John did not know this elderly white-haired man whose full beard covered a square, determined chin, nor that he was primarily interested in the mirror under his arm that was bound for Mt. Whitney with Langley, because he had helped finance the expedition. John hesitated, and would have turned away to wait a more auspicious moment for presentation if Langley had not called to him.

He was more than a little astonished when they immediately uncovered his precious package in the damp night air, and demurred. And he was surprised that the aristocratic gentleman seemed as interested in it as Langley. Together they pronounced the silvering beyond cavil, and he was introduced to William Thaw.

Even the millworker, John Brashear, had heard of this man whose name resounded through all the valleys wherever boats plied the rivers or railroads followed their shores, but he had never expected to meet him sitting out on any steps. Nor did he know that he had been under discussion before he arrived. What he had overheard was Sam Langley elaborating on his favorite theory of how the dust in the Pittsburgh air made it better, instead of worse, for his observations on the sun because it dulled the direct rays.

Mr. Thaw asked John if he were the Brashear writing articles on the stars for the *Evening Chronicle*, and John was embarrassed to admit his authorship before the scholarly Langley who, he knew, was writing a book. The light quite faded out of the summer sky as these three men, destined to become close colleagues, sat in the deepening shadow of the little ob-

71

servatory. It was John who finally suggested they might have a look, while he was there, at the new comet which Langley confessed he had not yet seen, and seemed to doubt John could locate as it was not visible to the naked eye. Going inside, John quickly found it for them with the observatory telescope that he had approached so timidly five years ago but now handled like a master. Langley was satisfied and Thaw grew positively cordial.

"Young man," he said in his decisive way, "I want to know you better. Come over to my house tomorrow night and let us have a talk together."

John was mystified. He thanked him, wished Langley good luck on his trip to the west, and departed.

The following night he obediently washed up, put on his other pair of trousers and took the horse car over to Penn Avenue in the triangle. The home of William Thaw stood at the corner of Fifth Street, now Stanwix, with a view of the Allegheny River. It occupied most of a city block and its huge rooms were crowded with the art treasures Thaw collected. Many of the early homes of Pittsburgh were on lower Penn Avenue around the Pittsburgh Club, for Liberty Avenue had been ruined by allowing the Pennsylvania Railroad to run on raised tracks down the center of the street. Those who could afford to move had made a hurried exit to Allegheny. But Thaw loved the railroad at his elbow, for he was one of its founders, and he denied that it was a nuisance to his neighbors.

Tired now, with his vast affairs centering around transportation both east and west of Pittsburgh, he received John lying on a sofa in his "back parlor," whose horsehair furniture and high secretary did nothing to make the room seem comfortable. Without rising, he made him sit before him like a schoolboy, and with terse inquiries soon learned more about him than John knew himself. Then he said,

"Tomorrow night I am coming over to see you."

John was abashed for many reasons, and said he was afraid he could not find the way. But Thaw opined that his coachman, Michael, could find his way anywhere, and he could. When Thaw arrived after dark, other people were using the outdoor twelve-inch telescope and he waited his turn to climb the ladder and view the binary star Albireo. It was not until he exclaimed, "I have never seen anything so beautiful in my whole life!" that John relaxed. He knew William Thaw was familiar with the Allegheny telescope, for he was one of the founders of the observatory, so it must be he judged his own effort not too amateurish.

At ease at last, with his usual enthusiasm he took Thaw into his shop and showed him how he had made his lenses, the first that he had broken, and the mirror that had cracked in silvering, and what he was doing with them and what he hoped to do. He recounted his ambition to make telescopes and optical goods for others, and confessed he had been obliged to give up his work in the mills in order to carry on in the shop, and what part Phoebe had played. Together they went into the house and sat down in the kitchen and talked to her over a cup of coffee.

"I see you have the boat, the captain and the pilot," said Mr. Thaw. "Now what you want is some water to float the vessel in. You must have a better and larger shop, better machinery, better equipment. Study your plans, then come to see me as soon as you can. Good night."

With a courtly, old-world bow he left them. They could hear Michael softly complaining as he turned the trap around on the narrow road and put on the brakes as they rattled off down the hill.

William Thaw was one of the few great men in Pittsburgh's period of expansion in the past century who was born there. A tablet has been placed on the Y.M.C.A. building on Wood Street, marking the very house, with dates, "Born October 12, 1818–died August 17, 1889." His father was John Thaw who founded the first bank of Pittsburgh, established as a western arm of a Philadelphia bank, and early the Thaw family was identified with high finance rather than the mills, a distinction they have always wanted people to observe.

William was educated at the old Pittsburgh Academy which became the Western University of Pennsylvania, and later the University of Pittsburgh; and when a boy of sixteen, working in his father's bank, was sent "down river" to make collections at various branches. He traveled alone on horseback, and did much thinking with his feet in the stirrups. For he saw that what the country needed most was new modes of transportation, an ambition to which he devoted his life.

He was one of the founders of the early canal system in the thirties, and helped build the remarkable steam-portage to haul canal boats over the mountains at Altoona. Soon, with others, he extended steam railroads from Philadelphia to Pittsburgh over the Pennsylvania System, completed in 1852, and after the new railroad had ruined the earlier canal venture he started a through boat line to New Orleans, connected with eastern train service, and operated a daily packet from the Point to Cincinnati. This transformed the billing of freight, which had begun with no connecting link between railroad and river, and in order to handle it efficiently he created the Star Union Company, as well as the Pennsylvania Company, formed to manage the interests of the railroads which were rapidly expanding toward the west. Subsequently he became interested in transatlantic shipping, and helped establish the Red Star Steamship Company and an American freight line from Philadelphia to Antwerp.

But it is in his relationship to Pittsburgh that he is best remembered. His personal benefactions began each morning anew, when he is said to have carried a bag of one hundred silver dollars to his office in order to have cash on hand to give away. Leaders of social causes were met with cordiality, and individual beggars were seldom turned aside. In this simple way he began the well-known society called The Improvement of the Poor, and in 1869 started the Workingmen's Savings Bank.

There was, however, another side of William Thaw's nature which prompted him to take part in the founding of the Art Society, to donate prizes for painting and music, and not only to buy canvases from local artists but to hang them on the walls of his home beside his European masterpieces. He gave generously to the Presbyterian Church and to the Western University, and after endowing the old observatory he furnished funds for Samuel Langley's research in astronomy. It was during the eighties that he financed the work of John Brashear, and doubtless for the reason he gave him at the time, "to help push outward the boundaries of human knowledge."

When John demurred, and hesitated to present the plan for his new shop, Thaw quieted him by saying that if John ever became wealthy he could do the same thing for someone else. What John did for thousands later was a different sort of return. He was able, however, to carry out the spirit of William Thaw in a way that would have justified Thaw's investment had he lived to see the result of his example. Thaw was the first man of wealth whom John had ever met, and John expected all the others to be like him. Strangely enough, in their relationship to him, they were. None of the millionaire steel men who coöperated with John Brashear as time went on would be outdone in matters astronomical by the banker of the preceding generation.

Phoebe and John sat up all night deciding what they must have and what they could do without. The plan, as presented to Mr. Thaw within a few days, called for a building twelve by twenty feet, on the same lot, with engine, boiler, two lathes, a drill press, better grinding and polishing machines, and a few new tools. Thaw was satisfied and told them to begin. A contract for the building was let to an old neighbor by the name of Davis, and by the time the shop was finished, the new machinery was in readiness.

The greatest difficulty was in installing the six horsepower engine and getting the boiler up the grade. Four men and their boss worked all day to accomplish this heroic feat, and Phoebe, in gratitude, prepared them a huge dinner, although John doubted there was enough in their lean larder to go around. In December of 1881 the dream was an actuality.

Contracts came very fast now there were means to fill them. George Klages joined the plant as mechanic, and soon young McDowell gave up his position in the glass company to work with John permanently. Before the shop on Holt Street was given up five assistants were employed.

It was after the new shop had been financed that John issued his first advertising pamphlet, a masterpiece of understatement. He must have been advised to do this by his patron, for the whole tone of it is an apology for being forced into a sales talk. John had only visualized himself as the benefactor of amateurs; he had no desire to charge them money. The little paper-covered booklet reads with many a scroll and flourish:

Silvered Glass Reflecting Telescopes and Specula
For celestial observations
By John A. Brashear, no. 3 Holt St.
Best and Co. printers, no. 41 Wood St. 1882

It opens with a short description of astronomy both before and after telescopes were used, and tells what had been added to science by their invention. "A working amateur can now own a telescope that was at one time only within the reach of kings." Then he gives a complete history of the reflecting or silvered mirror type of telescope; compares its cheapness to the cost of the refractor type; and says in learned fashion:

For bringing out the colors of such stars as Gamma Leonis, Eta Cassiopeia, Beta Cygni, Gamma Andromeda, nothing exceeds the beauty of the images in a well corrected reflector, and for seeing the delicate tints of the belt system of Jupiter, and the gradations of light and shade of the rings and surface of Saturn, the reflector is especially suited.

Having thus explained with enthusiasm what a telescope could do, he finally comes to the point he hates to mention:

Within the past year I have increased my facilities for manufacturing all parts of these telescopes to the amount of several thousand dollars, and I am now prepared to turn out good work, fitting each telescope neatly but not fancifully, aiming at effectiveness for work rather than outside show.

Then he tells exactly how they are fitted out, what materials they are made of from tube to eye-pieces, so that anyone might copy them, and continues:

As many mechanics and artisans cannot afford to purchase the telescope complete but can afford the optical parts and construct the mountings themselves, I have had complete drawings made of all the parts which I furnish free to purchasers, and I will be pleased to give any information in construction that may be required by amateur workers.

Having told his customers how to construct a telescope so that all they need to buy is the object glass, he proceeds to tell them how to make that. He reprints his entire formula, as he did in the science magazine, with directions aptly headed, "To clean mirror," "How to support the mirror," "To make the reducing solution," four pages on the precious "Silvering Solution," and concludes with "Remarks to those who mount their own telescopes," which he numbers neatly.

Number Five is:

If using the telescope in an observatory never have many observers at a time as the heat from the bodies passing out the slit in the dome caused bad definition.

Remark Six:

Never discard a hazy night, as hazy nights are frequently best for double star work. A good telescope is well worth the best of care as it is always a source of genuine pleasure and profit. I have frequently said that a single hour's sweeping through the constellations of Sagittarius on a moonless night has many times repaid me all the pains I have taken to make a good telescope.

He does take the trouble to reprint some letters from satisfied customers, among them Francis G. du Pont, and includes a price list which, in the old booklet we saw, had been rewritten in ink, either scaled downward by himself or upward by William Thaw, the prices running from $135 for a fully mounted telescope with 5½ inch lens, to $700 for one of 12½ inches, but he is careful to add smaller sums, from $4 to $12, for the glass alone, proving he thought it folly to invest in the completed instrument. Then, having said too much about costs, he retracts all his business suggestions.

In concluding this little booklet may I say, that my best wishes are for those who with limited means are struggling to get a practical knowledge of the stellar universe. My motive is not merely a mercenary one, as many can attest whom I have assisted to obtain good telescopes without any remuneration for the time spent and advice given. I shall ever hold myself in readiness to give advice so far as my time and ability will permit, *whether you choose to get one of my telescopes or not.* I extend a cordial invitation to anyone interested in this study to call at my shop if they ever come through the city.

But while telescopes were John Brashear's introduction to science, and the thing he taught himself and others to make for the better understanding of the stars, they are not by any means the whole story of his remarkable career. Telescopes are only a single element of the apparatus necessary for astronomy, and it was in the construction of all other sorts of delicate instruments of precision that the great toolmaker became famous.

What could be known of the position of the stellar bodies, their movements and distances from the earth, had been largely solved by the first telescopes made in America by Alvan Clark, and many credulous people were vastly disappointed when they disclosed no men on Mars, and no castles in the moon. Astronomers were now beginning to turn their attention from "position" to the study of the physical nature of the stars, and the great advances at the end of the nineteenth century were in the field of astrophysics, through the invention of the spectroscope and Langley's bolometer, built by Brashear, and the advance he made possible in sky photography. It was in apparatus for scientific investigation that John Brashear excelled. Telescope making was child's play compared to the work that was later done in his shop.

One of the first orders was for a solar-energy box for his friend Professor Langley. The results determined by experiments on this machine formed the basis of his book, *The New Astronomy*, which he read over with John, page by page, before submitting it for publication. At first shy with one another, they gradually overcame the difference in their temperaments and roamed the hills of Allegheny, warm friends, while Langley outlined his future investigations and John decided what sort of instrument he would have to invent to make them possible.

Dr. Charles Hastings, Professor of Physics at the Johns Hopkins University, asked the new shop to polish a prism of glass taken from one of the disks made for the Lick telescope objective. This was done so well by John's assistant, young James McDowell, that it attracted the attention of Professor Henry A. Rowland, who asked that they polish and correct some plates for the "Rowland Diffraction Gratings," a task which almost put the shop out of business.

These plates had to be prepared to be ruled a thousand parallel lines to the inch, and to do this required a plate with "no error of one-fifth of a light wave." To polish them was the task these amateurs had undertaken. When they were returned to Johns Hopkins, John's friend Langley, who happened to be there, wrote him that he had been with Rowland all afternoon testing them and they were right. "If you have thus satisfied his most critical requirements you need not be afraid to work for any scientist in the world."

This success opened a new field, for subsequently John made all the plates used by Rowland, who ruled them and sent them back to him as distributing agent. Several thousand were sent out from his shop and became highly prized by laboratories all over the world. Previous to 1900 he had supplied spectroscopes with these large gratings to the West Point Military Academy, the Sloane Physical Laboratory, the Royal University of Dublin, Cambridge University in England, University of Turin in Italy, McGill University in Canada, and the University of Paris. One of the gratings was presented, as a very special gift, to Sir William Thompson, who became Lord Kelvin, on the occasion of his lecturing at Johns Hopkins. When Professor Keeler, at a later period, showed one of them to Dr. Quincke while attending his lectures in Germany, the scientist was astonished, for he had just told his audience that the one he owned (made by Nobert) was the finest and largest in existence. The Nobert grating was less than an inch while Brashear's plate measured three.

Only once did John have any difficulty after he had commenced this highly specialized work. Professor Rowland tried to measure the accuracy of some of the Brashear plates at one time, with a test-plane made by Steinheil of Munich, and complained he found them uniformly depressed in the center. John hurried in dismay to Baltimore and was greeted summarily with, "Those last plates you made were all wrong."

In the ensuing grief, his first friend in the department, Dr. Hastings, suggested that the test-plane might be defective. Dr. Rowland thought this impossible, but when he compared a plate which he had on hand, made by Steinheil, with the test-plane also made by Steinheil, he found the error was doubled. John was vindicated and all he lost by their mistake was his time and train fare.

This matter of figuring the expense of his work was something John never could master. He could prepare a plate to within one two-hundred-thousandth of an inch, but he could not estimate his prices. William Thaw wrote to him in 1885:

You have to make up a method of computing the cost of your products, including materials, time of skilled work, proper charges for use of plant; and having that, add ten percent for your supervision.

But John never did this. At the outset Mr. Thaw had paid off the indebtedness on his house, and he felt so free from

worry that he plunged into contracts with no thought of reward. As his benefactor, Thaw felt obliged to see him through
and wrote him another letter more tart in tone:

I must insist on your requiring payment before delivery here-
after, for everything you sell. . . . As to . . . and they discover instinctively that you are a devotee to your specialty and
without any commercial greed or experience, and they simply
trifle with you.

So Thaw decided to put John on a salary after building his
first shop. It was not too much, six hundred dollars a year, and
it was to be paid in quarterly installments. This humiliated
John. Attempting to resist further donations, he received a letter which must have humbled him the more.

While I think highly of you and your wife and take pleasure
in opening the way for your work, nevertheless my appropri-
ations to your enterprises are primarily contributions to original research in science, it being my privilege to judge for
myself in the matter, and to regard you and your work as being
entitled to support as if you were a chartered institution and
bore a sounding title. It is not a personal question in my estima-
tion, but a public interest I am serving in keeping you at your
special work.

It is a great responsibility to be considered in the light of a
"chartered institution" or a "public interest." However, it was
only on some such impersonal basis that John would have accepted what Thaw offered him, and doubtless that humanitarian was shrewd enough to know it. Many a scientist since
has wished that someone would endow him like an institution,
for most of the public funds left for research by wealthy men
are stipulated for that purpose. They are for "sounding titles"
and are not open to individuals. John was fortunate in having
both endowment and proceeds, if he could make any profit,
and it seemed to annoy Thaw that he could not.

But there was only one William Thaw, and his unique benefactions died with him before ten more years had gone by.

X

WINGS OVER ALLEGHENY

ONE of the important achievements of the new shop on Holt Street, which, after all, existed only five years when it was forced to leave the South Side for a larger building in Allegheny, was the making of highly polished half-meter bars for Professor William Rogers, who had evolved a new ruling engine for investigating standards of measurement. These bars were not to vary over one fifty-thousandth of an inch from straightness.

After John's experience with Rowland Gratings this was easy. All he had to do was devise a machine on which to teach McDowell to carry out the order in quantity! An aurora spectroscope was made for Professor Edward S. Holden, provided with a single carbon-bisulphide prism, for which John designed an especially thin frame to prevent the expansion of the nauseous liquid from injuring the glass. Inventing new machines for building the parts of someone else's hobby was a privilege to John Brashear. He was the toolmaker. He let others have the credit of being scientists.

In 1884 he read his first paper before the Philadelphia meeting of the American Association for the Advancement of Science. Langley had urged him to lecture on his new method of correcting optical surfaces, and to his dismay he found he was to stand up before savants from England as well as from all over the United States. He had taken Phoebe with him for support (Thaw had paid his carfare), and they were both startled by a criticism from a member of the British Association who had come down from Montreal, and announced didactically that they made lenses and mirrors in England much better and more easily. The well-known Professor Young, however, saved John's reputation by pointing out that his paper was on lenses for astronomical purposes, while his critic was talking about lenses for lighthouses. John's report was published in full, and the following year, after his paper on Rock Salt Surfaces, he was proposed for fellowship by three sections and unanimously elected.

This work on rock salt prisms was undertaken for Professor Langley. Rock salt crystallizes in cubes, and because of its softness and dull color it is difficult to obtain prisms or lenses from it with a high polish. It has, however, a remarkable property for transmitting heat rays, and therefore was especially adapted for Langley's research into heat radiation from the sun. He had tried to secure some prisms made from rock salt with a perfect optical surface from Paris, and although they were shipped hermetically sealed, the very nature of the salt ruined the prisms as soon as they were exposed to Pittsburgh's damp air. This necessitated their being returned again and again to be repolished, and in the meantime all work stopped.

Many skilled workers in this country tried to prepare the perishable rock salt but gave up in despair, and at first John Brashear thought he would have to give up too. But suddenly he woke one morning with an inspiration which mastered the problem forever, an idea which was immediately adopted by astrophysicists all over Europe. Ten years later, after Langley was connected with the Smithsonian Institution, John found some magnificent crystals in the Russian exhibit at the Chicago World's Fair which he advised Langley to procure for him, and from one large piece of rock salt he succeeded in making a five-inch lens and a five by seven sixty-degree prism, an unheard-of achievement. With them, just before his death, Langley finished one of the most valuable researches ever made in solar physics.

In 1886 Thaw moved John's shop from Holt Street to some property he owned in Allegheny, near the old observatory. This site was on Perrysville Avenue, at the top of a long hill, and commanded a fine view of the Ohio so that John would not be too homesick for the Monongahela, where he had lived all his life. "The House of Inspiration" had served him well, and it was with strong emotion that the former mill worker and his wife said goodbye to the South Side where they had been married, and where they made their first lens.

Mr. Thaw stipulated that the shop should be a "firm, solid building," and it stands today, as useful as ever. The testing cellar was the most complete in the country, a startling change from the space under their former home on the slanting hillside. The financial agreement was that John should use the new equipment and premises rent free for five years, the arrangement to be renewed at Mr. Thaw's discretion, or that of his heirs, and although Thaw died a few years afterward the plan was continued for thirty-five years, or as long as Brashear lived.

John moved his family immediately into a small house in the neighborhood, and later built an adequate residence on the same Thaw property near the shop. The fourteen-room house was a delight and an amazement to Phoebe. Previously she had spent much of her time with John in the shop, but now, with the addition of more men to its distinguished personnel, she was relegated to the position of housewife, and would have been very unhappy if it had not happened that she had a natural gift for hospitality, and that her husband was so genial that his house was always full of visitors. Phoebe, as well as John, was over forty now; perhaps it was time she took a rest.

Their family had also increased so that the little house on Holt Street could hardly hold them and the new one was soon filled to overflowing. Their adopted son, Harry, was at this time eleven years of age. The adopted daughter, Effie, who had married James McDowell six years before, had two small sons, John Alfred and James Walter, five and three years old, both born on the South Side. They grew up and married in this house on Perrysville Avenue and continued to live there with their wives and children. Everyone was welcome.

The shop, too, was more than a one-man plant. Besides several helpers who had come from the South Side with him, John soon engaged his two younger brothers, William and Frank, who had started out like himself as mill workers, and became efficient assistants. William R. Ludewig grew up in the shop. John's old friend from Baltimore, Dr. Charles S. Hastings, agreed to become consultant on lenses and continued in the same capacity after he joined the staff at Yale. Professor Very of the Observatory managed special work for a time, and later Fred Hageman became an important figure.

But before he could enjoy his new premises John had to prepare two lectures for the American Association for the Advancement of Science in Philadelphia, where his paper on "Natural Gas in Reference to Its Use in Vertical Boilers" made a sensation in 1886.

Pittsburgh had suddenly discovered ten years before that it was located over a natural bed of gas, and while the coal barons were loath to have its acceptance general, other promoters decided to exploit it not only for illumination but for mill furnaces. No thought was taken of conserving what seemed to be a limitless supply, and on Saturday nights open standpipes on Herron Hill were allowed to blaze to the skies in order to reduce the pressure left by the closing of the mills. For many years persons who had private gas wells on their premises, and there were many such throughout the country-side, let their gas lamps burn night and day on their driveways or kept a flame lit on some outside waste pipe. Brashear was one of the first to recognize the value of gas over the dust of coal for engines designed for laboratories, and used it exclusively in his new shop.

One of John's early accomplishments in Allegheny was the rotating mirror he built for Professor Michelson's experiments in determining the velocity of light. This had to be constructed to withstand fifty thousand revolutions per minute, and in order to revolve so fast, was required to have its four faces absolutely equiangular as well as no deviation in its surface. In a discussion before the American Society of Engineers, of which he later became president, John told of the difficulty of obtaining glass hard enough for this intricate rotating mirror. One soft spot would have ruined its experiments.

At this period, 1886, the five-year-old firm of Warner and Swasey in Cleveland, Ohio, was awarded the building of the great thirty-six-inch telescope for the Lick Observatory to be erected on Mt. Hamilton, California. The firm had commenced by making fine mechanical tools for ordinary usage, and through the enthusiasm of Mr. Warner for amateur astronomy became interested in solar equipment. The Lick telescope was the first to include visual, photographic, and spectroscopic lenses, and because of its size and weight, its installation was a tremendous undertaking. Thousands of tons of rock had to be blasted off the face of the mountain before the observatory could be built.

John Brashear made the spectroscope for it; up to that time the largest ever built in the world. Instruments weighing forty tons were hauled to the top of the four thousand-foot peak, and in 1888 the observatory was finished.

This was the beginning of the long friendship between Ambrose Swasey and John Brashear, culminating in their trip to Japan together thirty years afterward. During the lifetime of these men the Brashear shops made most of the lenses and spectroscopes used by the Cleveland firm, who constructed the gears and mountings for the great telescopes at the turn of the century.

John Brashear had no sooner moved over to Allegheny, hoping to be near his friend Samuel Langley, than Langley was called to the Smithsonian Institution. Soon afterward, in 1887, he was made secretary in charge, but did not relinquish his work in Allegheny for four more years.

This was largely because he had received a grant from his liberal patron, William Thaw, to carry on his experiments in aerophysics, and to carry them on with the help of the new Brashear shop. In this way Thaw could kill two birds with one stone, or one endowment. Aeronautics had long been in Langley's mind, and he had talked over his plans with John in their walks through the Allegheny woods. The astronomer considered that the same toolmaker who had prepared his optical glass for the Mt. Whitney expedition, which led to the bolometer, and to rock salt prisms, was exactly the man to engage on his experiments for a flying machine.

The endowment for this project was Thaw's last and greatest effort to "push outward the boundaries of human knowledge," and the one that he must have enjoyed most. At a time when no one had ever flown, what would such a promoter not have given to send someone soaring into the air from Observatory Hill? But Thaw lived to see neither the success nor failure of the great adventure, and most people have forgotten that it was due to his financial backing and his faith in these two men that Langley was able to commence his work in aerophysics with apparatus executed by Brashear.

One reason for this lack of public recognition is that Thaw made his gifts anonymously. Langley's articles telling of his findings in science read, "This research was made possible through the liberality of a citizen of Pittsburgh." It is John Brashear, in his writings after both Thaw's and Langley's deaths, who explains who this citizen was. In relation to his own endowment he had broadcast the donor to the world from the beginning.

In order to expedite matters, Professor Very was installed in the new shop to help carry out their exciting schemes while Brashear was engaged in other matters simultaneously under way. Langley would leave his plans under Very's supervision while he went off to Washington. John would build the exact apparatus specified and when necessary invent tools and machinery for its completion. This went on until 1890 when, after William Thaw's death, the work was transferred to the Smithsonian Institution.

Perhaps it was his love of fairy tales that made all things seem possible to Samuel Pierpont Langley. Presbyterian Pittsburgh had long been shocked by his unabridged collection of the *Arabian Nights*. To him a flying machine was nothing more than a magic carpet. Or perhaps it was because he, as well as John Brashear, had preserved the wonder and enthusiasm of a child, to whom all things were possible. For children were his only intimates, and one of the first things he did at the Smithsonian was to build a room for them. A lady in Washington, discouraged with his lack of response to her prepared questions in science, asked him what he did like to talk about. "Children and fairy tales," he answered.

Before he became an astronomer Langley was an artist, and his drawings of solar phenomena anteceding photography were remarkable. Artist and dreamer, the force that motivated him was the same that inspired John Brashear: imagination that refused to be limited by boundaries.

But that John was willing to spend his time and energy on this preposterous plan shows not only his genius in adapting machinery to new uses, but the investigating spirit of the scientist. Langley's purpose at this time was not so much to construct an airplane as to discover the unknown laws relating to flight, and therefore he began at the bottom of the problem and worked up. And it was at the very bottom that John began with him in 1886, in the Perrysville Avenue shop.

One of Langley's experiments was the "whirling table" which he constructed behind the old observatory, and on which he fastened little models with light wings of tin or cork, to catch the wind. "There is no miracle about the flight of a bird," he said. If the breeze failed, he attached an ordinary threshing engine. When these curious creatures began to revolve, his back yard must have resembled the lawn of some of the sea captains on Cape Cod full of miniature windmills they made in the winter months to catch the tourist trade in summer.

No tourists, however, were allowed to look over Langley's high fence in Allegheny. One of the young men who began his career there was William Ludewig, afterward on the faculty of the University of Pittsburgh, for which he made a model of this strange merry-go-round as well as models built to scale of the first flying machine of Langley and of the old observatory, on the occasion of the sesquicentennial of the university. Referring to the whirling table, whose engine he stoked as a boy, Ludewig says, "With this attitude, Samuel Pierpont Langley, member of the University Faculty from 1867 to 1891, approached the problem of flight and solved it by careful, painstaking experiment."

Many a "painstaking experiment" must have been made in the shop where Brashear patiently worked out Langley's specifications and as frequently saw his labor destroyed because Langley had already outgrown some plan. One of the most complete orders has been saved, a letter dated Allegheny, March 8, 1887, outlining a small model that had been talked over in detail the day before.

This model was to be one hundred centimeters long, constructed on two horizontal hollow brass rods containing rubber springs in which could be stored up five hundred turns to react on the wheels that were to support four adjustable vanes. "The rudder to be shaped like the tail of a child's dart . . . the weight about one kilogramme to every two centimeters of the sustaining plane surface . . . and the whole to be constructed with a constant eye to future modifications." Langley estimated that it would fly twenty feet.

The principle is somewhat similar to the toy gliders now played with by children, but at that time children played only with kites, and adults with basket-balloons. Such a plane, with all its intricate mechanism, and about six feet long, was no toy.

When Langley had gone to Washington he continued his experiments, trying out his airplane model by drifting it off the balcony of the Smithsonian. He also erected another whirling table, forerunner of the modern wind-tunnel, in that venerable institution; and on one occasion mounted a large propeller on the rear of a handcar and tried it out on the Pennsylvania tracks before building a small stretch of his own.

As his planes grew larger he recognized a lack of balance, and attached a tin can whose contents could be altered, like the old-fashioned pail-weights of a grandfather clock. When he swung it under the front of the body, the plane went down by the nose—under the back, and it dived tail first. But when he put the balance dead center the plane swung round and sailed off out of sight. This was his first successful flight.

Dr. C. G. Abbot of the Smithsonian says in his book about his predecessor:

Langley, on May 6, 1896, in the presence of Alexander Graham Bell and others, successfully catapulted from a houseboat on the Potomac a thirteen-foot steam powered model which flew over one half mile and landed, softly, unharmed, on the water. In November of the same year another large model made an even longer flight of three quarters of a mile.

The steam power was generated by a tiny engine with a very fine burner, and he was criticized (among other things) because it burnt too much fuel. "I would burn gold," said Langley, "if it would make it go."

Everyone was surprised when it did—except his former mechanic in Allegheny and perhaps his former stoker of the whirling table. Luckily he had witnesses or the story would not have been believed.

As if he knew he would never fly himself, he wrote John Brashear, who always had faith in him:

I have now brought to a close the portion of my work which seemed to be especially mine, the demonstration of the practicability of human flight. For the next stage, which is the commercial development of the idea, it is probable the world may look to others. The great universal highway overhead is soon to be opened.

These first models that flew had not been designed to carry human freight, as no one could guess whether they would stay up or not, and Langley had no idea of committing either suicide or murder. He worked for several years more, at first repeating the same mistake, the principle that a bird soars on motionless wings, a theory that the Wright brothers overcame by a slight warping. In 1903 the machine he finally constructed and considered able to sustain itself and a pilot fell into the Potomac.

A chorus of "I told you so" echoed around the globe. Tormented by an ignorant and hostile press which considered him no better than a fool, and overwhelmed by the astonishing success of the Wright brothers who profited by his mistakes and made their first flight over the sand dunes of Kitty Hawk shortly afterward, Langley became despondent and gave up.

Yet the Wright brothers freely admitted it was the knowledge that Samuel Pierpont Langley, the distinguished head of the Smithsonian, believed in the possibility of human flight, which led them to dare their own undertaking. Airplanes had a great lift upward purely through his example. "He recommended the right books for us to read," they said. "It was a helpful hand in the right direction."

Shortly after this disastrous experience John Brashear was at the Smithsonian in Washington when Langley heard his voice. Coming into the room where John was talking he took him by both hands.

"I want to talk to you," he said.

Then he picked up two little pieces of steel and handed them to John.

"This is what wrecked my life," he said. "My life work is a failure. This broke and turned my ship into the Potomac instead of up in the air."

Brashear says he replied, "Your work in the study of the earth's atmosphere and the possibility of life is enough for one man to do." And then adds, dryly, "But it was no consolation to him."

Langley died in 1906 without knowing that in 1914 that master of the controls, Glenn Curtiss, was to fly the same plane that had failed on the Potomac in a government trial over Lake Keuka, and that Curtiss would declare Langley could have flown it himself if he had installed a heavier engine. Langley always calculated his stresses to the breaking point of the material to insure lightness, and something—the little piece of steel he had shown John Brashear—snapped.

On the Langley airplane now on view in the Smithsonian Institution which has become the mecca of thousands, is this caption by Dr. Abbot:

The first heavier-than-air craft in the history of the world capable of sustaining free flight under its own power.

John, who had worked with Langley for the first fifteen of the thirty years he had known him, mourned his failure as a personal disgrace, and his last flight into what he always called the "Summerland of Song," as the passing of a brother.

XI

THE GODS OF THE MILLS

"THE mills of God grind slowly, yet they grind exceeding small." The gods of the mills in Pittsburgh moved in another orbit from that of John Brashear, who ground lenses, and the manner of their meeting was exceeding small. It came about because of a greenhouse and a penitentiary.

The old Western Penitentiary stood on a part of the Commons donated by the town for a city park, and in 1883 was abandoned, as being an unfitting mixture of playground and prison, and soon afterwards torn down. It had been considered a very fine edifice, with its classic façade and Norman towers even reproduced on china plates made in England, and perhaps because thrifty citizens bemoaned the loss of its elegance Henry Phipps conceived the idea of erecting a conservatory in the same place, where rose gardens were laid out on what was formerly the jail yard.

This conservatory was finished in 1887, a year after John Brashear had moved over to Allegheny, and because it was a fine new toy for the steel men to admire they formed a habit of meeting there every Sunday morning. Another reason for this was because Mr. Phipps had stipulated in his gift to the city that his conservatory should be open to the public on Sundays as well as weekdays, so as to give the working men an opportunity to enjoy beauty. Then, as now, this caused great anguish to pious folk who tried to block such an evil with their blue laws but were defeated by a more worldly city council. So if the conservatory was to be open, open it was, and to make sure of it Mr. Phipps himself, and several of his cronies, used to foregather there and weigh the merits of carnations against tea roses instead of attending church.

Here also came their new neighbor, John Brashear, a very religious man, who had once intended to go into the Methodist ministry, but became discouraged after his first disastrous sermon and had continued worshiping God in his own way, through the stars. All he had to do to join his neighbors at the "Conservatory Club" was to walk the few miles from his home on Observatory Hill, down the long winding road into Allegheny and keep straight ahead to the Commons. There, if Phoebe had accompanied him, he could leave her at one of the red brick churches and keep on past the statue of George Washington to the group of greenhouses.

As John had been a mill worker for twenty-five years, and all the interests of the Allegheny men of wealth centered that way, he became a favorite with the members of the impromptu Sunday morning club, sometimes called "Phipps' Sunday School." "Charlie" Schwab had told them how he had looked through John's telescope in the South Hills, and pronounced it better than the one at the observatory, and that he was some sort of genius whom Thaw had brought over to Allegheny to work for his hobby, astronomy. William Thaw, who lived in downtown Pittsburgh, was not a member of this group, but they knew him well, not only through their business interests but as one of the trustees of the Western University which had recently moved over to their side of the river and wanted to be permitted to build anew on the Allegheny Commons.

The Commons had been reserved for the use of all those who had adjacent lots, and was originally useful for pasturing cows. Now that one hundred acres had been donated for a park by landowners who had given up their rights, they were naturally particular about what disposition was made of it. The "Conservatory Club" took the position that the university could struggle along where it was for a while, crowded into the quarters of the Western Theological Seminary. Because the jail had been torn down was no reason to litter up the new lawn with more such buildings. None of them had ever been to college but they knew how such matters worked. First the trustees would erect one ornamental building and then, when no one was looking, erect so many more that soon there would be no space left for sitting under the trees.

Some of them suggested that the university might have used the old jail, after the prisoners had been removed to the larger one down the river, but it was already demolished and the conservatory stood in its place. Then why not move the university to the hill where the observatory stood? Anyone ambitious enough to go to college would not object to the distance.

So they would spend the morning discussing civic affairs and planning deals that controlled the business of coal and steel all over the nation. Henry Phipps, who had built the conservatory where they gathered, was one of the associate partners of Andrew Carnegie, but nearer the age of "Andy's" younger brother, Tom, with whom he formed a partnership within a partnership. When they were boys they had lived on the Allegheny Bottoms, where other gods of the mills were growing up—Henry W. Oliver, Robert Pitcairn, David McCargo, and Thomas N. Miller. It was a familiar sight in Civil War days to see Harry Phipps, a lad of twenty, walking back down the river road from Kloman's Mills with the firm's ledger under his arm. He had begun his bookkeeping career by borrowing a quarter from his brother and investing it in an advertisement in the *Dispatch*—"Willing boy wants work"—which in those days brought results and was worth the speculation.

When Andrew and Thomas Carnegie bought an interest in their first iron works, that of Kloman, their friend Tom Miller became another partner and invested $800 for Henry Phipps, which lifted the young bookkeeper on the road to fortune. It was a quick succession from Kloman's to the Cyclops, Lucy, and other iron mills, followed fast by the steel mills. Phipps became head of the Edgar Thompson Works at Braddock in 1883, and head of the Carnegie-Phipps Steel Company in 1886. In the division of labor of these steel kings it is said that Phipps "took in the pennies and kept the overhead down."

After the formation of the Carnegie-Phipps Company, each of the partners had money to give away. One of the first gifts of Carnegie was the public library to Allegheny in 1886; and, not to be outdone by his Scotch friend, Henry Phipps immediately started work on the conservatory for the same city. The men he gathered around him of a Sunday morning were those he had known from youth, and they all became friends of John Brashear. The only botanist in the club was William Hamilton, the park superintendent, who pointed out to the steel men the differences between the growing things that showed their green heads around them.

One of the conservatory philosophers was James Patton, a witty Irishman of the old private banking firm in Allegheny. One day when he was walking with Brashear beside the lake on the Commons where the swans were lifting their long necks, Patton remarked to a gardener, "We have things like that back home, but begorrah we call them Irish Geese."

"Go on with yer blarney," replied his compatriot. "Ye never had the loikes of them in any bog you nor me come from."

Henry Phipps loved to tell how his horse and buggy used to zigzag across Fourth Avenue, from bank door to bank door, when he was seeking loans for the growing iron and steel business. When the banks began to turn to him, he said, he tried to sell the familiar equipage, but the purchaser brought the horse back. "He's no good," he complained. "He can't keep a straight line down the street."

The most characteristic story about Phipps was told by Brashear at a later period. It seems he had presented another greenhouse to the new Western Penitentiary at Wood's Run, perhaps because of the fact that he had already built his first one on the site of the old Allegheny jail. He had returned from New York for a banquet at the Duquesne Club, and he read aloud to his assembled friends a letter that he had received from one of the prisoners. It told of the condemned man's reformation through being permitted to work with the beautiful flowers in the conservatory Phipps had built, and how the prisoner had turned from a life of crime to a true appreciation of God's blessings. The steel men present were so moved they furtively dabbed their napkins to their eyes above their turtle soup.

"What shall we do about a fine criminal like that?" Phipps asked John, who sat next to him.

"Get him out," said John briefly.

So Henry Phipps drove over to see the warden of the penitentiary, John Francies, and asked for the release of the prisoner who had written the letter, saying he would "see the right people about it."

"Fine," said John Francies, "pick out any man you like and I'll let him go. I wrote the letter myself."

Henry Phipps was disappointed, but agreed with the warden to save someone else as a symbol of regeneration. John Brashear remarked that it would make no difference in the sight of the Lord.

The Western Penitentiary was always on the minds of more fortunate men who had succeeded in keeping out of it, and John Brashear made a habit of going there often, to show the prisoners pictures of the moon and stars so that they would not forget them. Arriving on one occasion after he had described Halley's Comet to them, he found in the waiting room fourteen amateur telescopes, sent there hopefully for his inspection. The prisoners had made them from strips of paper wound around broom handles, stiffened with glue and drawn off again intact, so that they formed hollow tubes; and had somehow secured old spectacle lenses for eye-pieces, with the idea of using them through the bars of their cells to watch the midnight sky. He says it was one of the hardest things he ever had to do in his life, to tell them they were worthless.

Henry Phipps did not stop with endowing conservatories in Allegheny. Following Carnegie's gift of a great library in the East End of Pittsburgh, Phipps promptly endowed a second conservatory in 1903 that stands near-by in Schenley Park. Carnegie's first library had gone to Allegheny because the Pittsburgh Council had declined to support one, so they failed to receive their own impressive building until he forgave them for changing their minds ten years later. Henry Phipps also had ideas ahead of his times, and in 1907 endowed the Phipps Tenements in Allegheny, forerunner of all the great city housing plans. But his times were similar to ours in this respect, that the tenants to whom he offered bathtubs were universally ungrateful, and he had a hard time filling his model apartments with needy working men.

This experiment failed to discourage Phipps, however, for he gave a million dollars for the same purpose to New York. He later endowed a clinic for the Johns Hopkins Hospital and served as trustee both at Johns Hopkins in Baltimore and the University of Pennsylvania in Philadelphia, where he erected the Phipps Institute.

Twenty years before he met John Brashear, Henry Phipps and Andrew Carnegie and John W. Vandervort had made their first trip to Europe. To "Andy" it was a gay return. Being young men in their twenties and thirties, they tramped the roads of England with their knapsacks on their backs, and finally found their way to most of the capitals of Europe, ending by roasting eggs on the crater of Mt. Vesuvius.

They had agreed then that later they would go around the world, and "Andy" and "Vandy" had done so, but Henry Phipps was too burdened with vast affairs entrusted to him in Carnegie's absence to leave the country at the same time. However, he remembered the thrill of the crossing and wanted his son John, a lad of fourteen, to have the same experience. In 1888 he asked John Brashear to take the young boy at his expense, and make a simple tour of England, France, and Germany.

To John, this invitation from Mr. Phipps was as amazing as if Langley had asked him to mount his tentative airplane and fly to the moon—a journey they had both (and not too laughingly) contemplated. John had not only never been to London, he had never been to New York. Lake Erie was the largest body of water he had ever seen, and what lay beyond the Atlantic was to him simply a series of postal addresses. His correspondence with various astronomers had early taught him the value of a five-cent stamp, but the cost of steamer passage and the mysteries of procuring a passport were unknown. He was no rover, nor that sort of poet who journeys to far lands for "material." His material was all in his workshop, and his contentment with his wife in his home. Certainly he would go nowhere without her.

But when he told her that of course he was going to refuse, Phoebe insisted on her ability to carry on his work so that he might leave. Her offer, however, was not realized. John consulted his patron, Thaw, and that man of lavish habit not only decided that orders under way could be postponed for a few months or left with various other experts in the new shop, but added enough to the traveling stipend to insure Phoebe's accompanying him. Also he insisted on "money for cabs, so as not to waste time walking." (Phipps had walked all his life; the sort of millionaire who was open-handed in large affairs and had the reputation among his intimates of quarreling with the cabbie every time he drove up to a hotel.)

If John Brashear had been an educated scientist, these gods of the mills who came to know him at the "Conservatory Club" would not have been as interested in helping him. Nor were the vacations offered him at various times by steel men for the purpose of aiding science. The only science they were concerned with was the making of laboratory tests in their foundries, an innovation of Phipps. The reason John became popular with them was because he was their own sort. Their fathers had been humble artisans, as his had, in a pioneering country, and in their youthful days they had not reached such a skilled position as that of millwright, but had jumped from a few years on the fringe of the iron business to investment and management.

Yet these hard-headed Scotchmen and soft-hearted business men of the past century were astute enough to have respect for John's success, which to them was as significant as, and far more amazing, than their own. They recognized that he had endured everything they had endured and won all they had won, excepting money. And as the height of their ambition was always to get away from Pittsburgh, as far and as fast and as long as they could, Phipps decided to send John to Europe.

XII

THE GODS OF THE MOUNTAINS

HIGH in the Allegheny Mountains, where the old canal portage once lifted the boats from the valley of the Little Juniata and deposited them in two pieces in the valley of the Conemaugh, was a lofty summer resort at Cresson Heights frequented by the steel men, where Andrew Carnegie, the god of all the gods of the mills, had drawn around him a Valhalla, a place of peace for warriors from the city.

Carnegie had been a train telegrapher at near-by Altoona when a young man, and William Thaw had been one of the founders of the canal system and afterwards interested in the railroad that supplanted it, so that the vicinity of Cresson from the Horseshoe Curve to the great reservoir at South Fork was familiar to both. After Thaw had moved the Brashears to Allegheny in the middle eighties and had come to know John and Phoebe in more than a business way, he sometimes invited them to Cresson as he did Samuel Langley to get the soot out of their lungs, called locally "taking a breather."

Carnegie, who had lived in New York since 1867, returned every spring and fall with his mother, who compared these hills with the Scottish Highlands. When she became too old to accompany him on coaching trips in England, he would leave her here during midsummer, but always hurried back and often remained in the mountains until snow fell. Until Margaret Morrison Carnegie died in 1886 and Andrew married the beautiful Louise Whitney of New York, his life with his adored mother at Braeburn Cottage was part of his routine. The summer neighbors ate together at the Mountain House, and John had the opportunity when he visited Cresson Springs with Thaw to know Carnegie in the same informal way that he knew Henry Phipps through his conservatory—by chatting with him on an idle Sunday morning.

The cottages in the mountains reminded John of his old

* : Should be Whitfield (not Whitney!)

home on Holt Street, for they also were of the Steamboat Gothic period, decorated with cornices and balconies. In June the paths through the woods were bordered with pink laurel, and in the autumn the maples turned color quickly while the red oaks held their leaves until the chestnut burs lay under foot. Carnegie loved horseback riding over the mountain trails, but John walked them, followed by devoted Phoebe in her pointed laced shoes and ruffled skirts. Such people as Judge Josiah Cohen and his charming young wife, who played the piano for Carnegie's mother in the evening, became their friends. Here he met C. C. Mellor, head of the well-known music firm, as well as B. F. Jones, the steel magnate, and Edward Bigelow, the park commissioner.

A story is told of Bigelow at the time he was trying to persuade Mrs. Schenley to give the lands she had inherited from her grandfather, General O'Hara, for a city park. She was living in England, and Bigelow heard that her business manager in Pittsburgh was going there to dissuade her from such generosity. So he hurried over himself, on a faster boat, and won the race and the park, where his statue stands today.

One of the men who had a summer home here was Dr. William J. Holland, the paleontologist, who became president of the Western University of Pennsylvania when it was situated in the nineties at John Brashear's back door in Allegheny, and ten years later became director of the new Carnegie Museum. He said he showed "Andy" how to track the elusive snowbird to its nest under the mountain fern, and told how proud the steelmaster was when he located one all by himself; and how John Brashear looked more like an artist than a business man, with his soft black tie and loose coat, swinging with easy gait over the mountain paths, as alert as a bird or a deer.

Such men as these brought the group of mill men at Cresson into contact with the Pittsburgh artists who spent their summers on another near-by mountain peak, called Scalp Level. The painters did not own fine cottages like their friends at Cresson Springs, but boarded with mountain farmers, and were similar to their stylish neighbors only in that they ate at a common table. Here, for a dozen years, they wrote the history of art of Western Pennsylvania.

Joseph Woodwell was the Pittsburgher who started the painters' colony. After he had studied in France, he brought back the idea of establishing a painter's paradise in the mountains, similar to the Barbizon school near Versailles, and soon he became the center of a group who followed him to the woods and pitched their easels on the slopes of the Alleghenies. Martin Leisser, George Hetzel, A. Brian Wall, and John Alexander, who was commissioned by Andrew Carnegie to do the symbolic murals of the mills when he built his new institute in Pittsburgh, summered at Scalp Level. John Beatty, the first art director of Carnegie Institute, was a leading figure.

Across the valley and the railroad that followed the Conemaugh River, another mountain top became a third resort, that of the Fishing Club at South Fork. To make a proper lake for their sport they had erected a dam across the Conemaugh, forming a huge reservoir useful only to themselves, but never considered a menace until it broke. Colonel William Allen, who was the patron of John Alexander, the artist, was one of the charter members of the Fishing Club and it was he who started the saying that it was "easier to get into society from the Allegheny Bottoms than from the East End." The Fishing Club with its beautiful reservoir was a rival of Cresson Springs. Its members said that the railway at Cresson ran right by the hotel door, and "only railroad men could stand it."

Joseph Woodwell was popular with all three groups who spent their summers in the mountains, and when John Brashear went for a walk he sometimes stumbled on him setting up his canvas. One day when he was looking over Woodwell's shoulder he remarked encouragingly, with a gesture toward the view, "It looks just like it." Woodwell drew back, quizzically, and held his brush between his teeth, while he cupped his hands to squint at the subject matter.

"Do you want a telescope?" asked John, helpfully.

"No," said Woodwell, turning back to his palette to daub on another bit of paint, "and it ought not to look 'just like it.'"

"Why not?" asked John, and added, "My grandfather used to make daguerreotypes."

"That's what I mean," said Woodwell. "If you want a photograph, all right. A painting ought to be something more, ought to add something."

John repeated this at the Mountain House, and they all decided there was more to this business of painting than met the eye. At Cresson the steel men had their first glimpse of "life among the artists," and the men from the mills never seemed to tire of talking at the Springs about the painters at Scalp Level.

That the influence of these men of gentle manners had some direct bearing on the founding of the art gallery by Carnegie is quite probable, for here he met the artists face to face on his long rides through the woods, saw them working, and heard them discuss what ought to be done for the city. The seed was planted at Cresson that blossomed twenty years later into an endowment worth untold millions. For Carnegie was not the sort to build a treasure house blindly; he began with the personnel. If the steel men who remained at home while he toured Scotland were the ones who made his fortune for him, as they liked to claim, the artists of Cresson and Scalp Level were the ones who showed him a graceful way of spending it, when the time came that he decided to die poor.

Phoebe enjoyed a new life at Cresson Springs. In her draped and bustled dress of the Godey's Book type, and her pancake hat tied over her waterfall curls, she could wield a croquet mallet with the best of the champions on the hotel lawn. She did not think much of the Philadelphia scrapple they served for breakfast, nor the summer sausage always on the table for lunch with the *schmierkäse*, for she was a better cook herself than the Pennsylvania Dutch chef. However, she condescended to write down one or two of the recipes, such as fried chicken simmered in sour-cream sauce.

When the other ladies sat down to casino or took a hand with their husbands at double whist, she wandered off to the woods, fascinated by the steep chutes from the lumber camps to the river, and the ox sleds she met coming down the road, heralded by the loud "Haw! Buck!" of the burly drivers. She traced the deer runs near the old canal route and, when exhausted, sat in a wooden rocker on the porch and knitted her long strips for garters. The woman most congenial to her was Carnegie's mother, "Maggie Morrison," who knew, like Phoebe, another side of life before her gnarled hands lay in her lap at the age of seventy. Madam Carnegie often talked to her son about the kindnesses of these two dear people, Phoebe and John. She saw to it that Andrew never extended any little courtesy to the husband but that he included the wife, recognizing in Phoebe the steady hand on the wheel of John's destiny.

Phoebe was an experienced woman of forty now, with merry brown eyes and quick movements, a favorite with everyone who met her. The kind of woman of whom others say, "I know her husband wouldn't amount to anything if it weren't for his wife." In a daguerreotype of her at this period she has unusual grace. Her dark hair is parted in the middle as always, and her hands speak as much as her mobile mouth. Her dress is all ruffles and tucks and pleatings, and she seems amused by it herself, not self-conscious of her elegance as in the portrait of her youth.

Best of all the amusements of Cresson she liked the cool evenings, when John and she would sing duets at the melodeon of the Mountain House—"My Darling Nellie Gray" by Stephen Foster, or the Methodist campmeeting hymns, "Let the Lower Lights be Burning" and "When the Roll Is Called up Yonder I'll Be There."

John Brashear was greatly loved by these devotees to mountain views and happy valleys. They saw in him the white flame of the artist, as if his spirit had passed through the fire of one of the city's crucibles, as in truth it had. Haniel Long, the poet, said of him,

Brashear walked through Pittsburgh like a visitor from the Islands of the Blest. Maybe Brashear had a sixth sense, maybe he was reborn. Some people are not afraid things can overpower them. Some people can accept things without forcing their will on them. Could you imagine Brashear thinking that God was on his side?

In the symposia at Cresson Springs he contributed his enthusiasm for the stars, making them known to the painters by their colors, and to musicians by their motions in space. To writers he told stories of the moon that loomed larger over the Alleghenies than over the city of that name. Because of their admiration for him he became a member of their cultural societies in the city, and with the founding of the great Carnegie Institute he took his place on the first board of trustees for building the museum, music hall, and art gallery, with many other old friends of the days at Cresson—Dr. Holland, Joseph Woodwell, C. C. Mellor, Josiah Cohen, Edward Bigelow, and A. Brian Wall.

Five miles north of Cresson lay the village of Loretto, sacred to the traditions of Demetrius Gallitzin, who had left the halls of the Romanoffs and the courts of Europe to become Father Smith to the Indians. After receiving the first Catholic orders granted in America in the early part of the nineteenth century he had built a chapel in the wilderness and enshrined a piece of the "True Cross" near the altar. The Gallitzin coat of arms was set in the stained-glass windows. This remote shrine was one of the places John and Phoebe always visited when they spent a few days close by, for their friend Charles Schwab had come from this Catholic community and had been educated by the Franciscan brothers.

Schwab's father ran a stage that carried passengers and freight from the railroad stop at Cresson, and when a boy "Charlie" had often driven the coach for the summer visitors. He remembered having driven Carnegie when he met him again on different terms. But by the time Schwab was ready to build himself a country house at Loretto the days of the com-

mon table at Mountain House were over. After the death of
William Thaw in the late eighties and the withdrawal of Carnegie more and more to Scotland the summer cottages passed
into less prominent hands and the summer colony finally into
desuetude.

A stranger fate overtook the Fishing Club at South Fork.
In 1889, the private dam built across the Conemaugh River
broke and precipitated the famous Johnstown Flood.

The Fishing Club would have been as forgotten as Cresson
Springs has come to be, if horrified mountaineers had not per-
petuated its memory by pointing out in a forceful way that
they knew all the time that the dam was weak, and how did
these city folks get the right to dam the river? The tide of
indignation that followed the Johnstown Flood sprang from a
reservoir of anger. The cottages of the absent club members
were located too high to be swept away in the debacle they
had caused, but none of the occupants cared to return there
again for a great many reasons—one of which was that there
were no more fish. Only the artists at Scalp Level escaped the
contumely directed toward members of mountain resorts in
general by farmers who lived, and whose friends had died, in
the valley. Like artists the world over, in time of war, plague
or flood, the Scalp Level colony continued on painting its
gentle landscapes until mining operations eventually dug the
ground out from under their feet.

Carnegie was quick to understand that he was in the presence of genius when he met Brashear in the mountains. He
realized that as much ability went into creating a perfect lens
as into his own sort of tonnage. As soon as he heard that John
and Phoebe were taking the son of his partner, Phipps, to England, he asked them to visit him there.

XIII

"INNOCENTS ABROAD"

FORTIFIED with introductions from friends, and his own long correspondence with astronomers in Europe, John, with Phoebe and Johnny Phipps, set sail on the *Chicago* in the summer of 1888.

The *Chicago* was a one-class cabin boat of the French Line carrying freight and passengers, and took fifteen days to cross the water. But to John and Phoebe, it was as if they were crossing today on the *Queen Mary*. As they steamed slowly past the Statue of Liberty and rounded Sandy Hook they hung over the rail, clinging to the last sight of land, then sat down in their steamer chairs with their mail and watched the departing seagulls while Johnny explored the "dog deck." They were quite amazed when the steward told them that they were to sit at the captain's table.

It was not long before John was invited up on the bridge where he tried out his knowledge of the stars on navigation. Phoebe amused Mr. Phipps' son with shuffleboard and counted the times they trod the narrow decks round. John Phipps was the same age as her adopted son Harry whom they had left at home with Effie Afton McDowell, whose husband was running the shop, and there was nothing about a fourteen-year-old youngster that Phoebe did not understand. Uncle John let him use his wonderful binoculars, the finest on shipboard, and they never missed a porpoise or a flying fish all the way over.

When they arrived in Europe there was no problem of what to do with John Phipps at night, for the Brashears seldom went out after dark. Phoebe would scan her guidebook and make out an itinerary for the following day, while John took Johnny for a walk. By ten they were all asleep, and at seven in the morning up and dressed ready to start the day anew, the habit of a lifetime. Phoebe enjoyed the English breakfasts with a choice of kidneys or fish but her housekeeping ability was offended by the meager French coffee and rolls. In France they learned the word for rabbit stew, and in Germany for sausage, and ignored the rest of the unintelligible menu.

Phoebe was surprised that she did not see many elegantly dressed women on the streets of London or Paris. Like all Americans abroad for the first time she was looking for the Parisian styles, and did not know she was looking in the wrong places, public thoroughfares and simple restaurants. Most of the well dressed women she saw turned out to be Americans like herself. But once when they went to the theatre in London she was shocked to find the audience wore evening clothes, and several times John was embarrassed at private dinners in England by the same universal custom.

The benefit the youthful Phipps boy derived from the plan was to see the usual museums, galleries, parks, and mountain passes, free from cant, and under enthusiastic guidance. His father had made no mistake about his choice of a guide. To travel with John Brashear was a liberal education. What Phoebe and John received was a European course in astronomy.

The customs inspector at Liverpool became over curious about a wonderful six-inch grating that John was carrying along for delivery, and almost ruined it. These instruments were so sensitive that he always washed his hair, as well as his hands, to get rid of Pittsburgh coal dust before he worked on them. The touch of a hand, or the warmth of one's breath, would spoil the labor of months. A spectroscope fitted with such a grating sold for three or four thousand dollars. Thereafter he carried the grating in his pocket, and as it weighed ten pounds, officials must have looked the other way when they saw his sagging overcoat. Luckily he did not have to bring it back through the customs of New York.

Their first call, of course, was at the Greenwich Observatory, the official meridian from which longitude is reckoned. In London, as in every city where they stopped, they called on the famous makers of optical instruments. They spent an evening with the scientist, Dr. Maw, in Kensington, who knew all about John because he had recently published an illustrated article for the Royal Astronomical Society on the Lick Observatory, for which John had made the greatest spectroscope in the world. Sir James and Lady Dewar entertained them at luncheon, and Sir James not only showed them around the Royal Observatory but gave them cards so they could take their young charge to the London Zoölogical Gardens. And another thing that John claimed he would not have had time for, except to show it to the Phipps boy, was Madam Tussaud's Wax Works. But that trip proved to be like a father's excuse for taking his boy to the circus, and Phoebe never recovered from all the delightful horrors. Soon they had to leave London, whose foggy atmosphere made them feel at home, for the promised visit with Andrew Carnegie and his bride at Sunningdale.

This was the summer Carnegie was making a six-weeks tour of the English cathedral towns on his way to Cluny Castle. After a luxurious week as the guests of the "Star Spangled Scotchman," the Brashears and John Phipps were escorted in Carnegie's coach with footman and bugler to Slough, to see the home of Sir William and Sir John Herschel, "Observatory House."

Here they met the four daughters of the famous astronomer, Sir John, and his son Alexander, and with them mourned the great telescope left dismantled and rusting away in the garden. As he reverently embraced the grand old broken tube, John's thoughts turned back to the beginning of the century. An informed romanticist, he brought his own understanding to bear on whatever was before him. In London he had enjoyed seeing the original dynamo of Michael Faraday, father of all electrical energy, and in Cambridge, a reflecting telescope of Sir Isaac Newton, ancestor to his own reflector.

They were warmly received in Paris by Paul and Prosper Henry, young astronomers becoming famous for their astral photography. Following dinner in their *petit appartement*, the

Henrys brought out cobwebbed vintages from their hiding place, but their cordial French gesture was entirely wasted. To make up for their lack of appreciation of the wine, John and Phoebe furnished the song, sitting down at the new Mason and Hamlin melodeon with its bracketed oil lamps at either side of the music rack, and running through their repertoire of Stephen Foster ballads.

The Frenchmen's "Bis, Bis, Encore!" surprised them, and in letters received during a long ensuing friendship, the Henrys constantly referred to the evening of the *musicale charmante*. Foster and John Brashear had both gone a long way from Allegheny.

At the works of Bardou, makers of field glasses and small telescopes, John ordered a number of objectives at great cost, only to find on their delivery to his shop that they were so poor, judged by his own standards, as to be worthless to him. One of his gratings which had arrived before him and was in use at the national French Observatory assured his welcome at Meudon, as also at Leipzig and Potsdam.

But before entering Germany their young charge enjoyed climbing the Swiss Alps, and the party arrived in Munich in time to join in singing "Die Wacht am Rhein" with the crowds on the street serenading old General Von Moltke, hero of the Franco-Prussian war. En route, John had grabbed up a couple of steins by mistake at a railway station, but threw out their contents on finding what they held. He had no use for German beer or English stout, and never heard a cork pop all the time he was in France.

In Potsdam they bowed deeply to the wrong man in gold braid, supposing they were passing the entourage of the new emperor, Kaiser Wilhelm, a mistake made up for many years later when his son, Prince Henry, visited Pittsburgh. Upon being introduced to Brashear at a banquet, he asked what he thought of the new telescope at the Royal Observatory. John made no reply. The Prince insisted. "Not much," said John, "I made the lenses for it."

After visiting astronomical works in Hamburg they sailed for Scotland to see the Royal Observatory at Edinburgh, then crossed to Ireland before returning home. Their itinerary was well thought out, for of all the tours arranged for "Homes of the Poets," or "Birthplaces of Painters," theirs was probably the first for travelers interested in the stars.

The miracle lasted only a few months, and John and Phoebe returned to Allegheny with the same enthusiasm with which they had left. Crossing the state they sighed as they looked out of the train window and saw their engine ahead of them on the Horseshoe Curve. It seemed as if the mountains at Cresson must have shrunk.

The winter following, John went to say goodbye to Mr. Thaw, who was sailing for France to visit Dr. Janssan, president of the French Academy of Science, who had personally conducted John around the observatory at Meudon. His studies on the absorption of the earth's atmosphere were carried on with the aid of the powerful electric light of the Eiffel Tower, and he was using a spectroscope with a grating made by Brashear. Before he left, Mr. Thaw wanted to discuss with John how these French discoveries differed from those of Dr. Draper of New York, and how they compared with Langley's, but their farewell was for longer than either of them knew.

This was the last time John saw William Thaw. He died in Paris in 1889, the year that John was made president of the Engineers Society of Western Pennsylvania. Fortunately their meeting was full of that enthusiasm they both had for astronomy, undimmed by any premonition that their ways were parting forever. Not only John Brashear and Samuel Langley mourned the loss of their friend, but hundreds of others whom Thaw had befriended in his long life in Pittsburgh.

With the death of Pittsburgh's first philanthropist, Langley's work on determining the principles of flight with the aid of instruments constructed in the Brashear shops came to an abrupt halt. The great guarantor was gone, and Langley left to take up residence in Washington, where he had already been secretary of the Smithsonian Institution for five years.

John missed all the attendant excitement. But with the arrival of Professor Keeler, who had been with Langley on his Mt. Whitney expedition, and had since been located at the new Lick Observatory in California, matters quickly accelerated again on Observatory Hill. Soon John was engaged in building a great driving clock, and the finest spectroscope he could devise.

His new shop was so close to the old observatory that he could step back and forth. Across a little gully and up to the top of the highest hill, and he was under the great oaks that framed the low brick building where so many important things were taking place. Professor Keeler, like Langley before him, soon found his way to Phoebe's back door, and into the heart of their hospitality. Many were the midnight conferences on Perrysville Avenue, not only with local people but with scientists from all over the United States, and many from abroad. For each of them John designed the instrument he wanted for some special purpose.

After his first trip to Europe there was an interval of five years when he took no vacation whatever. Among many other orders, he had completed a stellar spectroscope for West Point, another for Cambridge, England, and one for the observatory at the Cape of Good Hope. He had made an especially fine grating for Piazzi Smyth, Astronomer Royal of Scotland, and had just finished the optical parts for an exacting spectroscope for Sir William Huggins of the Royal Observatory in England. As no British shop knew how to mount this grating after it was delivered, John had become involved in a mass of complicated correspondence. He could not sleep well at night, but carried his problems to bed with him, and would sometimes rise and pace the Observatory Hill.

Suddenly in the spring of 1892 his work was interrupted by a summons from his friend Andrew Carnegie, in New York, to come there immediately and take over a certain set of lectures that must be given in relation to a scientific exhibit from Germany. Not only Carnegie lived in New York, but his partner, Henry Phipps, had also moved there to manage the business interests of the great Carnegie steel companies which could better be handled in the metropolis. The happy meetings of the Conservatory Club were over, as well as the days at Cresson.

John Brashear was always a fine lecturer. He not only could write well, but speak well. His discourse was scholarly and at the same time so lucid as to make anyone who heard him understand the slightest nuance of his subject. He had humor, and that delightful manner of not taking himself very seriously, which endears the public speaker to his audience. All of his talks on astronomy were seemingly extemporaneous, for he never wrote them down and none of them are extant. Both for churches and schools, and as a dinner speaker for bored banqueters, he was becoming increasingly in demand. He refused any fee, preferring to give back to the world gratuitously what he was pleased to call the "little he had learned." So this invitation did not frighten him, but enlisted his interest. If "Andy" wanted him he would drop everything and go, hoping that thereby he would add his bit toward extending human knowledge.

The exhibit of astronomical and geological and related instruments had been so popular at the *Gesellschaft Urania* in Berlin, that ninety thousand people had poured through its doors. Carnegie had brought it to America at his own expense and installed it as an attraction in his new Music Hall in New York City. To his dismay it attracted nobody. The astronomical lectures were greeted with yawns rather than applause.

John had been made president of the Pittsburgh Academy of Science and Art this year, and he felt that the reputation of the society he had helped to found was at stake. His first endeavor on arriving in New York was to hear what was being said by the present lecturer, and he was horrified to find how

dull his beloved subject could become when read from a man-
uscript by someone who did not understand it. The lecture, he
felt, should at least be applied to the exhibit on hand, so that
its context would illuminate the subject. This required study.
He worked in his hotel room until after midnight, and finally
going to bed blind with fatigue, woke later to find the room
spinning round dizzily.

The hotel physician was called and pronounced his condition a physical breakdown, due to overwork and exhausted
nerves. Rest was ordered—complete, immediate, and of long
duration. Chagrined by his failure, John was hastily shipped
back home in one of Carnegie's Pullmans, and put to bed under Phoebe's care for six weeks.

But Carnegie was more upset than John, and felt a personal
responsibility for his health. Forgiving him for disappointment
to his own pride, he saw that he had unwittingly demanded the
last ounce of strength from an already overburdened expert
who was constitutionally unable to refuse. On one of his many
trips to Pittsburgh, he asked to see John when he was recu-
perating, and announced he was sending him abroad for a rest.
Nor would he discuss the matter. He thumped the table at the
Duquesne Club and told him he had a pair of tickets bought
and paid for and wasn't going to waste them, and he'd engaged
the best stateroom on the fastest steamer sailing, the one he
took himself.

John hesitated, too sick to care where he went or what he
did. The doctors told him his heart was bad, and he dreaded
the passage. He demurred at accepting so much, and worried
about leaving his shop. To this Carnegie replied that he didn't
deserve to have a shop if he couldn't leave it. Any good manager could delegate his work to someone else. To stick to it
more than half the time was inefficient—a theory that always
annoyed his partners.

But here, to John's surprise, Phoebe agreed he ought to
leave, and threw in all her influence with Carnegie. It is true

she was anxious about her husband's health, but she was, moreover, the sort of wife who considered that anyone ought to be flattered by being able to help her John.

When he would say, "Oh dear, I'm afraid I'll be late for that engagement!" she would reply, "They're lucky if you go at all!"

So, after the usual commotion about passports, these two innocents set sail again in May 1892. What tempted them most was that their friends Mr. and Mrs. Henry Phipps, hearing of John's illness, had invited them to visit for a week at Knebworth Castle, their summer home in England. "As good as a sanitarium," they had said.

Phoebe fortified herself with one new dress as they passed through New York, and with a farewell party from friends and presents of fruit and flowers in their staterooms, they were off—and again at the captain's table.

XIV

STEEL KINGS AND ASTRONOMERS ROYAL

EARLY in the nineties Henry Phipps was free enough from the details of the Carnegie interests in New York to have a little time and money to spend on vacations in England, and had leased Knebworth Castle, the ancestral home of Baron Edward Bulwer-Lytton, which his son, the Lord Lytton of the period, was glad to get rid of now and then for a sum that would keep him more modestly at the Lido or the Riviera. Carnegie and his wife were spending their summers at Cluny Castle in Scotland for several years before he purchased his more fabulous estate at Skibo. The steel kings lived more royally than the royalty of Europe.

John and Phoebe were met with the Lytton trap at the little station of Wellwyn, between London and Sheffield, and as they were accustomed to the various vehicles of the millionaires at Cresson, climbed in without staring at the white breeches of the footman. After winding three miles through the park, however, they silently grasped each other by the hand, for between battlemented water towers stretched a great Tudor castle, topped with copper turrets.

They had gone to Knebworth straight from Liverpool, for John was still uncertain of his strength, and they had expected a simple and quiet place to rest. It was quiet. One could have heard his footfall in the empty corridors, or failed to hear its sound on the deep-piled rugs of the vaulted rooms. Mr. and Mrs. Phipps received them with the same cordiality they always extended in Allegheny. A gold-braided attendant carried their battered suitcases up to a far away bedchamber and when Phoebe followed after a hearty English tea, a maid had laid out her new dress, much to her surprise, for her to wear to dinner.

John was startled by the armor standing in the baronial hall, and Phoebe by the massive bed decorated with carved cupids, so high it necessitated steps for entrance to its luxurious interior. Going to bed was like going up a gangplank. She could not imagine, at Knebworth, how seven of them had managed to live in a house on the South Side that had only two proper bedrooms, and less than ten years ago. It was days before they finished their tour of the picture gallery in the left wing, and John never had time to examine the books and papers preserved in the great library where Bulwer Lytton had written *The Last Days of Pompeii.*

They stayed over a Sunday, and John took exception to the family pew in the old manor church they attended. When a vested verger closed the gate on the square plush-lined cubicle, he cringed. He remarked afterward, when a long way off, that the entire congregation had as much right to hear the Gospel from a box as they had. To him all were equal, not only in the sight of the Lord, but in his own.

Spring in England was worth the trip across the ocean. The elms of Knebworth Park burst into tender green and under foot yellow primroses thrust delicate blossoms through the mold of the winter's leaves. John's health revived in one great rush. Standing before his open windows at night he felt like singing aloud, and often did, staring at the clear stars, which alone reminded him of home.

There came a day when they must leave, and without warning, as they said goodbye to their kindly host and hostess at the foot of the grand staircase and followed their shabby luggage to the waiting trap at the door, they found themselves walking through a double line of blankfaced servants. The uniforms of the first and second footmen, the head butler and his helpers, the parlormaid and the chambermaid, and several other capped or gaitered attendants whom they had never seen before, looked unusually crisp, as did the subservient bows. Phoebe, greatly touched by such courtesy and devotion, shook each one by the hand as she passed down the line, and said "God bless you," hardly noticing that her salutation took them by surprise. John was equally friendly, and saw nothing amiss with what he took for an old English custom (in which conclusion he was right), until he looked back over his shoulder and found the well-trained baronial servants staring mutely after their departing carriage as only the English, when unmasked, can stare. Then he began to realize that all those outstretched hands had a peculiar significance. John sighed and gave the footman a good American dollar when he lifted his bags into the third-class railroad rack.

One lesson was learned from this. When they were invited to the home of Lord Rosse, at Parsontown, Ireland, John declined. He had met this eminent Irish lord at the Royal Astronomical Society of London, and he had urged them to come to his father's home to see the great seventy-two-inch telescope. A week with these famous scientists would have been a wonderful experience, but "I had learned that the servants would deplete our pocket-book to such an extent we might have nothing left to finish our travels." John is not the only Yankee who has discovered this when visiting.

In London they came down to their own simple standard, and stayed at the old pension they had patronized five years before. Friends who had met them on their first journey again entertained them.

John had been made a Fellow of the Royal Astronomical Society this same year, and was asked to address them on the status of astronomy in America. His speech was so well received that at the following banquet he was the great man of the occasion, although astronomers from all over Europe attended. He noted that the rigid class distinctions of English social life had no place in the field of science, and was impressed with the number of amateurs included in the group. This plan of extending astronomy through the ranks of enthusiasts was one he furthered in America, resulting in the great amateur societies of the present day.

Sir William Huggins' home was especially congenial to John and Phoebe because, like themselves, Sir William and his wife worked together in scientific research. What impressed Sir William most was that after John had sent him the optical parts for a stellar spectroscope and he had replied that he could find no one in England to mount them properly, John had written him full directions. Sir William remarked that it was the first time he had ever heard of a business firm sending out its trade secrets for the free use of others. John Brashear's openhandedness with his inventions was a new thing in Europe.

Realizing how valuable John's presence could be to them, Sir William suggested he call at the works of Troughton and Simms who were trying to build a spectroscope for him with John's grating and going from bad to worse. At other firms John had always received courteous treatment and had made a point of granting more information than he could possibly have received. He soon saw what their difficulty was and where he could advise them to their advantage, but was stopped by a remark of one of the partners, Mr. Simms.

"I suppose you have come over to pick up methods that would be of use to you in your work at home!"

John had taken the trouble to drive a long way from London at Sir William's request, but declined Mr. Simms' invitation to lunch and departed.

Dr. John Tyndall was one of the astronomers of the Royal Institute to whom John had written for further data on his studies of light when he was a young man working in the rolling mills. In educational correspondence Brashear was far in advance of his times, for while young people today are encouraged by their teachers to write to authors for collateral material, in the sixties such a system was not practised. Uncle John had been very proud of the resulting friendship, lasting for thirty years, and now that Tyndall was an old man and retired from active duty, John had carried one of his precious diffraction gratings all the way from America as a present to his first adviser.

He also brought with him what he called "two very accurate optical glass bars." And when Brashear said a bar was accurate he meant corrected to within the wave-length of green light, which is about one fifty-thousandth of an inch. One day a customer had asked him for a bar of glass a yard long and "absolutely straight," and wondered why a man reputed to be so skillful hesitated. "Well, it will cost you two hundred thousand dollars," said Brashear. When the matter was gone into fully it developed that what the customer expected was a forty-dollar bar straight to within the sixty-fourth of an inch.

Tyndall was very ill at this time, so the presents had to be sent to him instead of the personal call John had come so far to make. However, Tyndall was able to send a letter of thanks in which he speaks of "the gift princely, in a scientific sense, which you sent me. . . . Surely I am richly repaid for any little kindness I may have shown you in earlier years."

He also sent John a copy of his last book, *New Fragments*, and the inscription signed by Tyndall on his deathbed reads, "To his friend, J. A. Brashear to whom he wishes length of days and the reward of a genuine worker, this book is inscribed by its author . . . John Tyndall, 1892."

This volume that John cherished contains Tyndall's essay on Sunday as a day made for man's rest, instead of man for its observance; a theory John Brashear was one of the first in his part of the country to endorse, dominated as it was by the Scotch Presbyterians. He felt that on every day of the week the enjoyment of music or books or nature should be open to everyone, which was the same point of view that had prompted his friend Henry Phipps to open his conservatory to the public on Sunday.

When John had begun his English tour by visiting Henry Phipps at Knebworth Castle he noticed his host was preoccupied. There had been cables and letters constantly coming and going connected with that difficult life on the other side of the water which they had hoped to forget for awhile. John was never curious; he thought these absorbing interruptions were merely a part of the steel man's routine. But while John Brashear was making speeches to the Royal Astronomers the

voice of his beloved South Side had risen to a war cry, and
the great strike to end strikes had begun in the Pittsburgh mills.

Phipps hurried back to New York, and as nothing of this
was permitted to appear in the papers John did not even hear
a rumbling echo within the ivy-covered walls of England's
observatories when the Battle of Homestead took place on
July 5, 1892.

Almost fifty years have gone by since that unrecorded war
on the Monongahela. The difficulty of understanding it at the
time was due to the policy of the steel company in refusing to
give out information to the newspapers, occasioning much confusion. Some said that Carnegie had deserted his partners and
left Henry Frick, the head of the Homestead plant, to face the
strike alone. But there is a statement that Henry Phipps made
to the *New York Herald* later, in which he says that Andrew
Carnegie offered to come home from Scotland but that his
partners did not want him because he "was always disposed to
yield to the demands of the men, however unreasonable."

To corroborate this sentiment one has only to refer to the
well-known story of how Carnegie said he was immediately
relieved of business worries as soon as he went aboard ship.
"My God," remarked one of his partners, "think how relieved
we are!"

Carnegie's methods were well understood, but not followed.
In former strikes he had advocated closing the mills until the
men came back of their own accord. But Frick decided to end
the unions forever, if he died in the attempt, and in both am-
bitions he was almost successful.

Berkman, an anarchist who was never employed in the mills,
tried to assassinate Frick in his private office, but only succeeded in making him a public hero. On the day he was twice
shot and stabbed, Frick cabled Carnegie that all was well and
that he had the situation under control. He managed the strike
from his bed, and kept the wires sizzling back and forth to
Scotland. Berkman served his thirty years in prison and after-

ward took his own life, while Frick, during ensuing years, became a benefactor to his city.

This is one of the forgotten endings. The beginnings too are lost in a Pittsburgh fog. But it is remembered that mill owners as well as mill workers suffered, and women wept within the great houses of the East End and Allegheny as well as in the seething district along the river on the South Side. The strike to end strikes failed as did the war to end war. When John came home his heart was wrung between compassion for the mill men with whom he had worked for twenty years and compassion for the mill owners who were now his friends.

XV

"MEET DR. BRASHEAR"

WHILE the mills were staging their battles in the valley, John Brashear became more and more involved in affairs on Observatory Hill.

From the time he had moved over to Allegheny there had been the noise of hammering, and shouting of workmen hauling bricks, as the great new buildings of the Western University of Pennsylvania were erected at his elbow. The observatory, which topped the highest pinnacle, occupied only a small part of the hilltop, and following a bequest of $100,000 from William Thaw, the trustees finished their new halls of learning in 1890.

Under the presidency of Dr. William J. Holland many departments were added, such as the beginnings of a medical school in Allegheny and a law school in downtown Pittsburgh. The campus was too small for these additional branches to function on the hill, but the engineering classes kept in close touch with what was going on in the Brashear shop, so near them as to seem part of their own college, which also embraced the observatory. More of the students were interested in astronomy than present-day educators would suppose, but the fine arts department had ceased to be as attractive as the courses in mechanics, and two-thirds of the boys who climbed the hill were studying new forms of engineering. Two-thirds of them—which means about one hundred—were also day students from Allegheny City, sons of the thrifty German settlers and the ambitious Scotch-Irish.

Dr. Holland was an educated man and a great educator. He had graduated from three universities himself (the Moravian College at Bethlehem, Pa., Amherst, and Princeton), and had ambitious ideas about creating one. He was an inveterate conversationalist, and explained to Professor Keeler at the neighboring observatory, and John Brashear at the neighboring astronomical works, and both if he could get them together on the intervening campus, how as a government naturalist he had accompanied the United States expedition in 1887 that sailed for Japan to see the eclipse, and how, in that same capacity, he had traveled to West Africa with another expedition. He showed them his great collection of white moths, and looked through their telescopes with interesting observations of his own on sun, moon, and stars. A learned zoölogist and paleontologist, whatever anyone's subject was, Dr. Holland could cap it with some appropriate experience of his own. He was astonished at John's lack of scholastic education, but one of the first to honor his genius.

John Brashear had been appointed to the observatory board in 1891, when James Keeler had arrived to replace Samuel Langley as director. In 1893 another greater recognition came, for under Dr. Holland John received the honorary degree of Doctor of Science. He had never aspired to enter the doors of any college as a student, but now he was to enter them as an honorary graduate, and to become, when over fifty, a member in fact as well as in sympathy of the Western University of Pennsylvania.

It was a glowing day in June when John walked across the campus, and the wind from the river turned the leaves of the oaks on Observatory Hill. As Phoebe saw the slender figure with its quick, light step, climbing up to the great buildings in borrowed cap and gown to receive the plaudits of president and trustees, her eyes filled with tears. She remembered the long nights in the South Hills, the borrowed books, the lens and the reflector they had broken, and the evening he carried his first completed lens to the observatory wrapped up in a red bandanna. John was not thinking about himself, he was thinking of his only teacher, George Wilkinson, in the two upper rooms over the market house in Brownsville.

He received many other degrees as time went on, but none that touched him to the quick as this had. For he loved this hill with its old, ivy-covered observatory, and its growing college, and he loved the shop that Thaw had built so thoughtfully for him, close at hand. All his life, no matter what gold medal he received, and he had already won the medal of the Massachusetts Charitable Association, he valued none of these trophies laid away in plush boxes as he did the pointed velvet hood, thrown over his shoulders by the hands of his friend Dr. Holland, which Phoebe hastily put away in moth balls.

But not so hastily was this done that he had not time to realize its significance. Looking back on the years that had led to this recognition he saw that he too had studied and worked to arrive at any such point in life so recognized by his colleagues. Beside what he had taught himself about science, he knew what his friends had taught him; that his contacts with men in the mills, both workmen and employers, and his contacts with men in Allegheny and Cresson, both artists and business men, had brought him as much in one way as he had learned from books and hard experience in another. He did not perceive that his own example had also taught others how to live. He set himself now to give more of himself, to live for the city and the people of the city; to make a gift of his few hours of leisure to those less fortunate. For he always considered his own work a kind of privilege and play. After laboring twenty-five years in the mills, to have been given a shop of his own where he could work continuously on perfecting instruments for his chosen field of astrophysics was a responsibility and a trust for which he felt he must make a double return to life. So after ten years of what he termed selfish concentration, he was ready now to look down from the sky to the earth. And it is interesting that, in looking at the earth to see how he could be most helpful, he always retained the impartial view of the star-dweller.

Nor was he alone in this going-outwardness. A sudden acceleration had struck the whole city. The Gay Nineties in Western Pennsylvania were the decade of a great expansion. Perhaps it was the warning of the striking steel workers that frightened capitalists into making some return to their fellow men. The Chamber of Commerce began to talk about a Greater Pittsburgh, and like pellets of bread on the angry waters of industry, benefits began to float downstream, and upstream, to the gargantuan city on the Point.

First among these gifts had been Schenley Park, followed soon by the purchase of Highland Park, where Christopher Magee with a touch of Republican playfulness had endowed a zoo. Then, moving to the other extreme, he endowed a hospital. "Boss Magee," beside controlling the city politics, was one of the old graduates of the university, and on its board, where he became a staunch ally of Dr. Brashear. Carnegie and Phipps transferred their benefactions to the East End, and when his disputed gift of a library was dedicated in 1895, Carnegie announced that he would expand his original foundation into sufficient millions to endow an "Institute."

The dispute had been because he stipulated that the taxpayers support his gift, so as to enjoy the pride of possession and feel that the library belonged to them. But of course the burdened taxpayers did not care to whom it belonged as long as they could borrow the books. In the matter of the Institute, however, he agreed to support it entirely because, he said, art and music were a luxury, while books were a necessity—a moot point.

The edifice, covering several acres, was in process of building for over ten years. From its inception, Carnegie formed a committee of eighteen able men to superintend its construction and the housing of its future exhibits. It included an art gallery and music hall, and everything that went into it had to be allotted certain space, from the murals of John Alexander symbolizing the spirit of the mills to the unintentionally symbolic Diplodocus, relic of a Carnegie expedition to the West, around whose mammoth skeleton his museum seems to have been built.

Some of the early trustees were Carnegie's friends of the steel-mill days, and some were the musicians, artists, and scientists he knew at Cresson. Forming a sub-committee of great importance were four men who worked together faithfully for a decade, Dr. Samuel Harden Church, Dr. Wm. J. Holland, Mr. C. C. Mellor, and Dr. John A. Brashear.

Dr. Samuel Harden Church, or "Colonel" as he is popularly called, has been president of the Carnegie Institute in Pittsburgh since 1914, and during the World War was made an officer of the French Legion of Honor. He is nationally known as a trustee of the Carnegie Corporation of New York, and as the author of various plays and biographies. He was writing the "Life of Cromwell" at the time he began serving on the committee with Brashear. He says that the four men mentioned above, of whom he was one, met as a planning committee for the fine arts and museum departments "often in the late afternoons or evenings, or frequently on Sundays," and that Brashear, in spite of his exacting work many miles distant, attended every meeting and offered and put through many constructive plans. It was Brashear who insisted that the music hall be used on Sundays for the organ recitals initiated by Dr. Archer, and urged that the museum and library be kept open also. In this he won a compromise, for the museum doors stand open on Sunday afternoons, and in the library the reading room is available.

The planning of Carnegie Institute was not the only civic activity that Brashear undertook; it was almost the least of them. His life turned more and more to the humanities. Many citizens in the period of Pittsburgh's expansion served on some committee until he grew tired of it and his patience was exhausted, but Brashear seems to be the only workingman who served on all until his death.

The same year, 1896, that he began crossing the city to sit up nights with the museum, he was appointed one of the trustees of the struggling university close at hand on the hill. And while he was creating the city-wide Academy of Science and Art, and serving as its president from 1892 to 1896, he was made chairman of the observatory board, the project nearest his heart. For when he thought what the greatest benefit was that he might confer on mankind, he always thought of the stars, and his original plan of making the study of them convenient and free to the people.

Realizing that the old observatory was inadequate according to modern standards, and its location inaccessible to the public whom he wanted to enjoy it, he selected another site, and when Riverview Park was laid out he arranged to have two acres set aside for a new building. Funds were not yet available for the project, but from this time on he set his face toward making his dream come true.

These extra-curriculum activities were not hindering the Brashear shop. At the time its master was elected to many important boards which to some men would have been an entire occupation, John was finishing off, day after day, orders for all over the world. Perhaps he had learned from Andrew Carnegie that it was not necessary to work all the time at one specific thing if he was efficient enough to delegate part of the labor to others. But the kind of instruments Brashear was famous for building could hardly be left to others; they could not even be explained, for no one had made them before.

One of the great successes of the nineties was the invention of the Photographic Doublets. The astronomical photographic telescope was developed in the Brashear shop to a degree hitherto unknown. Its lenses were constructed according to a solution for which John gave credit to Dr. Hastings, his consultant on refracting surfaces, and developed by Brashear until he produced a telescope using two camera lenses simultaneously, which could photograph twice as much of the field of the sky at once as any single lens previously in use. George P. Bond, director of Harvard Observatory in the sixties, and sometimes called the father of photographic astronomy, had expressed the hope that at some future date it would be possible to photograph stars of the seventh magnitude. Brashear built achromatic lenses that could take pictures of stars of the seventeenth magnitude, which are ten thousand times less bright. In 1895 he sent two sixteen-inch photographic doublets to Dr. Max

Wolf at the University of Heidelberg in Germany, whose discoveries with them astonished the scientific world. Afterwards he furnished them to Edward Barnard, celebrated astronomer of the Lick and Yerkes Observatories, who was given recognition by the French Academy and the Royal Astronomical Society of England for his discoveries in the skies. Using the Brashear photographic doublets, Barnard found sixteen new comets, and left the University of Chicago 1,400 negatives of comets and 4,000 plates of the Milky Way.

Nor was anything too small for Brashear's attention. His brother Frank, who worked with him for years, said that if results were delayed because the machinery was inadequate, John, with the sureness of the born scientist, would make whatever apparatus was needed. At one time Frank had difficulty grinding off the minute irregularities that appear near the edge of a glass under construction. John, noting his slow progress, made for him in fifteen minutes a new sort of tool that immediately solved the problem.

He had no formulas for duplication, but the work on the ordinary telescope lenses and mirrors was so well understood by all the experts in the shop that these constant orders, at least, could be carried on even if Brashear were away or engaged otherwise. In 1905 three state universities had contracted for large object glasses for their telescopes—Illinois, Ohio State, and Indiana. In the same year the Smithsonian Institution ordered a lens, and another went to Tokio to be used by Professor Holden on the August eclipse of the sun. Two lenses were sent to Cleveland, Ohio; one for the Case School and the other for the private observatory of Warner and Swasey, who mounted many of the object glasses made by Brashear. A twelve-inch lens was made for the Mount Wilson Tower Telescope in California, which was equipped with a tube of 150 foot length. Lenses of larger size were made for Yale, the Carleton Observatory of Minnesota, for Newport News, Va., for the University of Pennsylvania, and for the Dominion Observatory at Ottawa, Canada. Reflectors were constructed for the Dominion Observatory at Victoria, for the University of Michigan, Chabot Observatory at Oakland, California, and many other destinations.

The spectroscope he sent to Dr. Hans Hausewalde of Magdeburg, Germany, with a focus of twenty-one feet, made Brashear famous all over Europe, for Hausewalde was outfitting his private observatory at great expense and his wants were exacting. He had searched Germany before sending his order to America.

One after another, in the nineties—and each took months or years to perfect—his stellar spectroscopes were made under strict personal supervision and sent to government observatories in Canada, Ireland, Italy, France, and even to Chile, with Professor Campbell's expedition from the great Lick Observatory. Beside this usual business, which was unique, during the Spanish War he received a contract to supply the United States Government with fifty telescopes and 125 range finders for coastal defense.

The sinking of the United States battleship *Maine* in Havana Harbor had precipitated the prosperous nation into an unanticipated war, and from Key West north, the long and practically unguarded coast line began to scan the ocean for Spanish cruisers. Brashear's ably constructed range-finders, the best the government could procure after investigations covering two continents, were of incalculable importance.

Such a range-finder is an astronomical instrument, for it contains three reflecting prisms which must be perfectly accurate. A microscopic and indiscernible error might send a missile wild by a hundred feet, and Uncle Sam does not like to waste ammunition. There was no flaw, no error in John's prisms, only a hit and a strike.

The order was worth many thousands of dollars, but more significant was the attention it attracted. People were not surprised at the government's buying of range-finders, but having no conception of how they were made, they failed to understand the connection between them and a telescope, and wondered why the Brashear shop was producing war materials.

Nor did they comprehend why a telescope must be used instead of the old-fashioned binoculars held by the unsteady hand of a watchman. The startling juxtaposition of telescope and war-weapon piqued the imagination of the world, and newspapers placed the item on their front pages.

One of the scientific journals said, "If this be true, the telescope has come to be an engine of wartime which is in strange and awful contrast with those classic ideas of serene placidity which belong to the nightly vigils of the astronomers."

Brashear was a man of peace, not peace of a negative sort, but the kind he could best secure for his country by putting his skill to work on problems that would promote it. His range-finders were as much of a paradox as the army trucks that Ford supplied to the government during the Great War, after sending a peace ship to Europe; or the nitroglycerine and dynamite invented by the great Swedish scientist, Alfred Nobel, who bequeathed a fortune to found, among other things, the Nobel Peace Prize. Sometimes a humanist tries to circumvent the outcome of his earlier inventions by spending the wealth they have brought him to prevent their misuse.

But John Brashear's motivations were more simple. If any enemy threatened, the contribution of this native-born American, whose ancestors had settled in Virginia in the days of William and Mary was not to defend his country with one single gun, but to make sure that anyone who was obliged to do so would win a medal. He did for the United States, during the Spanish War, what a Baltic general is credited with achieving for Finland when the Russian battleships tried to bombard their forts. He made it probable that "at least one shot out of three" would hit the mark.

As for the telescopes he furnished the government, John would have liked nothing better than to man one himself. He had suffered long training in watching through the black night for fainter flickering than the luminous green or red of starboard or port on any enemy vessel passing far out at sea. The lights he watched were millions of miles away, in a sea as yet uncharted.

XVI

THE CREST OF THE HILL

A NEWS note in *Popular Astronomy*, 1898, says, "James Keeler of the Allegheny Observatory has been appointed Director of the Lick Observatory and they want to raise $200,000 to equip the observatory in Allegheny to keep him there." "They" was John A. Brashear.

When Keeler had come to Allegheny he had found the observatory facilities so limited that he immediately demanded new instruments and the remounting of the old thirteen-inch telescope, which was forthwith accomplished at the Brashear shop, and financed willingly by Mrs. William Thaw after her husband's death, and by William Thaw, Jr. The Junta Club, of which Brashear was a member, was persuaded by him to place a shutter in the dome. But William Thaw, Jr., had only survived his father by three years, and as every effort in the city was now directed toward embellishing the East End instead of Allegheny, it was difficult in the nineties to find other donors of the same mind.

Professor Keeler had made many discoveries in the sky and was ambitious to continue, but he felt he could advance astronomy best where conditions were more favorable. His spectroscopic studies of Saturn's rings were an important addition to science, and had brought him fame among his colleagues, but what were Saturn's rings to people building museums and city parks? Carnegie, already overburdened with obligations, is quoted as saying to John, "Wait till coke sells for a dollar a ton."

Unfortunately the Spanish War began in 1898, and in wartimes no stars shine. James Keeler departed for the West, and to fill his place in the interval before the appointment of another director, Brashear himself served as head of the Allegheny Observatory.

The long road he had taken over the hills from the South

Side had reached its termination. By a twist of fate, the man who had been a slave to astronomy all his life now found himself in the position of master. He would touch three score years at the turn of the century, and it seemed as if the pinnacle of success had been reached. If Phoebe was startled when he was offered a doctor's degree by the university, what must her reaction have been when he was made director of the observatory? But Phoebe was almost through being surprised. Neither of them could know this was only the beginning of destined honors. The crest of the hill had been gained, but what lay beyond was still hidden in the mist of two more decades to come.

The fund that John had tried to raise for the new observatory had fallen short of $150,000 when Keeler left, and much of it had been promised on the condition that he stay. Under the circumstances, John hesitated to continue his drive for further financing. He had only accepted the appointment of director provisionally, and although the trustees had left him entirely alone in raising the endowment, and were disposed to leave him to his own resources indefinitely, he realized that the observatory must obtain a professional astronomer who would make it his sole work to see that Allegheny retained the place that Langley and Keeler had worked so hard to give it. Brashear did not want the observatory to deteriorate under his own or anyone else's management.

So he began again, and finally finished his campaign for $200,000, which insured the erection of a new building. Professor F. L. O. Wadsworth accepted as director when he heard the observatory would have the finest equipment in the country, that is, made in the Brashear shop. If this had been guaranteed two years before, Keeler would not have been so discouraged. John stepped down to welcome Wadsworth, and the cornerstone was laid in 1900, the same year Keeler died of pneumonia on the cold and lonely heights of the Lick Observatory at Mt. Hamilton, California.

John Brashear in his short term of office made it possible for the observatory to continue in a new home, under modern conditions, with facilities for greater usefulness. With the financing of the institution he revered, and the expert telescopes and machinery he devised for it, he kept it forever for the citizens of Pittsburgh, as well as for whatever director was in charge. Without the aid given during his tenure, the old observatory would have faded into insignificance on the departure of Keeler. The eighteen months' service of John Brashear saved its life by putting the cornerstone of the new, round domes squarely into the ground.

As his spade struck the earth on that high hill, in the new location he had chosen in Riverview Park, and he turned to face the public who were watching him sympathetically, John knew that no other sound would ever seem so epochal as that faint gritting of gravel. He had no interest in managing the affairs of the observatory as a director. He had tried that for over a year, and knew as well as the next that his gifts lay in another sort of usefulness. He was a toolmaker, not an astronomer. With a light step he returned to his shop to commence making the two great telescopes that were to become its ultimate glory. More than any other kind of building, an observatory is an empty shell except for what is put into it. It is like the hangar for an airplane.

However, when he looked across to the old Observatory Hill, and saw the little, low building where he and his friends had worked so happily for so many years, he could not help but cry from his heart, "What have I done to you?"

For he knew the old must be denuded to furnish the new, and that after a few more years this building which had seen half a century of service as one of the earliest observatories in America would be abandoned. The worn lintel where he had first met William Thaw, sitting in the dusk with Langley, would be buried under dead oak leaves, the eyes of the windows would be boarded over, and the slit where the famous telescope craned its neck at the sky would be stopped against snow and rain. Which was true. The red bricks are covered with mold; yet even today there is a magic about that forgotten shrine, an aura that breathes the spirit of Samuel Langley when he was young and hopeful, before he died broken-hearted; and of James Keeler, whose ashes were so soon returned from the West, where he had insisted on going; and of John Brashear, who loved it, and left it standing there forsaken.

When Saturn's rings are just right, a poet can hear the sound of a "whirling table" spinning its curious legend behind the crumbling wall, and the hum of a ghostly flying machine that passes, like a tiny cloud, across the moon.

John and Phoebe were never alone in their large frame house on Perrysville Avenue. Effie McDowell and her husband continued to live with them, and the McDowell boys, who had been born on the South Side and were only half-grown in the middle nineties, rushed up and down the stairs, banging doors, so that John had to close his ears, if not his heart, to them. He loved children, which means he was a prey to their natural selfishness, and because they were never rebuked not only his foster-grandsons but all the other boys in the neighborhood gathered at his home where Phoebe fed them.

His shop, too, was overrun with young men from the college at his back door, and no matter how involved he was on some intricate order, he always had time to explain to the engineering students anything that pertained to their problems. John entered his adopted son, Harry, in the university and had great hopes for him.

In the spring of 1896, however, when Harry was nineteen, he contracted typhoid fever and died. Phoebe, worn out with nursing him after long, arduous days in her large household, made a misstep on the stairs one night and fell, breaking her ankle in four places—an injury from which she never recovered. Trouble descended on John's home in a twofold way, as it is apt to do, and in the midst of many new business enterprises he decided to drop everything and take his wife away for a rest.

It was to give Phoebe a change from grief and care, more than to lighten his own overtaxed nerves, that John first took a cottage at Muskoka Lakes. Many of his old friends the steel men summered in this Canadian resort and had built luxurious residences on wooded islands. The life of the sunny waters made a complete change for land-bound, fog-bound Pittsburghers.

The Muskoka Lakes are in the Laurentian glacial belt, and to reach them from Pittsburgh one changes trains at Buffalo and again at Toronto, arriving from a single-track spur at Muskoka Junction. To succeed in carrying a woman there who was unable to walk was in itself a problem only love could solve, but John felt these vacations saved Phoebe's life. Once arrived, life opened out like the flinging wide of windows.

Strong winds from the west blow from Georgian Bay across miles of intervening pine forest threaded with silver streams. Great boulders on the islands show veins of gold-bearing quartz; one of them near John's porch which he measured scientifically weighed 180 tons. Flowers grow in profusion from the natural rock gardens near the little landing stages of each home, and at night the aurora borealis plays its many colored lights across the dark forests and glimmering waterways.

John told his friends at home that he had never been to the Italian Lakes, but that he had been to the Swiss, and to Lakes George and Champlain, and little Stony Lake in Pennsylvania, and to him Muskoka Lake was like the story told about the strawberry, "Doubtless God might have made a better berry, but doubtless God never did."

In the beginning their way of living was simple in the extreme; a little rented cottage in which John did most of the housework, a small rented sailboat that he learned to manage through reading a book, and a dory which he fixed for his wife's comfort so he could row her around in the evening under his beloved stars. It was the first time he said that he ever took a vacation without having to "lug along a boiled shirt," for previously his trips had been for the most part engagements to speak in various cities. Before 1900 he had saved enough from activities outside his shop to buy an island across from the resort at Beaumaris, which he named Urania in honor of the goddess of astronomy. There he built himself a cottage and a boathouse. All of the neighbors befriended John and Phoebe, noting how devoted he was to her as she became more and more an invalid. Sometimes they asked each other if she had been very beautiful as a girl, for they saw that John still considered her so when to them she was a stout, plain woman over fifty years old, who could not walk very well.

Women are intuitive. Not many of them knew the story, now so long past, of how Phoebe had helped John make his first lens. They could not guess the special ability in those hands now inert, nor imagine how she had faithfully urged him on to success when he was discouraged. But they admitted that their own busy husbands treated them with no such marked respect, and understood without investigation that their relationship was sacred. Sometimes they were even a little envious of the loyalty that prompted John to sign every note he had occasion to write them, thanking them perhaps for a basket of peaches or an invitation to tea, "Phoebe and John," never "John" alone. When friends sailed across the lake to Isle Urania, which they frequently did of a clear summer night to look at the stars through the great telescope on John's porch, the whole evening's entertainment seemed to center around Phoebe, lying in a deck chair.

John planned to buy a launch after he had paid for his island and cottage, and had drawn up specifications with consideration for Phoebe's comfort, when his old friend "Harry" Oliver surprised him by making him a present of the very beautiful *Alleghenia*. In his letter he said the gift was "not for charity but as a recognition of a life work so often done without monetary compensation." Henry Oliver seldom came to Muskoka, but he lived in Allegheny and knew what was done on Observatory Hill. Three years later, however, John and Phoebe were wakened one night by the shouts of a frantic friend who had rowed across the lake to warn them that their boathouse was on fire.

John tried to put the flames out with a fire extinguisher, and finally succeeded, but the damage was so great that the repairs were going to run into prohibitive figures. Before they attempted to replace their loss, Andrew Carnegie heard of it and the following summer ordered a new boat for them. This luxurious craft, the *Phoebe*, was one of the sights of Muskoka for ten years, when it suffered a like fate by burning up in drydock one winter when stored in a friend's boathouse. John had always used his launch not only to give recreation to an invalid wife but to do many errands and kindnesses for his neighbors. Immediately they joined together and bought him another *Phoebe* which soon came to be called the *Good Samaritan*.

Knowing how hard and slow it was to get up steam in a hurry for larger craft, a friend across the lake from him at Beaumaris presented them with a supplementary motorboat for short hauls. Standing upright, steering his small boat with one hand, his bright eyes unshaded against the glare of the water, Uncle John would cruise the harbors daily on errands for his island household, buying oranges for Phoebe from the "grocery-boat" that plied the lakes every morning, or rushing to the post or telegraph office, always waving with a glad "Ship Ahoy" to barelegged boys and girls who called to him from their sailboats as the well-known figure went whizzing past.

The natives of the bordering Canadian villages made harder work of understanding John Brashear than the city islanders, who at least were conversant with his background. Noticing that everyone called him "Uncle John," he was so called by woodcutters and fishermen, by storekeepers and children on the streets. They had seen pictures, all their lives, of a man from "The States" called "Uncle Sam," and to them this slim figure with gray, pointed beard and deepset, brilliant eyes, seemed not unlike the Yankee depicted on the posters. They half expected to see him come skimming across the lake, coattails flying above red-and-white striped trousers, and although they had never observed him wearing a hat, were sure if he did it would be a tall "beaver."

Many children who saw him in the schools at home had this same impression, for he was a legendary hero in their eyes, related either to Heaven or History. A Muskoka vacationist suggested he adopt the costume of Uncle Sam for a Fourth-of-July regatta held on the lake, but he declined. Uncle John seldom attended regattas. When the music from the hotel floated across the lake on a Saturday night, and he could see the shadow of young people dancing in the ballroom, he carried in a pitcher of lemonade to Phoebe and, after she was asleep, kept his nightly tryst with the lady in the moon. Often, when the northern lights shone brightly, he could not sleep but, as when a boy in Brownsville, carried his blanket out of doors and lay there staring at the sky's changing colors until they faded at dawn.

The summers at Muskoka were not devoid of professional contacts. Everyone recognized that this little man whose feet were obviously not on earth or water had his head in the stars, and he was sometimes called on to give lectures at near-by churches on the mainland, or before learned societies in Toronto. Although he had gone to Canada to escape exactly this, he would accept graciously, and even though very tired, would take some of his precious time to enlighten anyone who asked about the stars, or the aurora borealis, which had seldom been understood by natives who had grown up under its majesty.

When the Falls View International Bridge was opened in 1898, between Niagara and Canada, he was asked to attend the ceremonies, and the long parade was held up by the officiousness of one man who ran back and forth giving directions in a loud voice and telling everyone to "Halt!" and "Go!"

"Is that the man who built the bridge?" asked a little woman in the carriage behind John's.

"No," he called back to her, "that's the man who built the falls!"

There was only one blight on the Muskoka summers. When they were very dry, forest fires would spring up in the encircling woods, and one year five hundred people were driven into the water, far to the north, to escape the flames. At another frightening period, the crackle and roar could be heard close to his cottage, and smoke blinded John's eyes when the conflagration swept to within a mile of the Isle Urania. Bears and deer, driven out of their deep haunts in the burning brush, flung themselves into the lake, along with the small folk of the forest, the foxes and red squirrels, the otters, raccoons, and mink who swam about ineffectually till they drowned. As their soaked, furry bodies washed up on his beach a few days later, John lifted them tenderly from the shallows and buried them all, under the pine needles, on what he named "Cemetery Hill."

Although the neighbors differed in their capacity to be intimate with a personality so unique, all of them agreed on one point, that he was utterly unable to see any difference in them, for he treated them exactly alike: young or old, dowager or débutante, mill owner or college boy, boatman or banker, hotel chef at the back entrance, or magnate smoking on the pier; and they found it a charming way to be treated. Uncle John sloughed off all the exterior shell that years of veneer had unwittingly built around worldly people, and met them where their hearts lived, biting into the sometimes bitter kernel of the almond.

A close friend of his in Muskoka tells a characteristic story of him at the beginning of the World War. She says Uncle John came chug-chugging over the lake in the long, light evening, with a letter in his hand he had received from Germany. He had been there so recently that he was well remembered, and the widow of a soldier whom he had known as an astronomer in Munich had written to beg him to help raise funds for a hospital. Raising money was not too difficult to John Brashear; everyone gave him anything he wanted, and he was utterly unable to comprehend why a deaf ear met this request. Hurt and mystified, he went put-putting back across the water in the misty twilight. And there was a lump in the gentlewoman's throat as she watched his frail figure, seventy-five years old then, climbing the steps to write back to his friend that he could not understand why, but somehow people in America would not give to German hospitals. To him, all need was the same.

XVII

"SUN, MOON, AND STARS FORGOT"

The Western University of Pennsylvania had only been housed in its red brick buildings on Observatory Hill for ten years when John Brashear was called upon to become its president.

The former head, Dr. Holland, had found it a small institution in 1890, of a hundred students or less, studying the classics after the manner of the old-world colleges which its founders in the early eighteen hundreds had taken as their model. He left it in 1900 an ambitious, but scattered, university, with so many new departments added on paper that neither Brashear nor anyone else knew how to coördinate them.

Holland did not resign in discouragement, however, but because he had been asked by Carnegie to become curator of the museum in his new Institute, and science was to him a clarion call, louder than his original call to the Presbyterian ministry, or his call to the chancellorship of W.U.P. Foreseeing that the college would require more buildings than the present campus could hold, as well as funds to buy out various foundations such as the old Western Pennsylvania Medical School, and the School of Pharmacy, he had already started a campaign for a million dollars. But when Brashear assumed office, this endowment was as visionary as the projected Law School and School of Mines.

A committee of trustees was appointed to secure someone to take Dr. Holland's place, and after a year's time, during which Brashear refused three times to serve, succeeded in convincing him that to save the university he would have to accept office himself. When he stepped across the campus from his shop to assume the presidency, the student body rose in chapel and cheered, and the faculty relaxed. All of them were sanguine that under Uncle John's genial guidance life in the classroom would become as simple as they considered star-gazing.

John had but recently been relieved from his onerous duties as director of the observatory, and was still trying to raise funds

for the project where his heart lay. He had been grateful for
the doctorate conferred upon him by the university, and had
faithfully served for several years as a trustee, but to become
chancellor, even temporarily, was never envisaged on his already crowded calendar. Moreover he felt a little timid before
these roistering students and erudite professors, who moved in
crowds, rather than with the single step to which he was accustomed in his workshop. Conducting chapel the first morning
appeared like an ordeal. The boys were required to gather in an
austere auditorium in the main building, dark with stained-glass
windows and portraits of past presidents, where they were led
in Calvinistic prayer, and when John insisted on their joyfully
singing "America," even if he had to teach them the words himself, they suddenly realized they had, indeed, found another
sort of leader.

President Brashear was the sort of chancellor a faculty dreams
of, one who leaves them alone. There were only a dozen professors, and they formed an intimate society of their own into
which John and Phoebe were soon admitted. In turn, the President soon admitted them to the back door of his house, the one
nearest the campus.

The Fine Arts Department held its classes in the Administration Building, and the Engineering Department in Science Hall.
These buildings, created to hold a hundred students, were, with
the advent of two hundred, already overcrowded. More professors had to be engaged. At various times John entertained the
faculty and the whole student body, for Phoebe was a born
hostess. In spite of her constant lameness she could prepare a
hundred sandwiches with her household staff between morning
and night, and often was called upon by her hospitable husband
to do just that. The students knew them both as well as if they
were members of their family, and brought their friends and
mothers and fathers along when they attended the President's
receptions. Anyone in Allegheny was welcome.

The college Glee and Mandolin Club was John's favorite
organization, and he encouraged the club to appear at Com-

mencement, and offered to lend his musicians to the Pennsylvania College for Women, over in the East End. There were a half-dozen girls attending his own university, enough to teach the boys to dance when they begged to hold their first Junior Prom in 1901. The students banded together to hire delivery rigs from Allegheny, and plodded up the seven bends of Perrysville Avenue to the top of Observatory Hill, with much singing of songs above their creaking wheels. Promptly at eleven-thirty they put on the brakes and went down again.

This innovation of having girls in the college department had been initiated a few years before, when the Reverend John Cracker White led the Commencement exercises in a downtown auditorium and mentioned that after the ceremonies he would make an important announcement. Everyone was expectant, hoping to hear that some "Old Grad" had died and remembered the college in his will. But the anxiously awaited message was even more astonishing, although considered an anticlimax at the moment. It was that two girls, daughters of a prominent German family, were to enter classes with the boys at the University.

One of the first women students to bring prestige to the university was Luba Goldsmith, who graduated from the Medical School in 1902, to become one of the best-known doctors in the city. When Uncle John found that she might be forced to discontinue her studies for lack of funds, he appealed to Henry Frick, who asked him what was needed, and furnished it. No one knows how many other students were carried through college because of his sympathy and his ability to enlist the sympathy of others. It is said that for years anyone who wanted a scholarship appealed first to Uncle John.

Cornelius Scully, Democratic Mayor of Pittsburgh, received his LL.B. from the University Law School in 1904. Dr. Alexander Silverman, head of the Chemistry Department at the University of Pittsburgh, graduated on "the hill" in 1902. He says that "Prexy" Brashear dismissed all the classes one day so that the boys could rush across the campus and see the wreck of his shop. A great hole had been torn through the wall by the explosion of a sixty-inch object glass, in process of being made for the Lick Observatory.

Herman J. Schmitz was Professor of German, which Uncle John had taught himself when riding the street cars to work on the South Side. Professor Schmitz had been very much annoyed one day by having his roll-book stolen and tossed into the Ohio. The students bore him no malice; they merely resented being counted absent when they took a day off without leave. Once on senior Class Day the undergraduates barricaded themselves in the balcony of the chapel and threw everything they could lay their hands on at upper classmen on the stage, who were trying to declaim. No one could dislodge them until the President arrived.

Luckily two maiden ladies sitting as guests upon the platform were not struck during the barrage, although their "waterfall" curls shook with excitement. The Misses Smith were gentlewomen of Allegheny who had become interested in the university when it was housed near them with the Western Theological Seminary, ten years before. They had furnished the President's office for him, framed his Doré Bible pictures, donated a hundred dollars' worth of books (of their own choosing), and presented a cabinet to the Science Department that held a collection of minerals from all over the world. After the collection had been moved to the new quarters on the hill, they used to trudge up there every week and dust it off and recount its stories to the boys.

"Woolly Horse Phillips" was a gentleman of the old school, to which he literally belonged, having taught chemistry in W.U.P. from 1875 to 1915. At the time of Brashear's presidency, the Professor was riding an unclipped pony up and down the hill to the campus. One day when he had a huge chain to carry home, as well as heavy books, he achieved distinction by winding the chain around his body like a coat of mail and clanking off down the hill on his woolly horse named Oxygen.

It was under Brashear that a French teacher joined the faculty from old Jefferson Academy at Canonsburg, but few of the boys signed up for his course as French was not considered as useful a language as German. There was a teacher of oratory, who encouraged debates and taught the boys to declaim their Latin speeches at Commencement. As long as they were in Allegheny, the college had the fine old custom of delivering student addresses in the classic tongue. This put a strain on the Latin professor, but guaranteed to the mill men that their sons were educated.

Professor Henry Scribner taught the classics and remained on the faculty (which was transferred to the University of Pittsburgh) until he retired as Professor Emeritus of Greek in 1933. When he was a young professor in Allegheny he was asked by Brashear to speak at the new Carnegie lecture hall on "The Golden Age of Athens." He wrote out a laborious address and tried to read it with the embellishment of lantern slides, but somehow they became turned upside down and the audience laughed. He never forgot how kindly Uncle John spoke to him afterward and showed him the easy way of presenting a speech from notes. Dr. Scribner has been for years one of the most popular lecturers at the University of Pittsburgh.

Another story he tells of a different sort is how, on St. Patrick's day, they entered the chapel to find that some ingenious student had climbed into the loft above it and suspended "Mrs. Gridley," the school skeleton, from the ceiling. This gaunt anatomical necessity had been donated for serious study but was so popular with the students she had to be kept under lock and key. However, there she was dangling, with bony arms outstretched to the pulpit, and fleshless feet protruding from under a flowing green skirt, all dressed up for the day. Uncle John never discovered who perpetrated this outrage—probably because he never tried.

The most frightened person who ever appeared in chapel was Charlie Robinson, the colored janitor, who was required to give an account of a Christian Endeavor convention in London, the fall that Uncle John assumed office. The students and faculty had banded together the year before and raised funds for him to attend this event during the summer, for Charlie was greatly respected as the most religious man on the campus. With the eloquence of his race, he used such long words in his characteristic report that in the ensuing applause, which he accepted as a gracious tribute, no one could hear his inimitable description of the reception by Queen Victoria.

Just before Brashear came into office, one of the great lights of the hill had left, Dr. Reginald Fessenden, who made the basic experiments on the W.U.P. campus that resulted in radio. Previously he had worked three years with Edison, and afterward perfected the wireless telephone used in transoceanic calls, and sound-ranging for airplanes and undersea craft. Fessenden's "detector" replaced Marconi's "coherer" and was adopted in Marconi stations all over the world.

In the nineties, Reginald Fessenden had astounded the whole city by showing his students how to install telephones from building to building on the campus. He was a friend of Graham Bell, who was also a friend of Langley, then in Washington working on his unsuccessful airplane, and Langley was an old friend of Brashear. If you add George Westinghouse, inventor of the air brake, who had insured Fessenden's joining the W.U.P. faculty by giving him a salary for outside work in his own laboratory, the chain is complete between many of the great inventors of their era: Westinghouse, Fessenden, Graham Bell, Langley, and John Brashear, who all upheld each other's hands.

John Brashear was the only guest present in the New York sending room beside Graham Bell and his grandson, when in 1915 the first transcontinental telephone calls went out to California. Connections were also open to Boston and to Washington, where President Wilson answered, and Theodore Vail, President of the company, replied from his home on Jekyl Island off the coast of Georgia. Uncle John said he was astonished to hear the sound of the surf. Little of scientific importance took place in his day which he was not invited to witness.

One of the honorary degrees conferred by President Brashear was to Edward G. Acheson, another self-taught genius, who accidentally discovered the method of making carborundum in 1891, while working in the old electric powerhouse for the new street cars at the foot of Perrysville Avenue hill. Unlike Brashear, to whose near-by shop he often came for assistance, his invention brought him a fortune, augmented by his development of Acheson Graphite, used in every tungsten lamp. It was one of his happiest gestures when John put the gold and blue hood of his university across his neighbor's shoulders.

John had too many other irons in the fire, or too many lenses on the lathe, to teach any classes in W.U.P. while he was President. But once when he was substituting for Dean Carhart in astronomy, a paper was handed him from a bewildered student that enlisted his deepest attention. The boy had written on a blank page: "Sun, Moon, and Stars Forgot, Upward I Fly," and laid it on the President's desk and walked out. John was a hymn singer. He passed him.

But the incident gave him pause. He felt he was in much the same position as the faithless student.

XVIII

THE DEMISE OF "WUP"

It was not as if work in the shop had stopped because its master had been elected president of a university. The making of astronomical instruments was growing more and more complex each year, and although no wealth came through their completion, honors piled up until they were ignored or neglected.

In 1900 John became vice-president of the American Association for the Advancement of Science. The same year he received the gold medal award of the *Exposition Universelle Internationale*. In 1901 he had been designated by President McKinley, who had known him through his range-finders furnished the government during the Spanish War, to serve on the United States Assay Commission, an appointment whose work was carried out under Theodore Roosevelt after McKinley's assassination in September of that year. The commission dealt with the testing and weighing of gold and silver and Brashear was an authority on instruments of precision. And again in 1901, which was the year he was made chancellor of the Western University of Pennsylvania, he was chosen by Andrew Carnegie to head his committee for founding the Carnegie Institute of Technology.

In 1902 the Civic Club, for which he had acted as chairman for six months when it commenced its important work five years before, inaugurated evening lectures in the public schools, and their records say their success was due to such speakers as Brashear, who supplemented his talks on the stars with lantern slides. A newspaper picture of the period shows him planting a tree on Arbor Day in a school yard, another activity of the Civic Club. The year 1903 finds John A. Brashear heading other significant names as president of the Crucible Club, a social organization of leading men unrelated to the mills.

There were already rumors that the university must be moved, when John became president, and he knew from the beginning that he was not equal to any such involved transaction. Perhaps it was the colossus to which he had given legs that frightened the former incumbent into Carnegie Institute. For what bothered Uncle John was not the engineering school, the observatory, nor the College of Fine Arts, but the various other departments Dr. Holland had added to the catalogue and had not stayed long enough to assimilate.

The University records call Brashear "Acting Chancellor," and he called himself a "Stop-Gap," yet although the trustees knew before he assumed office that they must secure someone who could give his entire time to the business of raising funds for a new location and more buildings, they failed to find such a "Moses," as he was dubbed by an alumni committee, until Brashear insisted on resigning in 1904. Then they were somehow able to locate Dr. Samuel Black McCormick.

Not only had a medical school been projected, but a dental school had been begun, and in 1902 so many students attended that President Brashear had to supervise the moving into another downtown Pittsburgh building. There was also the School of Pharmacy which had joined forces with them, and an even more difficult venture was the School of Mines. The trustees had succeeded in getting the state legislature interested to the amount of $80,000, but the university had no more ground on which to erect a building.

The Law School was particularly vexing, because already, in 1903, it was becoming so professional that it refused to admit students without a college degree, and was suffering growing pains at Commencement time because the legislature had passed a law requiring state examinations. In happier days law students had read Blackstone in some amiable lawyer's office and been examined by a friendly judge.

All this was rather upsetting to a millwright astronomer. John Brashear once made the statement that he had never resorted to law in his life, nor the advice of a barrister in all the international contracts he drew up for his astronomical instruments. Of course he never said he made money by this procedure. In fact, he has been quoted as the only well-known business man in the United States who freely admitted that he never made a cent. A curious failing in the president of a law school.

His talents lay otherwhere. It was because he was an exceptionally able manager of men that his admirers knew no bounds in their demands on his time. He could have served advantageously on any personnel bureau in the city industries. And he was wanted on various boards because, although he could make no profit for himself, he could raise any amount of money for anything outside himself. That is why he knew he could accomplish more for the observatory if he were not in the position of being its director, and he came to feel the same way about the Western University.

During his presidency there was quite another sort of intramural argument going on. So many of the incoming students elected engineering that some of the trustees thought it was time to abandon the hoary classics and concentrate on educating boys to become practical scientists in a city which had such great need for them. There were others, however, who as stubbornly held otherwise, and a slogan arose in an alumni committee: "Save the College of Fine Arts." A group of the teachers most concerned went to call on the trustees, and it was largely due to them that the matter was dropped. John Brashear was not in sympathy with the movement, although it was thought he might be, because of his engineering proclivities. However, when he heard that the faculty of Washington and Jefferson were closely watching proceedings and ready to pounce on the crumbs that fell from the Western University table with the abandonment of the art courses, he argued that a city as large as Pittsburgh, even if primarily concerned with industry, would only cripple its educational facilities if it dropped its ancient academic ideals.

And it was as well for the university that it finally adopted this attitude, for after the completion of the Carnegie Technical Schools they suddenly changed into an engineering university themselves.

When his technical school was built, Carnegie was enthusiastic about establishing such a school as he had recently seen in England, called the Keigley Institute, at York. He had made his first gift to Dumferline, the town of his birth in Scotland, by establishing the Lauder Technical School, named for his idolized uncle, whose son had been educated in the University of Glasgow, and arriving in America, had proved the value of a scientific education to Carnegie by making use of materials hitherto wasted. Other educated men on his large staff further proved the same thing. Carnegie's offices, however, had been constantly besieged by young men who were graduates of eastern universities and yet entirely unfitted for positions in the mills. As Carnegie knew that many workers, and the ones who needed education most, were unable to advance further than the equivalent of the four years' high school course, he endowed a school, more like our present technical high schools, to fit young men and women for work in Pittsburgh industries.

The accomplishment was left in the hands of three men, William Conway, Charles Schwab, and John Brashear. Carnegie had an uncanny, rather than canny, gift for choosing the right man for the right place. Just as he had closed out competing mills by taking over their presidents, as well as bargaining for their stock, so in the realistic field of choosing men for managing his philanthropies, whether the Institute or the Technical Schools, he lifted whom he wanted out of his present position and set him to work for "the Laird." That was how Carnegie removed Dr. Holland from W.U.P., after its trustees had put him on their board where he renewed his old acquaintance with their next president, Brashear. As soon as he came to know the men "on the hill" he began to use them. And to Uncle John he was especially devoted. He gave him so much power in the founding of his schools that Brashear was considered Carnegie's private representative. Some say he would have made him president of them, but "Prexy" Brashear had had enough of that. He had, although it would be difficult to prove it, what is called a "single track" mind. For others he would do any amount of service, but for himself all he asked was to be let alone in his shop (which seemed to be asking too much).

That the example of John Brashear's life was uppermost in Carnegie's mind when he offered his schools to the city is shown by his letter to William J. Diehl, Mayor of Pittsburgh, which the donor read at a banquet tendered him November 15, 1900.

It is really astonishing how many of the world's foremost men have begun as manual laborers. The greatest of all, Shakespeare, was a wood-cutter: Burns, a plowman: Columbus, a sailor: Hannibal, a blacksmith: Lincoln, a rail-splitter: Grant, a tanner. I know of no better foundation from which to ascend than manual labor in youth. We have two notable examples of this in our own community whose fame is world-wide: George Westinghouse was a mechanic: Professor Brashear, a millwright.

Carnegie had no interest in educating the sons of the steel men who could afford to pay their tuition wherever they liked. He was reaching out to help boys who had grown up like himself, and like John Brashear whom he quoted.

The first months of work in founding the Technical Schools, which so appealed to Uncle John that he put all his best endeavor into them, were spent by himself and Charles Schwab and Conway, in studying the problem and engaging a group of advisers, presidents and deans of other universities, to submit a comprehensive program. The plan, as first presented, proved too ambitious for Carnegie. It was sound in relation to what the schools have become, but no such extensive program was wanted by the founder.

In the second year a site was chosen by the city, which supplied the property adjoining Schenley Park, and another group of experts proffered simpler specifications that were acceptable.

The three men, called the Plan and Scope Committee, of

whom John Brashear was one, divided the school as outlined into four branches, each one of which was to support night classes. Uncle John was particularly interested in the departments for girls, for he was enthusiastic about their innovation on his own campus. The School of Fine and Applied Arts was coeducational, admitting artists and sculptors with the plan of teaching them useful plastic arts; the Margaret Morrison Carnegie School for Girls, was named for Carnegie's mother, and was to fit women for vocational work; the School of Science and Technology was to train engineer's assistants, not engineers; and the School for Apprentices and Journeymen was for the education of simple mechanics. None of these branches was designed to offer college courses.

The whole city was delighted, including the man who had helped work out the plans, John Brashear, at that time head of a rival university. He had spent as much effort on these secondary schools as he had on the Western University of Pennsylvania. One of the things he had insisted on was to keep the tuition low, and it began with twenty dollars a year for day students and five dollars for night. At present the tuition has mounted to that of any other college, for the endowment that was sufficient for a hundred students who entered in 1905, while raised later to take care of the two thousand who soon crowded its doors, could not stretch to the present proportions of the student body since it has become a full-fledged university. And of all the schools which were first planned for preparatory work, only the "Maggie Murphy," as it was soon called, retains its original curriculum, although it too has added college courses.

One can see that when Uncle John was serving on the Plan and Scope Committee, there was no conflict with W.U.P. When he resigned the presidency in 1904, he said in his letter to the trustees:

The completion of our great astrophysical Observatory, the development of the Carnegie secondary technical schools, and my own chosen pursuit in the construction of instruments of precision, all demand an amount of energy scarcely to be found in the storage battery that has been drawn upon for nearly half a century, so that I am compelled to ask you to relieve me from the acting chancellorship of the University.

I beg to assure you that the work has been a labor of love to me, and I am pleased to say that all I have done in my weakness has been accepted in a spirit of kindness and helpfulness by the Board of Trustees, the alumni, the faculty, and the students.

After adding that he hoped he could continue to serve on the board, as he had before his presidency, and that he had begun his association with W.U.P. thirty years ago, through his old friends of the observatory, Langley and William Thaw, he continued:

It is perhaps needless to say that Mr. Carnegie decided that the new technical schools should not usurp the prerogatives of the University in teaching the higher branches of technology, so that, for the present, at least, that great field of usefulness has been left to us.

If anyone of that period knew what Carnegie's purpose was, it ought to have been John Brashear.

Taking the matter at its face value, W.U.P. decided to move its own university over to the East End, not only to have more space, for land could also have been had more cheaply in Allegheny, but because all the great new activities of the city were being located in Schenley Farms, and they considered that to be near Carnegie Institute and the Carnegie Technical Schools would be a great advantage. They enjoyed a misapprehension that boys who had completed their education in the secondary schools would gravitate to their own campus for their degrees in engineering. As soon as it could be accomplished they changed their location and their name.

The faculty were tired of hearing the boys corrupt the title of their alma mater into "Wup," which it was called all over the city. The name of the University of Pennsylvania at Philadelphia was causing confusion, even to exchange of mail, and one luckless student shipped off by his parents from Nanty

Glo arrived in the wrong city. There was also the name of the Pennsylvania State College to be coped with. So the old Western University of Pennsylvania took down its sign and became the University of Pittsburgh.

Under the next chancellor, Samuel B. McCormick, who succeeded Brashear in 1905, with Dean Carhart holding the interregnum for six months, the wanted million-dollar endowment was raised, and in 1908 the first building was occupied by the School of Mines. In 1909, the following obituary appeared in the W.U.P. *Courant.*

The promised land is in sight, but who is not sad to leave the old home? We would not give much for a fellow who has been here any length of time who will not sigh as he passes down the path for the last time. It is true that the buildings were not all that could be desired, and that we were expecting for a number of years to go to a new site; yet that did not keep us from placing our affections in the buildings on the "Hill."

At the top of the seven bends of Perrysville Avenue leading up to Observatory Hill, the old college buildings of W.U.P. are forgotten but not gone. By a fortuitous circumstance they have remained there for half a century.

A hundred years ago, a "benevolent ladies sewing society" of Allegheny founded an orphanage. Before they discovered any orphans worthy of their care, they furnished a pleasant home for them on the banks of the river, installed a matron, and, disliking to see all their efforts wasted, permitted one of their members to place her own children in the "Home" while making a phenomenal trip to Europe in the forties. It was not until the civil war that the Protestant Orphanage Asylum came into full usefulness, when it was crowded with children whose fathers had died to preserve the Union. Its facilities increased, as well as its orphans and its funds, and by 1900 it was the largest, as well as the oldest, asylum in Western Pennsylvania.

Soon after John Brashear's perplexed régime, one of the trustees of W.U.P. was jogging back from a board meeting on Observatory Hill. When crossing the Sixth Street Bridge, he met, coming toward him, one of the trustees of the orphanage, and stopped to exchange the pleasantries of the occasion with the pretty lady. During the course of the desultory conversation it was disclosed that the University was trying to sell, and the Orphanage was trying to buy, at exactly the same moment.

The tone of the argument grew more animated. And before their square-box buggies moved on, the deed was as good as signed. No hand-money was exchanged because the lady had forgotten her purse, but the orphanage bought the university buildings and the whole Observatory Hill for $85,000, and generously stipulated that the college could take all the desks away because they were going to put in a hundred cots and add a double-decker porch. Nor did they want any of the telescopes, thank you, what they liked best were the stained-glass windows in the chapel.

The observatory was denuded of its instruments and left empty, as John Brashear had foreseen when he began planning for a new one. Even then, working on in his shop near-by, he could hear the faint tread of the ghosts that were to keep him company when all the professors and astronomers should be gone from the hill. Yet if he were lonely, he never showed it. The children themselves became his friends. One of the pictures stamped on the mind of an acquaintance is of Uncle John with his new neighbors at the orphanage. This acquaintance had driven over to Observatory Hill to see the lens-maker on a government contract, and could not find him in the shop.

"He might be over at the college," said his brother Frank.

Following the sound of singing, he saw John standing bareheaded, with white shirt, flowing black tie, and no coat, on the steep lawn beside the old Administration Building, with a row of youngsters ranged before him according to size, from big to little. He was beating time, as they nodded their heads and sang the words back that he was teaching them. And the song was the ballad he used to sing on the South Side when he and Phoebe named their adopted baby. It was "Flow Gently, Sweet Afton."

The children saw the stranger and stopped singing. John turned.

"They're easier to teach," he said, "than the college boys used to be. They never could learn 'America.'" He brushed his hand across his eyes as if the sunlight hurt him.

Scattering like multi-colored butterflies on the advent of a stranger, the children ran off, laughing, across the old campus.

XIX

SUMMONS FROM MUSKOKA

JOHN BRASHEAR remained on the boards of both the great city universities all his life, and was equally valuable to both. For while he regretted their later rivalry, he understood changing conditions too well to try to sabotage the wheel of time.

In 1905, when the night schools were opened at "Tech," he addressed three hundred entering students, and from that time on was a favorite speaker for the Tartans. It was on the Plan and Scope Committee that his recognized intimacy began with "Charlie" Schwab, whom he had known for twenty years, ever since the latter had arrived with other young workmen to look through his telescope on the South Hills. The founder, "Andy," was almost as old a friend, for he had known him since the days at Cresson, in the eighties. In a speech at an eastern university he said, "No one knows better than he who addresses you what the friendship of Andrew Carnegie means."

In this same address, at Lehigh, Uncle John laid down one of the principles of education which he was first to advance: "Every student should learn something of another profession, a knowledge of something different from his work." To the students at "Tech" he said, "Have a hobby, and let it be as different from your work as the stars from the mills." To the ambitious young theorists at Pitt, "There is no room for the mean man in science," and again, "If you haven't time to understand the mathematics of astronomy don't miss the beauty of it." And more fully to a group of amateur astronomers, always his favorites, "Learn all you can about the stars, but I would rather that star lovers should have the opportunity to study the constellations, find beautiful colored doubles, star clusters, than to devote your entire time to the mathematical achievements of astronomy." This was his own approach to the subject, and the reason for his making his first telescope.

In illustrating his talks to amateurs, he always dwelt on the beauty of color of the stars, and illustrated their sparkling brilliancy by holding a prism to the light. To point his description further he dropped into the florist shop of A. W. Smith, one day, and asked his old friend of the South Side if he could have a few flowers of different hues for an impending lecture.

"Certainly," said Anthony Smith. But his thrift was shocked when he saw Uncle John deliberately picking out the most rare and expensive blooms in his case: a handful of American beauties, branches of pale, hot-house lilacs, dozens of yellow tulips and scarlet anemones, delicate orchids and a bunch of purple violets.

"What do you want all those for?" he asked in dismay.

"For a colored church," said John, innocently walking out of the door with his flowers.

The Carnegie Technical Schools have their own story to tell of their trustee, Uncle John. In 1905 Robert C. Hall, a wealthy real estate promoter and a patron of art who enjoyed a fabulous modern collection, ordered John Brashear's portrait painted by the Polish artist Keszthelyi. He stipulated that this was to remain in Phoebe's possession as long as she lived and then be delivered back to the Institute of Technology and hung in the halls of the "Tartans."

The trustees thanked the donor profusely, the secretary closed the recording book, and the matter was forgotten by everyone concerned—including John, who survived Phoebe. Three decades passed, when suddenly in searching for something entirely different, the old minutes of former board meetings were glanced over by Dean Tarbell, and the gift disclosed.

A thorough search began throughout the city for the "Missing Portrait." In the meantime the painting had wandered from John's Perrysville Avenue house to his shop, afterward occupied by the J. W. Fecker Company, and from there to the new home purchased by Effie McDowell after Brashear's death, where it was finally located in the possession of the widow of Effie's son, Walter. This woman graciously returned it to the Carnegie campus as soon as she understood the situation, and in 1934 the

"Missing Portrait" was unveiled with proper ceremony in the hall of the Administration Building, and hung with honor opposite the bas-relief of the first president.

Below the name and date, the inscription reads:

ASTRONOMER, PHYSICIST, MECHANICAL ENGINEER, MAKER OF TELESCOPES

Honored by degrees from Princeton University, College of Wooster, Stevens Institute of Technology, University of Pittsburgh, Washington and Jefferson College; Member of Original Board of Trustees, Carnegie Institute of Technology. A vigorous and devoted worker for the institution during the first two decades of its history.

The "Missing Portrait" is one of great interest. The face shines forth from the depths of a dark background, and the chin rests on one hand. In Uncle John's various portraits, and there were four of them painted during his lifetime when he was an elderly man, more of his character is revealed than in his numerous photographs. His was the long, lean Yankee type common to many professors of his day but uncommon in its differentiations. The eyes are those of a seer, and at the same time hold the suffering of the world and the long life he had lived in it. It is no wonder that children who used to hear him talk in the schools thought he, like one of the Greek gods in their lesson books, came straight from the starry heavens he described. Charles Schwab said of the portrait he owned of him, that he considered it "a kind of mascot, that always gives me hope and courage."

After John had resigned as president of the Western University he bent all his energies toward raising funds for the observatory. In the summer of 1905, as he and Phoebe were about to start for Muskoka, he was asked to dine with Henry Clay Frick, and over the coffee and liqueurs, in the way most business deals are managed by the barons of industry, Frick offered to help him finish the endowment.

"Brashear," John quoted him as saying, "go and find out what it will cost to finish the building, and I will give you half the amount if you will raise the balance by October 15th."

John raised the balance. And although this was his opportunity to estimate enough on the equipment he was building in his own shop to insure a profit to himself, he thought only of the cost of mortar and bricks. Before he took his invalid wife away for the summer he made an estimate of $65,000, and set about asking for his half by mail from Muskoka. By the middle of September, when he returned home, he had secured the promise of $20,000, and had a month to find the rest. This he did, and shortly all the apparatus from the old observatory was moved into the new with the assurance of eventual completion.

As soon as the foundations for the great Keeler telescope were built, a personal project that Brashear had long had in mind was carried out. The thirty-inch reflecting telescope was in process of construction in the Brashear shop as a memorial to Samuel Keeler, who had died in the West shortly after leaving Allegheny for the Lick Observatory. The friends who gave the telescope decided to have Keeler's ashes brought back from California and interred in a crypt formed by its great circular base, thirty feet in diameter. In 1906 this was accomplished, and they remain there today, with certain others which followed in the course of life, and death. John Brashear had always mourned that he had been unable to complete raising the funds for the new observatory in time to prevent Keeler's leaving Allegheny, and felt it only fitting that the place where he had spent most of his working years should be his final resting place.

Brashear's relationship to Henry Clay Frick, who at this time contributed $32,500 to the new observatory, is one of the most important chapters in his contacts with the millionaires of his day. It was as if something as magnetic as the attraction of the compass needle to the north pole pointed the attention of the barons of industry to John Brashear. Their seeking out a man of his type was as far from their ordinary course as the North Star is to the mariner on a rough sea.

Henry Clay Frick was the grandson of Abraham Overholt, whose daughter, Elizabeth, married her father's gardener, Frick, and moved from the neighborhood of the famous distillery at Broadsford to live on a farm near Wooster, Ohio. Frick had been brought up a long distance from his wealthy forebears, a circumstance which must have rankled in the mind of a growing boy, and perhaps gave him his first determination to lift himself into worthy prominence by his own efforts. When a young man, he was encouraged to come back to Pennsylvania by his picturesque grandfather, an elder in the Mennonite church, who discovered him clerking in a drygoods store outside Pittsburgh and removed him to the higher sphere of a grocery store in Connellsville. Finding himself in the center of vast and unsuspected coal fields, his first investment was to borrow ten thousand dollars from Thomas Mellon and others, to buy an interest in the neighboring coke ovens, derisively called "Frick's cinders." In the panic of 1873 he was determined to keep the "bee-hives" burning so the men could continue to buy from his grocery store, and paid them in goods instead of money, forerunner of the company stores that under later abuse menaced the wages of all the workers in the coal valleys.

By the time the panic was over, in 1879, Frick had bought out all the dissatisfied investors in his first enterprise and owned a thousand ovens smoldering in the hills. He sold his coke to the blast furnaces down river, and his wares became necessary to the Edgar Thompson works at Braddock which shortly asked him to combine with the Carnegie Company. Due to his shrewd manipulations the price jumped from ninety cents to five dollars a ton.

In 1881, when he was on a wedding trip with his bride, Adelaide Childs, of Pittsburgh, he was entertained by Andrew Carnegie and his mother at the Hotel Windsor in New York. Over the dinner table Carnegie told him he had decided to make him a partner. Maggie Morrison bristled up. "That's a verra good thing for Mr. Frick, Andra," she interrupted, "but what do we get out of it?"

What Carnegie got out of it, with his usual astuteness in choosing men, was a partner with a remarkable genius for management. All through the eighties, and through the strike of 1892, Frick managed the destinies of the great Carnegie-Phipps company, buying out the shares of Tom Carnegie when he died. The break between Andrew Carnegie and Frick came in 1899, when Frick resigned from the Carnegie Steel Company. Sufficient to our pages is the fact that although these two old friends were friends no longer, each of them was a personal friend of John Brashear. In his warming presence care and bitterness slipped away, and "Solitary Frick" was so no longer.

When he died in 1919, Henry Frick left a great park to the city of Pittsburgh, and his daughter endowed an art department in the University of Pittsburgh in his name. He is also remembered with gratitude for the Frick Teacher's Training School, and his great library and art gallery have become one of the attractions of New York, where he prospered for many years after shaking the coal dust of Pittsburgh off his feet.

He had already built his fabulous mansion at Pride's Crossing, on the coast of Massachusetts, when he summoned John Brashear from Muskoka in the summer of 1909 and told him he had an important matter to discuss with him. Helen Frick, his daughter, who became an even closer friend of John's than her father, and whom Uncle John said he loved as a daughter, entertained him in the style to which he was accustomed (when visiting the steel kings) and gave him a bedroom looking out to sea, as large, he said, as the whole lower floor of the cottage where he had just left Phoebe lying sick. It had been difficult to get away from Muskoka and he was in a hurry to return, so he immediately asked what was wanted.

To his astonishment he learned that Henry Frick, abetted by his daughter, had conceived the plan of setting aside $250,000 for the education of Pittsburgh school teachers in the summer time, and wanted John to manage the whole sum without using Frick's name. John demurred, as usual, at so great an honor and so grave a responsibility, but in the end acceded to the unique request for the sake of the good that it would do. For seven years the identity of the donor was not revealed, and the many teachers who benefited by Henry Frick's liberality were not informed from whom the funds came that Uncle John was dispensing.

Refusing to take sole charge, however, John had immediately appointed a committee of administration composed of two judges, two members of the school board, and two engineers. In October 1909 these men chose him as president of the board of seven.

Henry Frick recognized that the purely intellectual work of the schools was well taken care of, and sought to aid such teachers as were ambitious along the lines of civic usefulness, or needed training in the arts in order to become more efficient along special lines. His trust continues today as the Frick Educational Commission, and because he had to sign certain legal papers to make it permanent Frick's name was finally disclosed, but he never took the management out of John Brashear's hands as long as Brashear lived.

Through his wide personal acquaintance with the teachers in the city, many of whom he had known as students, John Brashear knew exactly who was worthy to benefit by this unusual sort of opportunity. He had long had the theory, also held by Carnegie in the beginning of his schools, that most young people never reached courses in any university, but had to content themselves with whatever was taught in the secondary, or highschool grades. In this proposition, however, the endowment was put into the reverse of the Carnegie plan, and the emphasis placed on securing better teachers. If students only came in contact with the teachers of the lower grades, it was felt by Frick, and worked out by John Brashear, that these ordinary grade teachers should have the best equipment possible for their tremendously important responsibility.

One outcome of this plan was that the many grateful teachers who soon benefited by it wanted to show appreciation for their unusual summer opportunities (which included everything from manual training, art and music courses, to scholastic work abroad), by establishing what is known as the Phoebe Brashear Club, named in her honor. This club, composed for the most part of young women teachers, held one of its first meetings in 1911 at the home of Dr. Luba Goldsmith, who was the student whom Frick had aided in the days when John was president of the Western University.

A characteristic story attaches itself to the occasion. The day was very warm, and about a hundred people were gathered together and being served lemonade and sandwiches by a weary maid-of-all-work, who was shoving through the crowd, bumping people in the back with her heavy tray. John, long awaited, entered with his usual sang-froid.

"Let me help you, my good woman," he said to the startled maid. "You sit down now, you must be tired, and I will wait on you." And to the dismay of the hostess this was done. He seated the woman in the best chair near the window and passed the refreshments to her.

The house on Perrysville Avenue became more and more full of McDowells as the years went on. Beside John and Phoebe Brashear, the heads of the house, and always called "Pa" and "Ma" by the rest, were Effie and her husband, Jim McDowell, who was right-hand man in the shop, and their two sons who had married and brought their wives home to live. Soon Walter and his wife Caroline had a baby daughter, greatly beloved by her foster great-grandfather, and as years went on the delight of his old age. There was also a cook and a laundress to take care of the family of nine, which increased to ten when another great-grandchild was born. Life went on in happy confusion, and when the big brass dinner bell was rung the family sat down to a huge table laid habitually for twelve, for there were always guests. The men of the family came home from the shop for lunch and often John's brothers came with him. After the Frick Educational Commission was established, a secretary, Miss Martha Hoyt, came to the house daily to attend to the prodigious correspondence, and at a later date often worked with Uncle John at Muskoka.

In July 1910, John's mother, who was ninety, and had always lived on the South Side in the shadow of her favorite Methodist Church, was brought back to her son's rooftree to be buried. This was the forerunner of an even greater break in family ties.

More and more John looked forward to his summers in Muskoka, finding there a tranquillity with his dear wife denied him in the city, where he had formed the habit of refusing invitations if women were to be present, because Phoebe could not accompany him. Sometimes he took one of the young McDowell women with him to his lectures, and more and more Effie took over the management of domestic affairs. Phoebe preferred above all these tender months with her husband on the sunny island where they had been contented for fifteen years. The young people of the family spent their vacations with them in Canada, and John's greatest delight was to have the little children on the island, and his only worry was that they might fall in the lake.

He worked at his garden constantly, bemoaning the lack of good soil but managing to raise beautiful flowers even though the tomatoes sometimes failed to ripen. He spent hours gathering wild blueberries for the womenfolk to can, and although he employed a boatman, Harry, and a cook, Mary, who later married each other, he would go out by himself to trim the branches of the trees so that Phoebe could have an unobstructed view of the water. He liked to fish, and would bring home trout for the family table, cleaning the fish himself for breakfast. Long before his wife or their visitors were awake he would attend to his correspondence, so that Harry could mail his letters when he went across the lake for the Toronto paper. There was nothing that went on in the shop during his absence that he did not know all about, and often he would rush to Pittsburgh to attend to details, and rush back again, probably bringing a young McDowell with him for a visit.

Phoebe, who had been so ill the year before that John hesitated to leave her when he went to Pride's Crossing to interview Frick, failed rapidly during the summer of 1910. The stars they had discovered together grew jealous for her companionship, and in the September after John's mother died, she slipped peacefully away under the glancing, northern lights, at the Isle Urania in Muskoka.

Her death, however much it left her husband bereft, was at least an end to the suffering he had been obliged to watch for years. Life could never be the same again with half of his buoyant spirit buried and gone, but remembering the long years of happiness they had spent together, undimmed by any sort of misunderstanding or loss of faith, with nothing to wish undone and nothing to regret, he tried to find courage to face inevitable loneliness.

He brought her ashes back and buried them in the crypt of the observatory. But when he began to think of notifying their friends all over the world, and of what he could say in relation to what was due her, he sent instead, the following beautiful lines, composed previously by his friend Albert Bigelow Paine, biographer of Mark Twain, which read as if they had been written expressly for Phoebe: Phoebe of the deft hands, working so long ago, so hard, for their success, in the beginning of their life's partnership in the little house on Holt Street.

> Poor tired hands that toiled so hard for me,
>   At rest before me now I see them lying.
> They toiled so hard; and yet we could not see
>   That she was dying.
>
> Poor, tired hands that drudged the livelong day,
>   Still busy when the midnight oil was burning;
> Oft toiling on until she saw the gray
>   Of day returning.
>
> If I could sit and hold those tired hands,
>   And feel the warm life-blood within them beating,
> And gaze with her across the twilight lands,
>   Some whispered words repeating;

I know tonight that I would love her so,
  And I could tell my love to her so truly,
That e'en though tired, she would not wish to go
  And leave me here so lonely.

Poor tired heart, that had so weary grown,
  That death came all unheeded o'er it creeping,
How sad it is to sit here all alone,
  While she is sleeping.

XX

BAGPIPES AT SKIBO

UNIVERSITIES all over the world were asked to send representatives to St. Andrews in 1911, when the old Scottish university celebrated its five-hundredth anniversary; and from the University of Pittsburgh John Brashear was chosen delegate.

The honor was the more acceptable to him because it gave him an opportunity to investigate various European trade schools in relation to the endowment for teachers' training that he was managing anonymously for Henry Frick. Furthermore, Carnegie had not only invited any of the board of trustees of the Institute to attend, of whom John was one, but wanted to entertain him after the celebration was over as John had worked so long with him on the founding board of his technical schools.

The winter previously, which was soon after Phoebe died, John had been with Andrew Carnegie and his wife at Dungeness, the island estate off the coast of Florida built by Tom Carnegie, where his widow used to entertain lavishly. It was John's first trip to the South, and his letters tell of the surf rolling up on the "outside" beach, the cranes flying over the inland marshes, the flowers and fruit that were strange to him, and the fish brought in by the boatload for the table at Dungeness. He made his own contribution by lecturing for his hostess in the schools of the old Spanish town of Fernandino. Perhaps it was here that plans were made for his trip to Skibo, for Andrew would have wanted to show him his own estate after he had seen his brother's. The following summer all roads led to the land of the pibroch, and John could hardly wait to hear the bagpipes play.

Andrew Carnegie had been made Lord Rector of St. Andrews in 1901, and had served two terms, a matter of six years. The appointment, which was purely honorary, came from the

students of the ancient university, founded by Roman Catholic
bishops in 1411 and presided over by them until the Reformation. Under John Knox's sway, Scotland became what is today
called Presbyterian, but St. Andrews preserved the pageantry
of the times of the popes, in its renowned celebrations. The
city was also known to quite dissimilar admirers as the parent
of golf links.

John Brashear was not the only American whose expenses
were paid across the ocean. Many college presidents whom he
did not know were present until he saw them introduced, were
beneficiaries of Carnegie's invitation from "door-step to door-
step." This was an ordinary routine with him. For although his
guest-book at Skibo was a register of empire builders, it also
contained the names of musicians, writers, educators, and artists, both famous and obscure, who arrived under this heading
in his secretary's ledger.

The trip was to be so short that John intended to confine
his attention to what was now his major occupation, the furthering of educational work in the humanities. His life after
1900 was a fulfillment of that side of his nature which had
been thwarted in his youth when he had been discouraged with
the ministry and gone into the mills but could now develop simultaneously with his successful shop.

Embarking in early September on the *Kaiser Wilhelm II*, he
stood at the rail, on the high bow, as the vessel steamed out of
New York harbor. He was thinking how he missed Phoebe,
and how she would have enjoyed being with him on the deck
again, and how hard it was going to be to manage without her
cheer and companionship. A Scotchman, also returning for the
great occasion, edged up beside him, guarding his Dunhill pipe
against the wind. John recognized him for a well-known figure
from the steel mills at home.

"I suppose this is the finest harbor in the world," said John
by way of friendly greeting. "The most beautiful, anyway,
that I have ever seen."

The Scotchman took his pipe out, and there was no change

of expression in his steel-blue eyes, as he replied, "Ye never war in Dundee, war ye?"

John remembered this when he came to that old shipbuilding town, so cherished, on the Firth of Tay.

Ten thousand delegates had overrun the village of St. Andrews, and there was no possibility of housing them in its few inns along the bay. Fortunately arrangements had been made for John to stay at the near-by estate of Sir Thomas and Lady Gertrude Cochran, who rescued him every night and took him to Crawford Priory, a modern Gothic edifice in the same county of Fife. Again John missed Phoebe, cruelly, but this time he had his tips for the household well in mind.

The color of the ceremonial delighted his artist's eye, many of the costumes worn being hundreds of years old. There was a huge procession followed by a pageant, but more impressive to him than the red robes of St. Andrews' scholars and the various regalia from all over the earth were the simple black suits of the French delegation, decorated with a crimson ribbon that crossed the stiff white shirt. To be present in this old-world ceremony was inspiring, although John could not help but realize that little learned there would be of use to his mission of investigation. It was in order to conduct matters in a more modern way that the universities in which he was interested had been founded.

Andrew Carnegie, who had worked hard for the success of the celebration, did not stay until it was over at the end of the week, but left instructions how John was to reach Skibo Castle, and preceded him with his popular young wife. This gave John an opportunity to accomplish one of the things he had come for, en route to their home.

A final meeting of the delegates was held at a branch of St. Andrews, the old University College at Dundee, where John unexpectedly had the opportunity to look over the beautiful harbor recommended by his shipboard friend. Then, having finished his scholastic and scenic duties, he hurried to near-by Broughty Ferry, where he had an appointment with himself.

He wanted to visit the home of Dr. Thomas Dick, author of the *Dick's Works* which his grandfather Smith had given him to read when he was a boy. He recognized that the influence of Dr. Dick on his beloved and scholarly grandfather, and through him on himself, had been one of the first unnoticed milestones on his journey of three score years and ten. "What reverent joy was mine that afternoon as I paid homage to the dear man who had done so much to rouse my interest in the science of astronomy in my youth."

It had been a long journey from Dr. Dick's cottage at Broughty Ferry to the farm of Nathaniel Smith at Brownsville, but at last the seed of knowledge Dr. Dick had planted had returned in full fruition to his humble door.

When John took the train for Bonar Bridge and Skibo he recognized no one in the carriage. On arrival, however, he found he had been traveling with Lloyd George and other notables. They had come to hear first news over Carnegie's private wire of an important election in Canada, and were part of the audience that night when he was asked to lecture on the stars. Mrs. Carnegie had had some copies made of sky photographs taken at Mt. Wilson, California, to be used in a transparency illuminated from the rear, and for three nights Uncle John entertained the castle guests. If Andrew Carnegie had not done so much for John, one would be tempted to quote the anecdote of Chopin, when asked to play after dinner at the home of an admiring friend—"But, Madam, I have eaten so little!"

Carnegie, however, had a fine sense of fitness, and knew that his friend would feel more at home immersed in his own subject, than in listening endlessly to British politics. That his judgment was right is shown by the fact that for some time afterward Uncle John kept coming across speeches of Lloyd George, quoted in Welsh papers in America and shown him by the mill men, in which he used material attributed to John's talks at Skibo.

Mrs. Andrew Carnegie says of the occasion:

We had a distinguished party of English friends visiting us, and dear Uncle John, in his modest way, sat quietly listening to the conversation. Later in the evening the talk naturally turned to the stars and the universe, and we adjourned to the morning room, where we had a large transparency, presented to us by the Mt. Wilson Observatory, brilliantly illuminated. Uncle John was in his element; he launched forth in his inimitable way, telling us of one marvel after another in the heavens, and pointing out on the transparency a little spot which he developed into a most wonderful example of the immensities by which we were surrounded. It was late before that party broke up, and it was with difficulty that we came down to earth.

Afterward one of the guests approached his host, Mrs. Carnegie relates, and complimented him on the success of John's lecture. "What a wonderful evening you have given us, Mr. Carnegie," he said. "In most country houses the conversation is of sport or politics, but this evening has lifted us out of our petty world and given us visions of things unknown to us."

The English were as fond of Uncle John as were the Americans. Not since Benjamin Franklin visited them had they met anyone whom they considered so typically Yankee. He disarmed their natural British suspicion. No one was too simple for him to inform, and equally, and more unusual, no one too great.

The castle of Skibo that Andrew Carnegie built bore no resemblance to the simple manor houses of the Scotch lairds which had preceded it in the same place for the past seven centuries. The exterior looked medieval, but no one knew better than the guest from Pittsburgh where the steel girders were made, and the electric elevators. Carnegie, however, had no pride in possession. All he cared about was a suitable setting for his adored wife and daughter. What interested him at Skibo was the surrounding acreage of moor, fen, and burn.

The gentle astronomer had been a little surprised when asked to fall in behind the pibroch and be escorted to the dinner table with wild Scotch airs. But he had been warned that

the din that would awaken him in the morning was made by
the same bagpipe player, circling the castle in kilts, and paus-
ing under each guest's window with an extra skirl on the pipes.
This to "Andra" was the height of hospitality. What caused
most argument among the visitors was whether the flag that
waved on the mast above the castle was the Union Jack or the
Stars and Stripes. Some said one, some said the other, depending on which way the wind blew. For the master mind that
had welded together the steel mills of the United States had
also caused his two equally loved flags to be woven together
and unfurled as one, above his cosmopolitan home.

One day, walking off from the others to be alone, John
found the Laird had the same idea, for he found him sitting
with his collie dog Laddie near his favorite burn, letting the
great of the world entertain each other. Andrew said he regretted for John that the heather was past its prime, and
John promised to return again and see it in its glory. Not that
either of them believed this; John was seventy-one and Carnegie seventy-six. When the World War made travel impossible
three years later, the Laird failed to return to Skibo himself,
but spent his winters as usual in New York, and his summers
in the Berkshires. An undercurernt of premonition prompted
him to say, "If Heaven is more beautiful than this, someone
has made a mistake!"

John answered him with his tender smile. He was a mild authority, he said, on the heavens, but not on Heaven.

On Sunday night the usual gathering of servants and family
took place in the great hall where Carnegie always chose the
hymns with due regard to their subject matter. John stood facing the household, a saintly figure, with his unworldly smile
and noble voice, leading the old hymn tunes they all loved
equally.

Carnegie's birthday fell on the day after John's, and they
often celebrated together and exchanged small gifts. This year,
six months after his visit to Skibo, the scientist made the steelmaster a characteristic present. On Mr. and Mrs. Carnegie's

twenty-fifth wedding anniversary, April 6, 1912, John built and sent to them a splendid telescope which is still in use on the lawn of the Scottish estate.

From Skibo, John investigated the industrial schools endowed by Carnegie at his native village of Dumferline, and traveling on in the interests of the Frick Educational Commission visited a girls' agricultural school at Crawford Priory. At Leeds he saw the apprentice schools for the woollen industry, and in Munich made a thorough study of their compulsory trade schools. He was disappointed that Germany failed to make the same provision for educating girls that they did for boys. In London and Cambridge he was entertained by old friends he had met twenty years before, and renewed his acquaintance with Madeline Pitt-Taylor and her aunt who had been to Pittsburgh in 1908 for the Sesqui-Centennial celebration of the old fort named for their ancestor. They helped care for him when he contracted influenza and had to spend most of his time in London, in a hotel bed.

John reached Paris just in time to attend the wedding of the son of Baron des Tournelles de Constant, who remembered John from lecturing at Carnegie Institute, and had left a formal invitation for him at the Hotel de Lille et d'Albion. Thanks to misinformation from an English lady at his hotel who assured him she knew French customs, he attended the church ceremony in evening dress, and found he was the only one so attired, for the wedding was in the afternoon. The Baron himself rescued him from his embarrassment at the following reception, by stepping out of the receiving line and personally introducing him to his family and friends as his *cher ami* from America.

The only business visits he made on the whole trip were to an observatory in Belgium that wanted help with a double lens camera he had made for them, and to the Schott Company in Munich who were trying to make the glass he had ordered for the great new lens of the Thaw Telescope. This imported glass was so difficult to procure that it was several years before it was ready for grinding and polishing in the Brashear shop.

Taking passage home in October, as a side issue en route he raised seven hundred dollars on shipboard for the Sailor's Fund, at the ordinary ship's concert held each trip. Usually about fifty is collected, and that with difficulty, for many of the more sophisticated passengers avoid being entertained by amateurs. Everyone, however, must have hurried to attend when they heard John was going to preside. Caruso was on board but had refused to sing, saying he was under contract. John was under none. His talks on the stars were sown on the winds of the sea, and at sea as elsewhere rumors of them were enough to draw a crowd.

XXI

"OVER A ROUGH ROAD TO THE STARS"

WORK in the Brashear shop, which had brought it early prestige in the eighties—the bolometer, rock-salt prisms, Rowland Gratings, aerophysics apparatus for Langley, and the first great stellar spectroscopes—was further advanced in the nineties by range-finders for the government, photographic doublets and telescopes sent all over the world.

After 1900 even more intricate machines were devised by the man who, by this time, was known as the greatest lens maker in the world. His work in astrophysics differed from that of Alvan Clark and Sons in New England who had concentrated on refracting telescopes, and of Carl Zeiss in Germany who perfected the microscope. Brashear, in America, was the outstanding figure of the "new astronomy."

The research of any scientist is at the mercy of his instrument maker, and particularly is this true in the department of astrophysics, whose discoveries at this time were newspaper headlines. Whenever anything new was learned through use of an instrument he had invented, a record and photograph were sent to Uncle John which he accepted as his reward. He seldom estimated a contract at a high enough figure to pay for the cost of material, nor the time he spent, which was endless.

The scientists who turned to him for the invention of a new machine needed for some particular research in the stars could not advise him how it was to be constructed. Geniuses are born and not made. In a city and age that measured success in terms of tonnage, John Brashear's life was dedicated to microscopic precision. He walked the streets of the world with the stars in his eyes, as could easily be seen by looking in his face. And strangers asking who he was were universally surprised by the astonishment in the tone of the answer given, "Why that's Uncle John."

One of the lasting achievements with which his name is linked was the perfecting of the interferometer for Dr. A. A. Michelson, famous scientist at the University of Chicago. Upon its invention, Dr. Michelson was called on by the International Bureau of Weights and Measures, whose headquarters were in Paris, to utilize it in settling for all time an international standard of length. Their single measuring device was a platinum bar kept locked in an underground vault and approached for testing purposes once every ten years. Michelson agreed to comply if he could find anyone who would make his optical surfaces so flat as to be within one-twentieth of the light waves he was to measure. He turned to John Brashear.

A carpenter works with a measure accurate to within a sixteenth of an inch: a cabinet maker, within a thirty-secondth. The finest scale the unaided eye can read is graduated to a hundredth, which is about five times a hair's breadth, or five one-hundredths of an inch, the accuracy claimed by the manufacturers of ball bearings. "The wave-length of green light" is not far from one fifty-thousandth of an inch, and Brashear's contract called for accuracy of one-twentieth of this, or one-millionth of an inch.

But with the remarkable surfaces that Uncle John constructed, the improved interferometer was able to check the world's standard meter in terms of a fraction of a wave-length of light, and establish an infallible length of measurement forever. Mention has already been made of the rotating mirror John devised for the same scientist, used in his experiments in measuring the velocity of light. Einstein's theory of relativity was founded on the work of Michelson, who was awarded a Nobel prize in physics. For his own use, Uncle John had built a most remarkable standard for comparing the flatness of surfaces before they left his shop. This was a testing mirror, so delicate that the touch of a hand or the warmth of one's breath would distort its surface. It was suspended on leather straps in an underground chamber, and when a lens was compared with it, by means of a tiny pin-point of light cast through a prick in the tin shade of a lamp, and reflected back to the surface of the lens, a defect could be noticed which was not visible to the eye, even under a microscope. Every inch of its surface was corrected as Michelson's glass was, to the twentieth part of a wave-length of sodium light, and the lenses of spectroscopes and telescopes were measured by it before John pronounced them ready for delivery. It was not for sale. But although it was called in its day "the flattest surface in the world," John Brashear disclaimed any pretense that it was perfect.

One of the astral cameras he perfected for the astronomer Wadsworth had a curved plate that could photograph a field of the sky eight times larger than any previous astronomical camera, and differed from the famous Brashear photographic doublets, arranged to take double views simultaneously. The first spectroheliograph ever made was built in the Brashear shop for Dr. George E. Hale, noted director of the Yerkes and later of the Mt. Wilson Observatory, and was used for automatic photography of the surface and surroundings of the sun. Dr. Hale's findings with it were epoch-making in the realm of solar photography. Deslandres, of Paris, ordered these lenses duplicated for the French Observatory. A fourth differentiation in camera lenses was constructed for the government, so that engineers might measure the speed of a projectile en route from a gun to its target. John Brashear was the Eastman of the skies.

The Mills spectroscope at the Lick Observatory, considered the finest in the world, not only contained Brashear lenses but was designed and constructed in its entirety at the Brashear shop. With it, Director W. W. Campbell discovered the drift of the solar system through space. The instrument with which the Flagstaff Observatory ascertained that there was vapor in the atmosphere of the planet Mars, was invented by John Brashear, and helped Percival Lowell to advance his contention that a race of human beings comparable to our own could inhabit that fiction-lover's planet.

Brashear also experimented with color photography, in which

his co-workers, McDowell and Dr. Charles Hastings, were particularly interested, and a picture they took of him with his own lenses, as early as 1913, is a fine example of this art, new at the time, which had originated in Germany. At about this period he built a kiln on his premises so that he would not be subjected to delays in importing glass from Europe, and engaged a French expert to oversee the work. But the plan was abandoned when he found, as other American firms had, that optical glass demanded too much attention to be a successful side-issue in a small shop whose staff of twenty-five experts were trained for other work.

Nor were all of the Brashear lenses and prisms made of glass. Some of them were composed of rock-salt, as for Langley's experiments, and reflectors were tried of hard rubber, calcite, obsidian, or even gold. A vary rare lens of quartz was made for Dr. W. H. Pickering of Harvard, when working on problems relating to the surface of the moon. Brashear said in a scientific journal that he had hoped for twenty-five years to succeed with porcelain for a mirror surface, as it was of such light weight, but that as yet it was not hard enough for his purpose, and would crack under grinding and polishing. The marvelous plates for the Rowland Gratings that were made so accurately they could be ruled twenty thousand lines to the inch, were of brittle tin or copper.

A curiosity of the shop was a set of huge binoculars with four-inch lenses and tubes thirty inches long. A spyglass was made for Commander Fish of the United States Navy, supported vertically, close to the body, while one gazed through a hole in the side, on the principle of a telescope. Microscopes and binoculars were the simplest things made in the Brashear shop.

One of the most ingenious things was the wheel for the Thaw Telescope at the Allegheny Observatory, six feet in diameter, part of the driving clock for turning the three-ton instrument, forty-six feet long. The wheel was split in two in the making, "like a pancake," and its teeth cut with utmost accuracy before the halves were placed together again, and once more ground with emery. Then a slight shift, and the process repeated until the greatest error in the teeth was less than a thousandth of an inch, said to be the most accurate wheel ever made. The facility with which the telescope could be handled by means of such a wheel has been for many years the pride of the astronomers in charge. Devices for saving time and strength were incorporated into all the Brashear inventions.

During these years more gold medals were put away in their plush boxes in the upper bureau drawer beside their predecessors: the Grand Prize of the St. Louis Exposition in 1904; the Elliot Cresson gold medal from the Franklin Institute in 1910; the Medal of Award for scientific instruments at the Panama-Pacific Exposition in 1915. And because of his honest judgment, he was appointed on two commissions for awarding medals, the Langley Gold Medal board of the Smithsonian Institution and the John Fritz Medal board of St. Louis.

Scientists from all over the United States and from Europe came to Allegheny not only to place orders, but to investigate the new things being made for others, for there were no secrets. Among the names in Phoebe's guest book, had she kept one, we should find Simon Newcomb from Annapolis, noted director of the United States Nautical Almanac; Sir William Thomson, astronomer royal of England, and Sir Robert Ball; Dr. Kayser of Bonn, and Dr. Wolf of Heidelberg, celebrated astronomers of Germany; and the great Deslandres of Paris. All were welcomed by Uncle John's simple hospitality in his home and, what is more rare, in his shop.

John's generosity with his inventions was phenomenal. He worked in the realm of machinery as an astronomer does in the realm of the sky, or a doctor in the realm of medicine, and gave his findings to the world, patenting nothing. There was no avarice or even ordinary self-protection in his make-up. He created a new order of business, in which every improvement he made was given to others so that science itself could ad-

vance. If other astronomical shops were afterward able to duplicate his efforts it is because he showed them how.

Nor is this a bad way of doing business. To ship lenses across
the water is one thing, to ship heavy pieces of delicate machinery is another. That is why it evolved that after he had sent
star spectroscopes to Europe, whenever he made one of his
rare trips, he was called upon to explain how they were to be
mounted. He made it a rule to send full written instructions,
pictures of his models, and plans drawn to scale, resulting in
a kind of correspondence school in astronomy. Without his
help, few would have known how to use what he was capable
of making. His system resulted in further orders, although this
was not his motive.

John Brashear, however, never had the heart-break of working for a firm that would usurp all the profits of his inventions,
as often is the case today. If he wanted to give them away he
was as much at liberty to do so as if he wanted to make money
on them. The amazing thing is that, even after thirty years of
scientific achievement, he still clung to his original theses, as
stated by Thaw, to "push outward the boundaries of human
knowledge." There was never a moment in all his busy life that
he would not drop what he was doing to show an impatient
boy how to make a telescope out of homemade materials. He
had set out to give eyes to the world, so that they might see
the wonders of Heaven, and he ended, not wide of the mark,
as most people do, but squarely on it. Few people in his generation, or any other, can be so estimated. What John Brashear
did in science may have been superseded since by newer methods with later inventions; he remains the pioneer. But what he
did to popularize astronomy can never be equaled. He brought
the knowledge of the skies down to the people who walked
the earth with him.

Nor did he stop with giving eyes to those who could see,
but was a member of the board for the School for the Blind,
and one of his favorite duties was to spend hours with little

children whose only contact with astronomy was through the stories he told about sun, moon, and stars. To them he was the whole hierarchy of the heavens.

He was as simple as the blind children he taught, much less worldly than the newsboys he addressed at their Christmas dinner for twenty-five years. He never wearied of helping people with cheer, with monetary aid, or with his good right arm. If any woman left a street car, staggering with a heavy suitcase, he jumped from his seat and carried it for her down the aisle and bowed her off the back platform. Sometimes he carried a stranger's load to the curb and waved her politely on her way, while the conductor held the car, too astonished to ring the bell and move on.

His faith in others was as absolute. One day when he had just come from the School for the Blind, and was carrying his valise before taking a train, he found he would have time to eat dinner in the neighborhood with his secretary, who was with him, but she demurred at his walking the ten blocks with his heavy bag. Before she could object further, he had rushed up the steps of a house they were passing, and left his luggage in a stranger's vestibule. Heaven defends its own. The bag was still there when they returned an hour later.

By 1912 John Brashear had raised almost $300,000 for the new observatory, and the trustees decided to dedicate it without waiting for the completion of the Thaw Telescope, which had been delayed for years, while glass was being made in Europe for John's thirty-inch refractor. The Keeler Memorial Telescope, with its thirty-inch mirror, silvered by John's special process, was already installed, as well as the old thirteen-inch refractor from the denuded building on Observatory Hill. This telescope of Langley's, which John had once thought so fine, with the completion of his own superior ones was used for the public lectures he inaugurated.

Uncle John had special aptitude for securing gifts for this city-wide project. The large sums necessary to guarantee the building had been subscribed earlier, and when crowds were trying to gain admission to see Halley's Comet in 1910, John not only gave lectures himself, but persuaded Henry Frick to establish a special fund of $15,000 so the work could be continued. And to be certain that the public could be seated before a lantern screen, John induced Robert Hall, the real estate promoter who had commissioned his portrait for "Tech," to install furnishings for the lecture room. Uncle John never ceased talking about this department, for it was the nucleus of his whole endeavor.

The structural steel for the observatory, the electrical equipment, and the instruments needed were all donated by friends. Not friends of one another, for half of them would not have given to any project of the other half, but they all gave to John Brashear. Their names compose a roll of honor typical of American manufacturers thirty years ago.

Professor F. L. O. Wadsworth, who had followed James Keeler as head of the observatory after the interregnum of John Brashear, was succeeded in 1905 by Dr. Frank Schlesinger, who was Director of the Allegheny Observatory until he was called to Yale in 1920. He was in charge during all the moving and planning of the new observatory, and much credit goes to him for its success. He was followed by Dr. Heber D. Curtis, who held the post for ten years, when he was succeeded by Dr. Frank C. Jordan, the present director, who assumed office in 1930, after serving on the staff since 1908. Under him the prestige begun by Langley, and the opportunities furnished by the new Brashear instruments have steadily increased.

At last came the long-awaited day of dedication, August 28, 1912, to Uncle John the culmination of the work of twenty years. His heart beat fast as he saw the flags on the lower gallery of the dome that was to house the great Thaw Telescope, and watched his friends gathering near him on its circular floor.

Astronomers from all over the country attended, and speeches were made by Professor Edward C. Pickering of Harvard, and Professor Frank Schlesinger, director of the new observatory. A memorial tablet to her father, William Thaw, and her brother, William Thaw, Jr., was unveiled by Mrs. William Reed Thompson. It fell to John to make the first address of the momentous day, when he presented the observatory, in the name of the trustees, to the University of Pittsburgh, by whom it was accepted in an answering address from Chancellor McCormick.

There was a catch in John's voice as he gave his own tribute to William Thaw, who had endowed the work of the old observatory so long ago, and to his other friends, now dead and gone, Samuel Langley and James Keeler. They had come "over a rough road to the stars," and he could not realize, in the midst of such crowds and confusion, that his dream was true: to have a "temple in the sky, where all the people who loved the stars could enjoy them." He did not speak of his own great telescopes, but of the lecture room for the public; praised the architect of the observatory, T. E. Bilquist, and that other young architect, Edward B. Lee, who had designed the crypt for him in the base of the Keeler telescope where the astronomer's ashes lay, and where Uncle John, two years before, had placed Phoebe's.

It was hard to finish, but he struggled on, thanking the men who had worked with him, and saying to the Chancellor in his modest way that he hoped the new observatory would continue to bring them honor, and ending by asking them to foster it in pushing forward the frontier of human knowledge.

The final congratulations were over, the last of the celebrated guests were gone. John walked back home from Riverview Park, wanting to be alone.

Crossing the former campus of what had since become an orphanage, he continued on up the little rise to the place where the old observatory stood, forsaken, its blind eyes searching the skies that it would never see again. The astronomers as well as

the professors were gone. The low red brick building seemed
to have shrunk under its withering ivy.

Sometimes he loved to sit on the worn stone step in the twilight, remembering how he had first found Thaw there, talking with Samuel Langley, one evening thirty years ago. Phoebe
used to like to sit there with him too, he remembered. And
they would watch the stars appearing one by one, far above
the starry lights of the city, which were increasing; while it
only seemed as if they were increasing in the sky, because
they were able to see more, year by year, through their telescope.

And he knew that if Phoebe were with him tonight, she
would lovingly point out the place of two asteroids that no
one had thought of mentioning that afternoon, small planets
that had written the name of their two cities between Mars
and Jupiter, far above the name of their observatory.

Almost ten years before, in 1903, Dr. Max Wolf of Heidelberg had won renown in Europe by discovering more of these
hitherto invisible planets with one of the Brashear double astral
cameras than anyone had known existed—about two hundred.
The astronomer wanted to honor the lens-maker by giving one
of these new planetoids his name, but Uncle John had no such
lofty aspiration, and "Phoebe" had been chosen several years
before. Dr. William H. Pickering had discovered the ninth
satellite of Saturn in 1899, through astral photography, and
designated the illusive lunar body which dismayed science by
revolving in a retrograde direction from the other eight Saturn
satellites, as Phoebe, for the Greek moon goddess.

So instead of calling any of his asteroids for Uncle John or
his wife, as Dr. Wolf had hoped until his good intention was
discouraged, the scientist accepted John's preference, and sub-
stituted the names of Uncle John's two cities to represent him
in the sky, Alleghenia, and Pittsburghia. Millions of miles away
from his own, or any other observatory on earth, they remain
an eternal memorial to the man whose genius devised a way
for other men to find them.

XXII

HENCHMAN TO THE SKIES

UNCLE JOHN was sweeping up the floor of the workroom in his shop when a reporter came to interview him about his appointment as "the most distinguished citizen of Pennsylvania."

As usual he wore no coat while working, and his spare frame was enveloped in a huge carpenter's apron tied over his vest and clean white shirt. The apron was immaculate too, and he intended the shop to be so, for not a speck of foreign matter could be tolerated near his lenses. He dipped the bristles of his broom in water and gently swept up invisible particles of glass dust. On his head was the puddler's black canvas cap that he had never given up, the sort worn by mill workers to keep the soot out of their hair. John did not wait for any chore boy to sweep up the floor for him, on the contrary he often cleaned up after them. At present he was engaged on a great seventy-two inch reflector of the Dominion Observatory in British Columbia, and was spending fifteen hours a day on its preliminary construction. He had contracted for it the year after he had dedicated the observatory, when he was seventy-three years of age.

In 1915 Governor Brumbaugh of Pennsylvania was asked to name a representative from his state to attend the Panama Pacific Exposition in San Francisco, and he chose Dr. John A. Brashear. In discussing possible candidates the committee had said that beside being their greatest scientist Uncle John had done more for education than any other three men in the state. When one thinks of the other names there were to choose from one would imagine that the decision must have been as difficult as awarding one of the present-day Rhodes Scholarships to a single student from the Keystone State, with its great universities both east and west. But the election was unanimous. John Brashear was born under skies that brooded over his destiny, although claiming him as henchman.

It was a summer morning when the reporter sent on by an eastern paper hurried over to Perrysville Avenue and sought the great man out in his shop. Uncle John leaned on his broom and gazed benignly at the representative of the press.

"There is some mistake," he said. "The names got mixed up in the hat. No, I have nothing to add—you know more about it, doubtless, than I do. You tell me."

He had a way of interviewing the reporters himself. He treated them much as children who had a job to perform to earn their living, in which it was his duty to help them, but when they finished they often found it was they who had told him the stories of their lives. John changed the subject.

"Young man," he said, waving his broom toward a sky map on the wall, "I don't want to tire you—but this is a picture of the moon. There are no reporters there, and no astronomers. If you went there for a story you would have to take an oxygen tank along. Besides you would have to encase yourself in a boiler plate about ten miles thick; the temperature is 250 degrees below zero." Then he handed the "young man" a bag of peppermints out of his desk drawer and told him not to smoke too much, and sent him back to his paper. The reporter had his story.

On September 22, 1915, "Brashear Day" was celebrated at the Panama Pacific Exposition, and Uncle John was awarded a bronze medal for his achievements in manufacturing and science. The presentation address was made by Colonel A. G. Hetherington of the Pennsylvania Commission, in the Court of Abundance, where thousands of tourists gathered to see the famous scientist from the place they called "down east."

John Brashear was already known in California through the lenses he had made for their great observatories, and had visited Los Angeles and San Francisco two years before with Ambrose Swasey, who made the mountings for the telescopes. Together, these two old friends had made their first trip in an airplane, flying over Mt. Holly in company with Professor E. C. Larkin of the Mt. Lowe Observatory, with whom they were searching for a new observatory site. Five public dinners had been tendered Uncle John in one week, and the newspapers ran his picture on the front page in goggles and aviator's helmet, referring to his work on aviation with Langley. California as well as Pennsylvania was pleased with his appointment as first citizen of the Keystone State.

This was a gala year for John Brashear, the year that he was three score years and fifteen, five years already stolen from the Reaper to add to the years of man, and five that had been the busiest in his life.

In November the Phoebe Brashear Club, composed of teachers who had received summer fellowships, decided to hold a great birthday party for Uncle John, and enlisted the help of the University of Pittsburgh and the Carnegie Technical Schools for a joint celebration. Their group had grown during its few years, but as yet no one knew where the funds for extension work were coming from, except that they were dispensed by Brashear. Frick's original endowment had soon been doubled, and subsequently amounted to four million dollars.

A banquet was held in the largest room available in the city, in Soldier's Memorial Hall, which proved not spacious enough to hold the seven hundred people who crowded in to attend. There were messages from the governor of the state, from President Wilson, and from all the associations of which Uncle John was a member, including the School for the Blind. Three hundred letters and telegrams arrived during the day and kept on arriving at night; from Graham Bell, from Edison, from scientists and educators all over the country. The toastmaster tried to read them aloud but could not keep abreast of the interruptions.

A fund of $50,000 was presented, as an acknowledgment of the unpaid lectures Uncle John had given for decades in the schools and at the observatory. It was arranged that he should draw the interest from this fund for personal use during his lifetime, and that afterward it would become an endowment to

administer the same sort of work in his memory. Donations
toward this gift were received from many outside the city, for
he had lectured in all the colleges and towns from the Mississippi to the Atlantic seaboard.

The speaker's table included the presidents of every university and school in Pittsburgh, including Duff's Mercantile
College, the only one John Brashear had ever attended as a
student, and that for a few months only, before the Civil War.
One of the guests was Daniel Delavey of Brownsville, an old
drummer who came with greetings from the band that John
had played in when a boy.

Charles Schwab, who sat most of the time with his arm
around Uncle John, afterward told reporters, "The gathering
was a spontaneous outburst of love and affection for the greatest man I ever knew." Henry Phipps summed up his address
with, "John and Phoebe, while showing us other worlds,
showed us how to adorn this one."

After the dinner he was led to the platform and asked to
stand before the audience while a procession of seventy-five
teachers of the Phoebe Brashear Club filed past him, each one
presenting a single American Beauty rose. His arms were full
of them as he stumbled back to his chair at the cheering banquet table. "Why should I be proud?" he asked. "I have done a
little, and that little you have helped me do."

A silver loving cup had been put before his place in his absence on the stage, but he was too bewildered to notice it until
it was called to his attention. "I don't know what else they are
going to do with me," he said. "Maybe they are breaking me
in for something else."

A significant remark. His mind must have rushed back over
all the difficult things he had undertaken for his beloved city,
as he tried to comprehend what was happening tonight. He
could hardly believe that anything purely laudatory could be
offered him.

A masque, arranged by Thomas Wood Stevens, Director of

the Carnegie Drama School, was given by the drama students,
followed by a pageant depicting the early life of Uncle John.
One verse of Stevens' beautiful prologue reads:

> Days of high dreams and lowly toil may bring
> To this our part, some image of our love,
> And we the masquers bid you tread with us
> Some measure at the closing of the play,
> And see beyond our circling steps the range
> Of a calm spirit, walking amidst stars.

The following well-known sonnet by George M. P. Baird
was written for the birthday celebration and afterward re-
printed:

Son of the toiling many, brother of all mankind,
Pilgrim of starry trails, far traced to the last sun's bound,
Voyager of sapphire seas, sounder of depths profound,
Meeting the pregnant void, reck'ning the bonds that bind
Planet and Asteroid, with golden measures of mind:
Heart of a little child, thought of a mage renowned,
Simple of life and aim, humble in victory, crowned
By loves that his heart made warm and truth that his soul
 divined:
Though in these later years, the tears and the toils be done,
Though through the long day's heat he hath journeyed high
 and far,
Though the doors of ten thousand hearts are open every one
And the hearth-fires signal, "Come to the board where thy
 lovers are,"
Still strives the pilgrim on in the glow of the setting sun,
Joyfully to the crest where brightens the evening star.

The line before the last is particularly meaningful in the
light of Uncle John's last years. When it was written it seemed
as if life's twilight must soon close in, but following this anniversary there was no diminution of labor during the final five
years of afterglow that endured to the end.

That same winter he was appointed by Secretary Lansing
as delegate to the second conference of the Pan American Scientific Congress that met in Washington from December 27 to

January 8. The World War had been in progress two years, although the United States had not as yet been drawn into it, and scientists from South and Central America and Canada were taking this opportunity to come to some agreement in trade policy. Following the congress, and with his usual zeal for imparting what he had learned to others, Brashear gave six lectures in his own city to civic, commercial, and educational groups, on the international situation.

Apparently still unfatigued by attending and reporting conventions, he immediately set out again in January on a long-scheduled lecture tour, giving a ten-day course in astronomy at Boston, followed by single night addresses at Lynn, Schenectady, and Rochester. This, in the rigors of a New England and New York State winter, after celebrating his seventy-fifth anniversary.

He had been made president of the American Society of Mechanical Engineers the winter previously, and his first important engagement after his birthday party had been to make his outgoing speech before them at their annual meeting in New York on December 15, 1915. The custom is for the president of this important society to speak at the end of his term of office, and Uncle John's tenure had been extremely popular. When he had been installed the year before, an editorial in *Steel and Iron* referred to him as "the humanist of all scientists in America."

What was meant by this is clear from his presidential address to the society on "Science in Relation to Engineering," which was widely quoted. He gave a résumé of the remarkable uses made of simple mechanical inventions; spoke of the first dynamo of Faraday, and what evolved from it; told of the first faint telephone message he heard over the wire of Graham Bell, and the last long-distance call he listened to across the continent from the Panama Pacific Exposition; and how in the little shop on Holt Street he built his first spectroscope to determine when the last ounce of carbon had disappeared from the Bessemer converter, whereas now in his shop they had made such an improved spectroscopic lens that "We would be able, as it were, to plunge it into a storm on the sun, and photograph the burning hydrogen of any other planet in that maelstrom of fire, the temperature of which this earth knows no correlative."

This is the scientific Brashear speaking. The humanist is shown in his conclusion to the same speech: "The illimitable field of truth opens up before us; aye, I love to liken it to the 'widow's cruse.' Take from it as much as you will, it will never be emptied of its priceless treasure."

Another example of this same mixture of science and its application was before the students at Schenectady: "Have a hobby; studying the stars is mine. If you would ride from the earth to Alpha Centauri on a train, going at the rate of a mile a minute, it would take forty-eight years. *We have an exaggerated sense of our own importance.*"

But although Uncle John's hobby was astronomy, he did not insist that every engineering student follow the same. One of his most endearing characteristics was that whatever anyone wanted to do, that was what he was encouraged to accomplish. John never tried to twist and bend the young to preconceived ideas of what was best for them. Before there were any placement tests for freshmen, or mentors appointed to guide their courses in the universities, he would take it upon himself to advise the bewildered incoming students, but only after ascertaining what each actually was competent to do. Many a boy he lifted out of uncongenial engineering courses and set happily to work in the school of art, or architecture. That was why, whenever he spoke on the "Tech" campus, the hall could not contain the students.

His scientific articles were appearing in many trade journals at this time, a whole series on optical glass in *Popular Astronomy*, and a biographical story on Thomas A. Melville, who originated spectrum analysis in 1752, in the *Journal of the Royal Astronomical Society of Canada*. The research for this

British publication was done by correspondence with the head librarian at Edinburgh, through introduction by Carnegie.

It was well known that besides being an able speaker Uncle John had a facile pen. In the few summers remaining to him at Muskoka he began writing his memoirs, and used to compare notes with his eighty-four-year-old friend D. F. Henry, on how he was getting along with his.

One of the stories told by others is how Brashear made trouble for himself with the Post Office and Police Departments. On a fine spring day, with the enthusiasm of youth, this white-haired man emerged from his home on Perrysville Avenue with a bucket of aluminum paint, on the way to his shop. But catching sight of two dingy urns on his front lawn, he decided to paint them, before time for their annual planting of petunias. This accomplished, and the result being so refreshing, he stepped over to his neighbor's lawn and painted their urns. There was still something missing in the verdant landscape and there was yet more paint. So he ran down the slope and painted the mailbox and fire plug on the corner. It was not long before impressive sheets of printed rules were franked through to him from Washington, and he looked from behind his Nottingham lace curtains, abashed, to see a stern policeman repainting his artistic efforts with customary coats of dull green. His only remark was, "Anyway, I got them done." This is the favorite story of the Civic Club.

What turned Dr. John A. Brashear, the scientist, into "Uncle John," the humanist, was his desire to use whatever leisure he had by giving back to the world what the world had given him. Everyone understood this propensity of Uncle John's, and some imposed upon it, but if they did he never knew it. Dr. Henry S. Pritchett, president of the Carnegie Foundation for the Advancement of Teaching, in New York, said in an address about Brashear in the twenties that these dual influences showed all through his life, and rose from the same thing, a keen imagination. "His service to education was the gift of his own personality, alive with the twin passions for science and humanity . . . a missionary of kindliness to those working in formal education."

But John Brashear's own precepts speak for themselves, couched in past-century phraseology that breathes the biblical spirit of the ancient poets, whose manner of speaking and thinking was his own.

Today we are learning single notes. Tomorrow we shall blend them into choirs. The hour will come when all humanity shall know the law of harmony.

Nothing is lost, no dewdrop perishes, but sinking into the flower makes it all the sweeter.

The science best worth while in this world is that of extracting sunlight from behind the clouds and scattering it over the shadowed pathway of our fellow travelers.

It is not book learning young men need, but a stiffening of the vertebrae which will cause them to be loyal to a trust,—to act promptly—concentrate their energies—"Carry the message to Garcia."

Referring to the crowds attending the public lectures at the observatory, the fulfillment of his greatest hope: "Do you think that kind of people will get into riots, or fights, or anything of the sort? There is nothing I know of that contributes more to the ennobling of the spiritual in man than to see something of God's beautiful work."

His favorite quotation was from Carlyle's *Sartor Resartus:* "That there should one man die ignorant who had capacity for knowledge, this I call tragedy."

In a letter: "I may not be able or permitted to see the [next] great eclipse, but I hope you will, for to my mind it is the most sublime spectacle that can be seen in this round old world of ours. Somehow one feels such a sense of littleness, and of the majesty and magnificence of the Creator's work, in witnessing the blotting out of the sunlight, the bursting out of magnificent streamers." Then he said he would give up his efforts to describe it, and quoted Robert Service:

It was not good for the eyes of man,
It was a sight for the eyes of God.

The letters of John Brashear contained sentences never forgotten by those who received them. Many were written to young people who still cherish them, and to the daughters of his friends on their wedding day. Such letters were put away with the bride's veil and laces, and now, when daughters are to be married, are brought out again and read aloud to the next generation. Even the inscriptions Uncle John wrote on photographs were not casual, but personal and poetic.

When a bigoted woman wrote him copiously of her belief in hell and damnation he replied that he had not time to read the twenty-three pages of tirade that could better have been expressed in one, or not at all. "My religion you will find embodied in one verse of the Bible, Micah, 6th Chapter, 8:

He hath shewed thee, O man, what is good; and what doth the Lord require of thee, but to do justly, and to love mercy, and to walk humbly with thy God?

XXIII

"SWIFTER THAN A WEAVER'S SHUTTLE"

THE last important journey of John Brashear's long life was to China and Japan in the winter of 1916–17.

Ambrose Swasey, of the manufacturing company of Warner and Swasey in Cleveland, had agreed to attend the opening of a science building he had endowed for the University of Nanking, and asked John to accompany him. In fact, he refused to go himself unless his friend agreed. They had known each other since their work for the Lick Observatory had brought them together in the eighties, and the combination of their abilities, one working on the optical parts and the other on the machinery for the telescopes, had insured success to both. On the first of December they sailed.

Uncle John had sent many lenses to the Orient, and on his arrival received the same enthusiastic reception previously accorded him in Europe. After three trips to England, France, and Germany, it is astonishing that he was able to take this final journey in the opposite direction, at the age of seventy-six, and enjoy the acclaim that by this time had made the circuit of the globe; a reward for living long enough to participate in fame, often reserved until after a man is gone. In Uncle John's case, his advance reputation in the Orient was not entirely because he was a famous lens maker, but because he was known as one of the foremost educators of his period, and as having a point of view on the humanities important to those outside his own country. He was not only received in all the large cities as a scientist and lecturer, but because of his personality he was entertained by diplomats who recognized in his good will a liaison with the United States, and embraced the opportunity to advance international cordiality during the time of the World War.

Uncle John was not permitted to leave Pittsburgh, however,

without a suitable farewell. Invited to attend what he thought was to be a small gathering of teachers at their clubrooms in the Frick Building, he found the foyer crowded with people who had come to wish him Godspeed. Uncle John stood on one of the balconies that surround the great rotunda, waving to his friends below. What he said may have been forgotten, but no one in the vast throng ever forgot him.

The circumstance for this impromptu farewell was a new project in his honor which had been set in motion a few weeks previously by Mrs. John N. Phillips, at that time president of the Carrick Women's Club, and one of the old residents of the South Side where Uncle John had spent twenty years working in the mills.

This civic-minded woman had been east during the summer, and visited many colonial houses under New England elms, commemorating the birthplaces of illustrious men of letters. On arriving home, in the City of Forges, living above the mills whose smoke obscured the sun by day, and where the flames at night made the sky ablaze above the furnaces, she realized that the men of fame whom such a city as Pittsburgh might produce would not be like the gentle Transcendentalists of Boston, but men of science. And yet there was one celebrated millworker in the city who had not only become a scientist, but a philosopher and educator—John Brashear.

It was the year after Uncle John had been chosen the most distinguished citizen of Pennsylvania, followed by his prodigious birthday party. Immediately she determined to do him greater honor, and to make a characteristic shrine of his old home on the South Side where he and Phoebe had lived so happily when they were young, and where they had built their first telescope.

The interest of other women's clubs in the city was enlisted, and within a month they had secured the premises on the hill and felt assured in announcing their gift to the city as a surprise for Uncle John's seventy-sixth birthday. They held their public celebration on the twenty-second of November, before

John left with Ambrose Swasey for the Orient; and, whereas hundreds had attended his banquet of the year previous, thousands gathered for the farewell party in the center of downtown Pittsburgh.

Two days later, on the twenty-fourth, after Uncle John was safely out of the city, the occasion of his seventy-sixth birthday was taken for raising the money needed to complete the projected shrine. John had been appreciative of the plan, but objected to further solicitation, as he was still embarrassed by the fifty thousand dollars raised the year before. So, respecting his wishes, a committee of women stationed themselves throughout the city, to receive only what was voluntarily offered. Looseleaf notebooks carefully recorded the donors of small sums, and school teachers asked the children to bring in their pennies. It was some time before all the hundreds of pounds of cash could be counted, when it was found the single day's work amounted to over four thousand dollars, almost as much as was required.

On January 27, while Uncle John was in China, a permanent organization was formed, called the Brashear Memorial Association, whose avowed purpose was to carry on the work and influence of John and Phoebe Brashear. The original plan was altered to suit the needs of the day and place, and resulted in the use of the premises on Holt Street for social settlement purposes.

Behind John Brashear's old home and shop stood a larger dwelling that was reconstructed into usefulness, and a smaller building was torn down to make room for a playground. The World War was raging, and the women in the congested neighborhood needed a meeting place for their Red Cross society, and a yard where their numerous progeny could play while they were knitting socks for their cousins across the sea. The district was called Polish Hill, and was crowded with families of immigrant workers of Slavic descent, a complete change from the Scotch-Irish of Uncle John's early days when he was the first to move there in the eighties. It was his own wish

that no single inch of the property now be wasted on senti-
mentality.

When they were renovating the premises his name and
Phoebe's were found scratched on a window-pane.

"Did you do it with a diamond ring?" someone asked him.

"There were no diamond rings," he replied. "Phoebe never
had a diamond ring—she had a glass cutter."

Except for the tablet on the door, there is no reminder that
the House of Inspiration was first thought of as an ornamental
shrine. Yet the growth of the important Brashear Settlements,
which now number four, has resulted in an even greater tribute than the original plan. Through the work carried on in his
name, in the "Melting Pot of America," the people of the
neighborhood know Uncle John as well as if he still moved
among them as he did two generations ago, carrying his dinner
pail in and out of the roaring mills, back and forth to his home,
which is like their homes. His spirit has not died, it is part of
the cosmos in which he lived on a higher plane than most of
his contemporaries—or ours.

Pittsburgh during the World War had only one ambition, to
make more armaments than were turned out by the great
Krupp works in Germany. Other exports almost ceased, and
looking down toward the mill yards on the river front, all that
could be seen were piles of great shells waiting to be hauled
off in the long lines of freight cars ceaselessly plying between
the city and the seaboard. As in the Civil War, when John
worked in the mills, prosperity briefly affected the highly paid
workers, who were buying beefsteaks and strawberries while
their brothers in Mittel-Europa were starving in the armies of
their Emperor or Tsar.

It was not until the United States entered the war in the
spring of 1917 that so many of the younger workers were
called out in the draft that their places had to be filled with
thousands of colored people from the Deep South. This new
type of imported labor suffered in the rigors of the climate,

and in the makeshift quarters where they were permitted to live, as no immigrants had ever suffered in the box-cars offered them during the Civil War, and they had their revenge by remaining a major problem, "when the boys came home."

There was a buzz and confusion in the air that unsettled all the social conditions in the city. But the hard facts of the mills were, as usual, only rumors by the time they crossed the river where chauffeured cars honked continuously through the narrow streets of the Golden Triangle, demanding right of way from army trucks and platoons of marching soldiers that suddenly appeared from nowhere.

Uncle John returned from the Orient in plenty of time to be harassed by what was taking place. His shop, too, was turned over to war orders, and instead of making astronomical lenses for his beloved stars he was called on to provide range-finders, panoramic sights, and gun-sights for the Navy. He perfected a photo-chronograph, which measures the speed of a projectile after it leaves the gun. During 1918, Professor Peters of the United States Naval Observatory arrived to plead with the Brashear shop to make sextant mirrors, which at that time could be procured from no other place in the world, and although rushed with other government orders John agreed to supply four or five hundred. During this period Jim McDowell and Fred Hageman were doing important work in the shop, and many extra helpers were engaged, although Brashear himself, at the age of seventy-eight, was working seven hours a day, and speaks of coming home so hot and perspiring with exertion that he had to bathe and change his underwear before sitting down to dinner.

Yet his heart was more troubled than his body was tired. These achievements brought no content. He had long known many scientists in Germany, and at first had been as concerned for them as for any other belligerents, pitying them as much as his English friends who wrote of losing their sons. But as time went on, and the newspapers spread their stories of atrocities, and his Belgian mail told of the devastation of the "Huns," while the French dwelt on the horrors of being taken prisoner, he suffered the same disillusion with the *Vaterland* as did his Teutonic neighbors; a humiliation that was one of the hardest things these old settlers had to bear. Uncle John spoke German, and received letters in that language that sometimes escaped the censor. One of them said, "If everyone thought as you do, there would not be this dreadful condition which almost makes me lose my faith in humanity." This was from Heidelberg, the center of the ancient university culture of the Reformation.

John grieved that many friends who were teachers of German in the schools lost their positions; that small tradespeople in Allegheny, butchers in the old market, and tinkerers and shoemakers, lost their business and livelihoods. During the war he helped these people with his modest means, and afterward aided the boys who returned home broken in body and spirit and could find no work. He gave talks to young soldiers in the great training camp that sprang up on the Carnegie campus; told the recruits all about making the world "safe for democracy," and how they were fighting a "war to end war," which he, with the rest of the world, firmly believed. Other leaders were making "four minute" speeches and sales talks for Liberty Bonds, which John bought, but most of his work was with the students who were drafted.

Many temporary war buildings were erected on the grounds of the Institute of Technology, and one of them, required in a hurry for the housing of airplanes which the government was sending for instruction purposes, was finished in twenty-three days, although constructed of iron and steel, with glass walls, and substantial enough to remain in use today. It was dedicated with a military band of a hundred pieces, while a thousand soldiers stood at attention and airplanes flew overhead. John Brashear was the speaker for this great occasion, as he was for other events at "Tech," and named the building Langley Laboratory for his friend who had been a pioneer in aeronautics. This military spectacle, in which he played a prominent part, was the single lift of the whole dreary period.

When Uncle John returned from a brief holiday in Muskoka, he had been depressed by the wounded he saw in the railroad junction at Toronto. The Canadians had been his summer neighbors for years, and his wife had died at Isle Urania. Whatever happened to Canada happened to him too, and hurt him. He knew personally many of the boys who had died in the Princess Pat Regiment, and raised a fund for Canadian volunteers who lived in the States and returned to join the British forces under Brigadier General White. John also knew many of the soldiers who had gone to the Mexican border with General Pershing, lads who had enlisted for adventure with the old National Guard. Later they had followed Pershing to France, and Uncle John attended their funerals in Pittsburgh when they were shipped back, finally, in unopened boxes, after the battle of Château-Thierry.

John Brashear had only one more task to complete before he folded his hands. For five years he had been working on the great mirror for the Dominion Observatory in Canada, and in June of 1918 he attended its dedication.

On the eighth of the month Uncle John had arrived in California to see the eclipse of the sun with a party from the Lick Observatory who set up their astronomical apparatus at Goldendale. Up to the last minute clouds obscured the sky, but he said "as if brushed aside by a good angel's wing," at the last moment the heavens were clear and he was satisfied. He was seventy-eight years old. The photographs taken with his telescopic lenses were entirely successful, and this, his third eclipse expedition, was his final one. He had seen his first eclipse almost thirty years before at Winnemucca, Nevada, in 1889. And he had sponsored an expedition from Allegheny Observatory to see the second at Union Springs, Alabama. It was in writing of the eclipse of 1918 that he stated his premonition that he would not be permitted to see another one.

Leaving California with scientists from the Lick and the Dominion Observatories, and accompanied by that faithful traveling companion, Ambrose Swasey of Cleveland, John immediately went north to Victoria, British Columbia. The seventy-two-inch reflector that he had made for this telescope had been a discouraging business from the first. When it was almost perfected, on two different occasions, due to an unforeseen scarcity of gas for his engines during war times, the "figure" was lost and work had to be commenced all over. But in final testing none of its huge surface differed by more than one-eighth of a light wave, or one sixteen-thousandth millimeter. It was the second largest telescope in the world, only exceeded by the one-hundred-inch at Mt. Wilson.

When the mirror was finally finished in the Allegheny shop, and had been sent off on its long journey to the north, a friend found Uncle John pacing the paths at Riverview Park at midnight. He could not sleep, he said, until he learned that the work he had spent so many years upon had safely arrived at its destination. The packing, alone, of this six-foot glass had been a precarious undertaking, and to haul it to a freight car and get it out again, without a scratch, was a problem its maker must leave to others, although it made him wring his hands. But John's back was still unbent and his eyes were on the stars. His friend went on and left him there, walking the dark roads that would lead him to defeat, or victory.

So many people claim that Uncle John had dinner with them every week during the war, or after Phoebe died, that allowing for pleasant exaggeration it would still seem that he must have been lonely in his home, notwithstanding that it was full of people. The two married sons of Effie McDowell had already died quite young, but their wives continued under the family rooftree, and one of them, the widow of Walter, had two children, a girl of ten and a boy of three, who were Uncle John's delight. But the face he wanted to see at the dinner table was Phoebe's. He had lived with her almost to their golden wedding, and hardly knew how to pass the remaining years without her. Wherever he went he spoke of her, carry-ing her image in his mind like a living presence.

Sometimes, and not only when he was old, Uncle John for-got where he was supposed to go. One night when he was expected at the table of a professor at the University of Pitts-burgh, who had asked an out-of-town scientist to meet him, he went instead to someone's house where he had been invited for the night following, sat for an hour wondering why dinner was not served, and then departed hungry when he discovered the family had eaten an informal supper and asked him to be sure and come "tomorrow." Even then he did not recall where he ought to be, but bought a sandwich at a drugstore, while a fine repast grew cold waiting for him at the home of the dis-appointed professor.

While in New York John often stayed at the mansion of Andrew Carnegie or Henry Frick or Schwab. He felt per-fectly at home on upper Fifth Avenue at Andrew's, for that famous little man was still Scotch enough to go around the house at night turning out the lights. Sometimes he would not announce himself, but preferred a modest hotel. Once at "Charlie" Schwab's, John had noticed that his suite had a bal-cony overlooking the sparkling lights of the Hudson from Riverside Drive, and had stolen back to it, tired and bored, to spend an hour communing with his friends the stars. But when he pushed the velvet draperies aside, he found that the long French windows had been locked to the floor, and although there was no mechanism Uncle John could not master, he hesitated at house-breaking in the palace of a friend. So he stood for a few disappointed moments with his face pressed to the pane, seeing "through a glass darkly" the lights on the bridges and moving ships, the distant glitter of passing cars, and the moon riding high in a sea of stars above the river.

After the armistice, when the world had time to resume its normal pleasantries, someone remembered Uncle John's birth-day again and arranged, in the fall of 1919, to send him a postal shower. To his complete undoing and the vast annoy-

ance of the postman who had not forgiven him yet for painting the mailbox, three thousand greetings arrived on November 24. At first John thought he would try to answer them, for
he kept up a correspondence all over the world, but by nightfall he gave up. However, they lasted him the whole winter,
for it took months to read them, and he was grateful for the
amusement while he was housebound.

One name he could not help but miss, that of his old friend
Andrew Carnegie, who had died the past summer in New
Hampshire, after hoping all through the years of the war to
return to Skibo. And shortly afterward, on the second of December, he attended the funeral of another good friend, Henry
Frick. This was one of the two occasions when he left the
house in the winter of 1919. The other was to say farewell at
the dinner given for Dr. Frank Schlesinger when he left the
Allegheny Observatory for Yale. It is not well for a man to
find himself the last of the autumn leaves. One looks around
for familiar faces, and comes to know the children of one's
friends even better than their fathers. Most of the men of the
old Conservatory Club were gone, and those who had spent
their summers at Cresson; even some of the group at Muskoka.
Four score years is too long for a man to keep his own beside
him.

Uncle John had never been very well since that triumphant
trip to the Orient two years before. He had gone on with his
contracts, working for the government during the war and
finishing the last great reflector for Canada, but the Flowery
Kingdom had taken its toll. He had arrived home with amoebic
dysentery, and although he tried to ignore all illness, he could
not help but know his days were numbered, and what their
number was.

He would live until spring, he said, turning the pages of his
Bible to the prophet, Job. "My days are swifter than a weaver's
shuttle, and are without hope." He repeated the phrase as if it
were a hymn. "When his candle shined upon my head, and
when by his light I walked through darkness." But if friends

came to see him, he did not quote the Scriptures. He cheer-fully showed them his birthday cards, souvenir of his last anniversary.

He was looking further back than that, one afternoon, when the sun was slanting through his open bedroom windows. "Do you remember the first inclines on the South Side?" he said to that nice young woman who had entered his room with a tray. At first he thought she was Phoebe, but then he remembered she was a McDowell. And as she smiled affectionately but did not answer, he said reproachfully. "Why, I suppose you don't even remember the mule cars that used to run over the Sixth Street Bridge!" He was going to add something about the canal, but it was too much effort. No one would know today where it was, nor care that his mother had fallen into it when a child, a hundred years ago . . . Now he was alone again, with the sounds he loved coming in on the wind from the river.

That was the call of a steamboat at the locks on the Ohio—that louder wail, the siren at some mill—that screech, the brakes of the street car going down the seven bends of Perrys-ville Avenue. The laughter on the sweet spring air came from the orphans playing on the old college campus. Was that an airplane he heard over Observatory Hill? And he thought of that other hill, where he had lived with Phoebe, above the Monongahela; and before that, the old hills of Brownsville, which did not look the same when he had returned there lately, as the river town where his grandfather used to keep an inn. What was the name of the man who had brought the telescope there, that he made from glass picked up in the Pitts-burgh fire? Nathaniel Smith? No, that was his grandfather, who had taken him to see the heavens through it.

And he remembered the star he saw, but could not recall its name either. It seemed as if it were an Indian name, like Alle-ghenia—but that came later. This one he searched for was gir-dled by three star-filled rings, and followed by many moons. The name eluded him, although he could see the ninth moon

plainer than anything else, for the rest of the sky had dark-
ened. And the star-like moon was not at the end of a telescope,
after all; there was no need for lenses any longer—it stood quite
near, as if waiting. "Phoebe," he said.

John Alfred Brashear died on April 8, 1920, and was laid in
state at Soldiers' Memorial Hall. A guard of honor, composed
of students from both his beloved universities, watched at his
flower-laden bier. All the flags of the city stood at half mast,
and on the day of his funeral, at eleven o'clock, the school bells
rang for five minutes, and church bells tolled from the South
Side to the North Side and throughout the Golden Triangle.
His ashes were laid in the crypt of the observatory with those
of his wife, under an inscription that he had placed there, ten
years before, for Phoebe.

> We have loved the stars too fondly
> To be fearful of the night.

Among the many accounts of his life that immediately appeared all over the country, was one in the *New York Evening
Sun* of May 14, 1920.

One of the noblest men of our times has risen from a wistful
contemplation of the firmament, through lenses of his own
making, to the freedom of the starry fellowship. He has gone
to see the source of light. . . . Philosophers, Mathematicians,
Physicists,—they all base their calculations and deductions in
some degree on the work of this mechanic of Pittsburgh. . . .
However intensely he labored with material substance, the real
meaning of this man's life is a spiritual meaning. . . . No one
can yet say what part the work of John Alfred Brashear may
play in the knowledge of the universe.

What was this part? Men saw in him a mirror of something
lost, which in his presence they regained, the dreams of their
boyhood, the working out of the precepts of their mothers,
and a faith in the stars which they came to see and know
through his eyes, as much as through the means he gave them
to approach infinity.

At a time when men ruthlessly built up a fortune, only to give it back in the end to the people, John Brashear failed to find any need for fortune. He himself was the people. And what he reaped was not what he planted to harvest, but star-dust sown on the wind.

The winds of time have blown for a hundred years since John Brashear was born. Countless times the earth he loved has circled round the sun he served. Yet the echo of his life re-sounds like a beloved footstep on the city streets, where they have ceased to wonder whether he was astronomer, scientist, or millwright, and have forgotten the tools he made the stars, but remember him forever as "Uncle John."

BIBLIOGRAPHICAL NOTE

Much of the new material used in this book was derived from articles published in the science magazines in John Brashear's lifetime; either by him on some timely astronomical subject, or by others who wrote of his work.

ARTICLES BY BRASHEAR

A. The most important of these scientific articles was John Brashear's own contribution to the *English Mechanic and World of Science*, June 1880, Vol. 32, containing directions for silvering a telescope mirror and divulging for the first time, the formula he invented, which has been in use ever since. Second in importance was an advertising pamphlet from his first shop, dated 1882, which was presented to the Technical Room of the Pittsburgh Carnegie Library by the late Charles M. Woodside of that city.

B. In the *Transactions of the American Society of Mechanical Engineers*, Vol. 30, 1908, is an article by Brashear on "Stone Ware and Porcelain Strength," and under the heading "Present Status of Military Aeronautics," his discussion of the failure of Samuel Langley's airplane. In Vol. 36 appears Brashear's contribution on "Factors in Hardening Steel."

C. News items in *Popular Astronomy* furnished material about contracts in the Brashear shop; orders for telescopes and spectroscopes as found in Vol. 3, 1895; sales to Germany are listed in Vol. 4, 1896; range-finders in Vol. 6, 1898, and in the same volume news about Keeler and the Allegheny Observatory. Also in *Popular Astronomy*, Vol. 1, 1893, appeared "Glass for Optical Instruments" by John Brashear, and later were articles he wrote about his friends: Vol. 7, 1899, Ambrose Swasey; Vol. 14, 1906, Samuel P. Langley. Vol. 24, 1916, contains an argument Brashear carried on with a critic of the new observatory lecture system; Vol. 34 discloses the later history of the Brashear shop after John Brashear's death.

ARTICLES ABOUT BRASHEAR

A. During John Brashear's lifetime two long magazine articles
were published about him, one a full account of his achievements by Edwin Tenny Brewster, which appeared in
McClure's Magazine, March 1911. After Brashear had been
designated first citizen of Pennsylvania, a discussion of his
work in the humanities was written by Merle Crowell,
which appeared in the *American Magazine* of July 1916.

B. After John Brashear's death two brief biographies were
published: one by Frank Schlesinger, former director of
Allegheny Observatory and then located at Yale, who
wrote of Brashear the scientist, in *Popular Science*, Vol. 28,
1920: and the other, a reprint in the *Transactions of the
American Society of Mechanical Engineers*, Vol. 42, November 1920, of an address made by Henry S. Pritchett,
President of the Carnegie Foundation for the advancement
of Teaching, entitled "John Alfred Brashear, Humanitarian
and Man of Science." The *New York Sun* of May 19, 1920,
also contained a long article on Brashear's life and influence.

NEWSPAPERS AND LECTURES

A. Although John Brashear won recognition as early as the
seventies for his popular articles on astronomy that appeared in various Pittsburgh newspapers, the files of these
papers were lost in the Pittsburgh flood of 1936, when
many records stored in downtown basements were destroyed. Their value is proved, however, by constant references to them in all articles about Brashear.

B. None of the lectures that John Brashear gave in the public
schools of the city, and in colleges throughout the country,
have been preserved, as he spoke extemporaneously. Their
contents, however, are still quoted by men who heard him
speak when they were students. A speech that has been
preserved, is his outgoing presidential address before the
American Society of Mechanical Engineers, found in their
Transactions, Vol. 38, December 1915.

C. More recent files of Pittsburgh newspapers preserved in
libraries give accounts of such events in John Brashear's life
as his birthday celebration in 1915, his farewell reception of

1916, and references to the founding of the Brashear Association, the Phoebe Brashear Club, and the Frick Educational Commission. (See *Pittsburgh Post, Press, Sun, Gazette Times,* and *Index.*) The *London Times* of September 1911 gives a full description of the five-hundredth anniversary of St. Andrews University in Scotland; and the *Los Angeles Tribune* of December 1911 contains an account, with photograph, of Brashear's first trip in an airplane.

BOOKS

A. John Brashear's own autobiography supplied material for background, as did certain biographies of other men in his period whose lives were interwoven with his: the *Life of Andrew Carnegie* by Burton Hendrick; *Henry Clay Frick, the Man* by George Harvey; the *Life of Samuel P. Langley* by C. G. Abbot, and a shorter one of Langley by Mary Parkman.

B. Material about the city of Pittsburgh was culled from the works of such authorities as Sarah M. Killikelly, James Park, Haniel Long, Leland Baldwin, Clarence E. Macartney, Arthur W. Tarbell, and Agnes L. Sterrett. Early Pennsylvania history was checked from standard sources. Astronomical material was better understood through the study of books quoted by Brashear himself: Dr. Dick's works; *Construction of a Silvered Telescope* by Henry Draper; *The New Astronomy* by Samuel P. Langley; and *The Moon* by W. N. Pickering. A more modern work studied was *Amateur Telescope Making* by Harlow Shapley; and for the iron industry in which Brashear was at one time a worker, *Iron Brew* by Stewart M. Holbrook.

SECONDARY SOURCES

The authors are uncertain whether this section ought not to be considered the primary one, for the word-of-mouth stories about John Brashear comprise the better half of their volume. From all walks of life, people who knew John Brashear when they were young eagerly contributed stories, definite information, and character analysis that has been invaluable in the study of his unique personality.

Thanks are due Uncle John's brothers, George Brashear and the late Frank Brashear; Dr. Frank C. Jordan, Director of the Allegheny Observatory; Dr. Samuel Harden Church, Director of Carnegie Institute; the late Frank J. Skalak, former Director of the Brashear Association; Miss Martha Hoyt, Secretary of the Frick Educational Commission; Dr. Henry S. Scribner, Professor Emeritus of Greek and Latin, University of Pittsburgh; Leo J. Scanlon, Head of the Valley Observatory and Secretary of the Astronomical Section of the Academy of Science and Art; Fred M. Garland, former President of the Amateur Astronomer's Association; Miss Marie Dermitt, Secretary of the Civic Club; Jesse Caldron, Historian of Brownsville, Pa.; Mrs. Wm. Reed Thompson; Mrs. Caroline Malseed of Allegheny; the late Martin Leisser of Allegheny; Mrs. Andrew Carnegie of New York City.

Acknowledgment is also made to Mrs. Florence G. Bernstein of Los Angeles, California, for her aid in collecting material; and to Mrs. John M. Phillips, who founded the Brashear Association and who has always been an enthusiastic supporter of any project bearing Uncle John's name.

Many letters from Dr. Brashear were read, and from them several important episodes and journeys were disclosed. Of especial value were those offered by Mrs. Enoch Rauh of Pittsburgh, Mrs. Caroline Malseed of Allegheny, and Mrs. Charles Boyer of Brentwood, Pennsylvania, whose etching of Uncle John was made for the frontispiece of this volume.

The authors wish to express their appreciation to the American Society of Mechanical Engineers for permission to use material from the *Autobiography of John A. Brashear*, compiled from his memoirs shortly after his death; and to George M. P. Baird for the sonnet written for the Brashear Masque given at his birthday celebration in 1915.

INDEX

Abbot, C. G., 90, 92
Acheson, Edward G., 148
Adams Company, 39
Advertising, in *Scientific American*, 67; pamphlet, 76-78
Airplane model, 89
Alexander, John, 103, 127
Alleghenia and Pittsburghia, asteroids, 187
Allegheny Commons, 93-94
Allegheny Observatory, new, 134-135, 161-162, 184-186; old, 47, 49-50, 71-72, 125, 128-129, 186-187; head of, 133-136
Allegheny Observatory Board, appointed to, 125
Allen, Col. William, 103
American Association for Advancement of Science, 82-83, 85; vice-president of, 149
American Society of Mechanical Engineers, president of, 193
Anderson Library, 48
Arsenal, Allegheny, 21
Articles published, 66, 71, 82-83, 194-195
Art Society, 32, 75
Assistants and associates, 76, 84-85, 202
Astral cameras, 180

Baird, George M. P., sonnet of, 192
Bakewell Glass Company, 3-4
Ball, Sir Robert, 182
Bardou Works, 111
Barnard, Edward E., 63-64, 130
Bayardstown, 39-40
Beatty, John, 103
Bell, Graham, 147, 190, 193
Berkman, anarchist, 122
Bigelow, Edward, 102, 106
Bilquist, T. B., 186
Bingham Street Methodist Church, sermon at, 28-29
Binoculars, 181
Birmingham, 31-34

Boats at Muskoka, the *Alleghenia*, 138; the first *Phoebe*, 139; the second *Phoebe*, 139
Boggs & Buhl Company, 26, 46
Bolometer, 49, 178
Bond, George P., 129
Brashear, Basil, 5-7, 10
Brashear, brothers and sisters, 12, 19, 33
Brashear, "Brown," 10, 12, 14, 17, 19, 34, 36, 39
Brashear, Frank, 33, 84, 130, 157
Brashear, George, 33
Brashear, John, birth, 12; school, 15, 17; apprenticeship, 18; mechanic, 20; marriage, 23; millwright, 30; completes and breaks first lens, 42; completes telescope, 43; meets Langley, 47; finishes 12-inch reflector, 59; discovers silvering process, 59; meets Charles Schwab, 65; meets William Thaw, 71; builds new shop, 76; makes rock-sale prisms, 83; makes spectroscope for Lick Observatory, 86; meets Andrew Carnegie, 101; goes abroad, 108, 116; Doctor of Science, 125; trustee of Western University of Pennsylvania, 128; director of Allegheny Observatory, 133; chancellor of Western University of Pennsylvania, 142; trustee of Carnegie Technical Schools, 160; relationship with Henry C. Frick, 162; administrator of Frick Educational Commission, 164; death of wife, 168; delegate to St. Andrews University, 170; delegate to Panama Pacific Exposition, 189; celebrates seventy-fifth birthday, 190; visits Orient, 200; death, 209
Brashear, Julia Smith, 7-9, 12-14, 17, 167
Brashear Memorial Association, 200

Brashear, Otho, 5

Brashear, Phoebe, marriage of, 23-25; as working partner, 25-28, 32, 35, 37-38, 40-41, 52-59, 62, 64, 73, 75, 201; as wife of famous man, 84, 94, 99, 104-105, 108-109, 111-112, 115-118, 125-126, 134, 160; becomes invalid, 136-138, 143, 164, 167-169; epitaph of, 209

Brashear Process, for silvering, 55-56, 59-60, 184

Brashear Settlements, 201

Brashear, William, 33, 84

Brown, Thomas and Basil, 5

Brownsville, 5-8, 12, 19, 22

Brownsville Clipper, 17

Brumbaugh, Governor Martin G., 188

Bulwer-Lytton, Baron Edward, 117-118

Burt, Prof. Andrew, 62

Campbell, W. W., 131, 180

Carhart, Dean, 148, 156

Carnegie, Andrew, early years of, 9, 48, 95, 98; industrial life of, 30-31, 95, 122, 163-164; life of, at Cresson, 101-102, 104, 107; philanthropies of, 95, 97, 104, 113-115, 133, 139, 152-153; life of, in Scotland, 110, 117, 170-176; later years of, 206-207

Carnegie, Mrs. Andrew, 101, 172-176

Carnegie Institute, founding of, 106, 127-128

Carnegie Library, Allegheny, 95, 97; East End, 97, 127

Carnegie, Margaret Morrison, 101-102, 105, 154, 163

Carnegie Mills, 30-31, 95

Carnegie Music Hall, New York, scientific exhibit at, 114

Carnegie-Phipps Steel Company, 95, 164

Carnegie Technical Schools, founding of, 149, 152-155, 160-161; during World War, 203

Carnegie, Tom, 95, 164, 170

Celebration of: Brashear Day, 189; seventy-fifth birthday, 190-192;

departure for Orient, 198-200; seventy-ninth birthday, 206-207

Chautauqua classes, 62

Children, adopted: Effie Afton, 25, 27, 33, 43, 52, 56, 68; Harry, 52, 53, 56, 84, 108, 136

Church, Col. Samuel Harden, 128

Civic Club, 149

Civil War, Pittsburgh in, 19-22

Clark, Alvan & Sons, 48, 66, 69, 78, 178

Coal Hill, 20, 27, 44

Cohen, Judge Josiah and wife, 102, 106

Color photography, 180-181

Conservatory Club, 93-96, 99

de Constant, Baron des Tournelles, 176

Conway, William, 152-153

Cressap, Capt. Michael, 6

Cresson, Pennsylvania, summer colony at, 101-102, 104-107

Crucible Club, president of, 149

Curtis, Heber D., 185

Curtiss, Glen, 91

Dean, Prof. Philotus, 44-46

Degrees, honorary, 17, 125, 161

Deslandres, of Paris, 180, 182

Dick, Thomas, 10, 173

Diehl, William J., 153

Director, acting, of Allegheny Observatory, 133-135

Dominion Observatory, reflector for, 188, 204-205

Draper, Henry, 48, 54-55, 57, 64

Driving clock, 113; wheel of, 181-182

Duff's Mercantile College, 17, 191

Dumferline, 176

Dundee, 172

Dungeness, 170

Duquesne Club, 96, 115

Eclipse expedition, 204

Edgar Thompson Works, 31, 65, 95, 163

Engineers Society of Western Pennsylvania, president of, 112

English Mechanic and World of Science, article in, 56, 59-60

Epitaph, for Phoebe, 209

Estimates, for contracts, 80-81
Experiments, with materials, 181

Faraday, Michael, 110
Fecker Company, J. W., 160
Ferries, 23
Fessenden, Reginald, 147
Fishing Club, 103, 107
Flagstaff Observatory, 180
Foster, Stephen, songs of, 14, 105, 111
Francies, John, 97
Frick Educational Commission, 165, 176
Frick, Helen, 164
Frick, Henry C.: philanthropies of, 63, 144, 161-162, 164-165, 170, 185, 190; business affiliations of, 122-123, 163-164; death of, 207
Fund, for 75th birthday, 190-191; for buying old home, 199-200

Gallitzin, Demetrius, 106
Glass bars, accuracy of, 120-121
Goldsmith, Dr. Luba, 144, 166

Hageman, Fred, 85, 202
Hale, George E., 180
Half-meter bars, 82
Hall, Robert C., 160, 185
Hamilton, William, 96
Hastings, Charles, 79-80, 85, 129, 181
Hausewalde, Hans, 131
Heliostat mirror, 68-69, 71
Henry, Paul and Prosper, 110-111
Herron, Dr. William, 68
Herschel, Sir John and family, 110
Herschel, Sir William, 110
Hetherington, Col. A. G., 189
Hetzel, George, 103
High, Rev. John C., 28-29
Holden, Edward S., 82, 130
Holland, Wm. J., 102, 106, 124-125, 128, 142, 152
Homestead Mills, 65; strike of, 122-123
House: on Holt Street, 12-13, 33-38, 44, 55, 62-63, 200-201; on Perrysville Avenue, 84, 113, 136, 166, 182, 195
Hoyt, Martha, 166-167

Huggins, Sir William, 113, 119-120

Interferometer, 179
International Bureau of Weights and Measures, 179
Isle Urania, Muskoka, 138, 141, 168

Janssan, Dr., 112
Johnstown Flood, 107
Jordan, Frank C., 185
Junta Club, 133

Kayser, Dr., 182
Keeler, James, 113, 133-134, 186; Memorial Telescope, 162, 184
Kiln, at Brashear shop, 181
Klages, Edward, 55
Klages, George, 76
Kloman's Mills, 95
Knebworth Castle, 116-119
Knox, Philander and Richard, 15

Lafayette, Marquis de, 7
Langley laboratory, 203-204
Langley, Samuel Pierpont: at Allegheny Observatory, 45-50, 66, 68-72, 79, 83, 112-113, 147, 186; work of, on flying machine, 86-92
Larkin, E. C., 189
Lectures and addresses, 82-83, 85, 97, 106, 114-115, 119, 140, 149, 159-160, 170, 184-186, 193-194, 198, 203
Lee, Edward B., 186
Leisser, Martin, 103
Lens: breaking of, 41-42; the first five-inch, 42-43, 46-48; orders for, 130
Lewis, Oliver, & Phillips, 17
Lick Observatory, 86, 110, 113, 133-134, 180, 198, 204-205
Lincoln, Abraham, 21-22
Lloyd George, David, 173
Long, Haniel, quotation from, 105-106
Loretto, Pennsylvania, 106
Louisville, work in, 18-19, 28
Lowell, Percival, 180
Ludewig, William R., 85, 88-89

Magee, Christopher, 127
Manchester, 22
Medals, 126, 149, 182, 189

Mellor, C. C., 102, 106, 128
Melville, Thomas A., 194
Miller, Thomas N., 95
Millwright, work as, 30, 37, 41
Monongahela Incline, 31
Moon craters, 64
Michelson, A. A., 85, 179
Music Societies, 32
Muskoka Lakes, home at, 137-141, 167-168

McCargo, David, 95
McCormick, Samuel Black, 150, 156, 186
McDowell, Effie and family, 84, 108, 136, 160, 166-167, 205
McDowell, James, 68, 76, 79, 82, 166, 181, 202
McKinley, President, appointment by, 149
McKnight-Duncan Mills, employed by, 30, 32, 39

National Pike, 8, 16
Natural gas, early use of, 85
Newcomb, Simon, 182
Newton, Sir Isaac, 110
New York Evening Sun, quotation from, 209

Oliver, Henry W., 95, 138
Orders for U.S. Government, during Spanish War, 131-132, 178; during World War, 202
Ormsby, John, 31
Overholt, Abraham, 163

Paine, Albert Bigelow, poem of, 168-169
Pan American Scientific Congress, delegate to, 192
Panama Pacific Exposition, delegate to, 188-189, 193
Parks, founding of, Schenley, 102, 127; Hiland, 127; Riverview, 129, 135; Frick, 164
Patton, James, 96
Pennsylvania Canal, 8, 74, 101
Pennsylvania Railroad strike, 57-58
Pershing, General, 204
Philadelphia Exposition, visit to, 51
Phillips, Mrs. John M., 199

Phipps Conservatory, Allegheny, 93, 95-96; Schenley Park, 97
Phipps, Henry, in Allegheny, 93-100; further endowments of, 97-98; in New York, 114; at Knebworth Castle, 116-117, 121-122; statement of, 122, 191
Phipps, John, 98, 108-111
Phoebe Brashear Club, 166, 190-191
Photo-chronograph, 202
Photographic Doublets, 129, 178, 180
Pickering, Edward C., 186
Pickering, W. M., 64, 181, 187
Pitcairn, Robert, 95
Pittsburgh Academy, old, 66, 74
Pittsburgh Academy of Science and Art, president of, 114, 128
Pittsburgh Fire, 1-4
Pitt-Taylor, Madeline, 176
Plan and Scope Committee, 153-154, 159
du Pont, Francis G., 77
Portraits, 160-161
Precepts and sayings, 159, 194, 196-197
Prince Henry, 111
Pritchett, Henry S., quotation from, 195-196
Protestant Orphanage Asylum, 156-158

Redstone Old Fort, 6
Reflector, breaking of, 54-56; the first 12-inch, 59-61; orders for, 130-131; 72-inch, 188, 205
Reporter, interview with, 188-189
Rock salt prisms, 83, 178
Rogers, William, 82
Rotating mirror, 85
Rowland, Henry A., 79-80
Rowland Diffraction Gratings, 79-80, 109, 111-113, 120, 181
Royal Astronomical Society, of England, fellow of, 119

Salary, in mills, 23, 26, 30, 33; in first shop, 81
Saturn, 4, 43, 50, 133, 187
Scalp Level, artist colony at, 102-104, 107
Schlesinger, Frank, 185-186, 207

Schmitz, Herman J., 145
School for Blind, 183-184
Schott Glass Company, of Munich, 176
Schwab, Charles, early life of, 31, 65, 106; friendship of, 31, 65, 94, 159, 161, 191, 206; death of, 66
Scully, Cornelius, 144
Service, Robert, quotation from, 196-197
Sheets, Will, 15, 33, 43
Ship concert, 177
Shop, first on Holt Street, 36-38, 55, 68-69, 73; reconstructed, 75-76, 82; on Perrysville Avenue, 82-84, 113, 160, 178-180, 182, 202
Silverman, Alexander, 144
Skibo Castle, 170-171, 173-176
Smith, Anthony, 160
Smith, the Misses, of Allegheny, 145
Smith, Nathaniel, 4, 7-11, 13, 16-17, 22-23, 26-27
Smyth, Piazzi, 113
Snowden, John & Sons, employed by, 18
Solar-energy box, 79
South Side, Pittsburgh, 23, 31-32
Spanish War, 131-133
Spectroheliograph, 180
Spectroscopes, 79-80, 86, 113, 131, 178-180, 193-194
St. Andrews University, 170-172
Steinheil test plane, 80
Stevens, Thomas Wood, 191-192
Stewart, Thomas, family of, 23
Swasey, Ambrose, 86, 189, 198, 205

Taylor, Rev. John, 66
Telescope Association, of Allegheny, 44-45
Telescopes, made by Brashear, first, 36, 43-44, 46; second, 55, 61-62, 64-65, 73; orders for, 76-78, 131-132, 178; used at Muskoka, 138; given to Carnegie, 176
Temperanceville, home at, 26
Testing mirror, 179-180
Thaw, John, 73
Thaw, William, endowments and gifts of, 45, 71-75, 80-81, 83-84, 86-87, 94, 99, 124; financial interests of, 73-74; summer home of, 101, 107; death of, 112; memorial to, 186
Thaw, William, Jr., 133, 186
Thaw, Mrs. William, 133
Thaw Memorial Telescope, 176, 181, 184-185
Thompson, Mrs. Wm. Reed, 186
Thomson, Sir William, 80, 182
Trip to Europe, 1888, 98, 100, 107-112; 1892, 115-123; 1911, 170-177; to Orient, 1916-17, 198
Troughton & Simms Works, 120
Tyndall, John, 120-121

Underground Railway, 20
United States Assay Commission, 149
University of Pittsburgh, 156, 170, 186

Very, Professor, 85, 87

Wadsworth, F. L. O., 134, 180, 185
Wall, A. Brian, 103, 106
Wampler, Squire, 3-4, 36
Warner & Swasey, firm of, 86, 130
Washington and Jefferson College, 17, 151
Wesleyanism, 14
Western Penitentiary, 93, 95-97
Western Theological Seminary, 94, 145
Western University of Pennsylvania, early days of, 74, 94, 124; degree from, 125; on board of, 128; acting chancellor of, 142-151, 154-158; departments of, 142-143, 150; students of, 144; professors of, 145-147; sale of buildings of, 156-157
Westinghouse, George, 147, 153
Whirling table, 88-89
White, Brigadier General, 204
White, Rev. John Cracker, 144
Wilkinson, George, 15, 32
Wilson, President, 147, 190
Wolf, Max, 129-130, 182, 187

Woodwell, Joseph, 103-104, 106

World War, anecdote of, 141; Pittsburgh in, 200-204; Canadian friends in, 204

Wright Brothers, 90-91

Zeiss, Carl, 178

Zug, Christopher, 39-41, 52-53, 57, 65; Sable Iron Works of, 39-41, 52-54, 57-58

Zug & Painter Mills, 20, 22, 26, 30, 39

The Words and Music of Melissa Etheridge

James E. Perone

AN IMPRINT OF ABC-CLIO, LLC
Santa Barbara, California • Denver, Colorado • Oxford, England

Library of Congress Cataloging-in-Publication Data

Perone, James E.
  The words and music of Melissa Etheridge / James E. Perone.
    pages cm. — (The Praeger singer-songwriter collection)
  Includes bibliographical references and index.
  ISBN 978–1–4408–3007–5 (hardback) — ISBN 978–1–4408–3008–2 (ebook)
1. Etheridge, Melissa—Criticism and interpretation. I. Title.
ML420.E88P47 2014
782.42166092—dc23   2013044660

ISBN: 978–1–4408–3007–5
EISBN: 978–1–4408–3008–2

18 17 16 15 14   1 2 3 4 5

This book is also available on the World Wide Web as an eBook.
Visit www.abc-clio.com for details.

Praeger
An Imprint of ABC-CLIO, LLC

ABC-CLIO, LLC
130 Cremona Drive, P.O. Box 1911
Santa Barbara, California 93116-1911

This book is printed on acid-free paper ∞

Manufactured in the United States of America

Contents

Series Foreword, by *James E. Perone*   vii

Acknowledgments   ix

Introduction   1
   Organization of This Book   3

1. Early Career   5
   Melissa Etheridge (1988)   6
   Brave and Crazy (1989)   11
   Never Enough (1992)   18

2. Yes, I Am   27
   Yes, I Am (1993)   28
   Your Little Secret (1995)   32
   Breakdown (1999)   41

3. Turbulence and Recovery   51
   Skin (2001)   52
   Melissa Etheridge Live . . . and Alone (2002)   59
   Lucky (2004)   62
   Greatest Hits: The Road Less Traveled (2005)   73

4. Maturity   77
    The Awakening (2007)   79
    A New Thought for Christmas (2008)   91
    Fearless Love (2010)   96
    Icon (2011)   106
    4th Street Feeling (2012)   106

Conclusions: Assessing Melissa Etheridge's Significance   119

Annotated Discography   127

Notes   133

Annotated Bibliography   139

Index   153

Series Foreword

Although the term *singer-songwriter* might most frequently be associated with a cadre of musicians of the early 1970s such as Paul Simon, James Taylor, Carly Simon, Joni Mitchell, Cat Stevens, and Carole King, the Praeger Singer-Songwriter Collection defines singer-songwriters more broadly, in terms of both style and time period. The series includes volumes on musicians who have been active from approximately the 1960s through the present. Musicians who write and record in folk, rock, soul, hip-hop, country, and various hybrids of these styles are represented. Therefore some of the early 1970s introspective singer-songwriters named here will be included, but not exclusively.

What do the individuals included in this series have in common? Some have never collaborated as writers, whereas others have; but all have written and recorded commercially successful and/or historically important music and lyrics at some point in their careers.

The authors who contribute to the series also exhibit diversity. Some are scholars who are trained primarily as musicians, whereas others have such areas of specialization such as American studies, history, sociology, popular culture studies, literature, and rhetoric. The authors share a high level of scholarship, accessibility in their writing, and a true insight into the work of the artists they study. The authors are also focused on the output of their subjects and how it relates to their subject's biography and the society around them; however, biography in and of itself is not a major focus of the books in this series.

Given the diversity of the musicians who are the subject of books in this series, and given the diversity of viewpoint of the authors, volumes in the series differ from book to book. All, however, are organized chronologically around the compositions and recorded performances of their subjects. All of the books in the series should also serve as listeners' guides to the music of their subjects, making them companions to the artists' recorded output.

James E. Perone
Series Editor

Acknowledgments

As has been the case for all of the writing that I have done for Praeger Publishers, I am indebted to the Praeger acquisitions and editorial staff, as well as to the copyeditors with whom they contract. I am grateful that this well-oiled machine raises questions that I had not considered, provides such a keen eye to help find every uncrossed *t* and undotted *i*, and manages to make the entire process as smooth as possible.

Thank you to my University of Mount Union colleagues Dr. Susan Haddox (Philosophy and Religious Studies), Dr. Kathleen Piker-King (Sociology), Dr. Andrew Price (English and Gender Studies), and Dr. Kevin Meyer (Psychology), all of whom made helpful suggestions for resources in the area of LGBT studies from the perspectives of their respective academic disciplines.

I would especially like to thank my wife, Karen, for encouraging me throughout the writing, editing, and indexing process over the course of this (and every previous) project; I could not have done it without your encouragement and support.

Despite all of the help of these individuals and organizations, there are bound to be some errors, some controversial interpretations of the words and music of Melissa Etheridge; they are all mine.

Introduction

American singer-songwriter-guitarist (and occasional pianist) Melissa Etheridge was born in Leavenworth, Kansas, on May 29, 1961. According to Etheridge, her older sister, Jennifer, physically and sexually abused Etheridge for years, beginning at approximately age "three or four."[1] Although Etheridge discusses this abuse openly in her autobiography, she overtly deals with this aspect of her life in her later work as a singer-songwriter very little. However, much of Etheridge's output as a writer revolves around themes such as betrayal, brokenness, and emotional torment, all of which could be rooted in the experiences of her childhood, or at the very least can be understood by the listener as being tied in part to Etheridge's childhood experiences. Etheridge began playing the guitar as a child, and by the time she was a teenager, she played in several country bands in the Leavenworth area as the lone female member. During her high school years, Etheridge came to grips with her sexual identity. Ironically, her first lesbian relationship was with a fellow Leavenworth High School student who mirrored some of the manipulative and abusive qualities of her sister.[2]

After graduating from Leavenworth High School, Etheridge moved to Boston, Massachusetts, to attend the Berklee College of Music, one of the most highly respected institutions in higher education for study in jazz, popular, and commercial music. During her time at Berklee, Etheridge began playing as a solo act at clubs around Boston. Sensing that the structured curriculum at Berklee was not necessary for her work as a singer-songwriter, Etheridge dropped out of college. After spending a brief period back home in Kansas, she moved to California to try to make it in the commercial music industry.

Etheridge's first major inroads in the industry were forged in 1987 when manager Bill Leopold signed her. Under Leopold's guidance, Etheridge undertook an increasingly prestigious round of appearances in the Los Angeles and Long Beach, California, areas. Because of the quality of Etheridge's songs and her success as a live solo artist, several major record companies attempted to sign her. Eventually, though, she signed with Island Records, with which she continues to record into the second decade of the twenty-first century.

Although producer Jim Gaines initially conceived of Etheridge's self-titled debut album as a pop album, Island Records founder Chris Blackwell intervened and directed that Etheridge rerecord the songs in a style suggested by a photo that had been taken in a shoot for the album's cover. The passion and edgy posture that blends ecstasy and torture that are embodied in that photo resulted in *Melissa Etheridge* being reconceived and reconstructed by Etheridge and her band in a harder-edged, classic rock style. The second version of the album—which Island released in 1988—established the classic Melissa Etheridge sound, a full-throated, guitar-oriented texture that has defined the majority of her recordings up to the present. To date, Etheridge has released a dozen studio albums, a popular solo concert DVD, two greatest hits albums, and popular and award-winning singles.

A longtime favorite of pop music critics, Melissa Etheridge received nominations for Grammys for Best Rock Vocal Performance, Female (but did not win) in 1989 ("Bring Me Some Water"), 1990 ("Brave and Crazy"), 1991 ("The Angels"), 2000 ("Angels Would Fall"), 2001 ("Enough of Me"), 2002 ("I Want to Be in Love"), and 2003 ("The Weakness in Me"). She also received Grammy nominations for Best Rock Song in 1995 ("Come to My Window" and "I'm the Only One") and 2000 ("Angels Would Fall"), and a nomination for Best Rock Album in 2000 (*Breakdown*). Etheridge's recording of the Greenwheel song "Breathe" received a 2005 Grammy nomination for Best Rock Vocal Performance, Solo, and her 2007 song "I Need to Wake Up" received a nomination for Best Song Written for a Motion Picture, Television or Other Visual Media. Etheridge won Grammys for Best Rock Vocal Performance, Female in 1993 ("Ain't It Heavy") and 1995 ("Come to My Window"). Her "I Need to Wake Up," from the film *An Inconvenient Truth*, won the 2007 Academy Award for Best Original Song. Etheridge won the Annual Juno Award in 1990 for International Entertainer of the Year and ASCAP's (the American Society of Composers, Authors, and Publishers) Songwriter of the Year Award in 1996. In 2001, Melissa Etheridge received a star on the Hollywood Walk of Fame, and in 2006, Berklee College of Music, the institution that Etheridge left after a year and a half, awarded her an Honorary Doctorate of Music.

In addition to her general commercial and critical success, Melissa Etheridge especially has been a favorite of female audiences. Throughout her career she has been one of the few prominent, highly visible female singer-guitarists in rock (as opposed to pop, country, or folk). Through her impassioned singing of her own lyrics of pain, desire, outrage, and the other emotions felt by Etheridge's characters—whether autobiographical or fictional—she reflects the very real emotional complexity and intensity felt by members of her audience, whether female or male. Since her own diagnosis of and successful battle against breast cancer in the early twenty-first century, Etheridge has been a tireless spokesperson for cancer research and an advocate for cancer sufferers and survivors. Ever since her somewhat casual coming out as a lesbian at an event celebrating the inauguration of U.S. President Bill Clinton in 1993, Etheridge also has been an outspoken advocate for same-sex marital rights, same-sex parental rights, and in more general ways for members of the LGBT community around the world. After her bout with breast cancer in the early twentieth-first century, Etheridge also became more spiritually and environmentally oriented in her songwriting. As a result of her environmentalism, Etheridge wrote and recorded the award-winning song "I Need to Wake Up" for Al Gore's film *An Inconvenient Truth.*

The compositions and recordings of Melissa Etheridge also remain important because of the gender neutrality of most of her lyrics. The objects of her desire, the characters that have wronged her, the characters to whom her character sings, and so on, can be understood as women or men, as often can her first-person characters. Therefore, even with her autobiographical-sounding storytelling and raw exposure of emotions, there is a universality to Etheridge's work that can be heard in few singer-songwriters of her generation; she absolutely destroys all the traditional gender-role stereotypes of rock and pop songwriting, and she falls within a long tradition in pop music of singer-songwriters who raise important and potentially challenging questions about identity on several levels. That being said, members of the lesbian community in particular praise Etheridge's songs, albums, and videos for their sensitive and accurate portrayal of lesbian relationships.[3] Despite the mostly gender- and sexuality-neutral nature of Melissa Etheridge's lyrics, some of her characterizations-in-song align with specific challenges faced by the LGB community, as identified by sociologists and psychologists; these will be discussed in the book's final chapter.

ORGANIZATION OF THIS BOOK

As suggested by its title, the focus of *The Words and Music of Melissa Etheridge* is on the music, lyrics, and recordings of Melissa Etheridge, and not on Etheridge's biography per se. The book is arranged chronologically and includes biographical information woven into the discussion of Etheridge's work as a songwriter and performer. Although I explore autobiographical references in Etheridge's music, I examine her work more globally, more universally: what does it say about the characters that Etheridge portrays and the characters that she observes, and what does it say about and to listeners who might not be familiar with the specific details of Melissa Etheridge's life story? I have also included a concluding chapter devoted to discussion of an overall assessment of Etheridge's work as a body of literature that raises questions about identity, gender roles, and sexuality, and as a body of literature that can be understood as an in-depth exploration of particular challenges faced particularly by members of the lesbian, gay, and bisexual communities.

This study revolves primarily around Melissa Etheridge's studio albums; therefore, I give her two "greatest hits"-style compilation albums and her singles less attention. Similarly, Etheridge's videos—studio and live—receive less attention than the studio albums. That being said, a number of Etheridge's music videos (e.g., that for "Come to My Window") have become so iconic that it is nearly impossible to address the song proper without also addressing the interpretation of the song as presented in the official video.

The bibliography includes many sources for further information about Melissa Etheridge and her work. Since the focus of this volume is on Etheridge's work as a songwriter and recording artist, I have not included references to concert reviews, with a few exceptions. I have included annotations for most of the bibliographical citations, especially for those that directly relate to Melissa Etheridge and her work. I have not included annotations for the bibliographical citations that are more general in nature (e.g., those that deal with sociological and psychological phenomena in general terms).

I have also included a selected annotated discography, which although it does not include full detail on instrumental and vocal personnel, includes information about awards and chart performance. For reasons of space, and because they are somewhat more transitory in the digital age, I have not included singles in the discography.

The Words and Music of Melissa Etheridge concludes with an index of names, places, and song and album titles. Song titles include those written and recorded by Etheridge, as well as songs by others that I discuss in relationship to Etheridge's compositions and recordings. It should be noted that I have included only the most extensive and most important discussions of Etheridge's work and life in the various subheadings of her entry in the index.

Early Career

After dropping out of Boston's Berklee College of Music, making her way to the Los Angeles, California, area, securing a manager, and performing a series of increasingly important and prestigious solo gigs, Etheridge's first recordings were released. In this case, Etheridge made her recording debut through her contribution of four songs to the soundtrack of the Nick Nolte movie *Weeds*.

Because of the relative obscurity of the songs and the movie *Weeds*, it was her signing to Island Records and the release of her first, self-titled album that marked the real beginning of Melissa Etheridge's recording career, insofar as the general public is concerned. During this early phase of Etheridge's career as a recording artist, she established a solid fan base as one of the few female rock stars. Her albums sold reasonably well and several singles enjoyed significant radio airplay; however, Etheridge did not become a truly iconic part of popular culture until later.

Some of Melissa Etheridge's early compositions resemble earlier rock and pop songs by her predecessors in the genre, especially melodically, harmonically, and in her use of accompanying instrumental figures. Etheridge's lyrics, while certainly not totally unprecedented, were more original. As a singer of her own material, Etheridge played the role of the lustful would-be lover, the jilted ex-lover, and the woman caught in a troubled relationship. In some respects, her songs reflected back to the songs that made Janis Joplin an iconic blues rock singer at the end of the 1960s.

MELISSA ETHERIDGE[1] (1988)

Over the years, Melissa Etheridge has been known as a frequent Grammy nominee, for her decision to candidly discuss her private life, as a gay rights activist, as an environmental activist, and as a cancer survivor. Her 1988 self-titled debut album presented a collection of 10 self-penned strong rock songs of loss, alienation, and self-reflection on identity in the face of betrayal. As a side note, throughout a significant part of Melissa Etheridge's career, the 10-song paradigm that this album established was the norm, even though Etheridge's career as a recording artist has been entirely within the digital age when lengthier albums certainly were possible. As noted by critics in the late 1980s and early 1990s, *Melissa Etheridge* and the songs on Etheridge's next two albums reflected some of the same aesthetics as found in the contemporary work of already established rock singer-songwriters such as John Mellencamp, Bob Seger, and Bruce Springsteen. Like these musicians, Etheridge championed independence, sang with powerful emotional expression, and presented a welcome alternative to the synthesizer-laden dance music of the time. In the words of *All Music Guide* critic Vik Iyengar, these attributes helped to make Etheridge "a role model for a generation of young women who found her to be an uncompromising artist unafraid to expose (and celebrate) her strengths and weaknesses."[2] However, Melissa Etheridge's songs, especially with their lack of references to any sort of stereotypes based on gender or sexual orientation, are more universal than Iyengar's review might suggest to some readers.

Ironically, *Melissa Etheridge* originally was conceived as a pop album, as opposed to a straight-ahead rock album. As Etheridge recounts in her autobiography, it "didn't occur to [her]" that the "layer upon layer of keyboards" that producer Jim Gaines overdubbed "might not be the best thing for [her] music."[3] Island Records founder and executive Chris Blackwell rejected the album as it was presented to him. He showed Etheridge one of the photographs that were taken as possibilities for the album's cover—in fact, the photo that eventually graced the cover—and told her, "Make *that* album."[4] Etheridge and her regular backing band commenced work on rerecording her songs with a stripped-down, tightly focused rock-oriented sound. The second version, which was recorded in a considerably compressed time frame, is what came to be released in spring 1988 as *Melissa Etheridge*.

The album opens with "Similar Features." Etheridge's character sings to a former lover, who is now with another woman who has "similar features [to Etheridge's character] with longer hair." Like the other songs about loss in love on the album, "Similar Features" finds Etheridge at once defiant, jealous, hurt, sarcastic, and angry. In short, the failure of her character's relationship elicits the range of human emotions that might reflect the complexity of real life. Part of the challenge of listening to the entire album in sequence, however, is that Etheridge so unrelentingly works her way through a similar range of emotions in song after song. This might tend to force some listeners away from the lyrics to a certain extent and experience the songs as musical pieces outside of their lyrical contexts. If the emotional jockeying becomes too much, it perhaps is best to think of and to experience the album as a collection of individual songs. In fact, in stark contrast to other artists of her generation, Melissa Etheridge's albums continued to consist more of collections of individual, stand-alone songs than reflect the aesthetics of integrated concept albums into her work of the early twenty-first century.

In a sense, then, Melissa Etheridge unwittingly anticipated the shift to a track mentality that emerged in the digital age, especially after the emergence of music file sharing at the end of the twentieth century. In fact, as the reader will see even in discussion of some of her more thoroughly conceived album packages, it makes sense still to think of Etheridge as a writer and performer of individual songs. Specifically, even some of her concept albums contain little in the way of chronological narrative, and little in the way of long-range musical connections and progression that might be expected in the full-fledged concept albums of other artists. In short, Etheridge's later concept albums, at least up to approximately 2009, tended to be loosely organized around themes rather than around a strict narrative structure.

The second song on Etheridge's debut album, "Chrome Plated Heart," finds Etheridge dealing with loss and desire more impressionistically and metaphorically. Here, she uses the image of "scratches and ... stains on [her] chrome plated heart" to symbolize her past losses. Perhaps even more interesting is the somewhat fatalistic image she creates when she sings, "The only way I know where the train will go is when I'm sleeping on the tracks." This image suggests the influence of the blues tradition, so similar is it in style to a clever turn of phrase such as "I've been down so long that it looks like up to me," from the 1920s Furry Lewis blues song "I Will Turn Your Money Green." The musical setting of "Chrome Plated Heart" is stripped-down acoustic guitar and rhythm section-based blues, albeit in a modified blues form. It is this kind of texture—as well as her blues-inflected vocals—that made Etheridge's sound stand out from the more obviously commercially motivated artists, especially the dance-oriented artists, of the late 1980s.

The rhythm section arrangement on "Chrome Plated Heart" hints at funk, particularly with the syncopations at the 16th-note level. The next song, "Like the Way I Do," also includes a mixture of rock and funk rhythmic styles. In the lyrics, Etheridge addresses a lover who is now with another woman. She puts her own prowess as a passionate lover and as a seducer up against that of her rival. Etheridge captures the bravado of the lyrics in her edgy, pointed singing. One of four songs on the album that made it onto the record charts as a single, "Like the Way I Do," is a standout. It was not necessarily the most commercially successful of the collection at the time ("Chrome Plated Heart" and "Bring Me Some Water" rose higher in the charts), but the emotion and the engaging and memorable tune both wear very well over a quarter century after the release of the song.

Curiously, the music of the next piece, "Precious Pain," bears a motivic resemblance to the Kansas hit "Dust in the Wind," a song written by Kerry Livgren. Like the well-known Livgren piece, "Precious Pain" is what can only be described as a "downer." While Livgren writes that "all we are is dust in the wind," Etheridge basically equates feeling pain in life with knowing that one is alive. The slow, largely acoustic setting and the dark lyrics of hopelessness suggest the 1970s singer-songwriter movement stretched to an extreme. In fact, the extreme darkness of the lyrics also suggests the rumblings of grunge music, which was first making an impact in the U.S. Pacific Northwest around this same time. What really makes the piece work, though, is Etheridge's understated singing style; she is entirely believable as the woman whose life has been filled with, and only with, such intense personal pain that were the pain to be absent, she might not be sure that she is still alive.

"Don't You Need" is one of the more interesting songs on the album from a structural standpoint. Etheridge includes tempo and texture changes as she contrasts her needs and desires with what would seem to be the lack of the same in an estranged lover. Interestingly, the stark changes of texture on this and other songs on *Melissa Etheridge* also suggest the grunge style that was emerging at the time. While the clearest connection between the songs on Etheridge's debut album is the emphasis on deeply seated emotions revolving around broken and dysfunctional relationships, some of the songs share specific imagery. For example, in "Don't You Need," Etheridge frames her explorations around a dream in which "the water was running low," thus allowing the heat of the desires of her heart to "abduct" her mind. In "The Late September Dogs," which is six and a half minutes long, Etheridge portrays a character who must now, after her loss, only dream that "the hand that touches you is mine, and mine alone." In the chorus, she pleads with the rain to "fall down on [her]" and thus to "set [her] free." In fact, despite its slow tempo, "The Late September Dogs" is one of the most potent songs on Etheridge's debut album, particularly because of the contrast between the quiet sparseness of the verses and the sharp edginess of Etheridge's plea to the rain in the chorus sections. Etheridge returns to the metaphor of water on the album's penultimate track, "Bring Me Some Water," probably the best-known song in this collection.

"The Late September Dogs" is followed by "Occasionally," the shortest track on the album. Here, accompanied solely by her own percussion work on the back of her guitar, Etheridge sings to a former lover (who she happens to see with the person's "new friends" and "new envoy") that she "only feel[s] lonely occasionally." She then provides a short and intentionally ironic litany of these "occasional" times, such as driving her car, watching television, and "after dark." In other words, Etheridge's character feels lonely virtually all of the time. As she does in earlier songs, Etheridge conveys feelings of sarcasm, hurt, anger, contempt, and so on. Her character seems to realize that she "is addicted" to being drawn into new relationships in which she ultimately will be hurt. This addiction hearkens back to the real-life story of Melissa Etheridge's childhood and adolescence, the period of her life during which she suffered sexual abuse at the hands of her sister, and experienced her first lesbian relationship with a schoolmate who turned out to be manipulative and similarly hurtful. Interestingly, this cycle of bad relationships also suggests the internalized sexual stigma that psychologists have identified in members of the LGB community, as will be discussed in the chapter, "Conclusions: Assessing Melissa Etheridge's Significance."

The stark a cappella setting of "Occasionally" is haunting. Etheridge sings the verses in the key of F major and the chorus in B flat major. The modulation to the key of the subdominant (F to B flat) is not in and of itself unusual in pop music or rock music; however, the fact that the song ends with the chorus and that Etheridge establishes the F major tonality of the verses more strongly than the B flat major tonality of the chorus (which is somewhat vague until the final cadence of the chorus sections) tends to give the piece a somewhat unresolved sound. To the extent that the listener perceives it, the unresolved feeling of tonality supports the unresolved nature of the pain of which Etheridge sings in her lyrics.

"Watching You," a slow ballad, is one of the richest pieces lyrically on the album. Etheridge's character can be understood in several ways. She braves even the harshest weather to watch someone else through their window. She sings that "if I can't love you, I don't want to love you." This, and the voyeuristic nature of the situation, suggests that Etheridge's character may be stalking a former lover. However, Etheridge includes several hints that her character lives in poverty and is homeless. In this scenario, the person she watches may be someone on whom she is fixated, even if they have never met. The sparse musical arrangement supports the image of the loneliness of Etheridge's character. The setting is also made more effective by Etheridge's performance of the opening few words of each verse as spoken text—this helps to give the piece a greater feeling of authenticity. The melody of the verses, too, with their short rise and fall, supports the text, in this case by suggesting the passing of time as Etheridge's character gives the object of her desire her secret scrutiny.

Interestingly, the theme of secret longing (and even implications of voyeurism) and desire that can be consummated only through hidden windows and through the back doors of residences is a theme that runs through Etheridge's songs for several years. Again, although I will detail this phenomenon in this book's final chapter, this theme seems to be consistent with the phenomenon that psychologists have identified as internalized sexual stigma.

In part because of the timbre of her singing voice and in part because she specializes in songs about brokenness, Melissa Etheridge sometimes has been compared with the late 1960s icon Janis Joplin. Because the song more closely resembles the hard-rock style associated with Joplin when she was a member of Big Brother and the Holding Company than any other on this album, the Etheridge song "Bring Me Some Water" is perhaps the most Joplin-like piece here. In her lyrics, Etheridge expresses how "weak" she feels because her former lover is now in the arms of another woman. However, the chorus plea, "somebody bring me some water," is so powerfully sung and performed with so much instrumental drive that the listener might feel that Etheridge is not just weakened by the breakup; she is also deeply angered.

Of all of the songs on *Melissa Etheridge*, "Bring Me Some Water" became the most widely recognized, and in some ways defined Etheridge's early voice as a lyricist, composer, and vocalist more fully than any other song. Curiously enough, the song's iconic nature is confirmed by the fact that in the twenty-first century, the title has become part of Melissa Etheridge merchandising: visitors to her official website, melissaetheridge.com, can purchase a pet water bowl emblazoned with the title around the outside and imprinted with Etheridge's distinctive trademarked logo on the inside.[5] While the inclusion of the phrase on a pet bowl trivializes the emotional content of the song itself to a certain extent, it also suggests the degree to which the song title has become a general part of American pop culture.

Etheridge's debut album concludes with "I Want You," a funky musical setting for the singer-songwriter's raw expression of desire. Despite an initial night of passion, Etheridge sings that now "satisfaction never comes," suggesting that her partner treated the event as a one-night stand. Interestingly, in this song—the most obvious statement of sexual desire—as well as in every other song on the album, Etheridge never defines the gender of the object of her desire. Even if Etheridge had never openly discussed her sexuality as she did beginning in the early 1990s, the gender-neutral nature of the relationships makes for interesting listening. This aspect of the songs allows the listener to imagine the characters whom Etheridge sets up in her songs in a wider variety of ways than would be possible if she explicitly told the listener that the character opposite her own was male or female. And, this is possible to do with the songs of Melissa Etheridge and throughout the singer-songwriter's career, in large part because the lack of gender specificity is supported by an avoidance of anything resembling stereotypical gender roles or emotional or physical responses.

Melissa Etheridge is a strong debut album with nothing that can be labeled as filler. Etheridge was unrelenting in her exploration of a wide range of emotions, all of which are caused by broken relationships; however, this is perhaps one of the most emotionally cathartic albums of the era and one that rocks throughout. In considering Etheridge's debut album, it is important to keep in mind that Island Records executive Chris Blackwell rejected the initial pop settings of Etheridge's songs. The stripped-down, rock style that emerged when the songs were hastily rerecorded came to define Melissa Etheridge as a rock artist. She has continued to wear that moniker as she has moved through the subsequent quarter century. *Melissa Etheridge* spawned two successful singles, "Bring Me Some Water" and "Similar Features," which topped out at No. 10 and No. 6 respectively on the Mainstream Rock charts. Perhaps even more notably, Etheridge's performance of "Bring Me Some Water" received a nomination for the National Academy of Recording Arts and Sciences' Grammy for Best Rock Vocal Performance, Female.

In 2010, Island Records released the CD *Rarities Edition: Melissa Etheridge*, a collection of nonalbum tracks and live acoustic versions of songs that were included on the *Melissa Etheridge* album. The material on *Rarities Edition* can also be found on Island's "Deluxe Edition" of *Melissa Etheridge*.

BRAVE AND CRAZY (1989)

Although Melissa Etheridge garnered favorable reviews and Grammy nominations for performances from her self-titled debut, her sophomore album—the 1989 collection *Brave and Crazy*—and her third album, *Never Enough*, it must be remembered that *Brave and Crazy* and the collections on either side of it sold well, and helped to establish a nationwide fan base for this new rock artist, but they failed to firmly establish Melissa Etheridge as a true pop culture icon. In part, this might be attributable to the fact that Etheridge was a newcomer and was somewhat unusual at the time as a female rock (as opposed to pop) singer-songwriter-guitarist, but it might be attributable in part to the fact that Etheridge had not yet entirely found an original, entirely distinctive voice as a songwriter. So, while an album such as *Brave and Crazy* is successful on many levels and never seems derivative in the strictest sense, there is something of the vaguely familiar about some of the songs.

Brave and Crazy opens with an attention-grabbing rhythmic stumble at the start of "No Souvenirs." The sparseness of the accompaniment and high degree of syncopation in both Etheridge's vocal melody and the accompaniment purposefully do not firmly establish the metrical feel and tempo of the song in the listener's ears at the offset. Once the band—and especially the drums—fully kick in, the rhythmic context of the opening becomes clearer. Thus, when the opening material returns later in the song, the listener is likely to understand how it fits within the overall feel of the song.

The melodic material of "No Souvenirs" is notable for a phrase in each verse that closely resembles a phrase in Bruce Springsteen's 1984 song "Dancing in the Dark," leading up to and including the title line in the Springsteen song. The apparent Springsteen influence is further suggested by some of Etheridge's lyrical images. These include a reference to running away (references to leaving or lamenting the inability to leave a desperate situation or place can be found in a number of mid-1980s Springsteen songs), and the feeling of desperation and alienation after her character's lover "packed up [her] heart and . . . left no souvenirs" (alienation is another persistent theme in Springsteen's work of the time period).

"No Souvenirs" is also notable for the high degree of textural contrast in the arrangement, which ranges from the minimalistic—and almost pointillistic—music of the opening to a full-toned, significantly louder, nearly power-ballad texture in the chorus. Although there is little reference to punk rock in this song—or in any of Etheridge's work—the contrast of textures and dynamics, combined with the alienation that is found in a song such as "No Souvenirs," connects the piece at least in a small way to the grunge music of the day.

The album's title track follows "No Souvenirs." Eventually, Etheridge received a Grammy nomination for Best Rock Vocal Performance, Female, for "Brave and Crazy." Although she did not win the Grammy for her recording of the song, it is easy to understand why the National Academy of Recording Arts and Sciences considered Etheridge for the award. As a singer, Etheridge pulls out all of the proverbial stops in expressing her character's frustration and even desperation. Given the title of the song, the reader might question the characterization of the character's feelings as those of frustration and desperation; however, in this song, Etheridge's character has the freedom, desire, and ability (at least in her own mind) to be as "brave and crazy" as she wants to be. The one thing that she cannot avoid, cannot explain, and over which she has absolutely no power is the character she addresses. As Etheridge sings, "What am I gonna do, about you?" Over the years, Etheridge has revisited this theme on more than one occasion, and the song "If I Wanted To," from the album *Yes I Am*, is a more lyrically and vocally successful—and ultimately more memorable—exploration of the theme.

"Brave and Crazy" is more than just its lyrics; the song is notable for the deft handling of a rock-funk hybrid style by Etheridge and her band. In the historical context of the development of Melissa Etheridge as a singer-songwriter, this stylistic hybridization is important to note, because the musical style and the vocal performance on this track represent a clear expansion of the work of Etheridge and her backing band from the songs of her debut album.

Etheridge turns to a more fluid songwriting structure in "You Used to Love to Dance." This is a song in which the chorus section does not contain the conventional pop-oriented, sometimes formulaic melodic hook of the most commercially successful rock songs. As a result, the piece fits more in the mold of some of Etheridge's contemporary singer-songwriters who were less rock oriented than Etheridge herself. For some listeners, the slight meandering feel of the form will create the impression that the piece was composed in an improvisatory manner, straight from the heart. Interestingly, though, the progression of the mood of the lyrics seems very much to be deliberately structured. Etheridge begins by recounting earlier times with her former lover, and the importance of the role of dancing in their relationship (but particularly for the former lover). Throughout the vast majority of the five-and-a-half-minute song, the listener easily can sense that the entire piece is about the sense of loss that Etheridge's character feels; however, at the end, Etheridge concludes by revealing that she is going to "go out tonight" and "dance 'til I get my fill." In other words, Etheridge's character is going to dance in spite of the loss, and, in fact, to recover from the loss—the dance, which symbolized what she lost when she lost her lover, is now that which she apparently believes will propel her into a future of happiness. On a deeper level, the listener can understand Etheridge's references to "the dance" as a metaphor for the dance of life, or as a metaphor for the search for love.

There are certain recordings from successful and well-known artists' careers that stand out as iconic—the songs that will forever define an artist and will remain remembered even when some of the artist's other—and sometimes better—material is long forgotten. In the case of Melissa Etheridge, one can point to "Come to My Window," "I'm the Only One," "Similar Features," and "I Want to Come Over" as perhaps four of the more iconic songs that define the best-known aspects of her work as a singer-songwriter. Although the song is not generally as iconic as some of those mentioned above, "The Angels" has remained a staple of Etheridge's performances, received a 1991 Grammy nomination for Best Rock Vocal Performance, Female, and eventually had the distinction of being Etheridge's contribution to the 2001 album *Earl Scruggs and Friends*, a tribute to the famed bluegrass banjoist and composer Scruggs. The song is notable for several reasons, not the least of which is the crossover rock-pop commercial appeal. Unlike a song such as "You Used to Love to Dance," "The Angels" is more conventional in structure, with clearly defined verses, chorus, and middle-eight sections, as well as a strong, instantly memorable melodic hook in the chorus. The song is also notable for Etheridge's integration of part of the well-known children's prayer "Now I Lay Me Down to Sleep" into the final verse. This foreshadows her more thorough integration of original and older, well-known, borrowed material in several songs on Etheridge's twenty-first-century album *A New Thought for Christmas*.

The lyrical focus of "The Angels," however, is not on the snippet of the children's prayer. The song focuses on the fate of Etheridge's character to be desperately in love with someone who is not true to her. The dysfunction in the relationship can be tied to some of the relationships that Etheridge discusses in her autobiography;[6] however, as is the case in most of her possibly autobiographical songs, Etheridge does not provide enough detail to definitively pinpoint any specific autobiographical references. While this may seem less than satisfying to the listener who wants to hear the songwriter's life story clearly played out in words and music, it gives a song such as "The Angels" a more universal reference point: it can speak for many people who have been involved in relationships in which their lover cannot remain true to them, regardless of how closely or how distantly the relationships might resemble those of Melissa Etheridge.

Despite the near-universal nature of Etheridge's theme of loss in love because of infidelity in "The Angels," it seems likely that listeners will not miss the extent to which the relationship in this song, and in the other songs on *Brave and Crazy*, either is totally dysfunctional or at the very least has some sort of dark cloud hanging over it. Although I detail this aspect of Etheridge's twentieth-century work in the Conclusions chapter, it may be helpful to consider that some psychological studies have established a connection between internalized sexual stigma that some members of the lesbian, gay, and bisexual communities feel as a result of discrimination and their minority status and difficulties in long-term relationships.[7] Perhaps this explains at least in part the popularity of Melissa Etheridge and her work within the lesbian community even years before she came out.

Although it is a gentle, acoustic guitar-based ballad, "You Can Sleep While I Drive" follows in the tradition of songs written by singer-songwriters about the reality of life on the road of a singer-songwriter, such as the songs of Jackson Browne's 1977 album *Running on Empty*. Like the title song on the Browne album, "You Can Sleep While I Drive" projects a feeling of emptiness. In Browne's work, the emptiness, the feeling that something is missing from life, tends to be felt by the first-person character Browne portrays. In the Etheridge song, it is more the lover of Etheridge's character who feels the emptiness, an emptiness that Etheridge's character detects in her lover's eyes. And this is the part of the song that seems to reflect the real story of Etheridge's life, a life in which she has found fulfillment in music (and later in motherhood), but in which her partners have drifted away from her possibly in part because of her attachment to music making.

"You Can Sleep While I Drive" was never destined to be one of Melissa Etheridge's great commercial successes, simply because the song is too slow, quiet, autobiographical sounding, and contemplative; however, it is one of Etheridge's most beautiful and artistically successful ballads. The next track on *Brave and Crazy*, "Testify," is not as successful. For one thing, some listeners might find some of the lyrical references hazy. For example, Etheridge sings about "stale headlines" and things that she has heard in the news; however, then she abruptly shifts to reflecting dramatically on a man who has made her "memories ache." Some listeners might find the identity of the man to be unclear: might he have been a former lover, a former husband, a public figure who was involved in those news stories, Etheridge's character's father? The other problem with the song is that the last line, adapted from the poet John Donne, "The bell tolls for me," hints at the self-pity and hyperbole with which Etheridge has been accused in some of her less than fully favorable reviews over the years.[8]

Etheridge returns to a more direct approach to dealing with dysfunctional relationships in "Let Me Go." In this song, her character is involved in a relationship in which she is not loved—she is desired, she is a fantasy lover, she is a "sweet temptation" for her lover, but she is not truly loved. Etheridge tells the other character that if she or he ("Let Me Go" is one of her gender-neutral songs) cannot love her, "let [her] go." The song shares in common with earlier tracks, such as "Brave and Crazy," not only the lyrical focus on wanting to get out of a dysfunctional—or even codependent—relationship, but also the musical mix of funky 16th-note-level syncopations with references to more traditional classic rock. It is almost as though the two disparate musical influences mirror the distinct differences of the characters.

The next track, "My Back Door," strikes an autobiographical-sounding note. In fact, it is the one song on *Brave and Crazy* that connects Etheridge's childhood—or that of her character—with her present. The song opens with Etheridge recalling the dreams of her childhood—that the stars she saw in the sky "cast a spell that [she was] under," and that she "was part of the earth" and thereby connected with all life throughout the world. In the chorus, however, Etheridge acknowledges that all of her dreams are "gone," and that they left her through the "back door" of the song's title. In the second stanza, Etheridge recalls falling in love, presumably for the first time. That stanza is followed by a repeat of the chorus and its reflection that the relationship ended, leaving through the "back door." In the third stanza, Etheridge reflects on her dismay, her questioning of why she has undergone these losses. The fourth stanza and the lyrical modification of the chorus that follows it are particularly interesting. In the fourth stanza, Etheridge recounts seeing people in the street, "their mouths all white and pale." Despite the appearance of the people's faces, Etheridge describes the men in the crowd as "painted proud." The references, although somewhat oblique, can easily be interpreted as the scene of a gay pride rally or parade in the post-AIDS era. Etheridge recounts that the men try to undo her dream, which could be interpreted as their reaction to a viral death sentence that, in the 1980s, was widely viewed by some people as being exclusive to the gay community. The song can also be understood in the context of an internal debate about coming out. In this interpretation, it appears that Etheridge's character might have a dream of living out her life quietly as a homosexual woman; perhaps the attention that the homosexual community received because of the AIDS epidemic and the highly visible nature of the rally that Etheridge seems to describe run counter to her character's desire to remain quiet about her sexuality.

Despite the resistance Etheridge's character encounters even as she "pick[s] up a sign" and joins the rally, she concludes in the modified version of the chorus that ends her text that she cannot let this dream "run away out [her] back door." She sings to the listener that the only way she can preserve this dream is to be vigilant: "Look out there [out the back door] every day." One can interpret the text as an early acknowledgment by Etheridge of her identity as a homosexual. Perhaps, then, the vigilance refers to her need to remind herself every day of who she is, to accept and be proud of it. By doing so, her "dream" of being able to freely and openly express her identity can come to pass. However, Etheridge's character can also be understood as a supporter of the marchers, and not necessarily as someone who is connected directly to the homosexuality of the marchers.

As one listens to *Brave and Crazy* in its running order, one can get the impression that "My Back Door" reflects back to and clarifies some of the lyrical references in earlier songs. For example, the "pride" of the "colorful" men in the street at the rally of "My Back Door" might clarify the reference to "stale headlines [and] others drenched in pride" of "Testify." If the listener senses this connection between songs, and hears the final stanza of "My Back Door" as an account of Etheridge's experience at a gay pride rally, then the reference to seeing people "marching to their drum with fear standing beside" in "Testify" is an acknowledgment of the pall that AIDS was casting over the gay community by the late 1980s.

Because "My Back Door" is so autobiographical sounding and because it is less oblique than some of the other songs on *Brave and Crazy*, it also tends to clarify the larger nature of gender references on the album and how they relate to the characters that populate the songs, as well as the possible roles that gender and sexuality play in Etheridge's real-life experience. The songs that are about love relationships, broken and dysfunctional though most of them may be, tend to be gender neutral. In other words, Etheridge does not identify her character's lovers, former lovers, or would-be lovers by gender or sexual orientation; neither does she reference any gender-role stereotypes that might infer the characters' gender identity. Interestingly, when Etheridge identifies characters as male, they are characters—either singularly or collectively—who dash, or at least try to dash, her dreams. This is true of the "men all painted proud" of "My Back Door," as well as the singular male character in "Testify." Conversely, the lone clearly female character, identified as "Barbara" in "You Can Sleep While I Drive," is supportive of Etheridge's character and her lover ("Barbara . . . says we're welcome to stay.").

Despite the fact that *Brave and Crazy* finds Etheridge and her band exploring funk-rock hybrids, some listeners may find that the ballad "You Can Sleep While I Drive" and the driving rock songs, such as "My Back Door," are the most successful and most memorable. "My Back Door" is a classic example of the Etheridge style that would propel her from being a moderately successful rock singer-songwriter to a popular culture icon within a few years of the release of *Brave and Crazy*. Although Etheridge does not play lead guitar, her distinctive acoustic rhythm guitar features prominently throughout "My Back Door." The piece includes wide dynamic shifts, which are first apparent between the quiet, introspective level of the first verse (in which Etheridge's character recounts the dreams of childhood) and the harder-edged intensity of the chorus (in which Etheridge first tells the listener that her dreams are gone forever). While Melissa Etheridge could never be lumped with the Pacific Northwest grunge scene of the time, the abrupt wide dynamic shifts, as well as the introspective lyrics of pain, certainly were a part of grunge and other alternative rock styles of the time. Therefore, even though the arrangement and general melodic, harmonic, and rhythmic style of a song such as "My Back Door" can be heard as part of a so-called classic rock continuum that included older artists such as Bruce Springsteen and Bob Seger, the song also fits squarely into what was *au courant* in 1989. And like the most commercially successful and memorable songs of Melissa Etheridge's entire career, "My Back Door" includes wide melodic contrasts between the verse and chorus sections, as well as a memorable melodic hook in the chorus.

Etheridge and her band turn to a swamp rock, funky electric blues style for the next track, "Skin Deep." Here, Etheridge's character expresses her physical desire for the would-be lover to whom she sings. She readily admits to the other character that her desire is only physical ("My love is only skin deep") and that it revolves at least in part around the other character's dark eyes.

Brave and Crazy concludes with the song "Royal Station 4/16." The reader might recall that the earlier track "You Can Sleep While I Drive" referenced Melissa Etheridge's career as a traveling singer-songwriter. "Royal Station 4/16" also does so. Here, Etheridge links the sound of trains to the sadness her character feels because of a just-ended relationship. Although the linkage of the mournful sound of trains and railway stations with sadness, lonesomeness, and so on has been a staple for country singer-songwriters from Jimmie Rodgers to Johnny Cash and beyond, this seven-minute-plus opus is not a country song. And, although the piece involves loneliness, identifies the protagonist as a guitar-playing musician, and is named after a train station, it is not really part of the folk music continuum of, say, Paul Simon's "Homeward Bound." What "Royal Station 4/16" is instead is a song that connects lyrically to the work of songwriters such as Simon, Cash, and Rodgers, but with a funky blues, folk, rock musical mix. By breaking down traditional genre boundaries, while maintaining a connection to the aesthetics of the blues, "Royal Station 4/16" seems to be a spiritual descendant of the work of the famed roots musician Bonnie Raitt. While Raitt does not come up as frequently in discussions of artists who influenced Etheridge as names such as Rod Stewart, Bruce Springsteen, Janis Joplin, and Bob Seger, it should be noted that in a 2002 interview in *Rolling Stone*, Etheridge acknowledged Raitt as an influence.[9] In the case of this song, it is not necessarily the roots-blues music with which Bonnie Raitt is so closely associated that comes to mind as much as the more general ability of Raitt to defy genre and stylistic boundaries, sometimes even by combining what might appear on the surface to be mutually exclusive styles. Of all of the stylistic combinations and hybridizations on *Brave and Crazy*, "Royal Station 4/16" is perhaps the most difficult to pigeonhole, so rich are the stylistic references.

If one were asked what the album *Brave and Crazy* is about, the answer might reasonably be that it revolves around the general theme of dysfunctional relationships and dysfunctional lives. In some songs, Etheridge's character cannot resist the urge to remain in a dysfunctional relationship, in some cases her character delivers an ultimatum to a lover, in some cases her character tries to reassure a lover who is not entirely fulfilled in the relationship, and in some cases Etheridge's character finds a way to work through the pain that she feels after a relationship ended. In the songs in which there is an ongoing connection between two lovers, the relationship is never entirely well rounded. For example, the relationship may revolve entirely around physicality and lack any sort of spiritual or emotional component. Musically, *Brave and Crazy* includes Etheridge's take on the so-called classic rock style; however, it also includes several funk-rock-blues hybrid pieces. The entire package is not as fully consistent and integrated as Etheridge's later more commercially and more critically successful albums, and it suggests at least a bit of grappling with just exactly how Etheridge was going to define herself as a composer, lyricist, and arranger.

NEVER ENOUGH (1992)

The female singer-songwriters who emerged in the late 1980s and the 1990s tended to suffer from somewhat mixed success in the recording industry, despite some strong, well-deserved critical approval, a strong live performance presence, and a solid fan base. That is to say, unlike already established musicians who maintained a fairly regular schedule of releases, for a variety of reasons artists such as Melissa Etheridge, Tracy Chapman, and Suzanne Vega, all well-respected and well-received musicians, sometimes went two or even three years between album releases. For that reason, and possibly for others, artists such as these did not enjoy commercial success in the late 1980s and early 1990s equal to their fan popularity and critical reception; nor did they enjoy the degree of commercial success afforded to the pop divas of the day. When Etheridge's *Never Enough* appeared in 1992, almost three years after *Brave and Crazy*, it was clear that Etheridge had not been stagnant as a songwriter between releases. In fact, *Never Enough* exhibited clear lyrical and musical development beyond what Etheridge already had achieved on her first two albums. As *All Music Guide* critic Johnny Loftus wrote, "The songs were challenging not only from a musicianship and songwriting standpoint, but also as the next steps in Etheridge's still-young career. It was a risk to issue a record like *Never Enough* after a three-year hiatus and into a market that might have expected 'Bring Me Some MORE Water.' "[10] To put it another way, Etheridge continued to redefine herself as an artist. Ultimately, listeners might have different reactions to *Never Enough*, especially after Etheridge achieved widespread fame and notoriety within a year. In retrospect, to fans accustomed to the more focused stylistic range on Etheridge's fourth album, *Yes I Am*, *Never Enough* might seem to be a bit too wide ranging. On the other hand, while the album can leave the listener with a sense of further grappling with self-definition for Etheridge (and her coproducer Kevin McCormick), the album proves that Etheridge could convincingly write and perform in a variety of styles.

While *Never Enough* did not perform on the album charts substantially better than had Etheridge's first two albums, the single release of the song "Dance without Sleeping" marked Melissa Etheridge's first appearance on the Adult Contemporary charts. This suggests that her continuing redefinition was broadening her audience at least somewhat. Topping that, however, is the fact that Etheridge won a 1993 Grammy for Best Rock Vocal Performance, Female, for the track "Ain't It Heavy."

Never Enough opens with the aforementioned "Ain't It Heavy," a straight-ahead rocker in the mold of the Rolling Stones. In fact, a few of the licks that lead guitarist Steuart Smith incorporates come right out of the late 1960s/early 1970s Keith Richards repertoire, including one figure that seems to have been inspired by a key figure in "Honky Tonk Women." The addition of open harmony vocals in the chorus sections, too, would not have been out of place in the work of the Stones' Mick Jagger and Keith Richards. Similarly, the harmonic progression of the chorus, B major (V), A major (IV), E major (I), is somewhat uncustomarily simple for Etheridge (who tends to include minor chords and added-note/suspended chords in her compositions) and recalls the straight-ahead rock songs of the Rolling Stones. Etheridge's lyrical theme of being on the prowl for a late night sexual encounter likewise falls in the tradition of Jagger and Richards's more provocative work of the late 1960s and the 1970s.

Despite the undeniable ties to the rock-and-roll style of the Rolling Stones, "Ain't It Heavy" is highly effective. Perhaps most notable is the way in which Etheridge, her band, and her coproducer Kevin McCormick use dramatic volume contrast to vary the intensity level. Specifically, after a gradual buildup in volume, fullness, and intensity from the first verse, through the first statement of the chorus, through the second verse and second statement of the chorus, the entire texture thins suddenly approximately two minutes, 43 seconds into the four-minute-and-24-seconds song. From that point the intensity level again increases until the final fadeout, which occurs very near the end of the song. Whether by intuition, accident, or design, the sudden thinning of the texture and decrease in the dynamic level takes place approximately 61.7 percent of the way through the song, curiously close to the point of the classical Golden Mean of ancient Greek aesthetic significance.

While the song "Ain't It Heavy" falls easily within the classic rock tradition of which Melissa Etheridge perhaps was the prototypical artist of the time, the second track on *Never Enough*, "2001," incorporates the "industrial percussion," minimalistic and edgy electric guitar, and syncopated at the 16th-note-level rhythmic feel of some of the period's alternative rock. Etheridge paints dark images of the state of individual people and the world in general of the early 1990s. She then asks the listener to "wake [her] up when we hit 2001." Although the two pieces share virtually nothing of consequence musically, one might be reminded of Prince's song of a decade before that projected forward to the end of the millennium, the well-known "1999."

Interestingly, both Prince and Etheridge present the listener with some mixed signals about what to expect leading up to and extending beyond the end of the twentieth century and the beginning of the twenty-first century. In the Prince song, the year 1999 represents being on the cusp of the biblical rapture, the end of the world. Even so (or, perhaps because of that), it is a time for partying. The eerie mix of world destruction and celebration presented Prince's listeners of the early 1980s with questions with which they had to deal. Similarly, Etheridge also raises questions, mostly suggested by her musical arrangement. In her lyrics, she paints a gloomy, fear-filled view of the world of the early 1990s that can only be described as a dystopia. The lyrics, when taken alone, suggest that the dawn of the new millennium might offer the hope that the "social suicide," the "homicide," the "fear," and the "dark age" of the late twentieth century, might give way to something better. The percussion, vocal looping track, and general tone color of the musical setting, however, sound as though they are supposed to be understood as futuristic. The dissonance, the edginess, and the mechanically inspired rhythms, if they are heard by the listener as representative of what the future might hold in store, evoke a twenty-first century more in keeping with such futuristic dystopian films as *Soylent Green* and *Blade Runner* than with the dawn of a bright new age of understanding, peace, and harmony.

The dissonance between the promise of the twenty-first century suggested by the lyrics and the more sinister implications suggested by the music of "2001" may tend to force some listeners to question just what Etheridge truly foretells for the future. And, that just may be the point of the song: to force the listener to consider the problems of the day and how they might be overcome. Curiously, Etheridge's request to be woken up in 2001 suggests not only a desire to be disengaged from the problems of the present but also a complete disengagement with any solutions that might be developed between 1992 and 2001. Given Melissa Etheridge's social consciousness and advocacy for social justice, this disengagement might seem unexpected—strange even. Some Etheridge fans might hear this uncharacteristic inaction as another attempt to raise questions among listeners. By presenting a litany of late twentieth-century social issues and then taking the stance that her character does, Etheridge seems to be inviting the listener to take the opposite track.

The next song, "Dance without Sleeping," is a collaboration of Etheridge, bassist and coproducer Kevin McCormick, and percussionist Mauricio Fritz Lewak. It is a more pop-oriented track than its predecessors on *Never Enough*, which probably accounts for the single release of the song's appearance on the Adult Contemporary charts. Like the prototypical Top 40 pop song, the melodic hook of the chorus is strong, and the melodic contours of the verse and chorus sections contrast, resulting in a chorus that stands out and tends to capture the listener's attention. Adding to the pop nature of the song is a decided muting of Etheridge's tendency toward vocal edginess and more rock-oriented rawness.

The lyrical message of "danc[ing] until I think I can overcome" reflects back to the *Brave and Crazy* track "You Used to Love to Dance." In both songs, Etheridge's character views dancing—or uses the metaphor of the dance—as a means of overcoming adversity, a means of achieving wholeness. From a musical standpoint, the two songs differ so widely that it would be entirely possible for the listener not to make the connection. And, despite the lyrical connection between these two songs, this is not a metaphor to which Etheridge returns frequently as a writer.

In the next song, "Place Your Hand," Etheridge presents the listener with the fourth discernibly different musical style in four tracks. Because the CD booklet for *Never Enough* contains the lyrics of the songs, it seems likely that listeners would take more than just a cursory look at the booklet. It is interesting to note that, just as Etheridge delves into a variety of subject matter and musical styles on the songs of the album, the 11 photographs in the album booklet present her in a wide diversity of ways. The booklet includes studio poses, photographs from live performances, photographs in which Etheridge appears alternately detached, engaged, chic, coy, focused on her guitar, and so on. Between the 11 photographs in the booklet and the 1 on the CD itself, Etheridge is shown literally from head to toe (the photograph on the CD itself focuses on her shoes). Therefore, whether by kismet or design, the entire package presents a far broader view of Melissa Etheridge as a singer-songwriter and as a pop culture figure than either of her first two albums. This can be something of a double-edged sword, as it might also suggest that Melissa Etheridge was not entirely clearly defined as an artist at this point in her career.

As previously mentioned, "Place Your Hand" is the first ballad on *Never Enough*. The arrangement is uncustomarily intimate for Melissa Etheridge, including instrumental contributions solely from Etheridge on 12-string acoustic guitar and Dermot Mulroney on cello. In this evocative song extolling the importance of a touch from a friend or lover, Etheridge's guitar accompaniment fits squarely within the acoustic singer-songwriter tradition. The suspended fourths and suspended seconds sound thoroughly contemporary; however, they connect the song to the work of 1970s introspective acoustic guitar-playing singer-songwriters such as James Taylor. Etheridge's guitar work on the track allows the listener to appreciate her playing to a far greater extent than in her more numerous classic rock-style recordings, especially since her finger picking is so rarely heard this clearly.

Although Melissa Etheridge's bread and butter as a performer generally revolves around so-called classic rock and heartland rock, as she has continued to develop the styles from predecessors such as Bruce Springsteen, John Mellencamp, and Bob Seger, the song "Must Be Crazy for Me" integrates touches of hip-hop-influenced double-time rhythms and touches of funk within the context of Etheridge's more characteristic style. Etheridge's character observes that the person to whom she sings does not like her car, tries to avoid her, resists her physical moves, and so on. To Etheridge's character, this behavior suggests that the other person "must be crazy for [her]." Although the lyrical theme of the proverbial playing hard to get is not especially noteworthy, the recording features infectious rhythms and an easy-to-remember tune that is based on short, narrow-range phrases.

While the music of the next song, "Meet Me in the Back," is not as immediately pop oriented and accessible as that of "Must Be Crazy for Me," the lyrics are more intriguing. Here, Etheridge's character invites another to "meet [her] in the back," presumably in a back room, or perhaps in an alley outside a dance club, for a sexual encounter. The music conveys a sense of urgency and nervousness of which the lyrics provide only a hint. As tends to be the case with Etheridge's songs, the gender of her character's would-be lover is left unstated; however, the lyrics hint at the possibility that the object of her character's desire for a casual sexual encounter is male, as Etheridge mentions the need for "protection." Characteristically, Etheridge's character lets the listener—and the other party in the song—know that her desire is purely physical; she discounts the possibility that any of her relationships can result in love and emotional attachment.

The next track, the ballad "The Boy Feels Strange," also reflects upon the impossibility of emotional attachment. On the surface level, Etheridge's lyrics find her character reflecting on the lack of emotional response she receives from a man who could be a friend or past lover; the exact nature of the relationship is murky. Just what it is that causes the male character's "miles and miles of pain," his "change," and his emotional distance is never revealed.

Taken as a pair of related songs, "Meet Me in the Back" and "The Boy Feels Strange" can be understood as an expression of the futility of male-female relationships for Etheridge's characters, or perhaps for Etheridge herself. In fact, it is possible to understand the new difficulty that Etheridge's character has in making emotional connection with the male character in "The Boy Feels Strange" as being a result not so much of the fact that "the boy has changed," as the lyrics state on the surface level, but really as a result of the fact that Etheridge's character's perception of "the boy" has changed. This might not be the most obvious interpretation of the song's lyrics, but there are some hints at the possibility of this interpretation. Most notably, in the third stanza, it is when Etheridge's character initiates physical contact with the male character that she senses that he "feels strange." The listener is left with the question of whether Etheridge's character senses some undefined change in the male character, or if she has come to some sort of new self-knowledge that makes him seem different, strange, inaccessible, or even less physically desirable than he used to seem.

Regardless of how the listener interprets the lyrics—who changed and in what way—the musical arrangement of "The Boy Feels Strange" supports the sense of distance and emotional detachment of the lyrics. The rest of the Melissa Etheridge band (save for lead guitarist Steuart Smith) supports Etheridge's voice and acoustic guitar; however, the texture is thin enough that the focus is always on Etheridge and her voice. The fact that bassist Kevin McCormick, percussionist Mauricio Fritz Lewak, and keyboardist Scott Thurston provide such a stark backdrop can be interpreted as a reflection of the detachment that runs through the song's lyrics. Most of the melodic phrases are low in Etheridge's vocal range and are sung quietly, which some listeners might interpret as support for the sense of resignation contained in the lyrics.

The next track on *Never Enough*, "Keep It Precious," finds Etheridge portraying a character whose relationship is ending. In this ballad, though, Etheridge's character and the "love" and "friend" whom she addresses seem to have separated amicably. Exactly what calls the other character away is left unstated; however, Etheridge's lyrics include nothing to suggest that anything other than a mutual understanding that the relationship—which in the past had involved the good and the bad—must end and that the characters must move on with their lives. Etheridge's character asks her former lover and (presumably) continuing friend to "keep [the memories of their relationship] precious."

Scott Thurston's keyboards in "Keep It Precious" are atmospheric in the beginning of the song, and suggest what might otherwise have been written for orchestral strings. As the first stanza moves into the refrain, the intensity level builds. Ultimately, the musical arrangement and tone colors bear a passing resemblance to the big, anthemic ballads of a band such as U2. That being said, "Keep It Precious" has a very interesting overall musical shape. Like some of Melissa Etheridge's other songs from her first three albums, this one includes sudden, wide dynamic changes. However, unlike the bulk of her work from this period, "Keep It Precious" includes an extended coda section. This lengthy extension—which sometimes is labeled the fadeout—lasts for nearly three minutes, certainly sizable considering that the entire song lasts approximately six and a quarter minutes. Unlike what is done in the conventional studio fadeout, in "Keep It Precious" Etheridge and her band create part of the diminuendo. And, in addition to decreasing the volume level, they thin out the texture, such that the ending of the song moves toward the atmospheric feeling of the opening. It may be dangerous to read a great deal into the possible emotional meanings of purely musical phenomena—such as a decrease of dynamic level, a thinning of texture, and an emphasis on ethereal synthesizer tones—because different people may understand the extramusical associations differently. That being said, the high level of intensity to which the music rises near the conclusion of each stanza might be understood to represent the intensity of the pain that the characters feel with losing what they once shared, and the fact that the song dies away might be understood as a representation of resignation, or a realization of the inevitability of the end of the relationship.

Etheridge continues to work with the same general theme in "The Letting Go," but with some important emotional variations. In "Keep It Precious," the wish of Etheridge's character was for her partner to cherish the memory of the couple's time together and the hills and valleys of the relationship they shared. Etheridge clearly conveys the fact that the two will remain friends. In "The Letting Go," Etheridge's character informs her opposite that "the letting go has taken place." In other words, she simply informs her lover that she has fallen out of love. Reading the lyrics without hearing the music might give those who open the CD booklet the sense that Etheridge's character has lost the ability to express any emotion. So, while "Keep It Precious" is about holding onto the memories, holding onto what can remain of the relationship given Etheridge's partner's new circumstances and new home, "The Letting Go" is about the death of any hope for any sort of emotional connection in the future.

Kevin McCormick collaborated with Etheridge in writing the album's final track, "It's for You." Including this song, *Never Enough* contains nine songs that deal with relationships between lovers, ex-lovers, or would-be lovers; the only song that ventures out of that general subject matter is "2001," which deals with more globally defined challenges and social ills. The first eight relationship-oriented songs on the album all revolve around relationships that have ended, are in the process of ending, or are in some way incomplete (e.g., a relationship that is built solely on physical attraction and desire [or just plain lust] with no emotional bond). In "It's for You," coauthors Etheridge and McCormick do not offer complete closure or a complete sense that Etheridge's character will necessarily live happily ever after (to use an old saw); however, they do present Etheridge with a character who is at least fully in the moment with the object of her desire. Still, Etheridge makes it clear that her partner for the night "is not [her] lover," which suggests that this is a somewhat casual encounter. Etheridge also tells her partner that she will be "1,000 miles away" the following day. Curiously, this is the clearest reference to Etheridge's life as a traveling musician on *Never Enough*. This fact helps to differentiate the album from its predecessor, *Brave and Crazy*, an album that included several even more clearly articulated references to Etheridge's profession and the amount of travel that it demands.

Drummer Mauricio Fritz Lewak incorporates 16th-note-level syncopations, although not to the extent that he does on some of the album's early tracks; therefore, the possible influence of hip-hop and alternative rock is more muted on "It's for You" than it was earlier on the album. Despite the accessible, pop nature of the song, the tempo of "It's for You" is on the moderate side of fast. Had the song been performed as quickly as it might have been, were it intended to be a radio hit, some of the sincerity of the lyrics might have been lost.

Over the course of her career, Melissa Etheridge has made it a standard practice to thank her fans, her family, her partners, her manager, and her coproducers in the liner notes of her albums. Significantly, of her immediate family (parents and sister), the only individual that she has singled out for special acknowledgment is her father. The last page of the CD booklet of *Never Enough* bears the inscription, all capitalized, "THIS ALBUM IS DEDICATED TO MY FATHER WITH ALL MY LOVE."[11] Etheridge's father had passed away shortly before the recording of the album; he was one member of Etheridge's immediate family who was accepting of Etheridge's homosexuality, as she later discussed in her autobiography.[12] The album *Never Enough* found Melissa Etheridge expanding her musical stylistic vocabulary somewhat over her work on her self-titled debut and *Brave and Crazy*. Perhaps most noticeably, the album contains a touch of mildly avant-garde experimentation, a higher proportion of ballads, and elements of alternative rock and hip-hop. But, was this by accident or design? The CD booklet for *Never Enough* includes 11 photographs of Etheridge, and the CD itself contains a 12th. Between the 12 photographs, Etheridge appears engaging, a bit elusive, coy, thoroughly absorbed with playing the guitar, smiling, in motion on stage, and posing statue-like with little overt expression. She is shown literally from head to toe. This packaging suggests a variety of identities for Melissa Etheridge. Lyrically, *Never Enough* expanded somewhat on Etheridge's work on her first two albums, and included one song with overt social observations, as well as several tracks that can be interpreted as explorations of the subject of discovery of one's sexual identity. While *Never Enough* and its songs helped to expand Melissa Etheridge's audience somewhat, it might seem to some listeners as a little too broad musically and perhaps a little too narrow lyrically to stand with her best work. While Etheridge expanded her audience base, made some inroads with critics, and continued to expand her musical and lyrical range through her first three albums, she still had not quite become a pop culture icon; that would come quickly in the next phase of her career.

Yes, I Am

In this phase of Melissa Etheridge's career she went from being a well-liked, critically respected rock singer-songwriter with stylistic ties to predecessors such as Bruce Springsteen, Janis Joplin, Rod Stewart, Bob Seger, and John Mellencamp, to being a popular culture icon.

There had been speculation among Etheridge's fans that she might be homosexual; however, until she made a casual announcement at a January 1993 gay party that celebrated the inauguration of U.S. President Bill Clinton and acknowledged her sexuality, Etheridge's sexual orientation had not generally been known. It must be remembered that the world of early 1993 had recently witnessed the coming out of Etheridge's contemporary and fellow singer-songwriter k.d. lang. Interestingly though, it would be several years before other celebrities of Etheridge and lang's generation—most notably, Ellen Degeneres and Rosie O'Donnell—would acknowledge their homosexuality. At the time of her announcement, Etheridge was in a long-term relationship with actress Julie Cypher, a relationship in which Cypher would eventually carry the couple's two children, Bailey Jean and Beckett (both fathered by sperm donor David Crosby), and a relationship that would end in the early twenty-first century. Etheridge gained public notoriety because of her relationship with Cypher and the identity of their children's father as the famous rock musician Crosby. However, during the time period between her public announcement and the end of the Etheridge-Cypher relationship, Melissa Etheridge became an outspoken advocate for equal rights, including parental rights, for gays and lesbians. Interestingly, much of her music from the period was more widely accessible than her earlier songs, more stylistically focused, and more reflective of Etheridge's sexual identity. So, while Etheridge cemented her relationship with the largely female and lesbian audiences that she already had developed before 1993, her announcement did little to narrow her audience; her growth as a singer, songwriter, guitarist, and producer actually seems to have helped to broaden her audience. The first album that she released after her January 1993 announcement, the provocatively titled *Yes I Am*, was one of the most notable albums of the entire decade. While the albums that followed in this phase of Melissa Etheridge's career did not achieve the commercial or critical acclaim of *Yes I Am*, *Your Little Secret* and *Breakdown* found Etheridge breaking new ground musically and lyrically.

Yes, I Am[1] (1993)

Between 1988 when Melissa Etheridge's self-titled debut album was released and 1992, she established herself as a hard-rocking powerful singer-songwriter, a writer whose songs about relationships could be understood on multiple levels because of her tendency to remain gender neutral in her lyrics. On Etheridge's 1993 album *Yes I Am*, she coproduced for the first time with the British producer and recording engineer Hugh Padgham, a figure perhaps most widely recognized for his work with the Police and Sting. The Etheridge-Padgham production team balanced power and popular accessibility such that *Yes I Am* brought Etheridge's music to a wider audience than had any of Etheridge's previous recordings. In fact, two of the album's tracks, "I'm the Only One" and "Come to My Window," not only were major hits, they remain among Etheridge's most popular songs into the second decade of the twenty-first century.

In her work that preceded *Yes I Am*, Etheridge focused on dysfunctional relationships. The edginess and power of her voice as well as the full electric guitar sound of many of her recordings conveyed a sense of raw, gut expression precipitated by the disastrous breakups about which she sang. Whether or not her songs truly were autobiographical, this raw expressiveness made them sound autobiographical to her fans. The opening track on *Yes I Am*, "I'm the Only One," is a highly effective example of the same degree of expression with the same sort of subject matter. Here, Etheridge's character reacts to her lover telling her that she or he (Etheridge remains gender neutral throughout the album in the first-person songs) has found another woman. Etheridge's text includes references to "razors a rippin' ... my heart apart" and similarly vivid images of the pain that her character feels. Her melody features a wide pitch range and some figures that suggest alternatively blues and country influences. The arrangement and performance include wide dynamic contrasts and an at times driving, electric guitar-based rock sound. While "I'm the Only One" cannot be characterized as a true example of grunge style, the gut-wrenching lyrics and the wide dynamic contrasts are in the same ballpark as the work of the Seattle-based proponents of grunge. One of the strengths of "I'm the Only One" is Etheridge's use of a catchy, memorable melodic phrase in the chorus as she assures her former lover that she is "the only one who'll drown in my desire for you."

Despite the instantly memorable nature of some of Etheridge's images and metaphors, the emotional intensity of her lyrics—and her manner of reinforcing the intensity in her singing—were something of a double-edged sword, particularly among music critics. For example, as early as 1990, Stephen Holden of the *New York Times* found favor with Etheridge as a live performer, but described her songs as "melodramatic."[2] Similarly, *Entertainment Weekly*'s Chris Willman wrote that Etheridge's first post–*Yes I Am* album, *Your Little Secret*, pointed "in just one direction: the next meeting of Overstaters Anonymous."[3] Etheridge's fans, on the other hand, tend to hear what some critics seem to believe to be hyperbole, to be very real expression of raw, intense emotion.

In the world of Melissa Etheridge songs, characters often are drawn into relationships and intense feelings of love and desire against their better judgment: physical passion and the heart override the characters' minds. Such is the case in "If I Wanted To." In this song, Etheridge expounds on all of the things (e.g., "dance with the devil on a Saturday night," "swear," "turn mountains into sand") that she would be able to do if she set her mind to it. The one thing that her character is unable to do, though, is to resist love. As she sings the chorus out in the most powerful part of her vocal range, it is easy to get the impression that in the realm of love, Etheridge's character is akin to a lemming being led to a cliff. As is the case with "I'm the Only One," this song combines pop melodic sensibilities with a more rock-oriented arrangement and guitar and vocal timbres. Unlike "I'm the Only One," however, "If I Wanted To" is not entirely successful: the melody is just not as memorable, and the auxiliary percussion seems out of place for the song's overall style.

One of the more curious features of *Yes I Am* is that the album is frontloaded with its best-known material: the first and third tracks were the album's successful singles. Like "I'm the Only One," "Come to My Window" is an impassioned cry for love. As a single track, the song was supported by a video that starred actress Juliette Lewis. In both the audio-only song and the video version, "Come to My Window" is a song that can be interpreted in a variety of ways. On one level, Etheridge's character could simply be hoping that someone to whom she is attracted passes by her window. However, the fact that she remains behind the window throughout the song raises several possibilities. For example, perhaps the character is homebound, perhaps an emotional problem makes her unable to face the outside world, perhaps Etheridge's character is enabling a voyeur, and so on. In the song's gutwrenching video, an emotionally disturbed or mentally ill character—portrayed by Lewis—paces in a small room, perhaps in an institution, alternately ranting, curled in a fetal position under an institutional bed, and writing on the wall. It is a scene of obsession and of stark and utter desperation, which is heightened by the fact that Lewis's character wears bandages around her wrists, which the viewer might reasonably assume that she cut in a suicide attempt. While detailed critical analysis of the video per se is outside of the realm of this study, suffice it to say that the brief opening spoken introduction (which is not included as part of the album track) generated debate about sexual orientation, the continuing lack of acceptance of gays and lesbians by society at large, and the emotional and psychological damage that this lack of acceptance can bring. In arrangement and performance, "Come to My Window" remains a quintessential example of Etheridge's use of sharp dynamic and stylistic contrasts. At the beginning of the song, Etheridge's voice is quiet and pleading; however, later she begs in desperation. Etheridge's performance earned her a Grammy Award for Best Rock Vocal Performance, Female.

Although most of the songs on *Yes I Am* come from the first-person viewpoint, there are notable exceptions. Etheridge plays the observer on "Silent Legacy" and "All American Girl," the fourth and sixth tracks on the album. The lives of the characters about whom she writes in these songs, however, are no less tragic than the lives of her first-person characters. In "Silent Legacy," Etheridge observes a woman who has been used by various men throughout her life. While some of the lines in the text are framed as questions, there is a distance to the song that suggests that Etheridge asks these rhetorically, from afar. The character she observes seems to personify all women who have been subjugated and sexually objectified by men. According to Etheridge, the cycle can be broken only by means of love, strength, and "refus[ing] to hand down" fear. She entrusts mothers with the charge to instill values in their children that will break the cycle of subjugation. Significantly, Etheridge sings the first two stanzas in the lower tessitura of her voice; however, she leaps upward an octave for the third stanza, in which she contrasts the subservient role that the woman played with the "alive" feeling that has been put down so much that now she feels "rage."

The other third-person song on *Yes I Am*, "All American Girl," is a hard-rocking riff-based song about a young woman who has sacrificed her dreams for a job that "pay[s] the bills." Etheridge equates the death of the character's dreams with her existence "in this man's world." The woman's lover left her without explanation, and her "best friend told her he's HIV." As an indictment of patronizing men and a male-dominated workplace and society, it is not as effective as "Silent Legacy," mostly because the HIV/AIDS piece of the puzzle tends to shift the focus near the end of the song. And, because the reference comes so late in the song, it, unfortunately, can be heard as an afterthought.

The song that separates the two third-person-voice tracks, "I Will Never Be the Same," represents a different sort of the song of loss for Etheridge. Here, she is more oblique than usual about the relationship between her character and the woman or man about whom she sings. Whether friend or lover, the other character touched Etheridge's character deeply, as evidenced by the title line. Because of the slow, gentle ballad setting, this song can be understood as a bittersweet recollection of the time the two characters shared together as well as the lasting influence of Etheridge's friend or lover. Musically, the piece stands apart from the rock-oriented material on *Yes I Am*, and the thinner texture comes closer to the confessional singer-songwriter style than the album's other songs. Rhetorically, too, it stands apart: the sense of resignation contrasts with the passion, assertiveness, and defiance that mark the album's other songs.

Perhaps mostly because of the album's timing—*Yes I Am* appeared just before Etheridge ended speculation about her sexual orientation—the album's title has been taken as a confirmation of sexual identity. However, the title can be understood as simply the name of one of the album's songs. The title track, like Etheridge's other first-person relationship songs from the start of her career up to this album, is in fact gender neutral. Neither do the lyrics of "Yes I Am" include any overt reference to sexual identity. Unlike the other relationship songs on the album, though, "Yes I Am" is a declaration of love and desire, absent the end-of-relationship intrigue that pervades the other songs. Perhaps the most interesting part of the piece, however, is Etheridge's treatment of musical meter. The verses tend to sound off-kilter: the rhythmic patterns of the percussion, guitars, and vocals all provide the listener with somewhat conflicting information about exactly where the downbeats are. Significantly, in the chorus sections—where Etheridge makes the title's declaration in response to any questions that her partner may have about Etheridge's commitment to be a lover—the 12/8 meter comes into focus. It is an intriguing example of text painting.

In the briefest song on *Yes I Am*, "Resist," Etheridge revisits the theme of "If I Wanted To." In "Resist," she paints her character as one who almost eagerly defies convention and others' expectations; however, she "cannot resist" the "forbidden" yearning she feels "for another burning soul." It might seem to be a calculated risk to include thematically related songs on the same album: listeners potentially could hear the lyrical sentiments as too repetitive. The musical settings, however, are quite different: while "If I Wanted To" includes wide dynamic contrasts and a melody that moves in the direction of pop music, "Resist" is a more thoroughly driving and more melodically concise rock song.

Etheridge returns to the role of the pained ex-lover in "Ruins." The premise of this song is that Etheridge's character was so fully damaged by a dysfunctional relationship that she now exists "in the ruins" and has yet to fight her way out of pain. While Etheridge's use of unexpected minor harmonies and her melodic sense is strong on "Ruins," the piece's synthesizer-heavy arrangement does not wear as well as the guitar-based arrangements of the earlier songs on the album.

The slow, introspective song "Talking to My Angel" is a better match to coproducers Etheridge and Hugh Padgham's arrangement. Here, James Fearnley plays the accordion, an unusual instrumental choice in the world of early 1990s pop music. In the text, Etheridge's character talks to her angel about the mistreatment and social isolation she has experienced. The angel assures her that "it's alright," effectively bringing a sense of closure not only to the feelings that Etheridge expresses in this song but also to the focus on despair of most of the album's previous tracks. In her autobiography, Etheridge writes that "Dad has always been my angel" and includes the lyrics of "Talking to My Angel" on a page that features a photograph of Etheridge with her father.[4] Just as Etheridge's character confides her deepest feelings to her unnamed angel in the lyrics of the song, Etheridge confided in her father as she was ready to leave Kansas for Los Angeles back in the mid-1980s. According to Etheridge, when she told her father that "I'm a homosexual," he responded "that although he didn't understand it, if it made [her] happy, he was fine about it." Etheridge concludes the story by writing that her father's acceptance and support helped her feel significantly more secure about her sexuality.[5]

In retrospect, it appears that Melissa Etheridge's *Yes I Am* became famous in the minds of some listeners for the wrong reasons. There is a universality to most of the songs that transcends gender and sexual orientation, but this became lost among all of the speculation about Etheridge's personal life. The beauty of much of Etheridge's writing on *Yes I Am* is that it can speak to and for so many listeners who have lost at love. The musical settings steer in the direction of pop music more than Etheridge's earlier recordings, but for the most part the album resists sounding overly slick. As a rock singer, Etheridge was one of the best of the late 1980s and early 1990s, and *Yes I Am* remains a powerful example of her talents as a writer and singer and as one of the strongest artists in the rock music genre during this time period.

Your Little Secret (1995)

In the wake of the success of *Yes I Am*, Melissa Etheridge, who already had built a strong following as a live performer, became a major concert attraction. Perhaps the best evidence of this was her performance at the 1994 Woodstock II festival, a venue that was a far cry from the clubs at which she performed less than a decade earlier. However, the success of *Yes I Am* and its singles proved to be something of a double-edged sword. It would be difficult for any artist to follow that kind of success with something that would match or exceed it. Etheridge, even going back to the beginning of her career as a recording artist, was not one to take the simple route and offer her fans more of the same recipe that had brought her success on any level. Therefore, just as nothing on *Brave and Crazy* or *Never Enough* represented a duplication of the same recipe that made "Bring Me Some Water" a commercial success, *Your Little Secret*, which followed the hugely successful *Yes I Am*, found Etheridge, her backing band, and her coproducer moving in new directions. Ironically, although *Your Little Secret* was not as commercially or critically successful as *Yes I Am*, it represents Melissa Etheridge's first complete artistic statement that fully addresses her sexuality. The lack of gender references that had marked the bulk of her work through 1993 (as well as much of her post–*Your Little Secret* work) gave way to songs in which the objects of her characters' desires clearly are female, and in which Etheridge addresses sexual orientation in other contexts as well.

Your Little Secret arguably is the first Melissa Etheridge album that can fully be appreciated on different levels of structure. Specifically, it can be understood as a collection of 10 individual songs—much like Etheridge's previous albums—and it can be understood as a complete overview of the progression of Etheridge's self-awareness, acceptance, and disclosure of her sexuality. In other words, *Your Little Secret* was the most concept-album-like opus of Melissa Etheridge's career up to that point. Let us first consider the album primarily as a collection of 10 individual—but connected—songs.

The album opens with its title track, a song that is typical of Etheridge's compositions on *Your Little Secret*, in that although the meaning of the lyrics is open to some interpretation, it is clearer than in her previous songs. Etheridge portrays a character who realizes that another woman is giving her the eye and is interested in her. The catch is that the other character is already in a relationship with someone else. Although the other character is interested in cheating on her partner—Etheridge sings, "One sugar ain't enough for you"—Etheridge's character has no interest in starting an illicit relationship, despite how attractive the other woman is ("I like the way you look"). Etheridge's character acknowledges that she used to just like the other character, apparently an autobiographical reference to her the fleeting relationships that she had during her nonmonogamous pre–Julie Cypher life. However, her character's rejection of the other woman suggests that a change that has come not only over Etheridge's character but possibly over Etheridge herself.

Although the rhetorical scheme of some of the songs of *Your Little Secret* contrast with the gender-neutral songs of *Yes I Am*, the coproduction team of Hugh Padgham and Melissa Etheridge instill the harder-rocking songs—such as "Your Little Secret"—and the louder more intense sections of songs that include dramatic textural contrasts with a power, edginess, and sonic impact that carries forth from Etheridge's 1993 *pièce de résistance*. In fact, if anything, songs such as "Your Little Secret" and "I Want to Come Over" are even more dramatic than the bulk of *Yes I Am*.

Musically, the title track of *Your Little Secret* is not without irony, whether intended or unintended. The melody at the beginning of the chorus, which opens with the line "I like the way you look," moves from scale-step three up to scale-step five and then back down again. In terms of melodic shape, rhythm, and the fact that the musical phrases opens a section, this tune bears more than a passing resemblance to the melody of the start of the verses of the old 1960s Wayne Fontana and the Mindbenders' hit "The Game of Love." The irony is that the melodic phrase to which Etheridge sets her acknowledgment of the Sapphic desires of her opposite in "Your Little Secret" so closely resembles the melody to which the line "The purpose of a man is to love a woman, and the purpose of a woman is to love a man" is set in "The Game of Love." Etheridge seems not to have made reference to any resemblance between "The Game of Love" and "Your Little Secret" in any of her interviews or in her autobiography, so it is unclear to what extent the melodic resemblance and the resulting irony is intentional.

The second track, "I Really Like You," continues the focus on a hard-rocking style. Here, Etheridge returns to the gender-neutral style that marked the bulk of her pre–*Your Little Secret* work. As a result, the person to whom her character expresses her affection could be widely interpreted, unless the listener reads the sexual orientation of Etheridge herself into the text. What is more important about the text from a structural standpoint is the fact that Etheridge's character finds herself to be so similar to her counterpart in this song. The reader might recall that the album's opening track, "Your Little Secret," also compares the woman who desires Etheridge's character with Etheridge's character at some point in the past. The thematic strand of similarity—or compatibility—of characters runs in and out of several songs throughout *Your Little Secret* and for some listeners might give the album a greater feeling of structural coherence than Etheridge's previous collections.

Although it does not directly relate to the song "I Really Like You," it is also worth noting that other musical and lyrical threads connect various songs over the course of the running order of *Your Little Secret*. For example, specific times of day are mentioned in the lyrics of "An Unusual Kiss" and "Change." Similarly, the subject of a change in one's life that results from self-awareness links the songs "Change" and "I Could Have Been You." Likewise, Etheridge's characters in "I Really Like You," "Nowhere to Go," and "Shriner's Park" invite the person that she addresses into her car. And, an automobile also figures prominently in "All the Way to Heaven." Another automobile, albeit a taxi, also plays a role in "An Unusual Kiss." On the musical side of things, Mark Browne adds a characteristic sliding touch on electric bass, which is especially noticeable at the opening of several of the ballads. The songs "Nowhere to Go," "Shriner's Park," and "Change" all open with brief fade-ins, which is highly unusual in the Melissa Etheridge canon. And, each of the 10 songs opens with a brief accompaniment riff, either in Etheridge's acoustic guitar, in Browne's bass, or in the electric guitar parts played by Etheridge and John Shanks. The entire album also exhibits an interesting, and not entirely conventional, shape. The album opens with two strong, hard-rocking songs, which are followed by two ballads (although the chorus of "An Unusual Kiss" abruptly moves into a hard-rock style). The fifth song, "I Want to Come Over," the best-known song on *Your Little Secret*, is another fast-paced, hard-rocking song—although it does feature dramatic dynamic and intensity contrasts. The last four tracks, although they are not all exactly the same pace or style, basically are slow-to-moderate ballads. So, the listener is left with a bit of a sense of the entire album dying away as it moves toward its conclusion.

The album's fourth song, "Nowhere to Go," is a conventionally structured rock ballad that contains a chorus hook that, while not as well known or well remembered as those of her most commercially successful singles, gives the track an easy accessibility. Etheridge uses the title phrase in such a way that invites hearing the words in a double meaning. The relationship between her character and her lover (gender not specified) can be understood at once as being easygoing (they have "nowhere to go" and all the time in the world on the Saturday night in question) and as a relationship that is outside of society's conventions. There is a hint that the nonconventional nature of the relationship might mean that the relationship itself has "nowhere to go," in the sense of offering no hope of a long-term future.

In the next song, "An Unusual Kiss," Etheridge seems to present a near play-by-play of the first time her character has spent the night with the other principal character in the song. Curiously, she also presents the listener with possible hints that a third person might be observing the two principal characters. For example, the line "My baby draws the shades as the taxi pulls away," which occurs at the end of the text, can be heard as a suggestion that the person with whom Etheridge's character made love has left. Could it be, then, that the longer-term lover of Etheridge's character was an observer, a voyeur? Etheridge offers the listener nothing concrete to suggest this, save an early reference in the song to "the thrill of eyes that capture this forbidden view" and the aforementioned reference to a possible third person. Alternatively, the song might be interpreted as a recounting of the experience of oral sex. Certainly, Etheridge offers clues—besides the title line—that the kiss to which she refers is not an ordinary kiss. The strongly sung chorus phrase "come on, come on, over and over," might be taken as a reference to the sexual orgasm that follows the "unusual kiss." The text can be understood, then, as highly suggestive, without resorting to being graphically explicit.

Etheridge continues the theme of sex that is viewed as the proverbial forbidden fruit by some people in the well-known song "I Want to Come Over." In this song, Etheridge's character tells a woman, who presumably is a neighbor, of her sexual desire for her. The other woman's female "friend," who apparently either lives with the object of Etheridge's desire, or at least visited her just before Etheridge's character tries to make her move, has warned Etheridge's would-be lover about Etheridge's character. The object of Etheridge's desires is now filled with "fear" and the belief that pursing a relationship with Etheridge's character would be "some kind of sin." Throughout the song, Etheridge the lyricist clearly defines her character as the pursuer, the aggressor. For example, Etheridge's character observes that the object of her desire is "weak" and therefore is subject to giving in to her. The illicit nature of the relationship is also suggested by Etheridge's request that the pursued "open [her] back door" to let her in; she presumably cannot afford to be seen entering through the front door.

The illicit nature of the relationship (as Etheridge clearly paints it) into which Etheridge's character desires to enter in "I Want to Come Over" brings up an interesting psychological phenomenon that seems to play into a fair number of the twentieth-century part of the Melissa Etheridge canon. Various psychological studies of the 1980s into the twenty-first century have delved into a phenomenon labeled internalized homophobia. According to researchers David M. Frost and Ilan H. Meyer, social pressures on members of the lesbian, gay, and bisexual communities create a negative self-image that "in its most extreme forms, can lead to the rejection of one's sexual orientation," and "is ... characterized by an intrapsychic conflict between experiences of same-sex affection or desire and feeling a need to be heterosexual."[6] Frost and Meyer's study details the negative impact that internalized homophobia can have on relationship quality among members of the LGB community. The fact that Etheridge paints potential sexual relationships as dark, illicit, and even taboo in a significant number of her twentieth-century compositions (whether the gender or sexuality of the object of her character's desire is specified or not) might be taken as a manifestation of the internalized homophobia described by Frost and Meyer, among others. Interestingly, the majority of the relationship songs that Etheridge has written throughout her lengthy career deal in whole or in part with rejection, the possible or the impending end of the relationship, or at least suspicion about the state of the relationship or about the fidelity of one of the partners. In short, the majority of her characters—autobiographical, semiautobiographical, or wholly fictional—seem to suffer from the sort of negative outcomes associated with internalized homophobia.

The music of "I Want to Come Over," like that of "An Unusual Kiss," is characteristic of Melissa Etheridge's most memorable work of the 1980s and 1990s. The verse section is relatively quiet and sung in the low tessitura of Etheridge's range, while the chorus melody is full-throated, in higher range, and supported by a more intense electric guitar-based backdrop. Unlike "An Unusual Kiss," however, "I Want to Come Over" contains the sort of chorus melodic hook that makes the song instantly recognizable and that invites singing along. In fact, the chorus, with its infectious tune and pointed sexual come-on, can be seen to generate widespread and hearty approval from the audience in Etheridge's 2002 concert DVD, *Melissa Etheridge Live ... and Alone*. The cheers that great the chorus are especially notable in the context of the concert video, because the audience's reaction is to an unadorned Etheridge on voice and guitar texture. In other words, the song does not rely on the instrumentation and production on *Your Little Secret* to elicit a strongly favorable response.

The album's sixth track, "All the Way to Heaven," is not the most memorable song on *Your Little Secret*. This tender love song includes the prominent chorus phrase, "all the way to heaven is heaven," which might be heard by some listeners as more oblique than Etheridge's most memorable and evocative lyrical hooks. That being said, the bulk of the song paints images that evoke Americana—a feature that links it with "Nowhere to Go" and "Shriner's Park," as well as with the much later songs on Etheridge's autobiographical album from the year 2012, *4th Street Feeling*. Musically, "All the Way to Heaven" is notable for the three-measure phrases of the chorus. Because pop songs, rock songs, blues songs, country songs, and R&B songs—in other words, the bulk of late twentieth-century and early twenty-first-century American popular music—conventionally are built in melodic and harmonic phrases of four and eight measures, the chorus of "All the Way to Heaven" stands out. The listener may, in fact, be left with a somewhat uneasy feeling, or a sense of musical instability. Interestingly, this may affect the way in which the listener understands the overall meaning of the song. Throughout the piece, Etheridge's character tells her would-be lover all the things that she would like to do (e.g., "find me a carnival," "roll you in sawdust," "tear off your chains," and so on). The slightly inconclusive and unsteady feel of the chorus's musical structure can be heard as a suggestion that perhaps Etheridge's character will never actually be able to do any of those things: she will never reach "heaven" (in the sense of emotional or sexual bliss) with the object of her desires.

Etheridge demonstrates her command of stylistic and structural variation in the next track, "I Could Have Been You." After a minimalistic and atmospheric instrumental introduction, Etheridge enters with a vocal melody that is built in short phrases of narrow range within the middle of her vocal tessitura. What is most notable about this is that the melody is perfectly in keeping with the nature of the introduction, thus exhibiting a strong attention to compositional detail by Etheridge and coproducer Hugh Padgham. This is one of Etheridge's songs with a high degree of melodic, dynamic, and textural contrast between the verses and the chorus. The significant uptick in intensity in the chorus sections results from Etheridge's full-throated, edgy singing style, the use of a higher vocal range, a significantly higher dynamic level, and the increased use of electric guitar distortion.

As a songwriter, Etheridge matches the high degree of contrast between the verses and chorus sections in "I Could Have Been You" with contrasting lyrical focus. The verses are defined by Etheridge indicting the character with whom she compares herself—or what they personify—for a variety of ills in the world. Principally, though, her concern seems to be with the lack of understanding that the unnamed character has for people who are different from themselves. In the chorus, Etheridge acknowledges that she "could have been you," the other character. The way in which Etheridge nearly shouts the title line, it seems that her character is recoiling in horror to think that she might have turned out like the other character. What is clear throughout the song, however, is that Etheridge's character really had no choice in who she is; whatever she is at the point in time in which the song takes place is a result of nature and her eventual self-knowledge and self-acceptance. In the context of Etheridge's public announcement of her sexual orientation, "I Could Have Been You" seems most likely to be a song that will be understood in the context of sexual orientation. Similarly, the album's final track, "This War Is Over," seems to refer to Etheridge's public acknowledgment and the weight that it lifted off her shoulders.

If one were to pigeonhole Melissa Etheridge as a performer, it seems most likely that she would be labeled a rock musician, as opposed to a folk, country, blues, Top 40 pop musician, and so on. What that definition tends to ignore are the songs that she has produced over the years that do not fit into the classic rock, heartland rock, blues rock, or any of the kind of conventional "rock" mold. In the song "Shriner's Park," Etheridge writes and performs in more of an introspective, acoustic singer-songwriter style than any of the other pieces on *Your Little Secret*. The texture focuses on Etheridge's voice and acoustic guitar accompaniment. Etheridge develops the melody of the verses of the song from short, narrow-range motives. Because of the separation of the rhymed lines, the motivic style of melodic writing, and the fact that some of the rhymes are relatively soft rhymes, the piece tends to sound spontaneous. This feel is entirely in keeping with the acoustic singer-songwriter style, which tends to favor autobiographical personal expression over conformity to pop songwriting styles and structures.

As mentioned earlier, Etheridge uses particular musical attributes and lyrical attributes to link some of the songs of *Your Little Secret*. In the case of the album's penultimate song, "Change," a reference to a specific time links the song to "An Unusual Kiss." In addition, whether Etheridge made the connection intentionally or not, some listeners may sense a connection with the song "All the Way to Heaven." In "Change," Etheridge's character expresses her desire not to have to face the coming day (she and her partner have just ended their relationship) by using the phrase, "hold back the dawn." In "All the Way to Heaven," she mentions to her would-be lover that she would like to go to a bar where the bartender is named "Dawn." Even if the listener does not pick up on the possible connections to earlier songs on the album, "Change" plays an important role in helping to define *Your Little Secret* as a concept album that chronicles Melissa Etheridge's coming to grips with her homosexuality, accepting her homosexuality, developing greater self-awareness, self-acceptance, and self-love in the face of society's mixed reaction to homosexuality, developing relationships, seeing relationships end, and finally keeping her sexual orientation a secret no more. What is significant to the structure of the album is that all of the songs that deal with relationships on *Your Little Secret* prior to "Change" deal with desire, lust, and love, but not with a relationship that has ended. That the sole song that deals with a breakup occurs just before the end of the album is entirely appropriate, even if *Your Little Secret* does not seem to be an entirely chronological autobiographical account.

The album concludes with its lengthiest composition, "This War Is Over." It seems as though listeners—especially those familiar with Etheridge's life story—are likely to interpret the song's lyrics as a reference to her own life. What might differ are the specifics of the interpretation. For example, the "war" to which Etheridge refers might be keeping her sexual orientation private, or the "war" might be coming to full self-knowledge and self-love in the face of mainstream society's rejection; however, the "war" could be any battle fought by virtually any character. For example, given the timing of *Your Little Secret*, a listener could understand Etheridge's character as a coalition veteran of the 1991 Gulf War. Perhaps the veteran suffered from Gulf War Syndrome, a mysterious illness with multiple symptoms that was being seen and discussed in the mid-1990s. While Etheridge leaves the listener with few specifics about the nature of the "war" of which she sings, it perhaps is clearer is that Etheridge's character feels a sense of relief, which is tempered by exhaustion or resignation that suggests the duration and intensity of her battle.

The weariness of Etheridge's character is supported, or even suggested, by the musical setting of "This War Is Over." The piece uses the G Mixolydian mode for its melodic material. The slow-paced tune is supported by a brief ostinato figure in the bass guitar that revolves around the pitch G, the tonic of the song. The slow pace, the length of the song—which clocks in at just two ticks under seven minutes—the use of modality, and the prominence of the ostinato bass line all add up to suggest the possible influence of 1960s modal rock, represented perhaps most clearly by a song such as the Doors' "The End."

Ultimately, *Your Little Secret* did not receive the amount of critical praise or exhibit the same high level of immediate commercial appeal as *Yes I Am*. Despite this, *Your Little Secret* is an important work within the Melissa Etheridge canon. For one thing, it represented Etheridge's first foray into songs that deal explicitly with lesbian relationships. Because of that, the listener can interpret this collection of 10 songs as the most personal, the most autobiographical (or apparently autobiographical) statements, to date from Etheridge, even the gender-neutral songs that accompany the gender-specific works.

The album is also significant because it exhibited a new facet to the characters created and portrayed by Etheridge. On all of her earlier albums, Etheridge seemed to fixate at times on the subject of relationships torn apart by a third party. Generally, Etheridge was the loser; she was not the sexual aggressor, nor was her character the party interfering in a couple's relationship. Such is not the case with songs such as "An Unusual Kiss" and, especially, "I Want to Come Over." In "Your Little Secret," Etheridge's character finds herself a potential third party; however, in this song her character rejects the advances of a suitor who is cheating on a partner. The result of this shift is that Etheridge's characters are not as monochromatic as they might sometimes be perceived in some of her earlier songs. On *Your Little Secret*, the characters are wider ranging, as are the emotional states and views of love and sexual relationships.

The other significant difference between *Your Little Secret* and any of Melissa Etheridge's earlier albums is that this collection finds Etheridge dealing with social issues head-on. Although the lyrics of none of the songs are necessarily as outspoken, pointed, and crystal clear as some of Etheridge's socially conscious songs of the twenty-first century, "I Could Have Been You" and "This War Is Over" both seem to be directed at homophobia in American society and the struggles of members of the LGBT community.

Perhaps even more significant than any of these individual differences that distinguish *Your Little Secret* from any of Melissa Etheridge's earlier albums is the fact that this album can be understood as a concept album. Although the progression does not necessarily follow in precise chronological order, *Your Little Secret* can be heard as a chronicle of Etheridge's self-awareness of her sexuality, early potential lesbian relationships that were never consummated or that did not last because of society's rejection of homosexuality ("Shriner's Park"), relationships that were consummated ("An Unusual Kiss") or that Etheridge's character wanted to see consummated ("I Really Like You," "I Want to Come Over," "All the Way to Heaven"), her plea to the world at large for acceptance and equal treatment ("Nowhere to Go" and "I Could Have Been You"), and the burden that was lifted off her shoulders by her informal announcement of homosexuality in January 1993 ("This War Is Over"). It is significant that "This War Is Over" concludes the album, as the song can be understood as Etheridge's statement of full acceptance of herself for who she is, and the acknowledgment that only by revealing herself fully to the world could she reach the state of complete self-acceptance.

In 1995, Etheridge inducted Janis Joplin into the Rock and Roll Hall of Fame. At the Hall of Fame's induction ceremony she performed "Piece of My Heart," one of Joplin's more iconic hits from the late 1960s. While it has been rare for Etheridge to so much as record or undertake a live performance of a cover song, "Piece of My Heart" has remained in her repertoire. So, why? In general, the vocal connections between Joplin and Etheridge are undeniable. And, although it is not always entirely obvious in her compositions, Melissa Etheridge has retained at least some connection with blues-rock (the style most closely associated with Joplin) throughout her career. Similarly, Joplin's most successful recordings found her playing the role of the scorned ex-lover, a role that Etheridge has played in more songs than can easily be counted. Perhaps the greatest irony of Melissa Etheridge's iconic performance of "Piece of My Heart" at the 1995 Rock and Roll Hall of Fame induction ceremony and her subsequent live recording of the song at the 2005 Grammy Awards ceremony is that although the piece is so thoroughly linked with Janis Joplin, Etheridge has enjoyed a far longer career than Joplin. In fact, to put it in perspective, Joplin died at age 27 and Melissa Etheridge's professional career has spanned more than 27 years. Etheridge has impacted popular music not only as a singer but also as a songwriter and guitarist. Despite her iconic status, Janis Joplin primarily was known as a singer, enjoyed a relatively short career, and was in reality a highly erratic live performer. Throughout her career, Melissa Etheridge has been a much more consistent live performer and recording artist than Joplin; she also has been a successful guitarist, a significant songwriter, and a social activist on gender, sexual identity, gay parental rights, and environmental issues, as well as a tireless advocate for breast cancer sufferers and survivors. Still, as a white, female, blues-rock performer Janis Joplin was a groundbreaker. As a rock musician who lived excessively during a time defined in some respects by excess, Joplin was an icon of individualism, hedonism, and ultimately deadly recklessness. In the world of popular culture, Joplin remains an icon over 40 years since her death. The great irony of Melissa Etheridge's continuing celebration of the work of Joplin (in part by maintaining "Piece of My Heart" in her repertoire) is that Etheridge arguably has contributed more to society than had Joplin, yet the specter of Joplin may well continue to remain in public consciousness longer and with a greater intensity than the more voluminous and arguably ultimately more important work of Melissa Etheridge.

In the year 1996, ASCAP awarded Melissa Etheridge the Pop Songwriter of the Year award—which she shared with the band Hootie & the Blowfish. Etheridge was honored for the commercial and critical success of the songs "I'm the Only One," "Come to My Window," and "If I Wanted To," from the 1993 album *Yes I Am*. Etheridge's prominence as a pop culture icon was also affirmed by her 1996 performance on the children's television program *Sesame Street*. For her *Sesame Street* appearance, Etheridge adapted her nearly-decade-old song "Like the Way I Do" to sing "Like the Way U Do," with a focus on words that begin with the letter "U."

BREAKDOWN (1999)

Despite the fact that *Yes I Am* and *Your Little Secret* and the singles generated by these albums established Melissa Etheridge as a major star in over the period 1993–95, it was not until 1999 that her next album, *Breakdown*, appeared. Etheridge was not entirely inactive during the period between album releases. She and partner Julie Cypher concentrated on their domestic life and had two children, Bailey Jean (born February 1997) and Beckett (born November 1998), both of whom were fathered by 1960s and 1970s rock music icon David Crosby (formerly of the Byrds, and Crosby, Stills, Nash & Young).

While *Yes I Am* was Melissa Etheridge's breakthrough into superstardom and biggest-selling album, and *Your Little Secret* was Etheridge's highest-charting album up to that point in her career (although it sold far fewer copies than did *Yes I Am*), *Breakdown* fared less well commercially. *Breakdown* is, however, Etheridge's only album to date that has been nominated for a Grammy for Best Rock Album, an award that ultimately went to the legendary guitarist Carlos Santana. The Grammy nomination from the National Academy of Recording Arts and Sciences does not necessarily signify that all critics viewed *Breakdown* as a groundbreaking recording. For example, in his review of the album, *All Music Guide* critic Stephen Thomas Erlewine suggested that a number of new significant and popular female performers had emerged during the interval between the release of *Your Little Secret* and *Breakdown* that posed a commercial threat to blues, rock, roots music-based artists such as Etheridge. Erlewine wrote that Etheridge and her stylistic sisters "by and large . . . were overshadowed by the bouncy pop of the Spice Girls and their ilk, Alanis Morissette and her offspring, and Sarah McLachlan and the Lilith Fair crowd."[7] It is interesting, then, that songs from *Breakdown* figured prominently enough in the playlist rotation on the video music cable television channel VH1 that their heavy play was mentioned in a *Time* magazine interview with Etheridge.[8]

Breakdown opens with its title track. Even from the opening instrumental introduction of "Breakdown," before Melissa Etheridge sings a note, it is clear that the album begins with a more spacious, less-punchy, and less of a hard-rock-oriented production than what tended to define—at least in large part—*Yes I Am* and *Your Little Secret*. In this respect, the production by John Shanks and Etheridge on *Breakdown* hearkens back somewhat to the early production work of Etheridge with Kevin McCormick, which tended to lean more in the direction of pop than did the production work of Etheridge and Hugh Padgham.

Lyrically, "Breakdown" is less direct than some of the more event-specific and situation-specific songs from Etheridge's previous two albums. The gist of the song is that Etheridge's character acknowledges that the person to whom she sings is headed for a "breakdown." The specific nature of the relationship is somewhat hazy. On the surface, the first verses and the chorus seem to imply that the characters are lovers, domestic partners, or something along those lines. Etheridge's character is trying to return home to be with the other person during her or his breakdown. She sings of driving and flying, moving between the different modes of transportation, which might suggest to the listener that this kind of emotional upheaval in the other party has occurred more often than once in the past, or at the very least that the two are separated by a considerable distance, thus necessitating several modes of transportation. Interestingly, however, Etheridge incorporates two lines from the text of the lullaby/nursery rhyme "Rock-a-Bye Baby," which throws a wrinkle into the listener's interpretation of the meaning of "Breakdown" and the relationship of the two principal characters of the song. The listener is left to consider if the other character is one of Etheridge's children, or if she is using the references to "Rock-a-Bye Baby" metaphorically, or perhaps if she considers the person to whom she sings to be childlike in their lack of emotional control.

The second track on the album, "Angels Would Fall," continues the album's focus on rock music with a definite pop bent. In fact, the jangling electric guitars, the muting of Etheridge's sometimes edgy, raspy vocal delivery, and the clear, pop song-oriented structure of "Angels Would Fall" combine to suggest an allegiance to the rock singer-songwriter style that made Etheridge's contemporary Sheryl Crow a popular success in the mid-1990s. Interestingly, the song opens with a relatively faint percussion part that sounds similar in style to the hip-hop-influenced sampled percussion parts that Crow also used in some of her recordings of the 1990s.

The lyrics of "Angels Would Fall," like those of the album's opening track, are more oblique than those of most of the songs on *Your Little Secret*. Because of this, the song is widely open to interpretation, and potentially more applicable to a wider audience. More specifically, several of the songs on *Your Little Secret* clearly dealt with lesbian relationships; however, "Angels Would Fall" seems to be a reaction to an infatuation with or a crush on someone of unspecified gender who is inaccessible and who perhaps is not as fully appreciated or loved by others as they are by Etheridge's character. Despite the religious references in the song's lyrics, the easy pop accessibility and somewhat indirect nature of the lyrics would seem to make "Angels Would Fall" a fully workable cover track for a wide variety of performers.

Throughout *Breakdown*, listeners might perceive that other songs are double-edged swords in the manner of "Breakdown" and "Angels Would Fall." Both of the album's first two tracks are memorable and accessible, and feature more a spacious and more muted production and performance than on Etheridge's previous two albums. Likewise, they are more universal in their lyrics, although they can be interpreted as autobiographical statements, particularly to the extent that the listener is aware of Etheridge's life story. All of this accessibility would seem to have been a logical formula for widespread chart and sales success. As mentioned earlier, it was not. Perhaps some Melissa Etheridge fans found these songs to be too general in nature, and too close to the pop side of the rock genre. That being said, one of the advantages that songs such as "Breakdown" and "Angels Would Fall" have over the more explicit, harder-rock, and more lyrically narrow songs that appeared on *Your Little Secret* is that logically they should be more adaptable to a variety of settings. It is surprising, therefore, that artists other than those who have recorded the songs for sound-alike or Etheridge tribute albums have not covered these songs.

One thing that is notable and that represents growth for Melissa Etheridge as a songwriter is the metaphorical richness of the lyrics, not only of "Breakdown" and "Angels Would Fall," but a richness that runs throughout the album. It would appear that the critical recognition that *Breakdown* received in the form of a Grammy nomination for Best Rock Album might in part stem from the growth in subtlety of Etheridge's writing, as well as the near-universal accessibility of the songs, arrangements, and productions. For the most part, Etheridge's earlier tendency toward extreme histrionics is tempered on *Breakdown*, so the opening tracks, in particular, tend to sound more like a part of the musical mainstream than some of Etheridge's earlier work.

Musical conservatism is probably too strong a term to use to describe the first songs of *Breakdown*, but the opening of the album does seem to be more firmly tied to pop-oriented rock styles of the 1970s and 1980s than some of the work on Etheridge's earlier albums. This tie to the past, this mainstream rock feel, carries forward into the song "Stronger than Me," which opens with a brief slide guitar figure that would not have seemed entirely out of place on a 1970s or 1980s George Harrison album. The song concerns a relationship that is falling apart. Etheridge's character tells her (gender-neutral) partner that they "must be stronger than [her]" because they appear to be so nonchalant in the midst of the breakdown of the relationship, and the near breakdown of Etheridge's character. Etheridge exhibits a feeling of resignation, which is enhanced by the slide guitar part. This adds to the emotional range of the album and contrasts strongly to the anger, passion, lust, and other emotions sometimes more frequently associated with Etheridge's compositions.

The album's next track, "Into the Dark," represents another example of Etheridge's move away from guitar-dominated rock into a more pop-oriented style on *Breakdown*. The song primarily revolves around the E natural-minor (Aeolian) scale. Etheridge's use of the minor mode and the atmospheric production and effects treatment of the guitars and keyboards all combine to provide a feeling of near melancholy. Etheridge's lyrics are, as they were on *Breakdown*'s opening tracks, more impressionistic and less explicit in autobiographical references than anything on her previous albums. In fact, "Into the Dark" is the haziest of the album's opening songs. It is an acknowledgment of desperation and the need to be saved from that feeling of desperation. However, the exact nature of the relationship between the characters is vague. Because of that, one could read it as a spiritual song, as a song about the demise of an intense love relationship, or possibly in many other ways.

As the listener moves into "Enough of Me," the Melissa Etheridge of old starts to emerge on a musical and a lyrical level. The reader might recall that on her first several albums Etheridge had a tendency to write songs in which she portrayed the injured party in a broken relationship. Such is the case in "Enough of Me"; however, this song contrasts with many of her earlier songs from the viewpoint of the jilted lover. The anger of old is replaced with what might more accurately be labeled as exasperation in "Enough of Me." In her 2001 autobiography, Etheridge discussed how, in retrospect, some of the songs that she wrote for *Breakdown* foreshadowed the disintegration and the end of her decade-long relationship with film director Julie Cypher (the relationship ended in 2000).[9] "Enough of Me" certainly sounds like an example of such a song. "Enough of Me" is slower in tempo and more relaxed in style than the previous songs on *Breakdown*. While the tempo and style of the music does not necessarily lend a complete feeling of resignation and weariness to "Enough of Me," it helps to move the overall mood of the song in that direction. The listener might also sense the exasperation of Etheridge's character; this mood emanates from the lyrics themselves and Etheridge's delivery.

The next track, "Truth of the Heart," is another ballad. This song, which is driven by Etheridge's 12-string acoustic guitar, is a heartfelt, autobiographical song to Etheridge and Cypher's children. Etheridge focuses her message on the need to overcome the fear and darkness in the world, the need to respect and try understand everyone who one encounters, and the need to follow one's heart. Near the end of the text, she refers to her parents, her sister, and her own struggles in life. None of these references are so specific as to be clearly autobiographical. Thus, there is a universal quality to the lyrics. If, however, the listener is familiar with Etheridge's life story, the events of her childhood and youth can easily be read into the song. For example, Etheridge refers to her "sister's pain." Listeners familiar with Etheridge's life might reasonably assume that the pain to which she refers is that which apparently led to her sister inflicting emotional, physical, and sexual abuse on the young Melissa Etheridge.

One of the perhaps overlooked qualities of Etheridge as a songwriter is her ability to use musical structure to help make her songs stand out from pop song stereotypes. "Truth of the Heart" is a case in point. The subtle structural peculiarities of the song are so smoothly integrated that it is easy to miss exactly how the song defies convention. Each verse includes an eight-measure section, which is followed by a four-measure phrase with a contrasting rhythmic feel. In a conventional pop song, the eight-measure section alone could constitute a complete verse. Etheridge's inclusion of the four-measure tag lends the song a through-composed[10] feel. To put it another way, the poetic structure seems to drive the musical structure, which generally is not often the case in much of the sometimes-cookie-cutter world of pop music.

Etheridge also uses unusual structure in the music and lyrics of the chorus. The chorus text consists of five lines, the third and fifth of which rhyme. Etheridge's musical setting of the first three lines extends through the whole of a four-measure phrase. This is followed by another four-measure phrase. Etheridge uses only the first two measures of this second phrase to set the remaining two lines of text; the third and fourth measures form a brief interlude. The asymmetrical nature of the combination of text and music in the chorus also gives the song something of an improvisatory feel.

Although the bridge (sometimes called the middle eight) section of "Truth of the Heart" is more conventional in structure, the somewhat unusual structure of the verses and the chorus helps to give the listener the sense that Etheridge wrote it from "the heart." That being said, it is thoroughly accessible both lyrically and musically. In fact, it may be the best song on *Breakdown* in terms of emotional balance and musical contrast between sections.

As one listens to *Breakdown*, one may sense that coproducers Melissa Etheridge and John Shanks possibly had an overall shape in mind for the sequencing of the songs. Generally, the opening tracks on the album, while they might be interpreted as autobiographical statements or reflections, tend to feature lyrics that are general and impressionistic enough that they do not have to be understood as pertaining only to the songs' composer. The opening tracks, too, tend toward moderate tempo and mainstream pop style. As the album reaches its midpoint, there is more variation of lyrical theme, of autobiographical focus, and of musical styles, intensity levels, and tempi.

"Mama I'm Strange" is not the best-known song on *Breakdown*; however, it is one of the more intriguing sleepers from Melissa Etheridge's output from the 1990s. Musically, the song is an intriguing combination of double-time hip-hop/alternative rock rhythms in the percussion, with electric guitar solo figures that resemble those in the famous 1960s Buffalo Springfield song "For What It's Worth." The result suggests the nearly psychedelic emotional disturbance of the lyrics. While the lyrics are not as clear and explicit as some of those of *Yes I Am* and *Your Little Secret*, they are more clearly autobiographical than those of the earlier tracks on *Breakdown*. Here, Etheridge confronts her childhood, her knowledge that she did not have the same likes and dislikes and aspirations and feelings of the majority of other girls. In short, "Mama I'm Strange" is about the depression, the anger, the bewilderment, and all of the other negative emotions that Etheridge suffered as she came to grips with her sexuality. The song's title line seems to suggest not only that the young Etheridge recognized that she stood apart from what she saw as the expectations of society, but that she had not developed a self-understanding, a self-love, or a self-acceptance.

After coming out in January 1993, Melissa Etheridge became a spokesperson for the rights of members of the LGBT community. Perhaps most visible was her advocacy for parental and spousal rights for gays and lesbians. It must be remembered that this initial period of activism was also a period in which Etheridge produced precious little new musical material, at least that which was commercially released. The great work of social commentary on *Breakdown* was "Scarecrow," a song that Etheridge dedicated to the memory of Matthew Shepard. Shepard (1976–98) was the young University of Wyoming student who was brutally beaten, robbed, and left for dead in what allegedly was an antigay hate crime in October 1998. Shepard died several days after being found—mistaken for a scarecrow—and hospitalized. Wyoming law and federal law at the time did not include provisions for crimes of violence against gays to be prosecuted as hate crimes. The brutal beating of Matthew Shepard and his subsequent death led to the expansion of the definition of "hate crimes" in some states and at the federal level, although it was not until over a decade after the young man's death that the Matthew Shepard Act was signed into law by President Barack Obama.

The brutal murder of Matthew Shepard symbolized the oppression of homosexuals not only to those in the world of politics but also to artists. A number of singers and songwriters referred to Shepard in their work, perhaps the most famous of whom was Elton John. Melissa Etheridge's "Scarecrow" presents a stark emotional contrast to the previous songs on *Breakdown*. It is worth noting that despite the high level of emotionally charged content in "Scarecrow," Etheridge does not overact in her vocal delivery, something of which she had been accused earlier in her career.

Although some overviews of *Breakdown* have labeled "Scarecrow" as Etheridge's first foray into topical songwriting,[11] she had made social commentary that certainly was timely, especially on *Your Little Secret*. "Scarecrow," though, does indeed revolve around the murder of Matthew Shepard and its implications. What is important to note, though, is that Etheridge goes well beyond documenting Shepard's murder and what it signifies for LGBT individuals. She expands the implications of the event to include anyone who is "different" (my quotes). But, she also goes further by moving into her own reaction, eventually concluding that she will "forgive, but never forget."

The lyrics, Etheridge's vocal restraint, and the topical subject matter are significant enough, but what makes "Scarecrow" a great song is in part the musical setting. Not all listeners might feel this way, but I hear the melody of the verses of the song as somehow implying a motion in the direction of a goal that never arrives. It seems as though Etheridge sets up a melodic expectation and then deliberately moves in a direction that is just as logical and conclusive sounding, but not exactly what the listener expected. Another attribute of the song that makes it stand out from the other works on this album is the pitch range of the melody in the verses. Etheridge's singing in these sections is in a generally higher range than is customary in her compositions. She also sings in the verses with a feeling of rubato (rhythmic flexibility). The tessitura (range) and rubato work also help to instill the verses with a floating, slightly unresolved quality.

The chorus of "Scarecrow," which deals more with the brutality of the attack, what it signifies about intolerance in American society, and Etheridge's reaction to that intolerance and brutality, contrasts starkly with respect to vocal range, vocal style, and the instrumentation that accompanies Etheridge's singing. As mentioned earlier, though, despite the greater musical intensity and vocal intensity of the chorus, Etheridge exercises a degree of restraint that suggests a new level of maturity: she tempers her earlier tendency sometimes to overact as a performer.

After building up to the emotional intensity of "Scarecrow," Etheridge provides musical and lyrical relaxation in the form of the song "How Would I Know." Strangely enough, in its rhythmic materials and feeling of space in the melody and the record production, the piece resembles early 1970s soul works, such as Marvin Gaye's "What's Going On" and Barry White's "Love's Theme." The music is pleasant and engaging; however, the text concerns the disintegration of a relationship. Some listeners may hear something of a sense of eeriness in the piece, especially those who sense a disconnection between the lyrics and musical setting.

In her autobiography, Etheridge is quick to point out that she does not write songs for music critics as much as she writes them as a form of self-expression and for her audience; however, she also points out that when *Rolling Stone* magazine compared "My Lover" to John Lennon's emotionally tortured and cathartic song "Mother," "I really drank that in and was grateful."[12] For myself, and possibly some other listeners, any connections to Lennon's tortured, primal scream therapy-inspired "Mother" and the Etheridge song are tenuous. Like Lennon did on his 1970 song, Etheridge employs a relatively stark accompaniment; however, it is not nearly as stark as that of the Lennon song. Like Lennon, Etheridge explores her own psyche; however, the piece—at least on the surface—does not find the artist pouring out her soul with a cathartic expungement of long-suppressed pain and rage to the extent that Lennon did in "Mother." "My Lover" is interesting as a work of inner probing for an entirely different reason. Throughout the piece, Etheridge points out the listener the ways in which she relies on, and essentially lives through, her lover. It is a pop song cliché to say something such as "without you I would die." Although Melissa Etheridge does not use that exact phrase, "My Lover" makes it clear that her character really would have absolutely nothing for which to live and no way to cope with the world (or with life) without her lover.

The original release of *Breakdown* concludes with the ballad "Sleep." This is a gentle love song that extols the beauty of Etheridge and her (gender-neutral) lover simply lying together and sleeping after lovemaking. Over the course of the last third of *Breakdown*, the listener is likely to sense that Melissa Etheridge is more of a composer of songs, each of which explores a particular event or a particular emotion, than a composer of albums. More to the point, the last three songs of *Breakdown*, "How Would I Know," "My Lover," and "Sleep," might not seem to make logical sense in sequence. This is curious, because the first half of *Breakdown* seems to have an overall shape and song-to-song progression.

Breakdown also was issued in a limited-edition enhanced CD format that included the bonus tracks "Touch and Go," "Cherry Avenue," and "Beloved," as well as computer-accessible materials. Unfortunately, the computer materials are likely to be difficult to access for today's listeners, because of incompatibilities between the 1999 technology that was used on the enhanced CD and the operating systems of the second decade of the twenty-first century. Despite that, Etheridge fans might do well to seek out the enhanced edition because of the inclusion of the three bonus tracks.

Etheridge turns to familiar lyrical territory for the song "Touch and Go," a piece that deals with the transitory nature of a relationship in which her character is more in love with her partner than the partner is with her. Despite the realization that her character's partner feels like a caged animal, and cannot truly commit to Etheridge, the two live for the "touch and go" of lovemaking. This is a more folk-oriented acoustic musical setting than what listeners probably expect from Etheridge. The atmospheric sustained notes in the synthesizer are reminiscent of some of the more ethereal settings of the Irish rock band U2. It should be noted that, for better or for worse—depending on the listener's appreciation of U2—the specter of Bono, The Edge, and their bandmates would continue to figure in Melissa Etheridge's work in the future. In "Touch and Go," Etheridge's harmonic writing—and the largely acoustic guitar-focused setting—also is reminiscent of some of the work of Paul Simon. Particularly Simon-esque is the motion to minor chords, a staple of Simon's harmonic vocabulary, particularly in his solo work of the 1970s and 1980s.

"Cherry Avenue," in contrast, is a song of seduction in a pop-oriented rock style; however, like "Touch and Go," it is a song with musical ties to the 1980s. Here, Etheridge's character meets a potential lover at a bar, which is located on the "Cherry Avenue" of the song's title. Various nicknamed characters who work at the bar are mentioned, which gives the piece an autobiographical/real-life feel. Etheridge's character and her (gender-neutral) partner dance until closing time. Etheridge offers the listener a suggestion that whatever the exact nature is of the relationship that her character wants to initiate with the other person might not be entirely comfortable for the potential lover. Although it is debatable if it was the intent, listeners may read the text (particularly the street name in the title) as a play on words: Etheridge's character easily could be understood as trying to seduce another woman into her first lesbian relationship.

As mentioned earlier, some of Melissa Etheridge's earliest songs occasionally sound similar to the work of other artists. By and large, any possible influences on her writing became less clear over time. However, just as the harmonic vocabulary and the use of sustained electronic tones in "Touch and Go" might cause the listener to think of the work of such diverse artists as Paul Simon and U2, the musical materials, arrangement, and musical style of "Cherry Avenue" also sound familiar. In this case, the focus on melodic motion in the opening instrumental introduction and in Etheridge's vocal line emphasizes the narrow range between scale-step one and scale-step three. This range, the shape of the short melodic phrases, and the near-1980s dance style of the piece suggest the possible influence of mid-1980s Prince, particularly Prince's work with the Revolution on songs such as "Raspberry Beret."

If one is familiar with sexual double entendres and overt sexual references in the compositions of Prince, and if one hears a relationship between mid-1980s Prince and Etheridge's work on "Cherry Avenue," then it seems more likely that the listener might make a connection with a double meaning in the Etheridge song's title.

Of the three bonus tracks on *Breakdown*, "Beloved" perhaps is the most interesting in many respects. Curiously, this song also reflects earlier popular music styles. Some of the electric guitar figures and the keyboards reflect back to the late 1960s and early 1970s. Etheridge also includes one harmonic touch that is unusual in her work, but that also links the song back to earlier rock styles. In the last line of the chorus of this D major song, Etheridge uses the minor-quality variant of the subdominant chord (G minor, or iv) as a passing chord between the standard major-quality subdominant chord (G major, or IV) and the tonic chord (D major, or I). This passing chord usage can be heard in pop music from the 1960s and 1970s, but was particularly notable in some of the British Invasion pop of 1964 and 1965.

Etheridge's lyrics for "Beloved" also have an interesting shape. The first two verses of the song find her character at odds with the world, presumably because of her sexual orientation: some people threaten her character with eternal damnation, in a more generalized way she is not accepted by society, and so on. In the chorus sections, Etheridge affirms that the only person who is supportive and who stands up for her is "[her] beloved." In the last stanza, Etheridge suggests to the listener that all of the injustice, violence, and intolerance she has seen in the world has caused her for the first time to become an activist. It is Etheridge's description of the birth of her activism that seems particularly autobiographical; it was shortly after coming out in the early 1990s that Etheridge became a spokesperson for parental rights for lesbian and gay couples, and shortly after the murder of Matthew Shepard that she turned to topical songwriting in response to the struggles of the LGBT community.

Breakdown plays a curious role in the recorded output of Melissa Etheridge. On one hand, "Scarecrow" is a powerful response to the murder of Matthew Shepard; "Angels Would Fall" is a fine pop song that could work musically, stylistically, and rhetorically for a wide variety of artists; and "Mama I'm Strange" and "My Lover" find Etheridge confronting the emotionally intense challenges of coming to an understanding of her sexuality as a youth. Several of the songs betray the possibility that all was not right between Melissa Etheridge and her partner, Julie Cypher; however, most of the songs lack the autobiographical-sounding detail of the songs of *Yes I Am* and *Your Little Secret*. Musically, the album seems safe, and despite the emotional intensity and autobiographical probing of a few of the songs, *Breakdown* generally does not sound as cutting-edge, emotionally charged, or musically fresh as the work of some of the singer-songwriters who had emerged between the release of *Your Little Secret* and *Breakdown*.

Turbulence and Recovery

The early twenty-first century was a period of intense ups and downs for Melissa Etheridge. In the year 2000, her decade-plus relationship with Julie Cypher ended when Cypher came to the realization that she was not gay, but bisexual. On the positive side, however, Etheridge contributed a new recording of her song "The Angels" to the 2001 album *Earl Scruggs and Friends*, thus connecting with the traditional country/roots music genre. Etheridge's musical response to her breakup with Cypher, the 2001 album *Skin*, found the singer-songwriter putting a thoroughly believable autobiographical face on the kinds of songs that defined the start of Etheridge's career back in the 1980s: tortured songs of loss in love. In 2002, Etheridge released her first live DVD, *Melissa Etheridge Live . . . and Alone*. Not only was this a document of Etheridge as a solo singer-guitarist, the title also played on the breakup of the Etheridge-Cypher relationship.

The period 2002–5 continued to be a time of extreme highs and extreme lows for Etheridge, both musically and in her personal life. She was nominated for a Grammy in 2002 for Best Female Rock Vocal Performance for the *Skin* track "I Want to Be in Love." In 2002, Etheridge collaborated with coauthor Laura Morton to write her autobiography, *The Truth Is . . . My Life in Love and Music*. By 2003, Etheridge had a new love interest in Tammy Lynn Michaels, whom she married in September 2003. The 2004 album *Lucky* celebrated this new relationship and was Etheridge's best critically received album since the early 1990s. Unfortunately, sales of *Lucky* did not match the heights of the critical reaction to the album; *Lucky* peaked only at No. 15 on the *Billboard* charts.

In October 2004, Melissa Etheridge was diagnosed with breast cancer. During the months that she battled the illness, Etheridge was absent from the music world. However, given the amount of time that passed between some of her previous albums, it was not the duration of her absence that was noticed. Rather, it was Etheridge's valiant fight with the disease and her triumphant reemergence for a live performance at the February 2005 Grammy Awards ceremony that was noticed by fans. Etheridge's successful battle and her activism on behalf of cancer victims and survivors have also helped to bring her, her music, and the disease to the attention of a wider public than her loyal fans. Etheridge was frank in her discussions of her experience; she gave interviews on the subject to print journalists from a wide variety of publications, and she made the rounds of morning, afternoon, and evening television talk shows.

This period of turbulence, recovery, and reemergence concluded with the release of the 2005 album *Greatest Hits: The Road Less Traveled*. In addition to containing some of Etheridge's most iconic songs of the past, the 2005 greatest hits package also included a number of new songs, at least one of which reflected the direction that the iconic singer-songwriter would take in the most recent phase of her career.

SKIN (2001)

Although this period of Melissa Etheridge's life and career was a veritable rollercoaster ride on all sorts of levels—including the most extreme—the twenty-first century opened with recognition of Etheridge as a pop culture, entertainment industry icon—this represented by the fact that she received a star on the Hollywood Walk of Fame in 2001. Ironically, this was one of the darkest periods of Etheridge's personal life since she became a widely known musician. The fact that the 2001 album *Skin* marked one of the darker periods of Melissa Etheridge's personal life, the breakup of her decade-plus-long relationship with actor/director Julie Cypher, is foreshadowed by the physical disc itself—*Skin* is stark black. *Skin* marked Etheridge's return to Top 10 of the *Billboard* album charts, suggesting that the highly personal nature of the material resonated with fans more than some of the less overtly autobiographical-sounding material on its predecessor, *Breakdown*. Generally, critics reacted favorably to the album, despite the fact that the subject matter seemed to be tailor-made for the sort of overstatement that led to some less-than-flattering words from critics earlier in Etheridge's career. *Billboard*'s Melinda Newman, for example, wrote a largely favorable review, but concluded that the best songs are those "where Etheridge uses a velvet glove rather than a hammer to make her point."[1] Perhaps the best, most concise statement on *Skin*, its successes, and the nature of its material comes from *All Music Guide* critic Kerry L. Smith, who writes, "If ever there was a perfect breakup album, this is it."[2]

Skin opens with the song "Lover Please." *Lesbian News* critic Heidi Hudson wrote a largely favorable review of *Skin*, but referred to the album as "over produced."[3] To the extent that the listener hears the album this way, she or he finds that the overproduction manifests itself in two primary ways: (1) some of the tracks include more overdubs than what might be expected on a Melissa Etheridge album; and (2) some of the tracks, such as "Lover Please," begin with a relatively intimate texture, only to expand into a full rock band arrangement. What is especially interesting about the work of coproducers Etheridge and David Cole is how they used relatively minimal resources to achieve such a full studio sound. Specifically, the album's liner notes credit only Etheridge with the multitude of guitar parts and with the keyboard parts on all of the songs except for one.

"Lover Please" is a plea with an estranged lover to return the telephone calls of Etheridge's character, and a plea to her (presumably) to return. Admittedly, there is something quite familiar about the lyrics—Etheridge plays the role of the jilted party in a rocky relationship just as she had done in songs on her earliest commercial recordings, over a dozen years before. Likewise, the passionate musical setting—particularly the jangling and slightly distorted guitar chords and Etheridge's edgy singing style—hearken back to her recordings of the *Yes I Am* era and before. Speaking of *Yes I Am*, there are some slight similarities of melodic material, texture, and tone color between that earlier album's title track and "Lover Please," especially in the chorus. Unfortunately for Etheridge in light of what she had experienced just before the recording and release of *Skin*, perhaps one of the things that gives "Lover Please" a sense of freshness is the fact that this rock-oriented song of heartache and longing can be understood as an autobiographical statement related to Julie Cypher's leaving.

I mentioned the similarities between "Lover Please" and "Yes I Am," and it is interesting to note that the *Skin* album represents what sounds like a conscious attempt to return to the style, textures, and vocal treatments of Etheridge's most popular and critically acclaimed work, that of the early 1990s. The production work by Etheridge and her coproducer David Cole does not mute the edge the way that was done in some of Etheridge's post–Hugh Padgham work. On "Lover Please," this does not seem as much like a retreat or some sort of calculated commercially driven attempt to return the singer to the levels of popularity that she enjoyed at the time of *Yes I Am*, as it does like an attempt to reestablish what had been Etheridge's defining style. Or, to put it another way, it sounds like a rejection of the movement toward the pop end of the rock style that Etheridge's work had taken in the mid- to late 1990s.

While "Lover Please" maintains some connections to classic Etheridge recordings up to the time of *Yes I Am* and *Your Little Secret*, this is not a completely retro-sounding recording. It opens with the sound of background, industrial-style drum loops, and it includes electronic processing of voice and guitar (especially noticeable approximately two minutes and 20 seconds into the song) that lend the piece a touch of an otherworldly eeriness. This might not be the most seamless integration of classic rock and electronics, but in the case of "Lover Please" some listeners might hear it as an enhancement of the depiction of the disturbed emotional state of Etheridge's character.

Some reviewers of Etheridge's 2012 album, *4th Street Feeling*, made much of the fact that Etheridge played all of the guitar parts on the songs of that collection.[4] Despite the proclamations of critics, the liner notes of *Skin* suggest that *4th Street Feeling* was not the first Melissa Etheridge album on which she played most or all of the guitar parts: she is the only guitarist listed in the *Skin* credits.[5] Upon listening to *Skin*, it seems plausible that the liner notes are accurate, because the guitar parts on the tracks are accompanimental and do not include much in the way of the virtuosic lead guitar work from Etheridge's more fully band-oriented earlier albums. Here, on *Skin*, there is a more stripped-down feel. This tends to result in a more personal, less commercially oriented sound.

In the album's second track, "The Prison," Etheridge turns to a more folk-like, acoustic singer-songwriter texture. The accompanimental focus, in fact, is on her acoustic guitar and harmonica; it is a considerably more intimate setting than that of "Lover Please." Musically, the texture represents an expansion of the creative range of Melissa Etheridge. It turned out to be an important expansion, because Etheridge's work after the release of *Skin* continued to move toward more frequent folk-like settings—and less out and out rocking. Just as the music of "The Prison" bring a higher level of intimacy to Etheridge's music, throughout *Skin* the lyrics seem more deeply personal than on some of her earlier recordings. What might be particularly noticeable is the fact that while Etheridge sometimes would make abrupt shifts between metaphorical, impressionistic lyrics and cut-to-the-chase, exclamatory lyrics in her earlier work, the lyrics of *Skin* sound more like they come from the voice and experience of the same character. There is stylistic variety, to be sure, but there also is more rhetorical consistency. In "The Prison," Etheridge uses a metaphor of a prison to describe her loneliness.

The lyrics of the next song, "Walking on Water," move in a more impressionistic direction. The gist of the text is that Etheridge's character, not sure what she failed to bring to a relationship (thereby making it possible for her lover to leave), comes to the realization that she needs "a miracle" in order to cause her former lover to regain "desire's spark."

The musical setting continues the move away from adherence to the rock style. The arrangement developed and executed by Etheridge, her coproducer David Cole, and the rest of the band is largely acoustic guitar centered, and includes a prominent flute obligato and mid-song solo. Although the flute sound is quite convincingly authentic sounding, the album's credits suggest that it is synthesized, as does the fact that the vibrato is so perfectly modulated as to be a touch synthetic sounding.

"Walking on Water" is also notable for Etheridge's effective use of narrow-range melodic phrases, which she sings in the middle of her vocal range. By avoiding the extremes of her range—and by singing with a minimum of dynamic and intensity change—Etheridge seems to offer a sense of resignation to the song. Therefore, the listener might be left with the impression that the "miracle" for which Etheridge's character longs is unlikely to occur. It is as though the Melissa Etheridge who used to rail against the injustices inflicted upon her character by cheating "lovers" and scream out her passionate desires now offers her listeners a character who has died emotionally, as if all of her hope has been lost.

Etheridge cements the end of the relationship in the next song, "Down to One." Her character ponders with more persistence than in "Walking on Water" "what went right" and "what went wrong" in the failed relationship. Perhaps the most striking thing about Etheridge's lyrics actually occurs later in the song when her character observes that her heart betrayed her. This observation ties the song in with much of Etheridge's earlier output as a song-writer. In other words, she once again portrays a character who fell in love with the wrong person: the one who ultimately left her. To the listener who is interested in trying to read autobiography into Etheridge's lyrics, this might suggest that her experience in being rejected by longtime partner Julie Cypher was a continuation of Etheridge's (or her character's) experiences from years and decades past.

The song "Goodnight" continues with the theme of lost love, and the inclusion of touches of mild hip-hop-influenced rhythms in the accompaniment. Here, Etheridge acknowledges the end of her character's long-term relationship and her newfound freedom (e.g., "called a new friend for the second time"). Her character still wants to be with her former lover, but the lyrics suggest that a certain emotional coolness has now replaced whatever extremes of pain may initially have accompanied the breakup.

Musically, "Goodnight" could be taken by some listeners as a confusing mix of noncompatible references. The hip-hop-derived rhythms are almost too fully emphasized, such that there is an anonymous quality to parts of the song. To put it another way, at times the style bears less of a "Melissa Etheridge" stamp than it otherwise might. The other thing about "Goodnight" that could alternatively delight some listeners and confuse others is the sheer number of things going on in the arrangement. These include brief and occasional accompanimental electric guitar chords with heavy tremolo (think of early 1960s surf music, or the original "James Bond Theme") and Etheridge's harmonica, which enters so late in the song as possibly to be perceived as an afterthought. The song's melody, however, is memorable. Ultimately, the catchy melody is overshadowed by an overly quick tempo and the feeling that the song's arrangement is less integrated than it is a collection of musical non sequiturs. It is unfortunate, because Etheridge's lyrical sentiments seem to come fully from the heart and from her real-life experiences.

Throughout her career, Melissa Etheridge has maintained strong ties to what is known as roots music. The genre of roots music is loosely defined and may include rural blues, early New Orleans-style jazz, traditional folk, traditional old-time country, and the like; however, Etheridge's ties to roots music generally revolved around blues references within her characteristic rock style. In her twenty-first-century songs, Etheridge has moved increasingly toward the folk and country sides of the roots spectrum. Such is the case with the song "It's Only Me." Etheridge's texture includes the mandolin and background hints of the sound of steel guitar. Interestingly, the composition and arrangement resemble some of the early country-rock music of Bob Dylan, specifically, the style of the songs of Dylan's iconic *Nashville Skyline*. The Dylan-esque attributes of "It's Only Me" go beyond the country-rock style. The harmony of the verses involves an oscillation between two chords, the sort of minimalistic harmonic style apparent in some of Dylan's songs of the 1960s. Also Dylan-esque is Etheridge's incorporation of her spoken voice in the verses. The use of minimalistic harmony in the verses allows the text to come fully to the forefront. The lyrics of the verses find Etheridge's character in a variety of situations, including praying, busy in the kitchen, on the morning after a night spent with "another angel" who she "taught to fly." In each case, Etheridge's character catches her image in the mirror and realizes that she is alone ("It's only me").

As is customary in Etheridge's most memorable compositions, the melodic and harmonic material of the chorus section of "It's Only Me" exhibits a high degree of contrast with the verses. This especially is the case in this song: while the verses include extensive recitation and minimalistic harmony, the chorus features high-register, emotionally charged singing. Similarly, the chorus sections are more harmonically active and include a harmonic cadential formula that is more directional than the oscillations of the verses. Lyrically, too, the chorus contrasts with the verses. In the chorus, Etheridge's character addresses her former lover—who clearly is not present—telling her that the only one who can ever truly give her the love and satisfaction that she needs is "only me."

"I Want to Be in Love" includes the same kind of prerecorded loop-sounding percussion tracks that are interwoven throughout *Skin*. Here, though, the loops are fully integrated into the arrangement. The song does present the listener with a bit of a departure from the established Etheridge sound because of the use of synthesizers, which, to some listeners, might suggest a bit too much adherence to the sound of commercial dance music. Etheridge's fast-paced, largely acoustic music, though, is as optimistic as the lyrical desire to be in love again.

Etheridge's pre-twenty-first-century albums tended to be collections of individual songs. Although two or more of the songs might revolve around similar themes and might even include parallel lyrical references, Etheridge's collections were so loosely connected that they could not be classified as concept albums. In the case of some albums, perhaps most notably *Your Little Secret*, the rhetorical progression of the songs defied concept-album-like linear progression of mood and situation.

Because "I Want to Be in Love" includes lyrical references to the past losses in love of Etheridge's character, but also a new desire to "be in love again," the album follows its predecessors on *Skin* quite logically from the rhetorical, storytelling standpoint. While recounting her character's past losses in the verses of the song, Etheridge includes the words "only me" at a prominent point. Coming immediately after the song "It's Only Me" as "I Want to Be in Love" does, it seems likely that some listeners may sense a direct connection between the two songs.

Although the percussion loops and synthesized drum sounds are well integrated by producers Etheridge and David Cole into some of the songs of *Skin*, on the track "Please Forgive Me" the synthetic sounds are intrusive. Principally, the problem is that the loops are so obviously artificial/synthetic/machine-made that they fundamentally are at odds with the human expressiveness of the song's lyrics.

Rhetorically, "The Different" really follows "I Want to Be in Love" better than it follows its immediate predecessor. In this song, Etheridge's character issues an invitation to love and physical lovemaking to the new object of her desires. It is notable that this is the one song on *Skin* that offers a hint of Etheridge's sexual orientation; however, that is open to interpretation. She describes the levels of ecstasy that she hopes to reach with her new lover and tells her (presumably) that it is something that "only the different know."

Of all of the tracks on *Skin*, "The Different" is the one that makes the fullest use of the resources of the synthesizer, electronic processing of the voice, and the various other electronic effects of the recording studio. The effect is that, despite the highly personal, sexually oriented nature of the lyrics, Etheridge's voice has a highly detached, impersonal quality to it.

The detachment, the self-description as "different," and the outsider status that runs through the words and music of "The Different" suggest the kind of stigmatization suffered by members of the LGBT community, as well as members of other minority groups within U.S. society, as described by social scientists, such as psychologists Herek, Gillis, and Cogan in their *Journal of Counseling Psychology* article "Internalized Stigma among Sexual Minority Adults: Insights from a Social Psychological Perspective,"[6] and humanists, such as poet and essayist Adrienne Rich in her essay "Compulsory Heterosexuality and Lesbian Existence."[7]

On *Skin*'s final track, "Heal Me," coproducers Etheridge and David Cole back off on the electronic effects and the use of synthesizers, which lend a somewhat impersonal, anonymous sound to some of the album's songs. Although the hip-hop drum rhythms—which probably struck listeners as novel and *au courant* at the time—seem dated in the second decade of the twenty-first century, "Heal Me" is more successful than its predecessor and more successful than "Please Forgive Me." "Heal Me" finds Etheridge acknowledging that a newfound relationship offers hope for her character's future: principally hope that the new relationship will heal her and free her from the pain of the loss that runs through the vast majority of the rest of the album. In its hopefulness, "Heal Me" brings appropriate closure to the album. It is as though the rest of the songs primarily look to the past and this one looks to the future.

One of the extramusical features of *Skin* that is notable is the documentation of Melissa Etheridge's "Skin" tattoo at the nape of her neck. In addition to the more conventional photographs, the performer and production credits, and the lyrics of the songs, the *Skin* CD booklet contains six photographs directly tied to the process, the instruments, and the final results of the tattoo process. It is as though the tattoo and the depictions of Etheridge receiving it symbolize the possibilities of her new single life, as well as the mark of her 10-plus years with Julie Cypher, the experience, the pain, the memory of which seem to have been as indelibly marked on Etheridge as the tattoo itself.

When considering *Skin*, it should be noted that as a breakup album, it is a near-universal breakup album. Etheridge provides no explicit or even slyly obscured references to the gender identity of any of the ex-lovers of her characters, save the oblique reference to "the different" in the song of the same name. More pointedly, although Etheridge's first-person characters express a wide range of emotional responses to the failed relationships that run throughout every song on *Skin*, Etheridge seems to studiously avoid any responses that could be considered stereotypical of any gender or sexual orientation. To put it another way, Etheridge's characters and her opposites could be just about anyone: she deals in wide-ranging human emotions and situations.

There is another aspect of *Skin* that some listeners might notice: it is a remarkably short album. The fact that *Skin* contains only 10 songs is not new: Etheridge had by that time in her career released several albums with exactly that number of tracks, including her first collections from back in the 1980s. With 7 of the songs under 4 minutes in length, *Skin* clocks in at less than 40 minutes, a length that was possible—and plausible—back in the days of vinyl albums. By comparison, Etheridge's next album, *Lucky*, a work that celebrated Etheridge's new relationship with Tammy Lynn Michaels, contained 13 songs and clocked in at a comparably effusive 55 minutes.

The year 2002 marked the publication of Melissa Etheridge's autobiography, *The Truth Is . . . My Life in Love and Music*. In the book, Etheridge—assisted by cowriter Laura Morton—was open and somewhat revealing about her childhood, including the physical, emotional, and sexual abuse she suffered at the hands of her sister. Etheridge also openly discussed her teen years, coming to self-realization about her sexuality, the early abusive lesbian relationships she survived, and her work during high school as the only female performer in otherwise-male country bands. As the book progresses, Etheridge discusses her work, her personal and professional life, and some of the relationships with which she has been involved. Etheridge focuses most of her attention on her relationship with Julie Cypher and their children. While some of the personal information had been reported in tabloids and in more widely respected media sources, including interviews with Etheridge herself, it was in one place and at one time for the first time in *The Truth Is . . . My Life in Love and Music.*

One of the interesting features of *The Truth Is . . . My Life in Love and Music* is that Etheridge discusses several examples of how her real-life experiences have found their way into her lyrics. Readers who are looking for details on Etheridge's music, though, are apt to be disappointed. The relatively small-scale scope of the book and the focus on biography results in little information about Etheridge's songwriting processes; how she views the intersection between music and lyrics; her approaches to melody, harmony, musical structure, style; and so on. It should be noted that in her interviews Etheridge also focuses on her life, her lyrics, and her general influences at the expense of her music.

Despite the insights that *The Truth Is . . . My Life in Love and Music* provides, the book received mixed—even highly contrasting—reviews. For example, Rob Brunner, writing in the mainstream popular culture magazine *Entertainment Weekly*, referred to *The Truth Is . . . My Life in Love and Music* as "banal" and overly general.[8] In contrast, Laura DeHart Young, writing in the LGBT-focused journal *Lambda Book Report*, gave Etheridge's autobiography a generally favorable review, especially noting Etheridge's openness in discussing her sexuality.[9]

MELISSA ETHERIDGE LIVE . . . AND ALONE (2002)

Before she became a rock star, Melissa Etheridge was highly active as a live performer. Although the venues became significantly larger once she assembled a band, became a recording artist, and became a widely recognized star, Etheridge remained active as a live performer. It might seem somewhat surprising, then, that the first live concert recording of Etheridge did not appear until November 2002. Given the success that Etheridge had achieved by that time as a singer-songwriter and guitarist backed by a powerful rock band, it might also be surprising that the DVD *Melissa Etheridge Live . . . and Alone* is, as suggested in the title, essentially Etheridge's first real solo gig since her days playing clubs before her debut album broke through nationally. Incidentally, fans of Melissa Etheridge might also understand the title as a pun on the end of Etheridge's decade-long relationship with Julie Cypher. This video release is somewhat controversial, as any perusal of fan reviews on numerous websites suggests. Despite her experience playing as a solo act in clubs during and just after her short academic career at the Berklee College of Music, Etheridge's work as a recording artist had all revolved around the use of rock band. In fact, the Etheridge sound has never been fully defined by her voice alone. Etheridge's rhythm guitar (or occasional piano) figures prominently in virtually all of her recordings; however, so do the drum set, electric bass, keyboards, and electric guitar parts played by members of Etheridge's touring band and studio musicians.

Various commentators and rock music critics have discussed the importance of the recording as an artifact in general, and the specific arrangement and record production on the best-known recording of a song in defining the song itself. Perhaps one of the most focused, dramatic, and pointed statements on this came from rock guitarist-composer Frank Zappa:

> On a record, the overall timbre of the piece (determined by equalization of individual parts and their proportions in the mix) tells you, in a subtle way, *WHAT* the song is about. The orchestration provides *important information* about what the composition IS and, in some instances, assumes a greater importance than *the composition itself.*[10]

If the reader accepts that Zappa is correct in his assessment of the significance of the arrangement, and all of the varied aspects of record production in defining a song, then it might be understandable why *Melissa Etheridge Live ... and Alone* is controversial in the view of some fans. By changing the entire musical arrangement and context of her songs, Etheridge in essence recomposes them. The connections that a particular listener might make between the vocal performance style, the instrumental arrangement, the placement of the rhythm guitar in the aural soundscape, a particular drum fill (and so on), and the message and emotional content of Etheridge's lyrics are challenged in a solo live performance setting. So, does this mean that *Melissa Etheridge Live and Alone* is a failure? No. While the DVD might arouse controversy among some fans, it is thoroughly engaging and presents Etheridge in an intimate setting that allows complete focus on the woman, her singing, her sometimes underappreciated guitar playing, and the tunes and words of her songs. Some fans and reviewers actually appreciate this intimate setting better than the rock band context with which Melissa Etheridge's songs are usually associated. For example, former Amazon.com editor Jeff Shannon writes that "this two-disc set is heaven-sent for Etheridge's loyal fans, offering a thorough and technically impressive survey of Etheridge's career thus far."[11]

One major contribution of the video is that it shows the extent to which Etheridge's rhythm guitar playing—more specifically her 12-string acoustic rhythm guitar playing—defines her work as a singer-songwriter. However, one of the attributes that has defined Etheridge's approach to record production, arranging, and performance throughout her career as a recording artist has been the use of dramatic textural contrasts. Without a band, Etheridge's songs do not have the ability suddenly to open up at changes of phrase and changes of section nearly to the extent that they do on her studio recordings. Therefore, what is gained in intimacy in this solo live setting is lost in overall impact and adherence to the structure of the songs as defined by their changes of timbre.

In addition to Etheridge's most iconic and most popular songs, the set list includes some pleasant surprises. Included among them is Etheridge's version of Joan Armatrading's early 1980s composition "The Weakness in Me." For this song, Etheridge accompanies herself on the piano. Perhaps in part because Melissa Etheridge has been associated for so many years with songs about the emotional upheaval that love and loss in love can cause, "The Weakness in Me" is a well-chosen piece for her to interpret, and she does so convincingly.

Other than the performance itself, what perhaps is most important about a live solo track such as "The Weakness in Me" is the fact that it shows that Melissa Etheridge can not only survive but thrive in a bare-bones, intimate musical setting. This puts her in the company of singer-songwriters on either side of her in the age spectrum, such as Armatrading and Ani Difranco. Despite their differences in age and their stylistic differences, Armatrading, Difranco, and Etheridge share a deeply personal, autobiographical-sounding writing style; however, Armatrading and Difranco, to name just two such artists, are much more closely associated with thinner accompanimental textures than Etheridge. Rock does not tend to lend itself to subtlety as much as acoustic singer-songwriter textures, and the texture on the Armatrading composition, in particular, seems far more appropriate to the style and intimacy of the song than the sound of the entire Melissa Etheridge band at full tilt.

For die-hard Etheridge fans, and for people who are interested in Etheridge's prefame work, *Melissa Etheridge Live . . . and Alone* also provides important documentary material in the form of archival footage of Etheridge performing solo just before she began her recording career.

Shortly after the concert dates that included the *Melissa Etheridge Live . . . and Alone* performance, Etheridge was diagnosed with breast cancer. In retrospect, the early twenty-first century must have been an especially terrifying time to receive the diagnosis. It must be remembered that this was a time period just a relatively few years after some well-known personalities in the music industry, specifically British singer Dusty Springfield and the American photographer-turned-rock-keyboardist Linda McCartney, both had succumbed to the disease. As a result of the deaths of Springfield, McCartney, and a number of other iconic popular culture figures, breast cancer was a disease that was very much in the news. Unfortunately, the prominent pop culture figures that recently had battled the disease were not successful in their battles, thereby making breast cancer perhaps one of the most feared cancers.

Between autumn 2004 and her triumphant return to live performance in spring 2005 at the Grammy Awards ceremony, Melissa Etheridge battled the disease. When she finally did return to live performance and as an interviewee on American television programs in 2005, Etheridge appeared bald, bald from the treatments that ultimately helped her to recover from cancer. Etheridge's comeback at the 2005 Grammy ceremony remains one of the more memorable and iconic moments from the Grammys.

LUCKY (2004)

Melissa Etheridge's 2004 album *Lucky* might cause listeners familiar with Etheridge, but unfamiliar with the album itself, to do a bit of a double take. The album art contrasts highly with that of every previous Etheridge album. Instead of the usual CD booklet, *Lucky* includes an approximately 14" × 14" double-sided piece of heavy paper with a poster on one side and the lyrics and credits on the other side. The side with the lyrics and credits also includes four different photos of Etheridge that capture four contrasting moods. In one photograph she appears smiling and wearing a cowboy hat; in another photograph she sports large round sunglasses and looks remarkably like Janis Joplin, and so on. The panel that serves as the CD's cover (which is reproduced as the larger poster) shows a horse's head, a rocket, and a female deep-sea diver or astronaut, all drawn in a cartoonish style. Further study of the cover reveals that all of these images are meant to be part of the art on a pinball machine. Fans who are familiar with Melissa Etheridge's up-and-down love life might find a touch of irony in the depiction of a pinball machine. And, in retrospect, Etheridge's fortunes in love and in health in the first half of the first decade of the twenty-first century seemed to bounce around as much as a shiny metal ball in a well-played pinball machine.

As mentioned previously, Etheridge's previous studio album, *Skin*, the album that followed her breakup from longtime partner Julie Cypher, contained 10 songs and clocked in at under 40 minutes. By contrast, *Lucky* contains 13 songs and lasts approximately 55 minutes. Apparently, then, Etheridge's new relationship with Tammy Lynn Michaels was a monumental inspiration. The songs of *Lucky* are not, however, solely focused on the subject of physical and emotional love. Melissa Etheridge's increasing sense of social responsibility, which developed even further over the course of the next several years,[12] is manifest on *Lucky* in the form of "Tuesday Morning" and "Giant." The former song was dedicated to the memory of Mark Bingham, one of the heroes of doomed September 11, 2001, United Airlines Flight 93, who Etheridge believed was not treated fairly in death by the U.S. government because of his homosexuality.[13] The latter song was understood by some music critics and by Etheridge's audience as an inspired statement against the discrimination against and oppression of members of the LGBT community.[14]

The album opens with its title track. "Lucky" includes an instrumental introduction that features a catchy lead electric guitar melodic hook. Some listeners might hear the lead guitar figure as a distinctive, song-defining hook on the order of, say, George Harrison's slide guitar part on the former Beatle's "My Sweet Lord." In many pop and rock songs with signature instrumental figures, the introductory material returns, perhaps mid-song, or at the very least during the coda, or fade-out section. By contrast, in "Lucky" the prominence of the figure is limited to the introduction. This defies pop-rock convention. For the listener who has had pop music conventions thoroughly ingrained in her or his ears, the arrangement's avoidance of convention can heighten awareness. For example, one might keep anticipating the return of the introductory electric guitar figure and focus in on sections of the song in which it might—either logically or based on past experience with pop songs—occur. Absent the expected instrumental lick, the listener might, then, focus on everything that is transpiring. At least for this listener, this seems to shift the focus to the overall aural experience, including Etheridge's ever-present acoustic rhythm guitar, the brief lead guitar fills, and the lyrics. It should be noted, however, that introducing a potentially important instrumental hook and then failing to take full advantage of its commercial potential can be understood as a deficiency of "Lucky," especially because it breaks all of the rules of commercially oriented pop music.

Melodically, "Lucky" is also notable. While Etheridge's better-remembered earlier songs emphasized the use of memorable melodic hooks primarily in the chorus, the chorus of "Lucky" might not stick in the listener's mind as thoroughly as the closing phrases of the verses. Here, Etheridge emphasizes the fifth scale-degree, however, not as conventionally might be done as a point from which she descends or ascends to a cadence on the tonic pitch. Instead, the fifth scale-step is emphasized as a goal unto itself. To the extent that the listener is familiar with folk-rock of the mid-1960s, this melodic trait of "Lucky" might seem to hearken back to Bob Dylan's "Like a Rolling Stone"-era work.

It should also be noted that *Lucky* is unusual in the Melissa Etheridge canon in terms of the number of coproducers with whom Etheridge collaborated. On "Lucky," Etheridge and her coproducer, David Cole, create an interesting soundscape. As described previously, the track's arrangement includes a signature-type electric guitar introduction. However, the coproducers separate all of the guitar parts of the arrangement in the final mix to the extent that Etheridge's rhythm acoustic guitar is given a prominence to which it was not necessarily afforded on her earlier harder rock-oriented songs.

The text—the lyrics—of "Lucky" finds Etheridge displaying a rare (for her) optimism. She portrays a woman who is ready for a new love relationship, ready for a brighter life. If one understands "Lucky" as an autobiographical work, then one could interpret this as a symbol of Melissa Etheridge's recovery from the pain of her breakup with Julie Cypher, a breakup to which Etheridge had reacted with her previous album, *Skin*.

Because the opening and title track of "Lucky" focuses on the promise of the future, the song works well as the album's opener from a rhetorical standpoint. In fact, the song also represents a logical connection to and progression from "Heal Me," the concluding track on *Skin*. Specifically, in "Heal Me" Etheridge's character begs or prays, depending upon how one interprets the entity to whom her character sings in "Heal Me," to be relieved of her emotional pain and suffering. By the time of "Lucky," it is apparent that she is, at worst, on the mend.

The fact that listeners might hear a connection between the end of *Skin* and the opening track of *Lucky* is significant, just as is the fact that *Lucky* has a more logical rhetorical flow than any previous Melissa Etheridge album. From the time of *Skin* up to her most recent album to date, *4th Street Feeling*, Etheridge has become more of a wider-visioned album artist than the writer and performer of stand-alone songs that she was earlier in her career.

Ironically, despite the greater structural coherence of the album, perusal of the reviews of *Lucky* suggests anecdotally that critics found more individual songs especially worthy of note on this album than on Etheridge's other twenty-first-century collections. The first of these is the album's second track, "This Moment." *Billboard* magazine's Christa Titus, for example, writes that this song, a collaborative composition of Etheridge and John Shanks, "is likely to become a new anthem at proms, graduation parties and wedding celebrations."[15]

Titus's assessment of "This Moment" is interesting on several levels. First, it does suggest that even on Etheridge's most concept-album-like collection up to that time, individual songs tend to define the album. On another level, though, the *Billboard* review suggests just as much that Melissa Etheridge and her music appealed across many traditional boundaries, including age, gender, and sexual orientation.

"This Moment," a collaboration of Etheridge and John Shanks, is a celebration of a new love. The musical setting features a slow large-scale pulse with a more foreground-level triple subdivision of the beat. The rhythmic activity exudes a musical exuberance that fits with the lyrical expression of love and sexual desire. In fact, compared with the less successful combinations of lyrics, music, arrangement, and production on *Lucky*, "This Moment" is a highly successful integration of all of the elements of a pop song.

Perhaps more importantly, "This Moment" can be understood as a pivotal piece in the Melissa Etheridge canon. In the chorus of the song, Etheridge references "the angels" who "will just have to wait." The angelic reference reflects back to such earlier Etheridge compositions as the *Brave and Crazy*'s "The Angels" and *Breakdown*'s "Angels Would Fall." Here, Etheridge puts off the angels, because "this moment" that she is sharing with her lover surpasses any heavenly experience that the angels might offer. The song does not, however, reflect entirely backward into Etheridge's past song catalog. The suspended-note chords that define the introduction and the verses tie the piece to the time period's singer-songwriter style. The arrangement and the electric guitar treatments include touches of U2's The Edge and alternative rock. In her post-*Lucky* recordings, Melissa Etheridge has continued to utilize this stylistic combination, a combination that represents a significant but thoroughly engaging shift from her bluesier heartland rock roots.

"This Moment" also confirms what Etheridge introduced in the album's opening track: that *Lucky* as a whole focuses on the promise offered by love to a far greater extent than any previous Melissa Etheridge album. In fact, "Lucky" and "This Moment" find Etheridge portraying far different characters than was the norm throughout the earlier part of her career. On "Lucky," she even dares to refer to a character as Lucky. Compare this characterization to the first-person characters of Etheridge's compositions at the start of her career, a period in which she typically played the roles of (1) the jilted ex-lover, (2) the sexual aggressor who lusted after the unattainable would-be lover, and (3) the alienated partner in a dysfunctional or disintegrating relationship. There were exceptions, to be sure, but it is safe to say that the one would not expect Etheridge to portray two happy lovers on the first two songs of an album. There is no darkness; there is no hint of romantic disaster lurking in the background; there is only hope and happiness.

This is not to suggest that *Lucky* is entirely populated by songs that anyone even casually familiar with Melissa Etheridge's life story will immediately interpret as autobiographical celebrations of Etheridge's new relationship with Tammy Lynn Michaels. The album is much wider ranging than that. However, the theme of love (as opposed to lust, rejection, and other more stereotypical Melissa Etheridge themes) runs throughout *Lucky*. Even the song that might logically be considered the least likely to adhere to the theme, Etheridge's tribute to September 11, 2001, United Airlines Flight 93 hero Mark Bingham, "Tuesday Morning," focuses as much on Bingham's love for his mother and for his partner as it does on his heroic actions and the discrimination Bingham faced in life and in death as a homosexual man.

Interestingly, "This Moment" exhibits one trait of Etheridge's writing and the arrangements of she and her band that listeners can find throughout her career: the tendency of some of Etheridge's musical settings to reference earlier songs. While the lyrics of "This Moment" seem to refer back to earlier Melissa Etheridge songs, the musical arrangement, by design or by accident, references Joe Cocker's late-1960s version of the Beatles' "With a Little Help from My Friends." The Cocker version of the song, arguably one of the better covers of a Beatles classic, includes a prominent three-note lead electric guitar line that moves from the lowered-seventh scale-step (solfege syllable Te), downward through the sixth scale-step (La) to the fifth scale-step (Sol). So prominent is the figure, and so different is it than anything that is found in the Beatles' original version on *Sgt. Pepper's Lonely Hearts Club Band*, that the Te-La-Sol guitar figure in part defines Joe Cocker's cover.

John Shanks plays the Te-La-Sol figure in "This Moment" approximately one minute and 50 seconds into the song. It should be noted that not only did Shanks play lead guitar on the track, he also cowrote and coproduced "This Moment" with Melissa Etheridge. Shanks adopts an electric guitar tone color that is not at all far removed from the timbre of the line in the Cocker recording, especially considering the fact that over three decades of rock music history had elapsed between the two pieces.

Whether Shanks's incorporation of the "With a Little Help from My Friends" guitar motive was by accident or design, it does provide an interesting subtext to "This Moment," at least possibly to listeners who are familiar with the late-1960s Joe Cocker recording. The John Lennon/Paul McCartney composition "With a Little Help from My Friends" concerns the extent to which, no matter what ills transpire in the life of the singer's character, he will "get by with a little help from [his] friends." To put it another way, the character's friends provide meaning to the character's life. Similarly, in "This Moment," Etheridge's character's lover provides a context for Etheridge's sense of being. Therefore, for listeners who are familiar with the early Cocker recording, Lennon and McCartney's song provides rhetorical support for "This Moment."

In the album's third track, "If You Want To," Etheridge's character reaches out to a potential lover. While it might be hyperbolic to characterize the singer's character as obsessed with the object of her desires, whom she calls on the telephone, Etheridge's lyrics suggest at least something approaching obsession. To fans familiar with the entire Melissa Etheridge canon, this might suggest a return to some of her earlier work that explored the slightly darker sides of sexual desire. While that might be the case with the premise of the song, Etheridge's playful approach to the rhyme scheme and the near-alternative rock nature of the music sound fresh and new, as opposed to anything that could be characterized as a replay of her work of the late 1980s and 1990s. Etheridge also strengths the overall impact of the song by matching the urgency of the lyrics with music that matches. In particular, the strong pulse that subdivides the beats and the rhythmic syncopations can be understood as a subtle form of text painting.

Over the course of her lengthy career, Melissa Etheridge has specialized in performing and recording her own material. In fact, her incorporation of the work of other songwriters is so rare that when it does take place, it truly is noteworthy. The choice of Greenwheel's song "Breathe" is curious for *Lucky*. This is because the album's first two tracks revolve around the possibility, promise, and exuberance of new love. "Breathe," with its tagline of "It only hurts when I breathe," finds Etheridge's character reflecting on a loss in love. In fact, if one takes the first four songs of the album as a whole, the published order seems to be close to a rhetorical retrograde of what one might logically expect on an album that was widely believed to be a testament to Melissa Etheridge's new relationship with Tammy Lynn Michaels.

What is not clear until one listens to the entire album is that perhaps the only way to logically relate *Lucky* to the at-that-time-rosy relationship between Etheridge and Michaels is to listen to the flow of the entire package. At that point, at least to some listeners, it may become clear that *Lucky* can be interpreted as a chronicle of the relationships in Melissa Etheridge's life up to the time of her relationship with Michaels. In other words, the album can be interpreted as a depiction of the ups and downs of love scattered over time, with the final track serving as a representation of the joy of the present. When understood in this way, a song such as "Breathe" makes more rhetorical sense.

Perhaps just as important as the rhetorical sense that "Breathe" makes when the entirety of *Lucky* is considered is the fact that the track represents strong performances from Etheridge and her backing musicians, particularly John Shanks on acoustic and electric guitars. Etheridge, Shanks, bassist Paul Bushnell, drummer Kenny Azonoff, and keyboardist Jamie Muhoberac perform the piece with so much distinctive conviction that "Breathe" becomes a Melissa Etheridge song.

"Mercy," a collaborative composition of Etheridge and Jonathan Taylor, represents a declaration of unconditional love from Etheridge's character. It seems likely that Etheridge fans would interpret the song as a declaration of love for Tammy Lynn Michaels, whom Etheridge thanks "for [her] unlimited love and patience" in the album's liner notes.[16] Despite the fact that the album appeared at the time at which the Etheridge-Michaels relationship was public knowledge, the song is, like the vast majority of Etheridge's compositions throughout her career, fairly general in nature. Etheridge's character could be of any gender, as could the person to whom Etheridge's character declares her love. To put it another way, the song could come from the voice of a woman to another woman, a woman to a man, a man to another man, or a man to a woman.

In "Secret Agent," cowriters Melissa Etheridge and Jonathan Taylor break down gender boundaries in an unusual manner, especially in the context of Etheridge's songs. The text profiles a somewhat stereotypical film noir-style femme fatale whose appearance generates sexual excitation for men and women alike. The song's arrangement pulls out all of the proverbial stops in utilizing every detective/secret agent musical stereotype and cliché, including a lead electric guitar line with a heavy use of tremelo. This effect calls to mind the famous instrumental theme music from the early James Bond films, as well as Elvis Costello's late-1970s track "Watching the Detectives."

Despite these references to Bond and Costello, the accompaniment rhythms and some of the electric guitar tone colors owe much more to alternative rock and hip-hop than to music of the 1960s and 1970s. Musically, this seems like a clever mix of the modern and the retrospective. However, the song seems like a stretch for Etheridge, as some listeners may hear the description of the femme fatale character and the song's combination of modern rock and older styles as contrived.

The next track, "Will You Still Love Me," is a solo Melissa Etheridge composition. Interestingly, this song, like the other solo compositions on *Lucky*, is relatively free of any feeling of being overproduced. The relative simplicity, especially when the song is compared with some of the more complex productions on *Lucky*, helps to provide the piece with a feeling of intimacy, immediacy, and emotional authenticity.

Interestingly, although Etheridge's lyrics are open about specifics, the gist of "Will You Still Love Me" is that her character's partner is on the verge of a "victory" of some sort. In an apparent expression of self-doubt, Etheridge's character asks that song's title question of her lover, wanting to know if the love will remain even after her partner achieves her goals. The song, then, can be understood as an expression of the concern of one partner when a relationship makes a fundamental shift in terms of its power structure. The lyrical references are so general that the listener can interpret this shift in many ways. For example, perhaps up to this point in the relationship Etheridge's character has been the primary breadwinner in the family; now her partner is poised to become the more dominant economic force, and as a result Etheridge's character's self-doubt is heightened. However, this is not the only possible interpretation, and arguably one of Melissa Etheridge's strengths as a lyricist is her ability to create near-universal expressions that can be applied by a wide range of individuals to their own lives.

Generally, Melissa Etheridge's musical settings follow current and sometimes long-standing practices within rock and pop music with regard to melodic shapes, harmonic patterns, rhythmic devices, instrumentation, and so on. This is not to imply that her music sounds unoriginal or derivative. In fact, many of her compositions, particularly after her first two or three albums, sound original, even if the basic materials and procedures are in the same ballpark as those of other late twentieth-century and early twenty-first-century rock songwriters. When Etheridge deviates from the rock song/pop song norm, it is noteworthy. Such is the case with "Will You Still Love Me." Notably, the verses of the song avoid full and complete-sounding cadences on the tonic pitch and tonic chord, at least until the verse gives way to the chorus. To the extent that the listener perceives this avoidance of closure, the melodic and harmonic openness can be understood as a reflection of the sense of unease that Etheridge expresses in her lyrics.

The album's next track, "Meet Me in the Dark," is another production that is free of the electronic trickery that mars some of the other songs on *Lucky*. Here, Etheridge trades in her customary Ovation 12-string guitar for the piano. The texture of piano, female voice, bass, guitar, drums, and orchestral strings would not have been out of place on singer-songwriter-pianist Carole King's iconic album *Tapestry*. In fact, listeners who are familiar with the ballad style of the early 1970s female singer-songwriter-pianists such as King and

Laura Nyro might perceive a possible touch of *Tapestry*-era influence in "Meet Me in the Dark." Although not as fully gospel inflected as the pianistic styles of King and Nyro, there is at least a touch of gospel piano influence in the Etheridge performance. Some of the harmonies that Etheridge employs also suggest a King and Nyro pop song influence. Specifically, Etheridge's guitar-based songs often contain chords with added notes. The guitar-based songs, though, are just as likely to contain suspended fourths and suspended seconds as other added notes. The suspended seconds that often result from open strings in guitar playing are replaced in "Meet Me in the Dark" by more piano-specific intervals and harmonies that focus on triads and seventh chords.

Etheridge collaborated with Jonathan Taylor in writing "Tuesday Morning," a tribute to Mark Bingham, one of the three heroes of doomed September 11, 2001, United Airlines Flight 93 who thwarted the efforts of the terrorists by crashing the plane into a field in rural Pennsylvania. Etheridge sings about Bingham's love for his mother (whom he called on his cellular phone just before he and two of his fellow passengers attacked the hijackers), his father, and "his man." Etheridge subsequently sings of society's refusal to acknowledge the relationship of Bingham and his partner, and the couple's inability to marry in the United States in the early twenty-first century. The song turns increasingly more pointed when Etheridge asks religiously conservative and mainstream Americans how they can look themselves in the mirror after considering how they treated Bingham—and presumably other gays—considering the fact that Bingham gave his life for the sake of other Americans and the nation in general. The progression of emotional intensity strengthens the juxtaposition of "Tuesday Morning" and "Giant," which is an even more pointed and more musically powerful statement against oppression and discrimination.

The music of "Tuesday Morning" exhibits a high degree of melodic contrast between the verses and the chorus. Specifically, the verses favor Etheridge's low vocal register, while the tessitura of the chorus is noticeably higher. The melody of the verse sections is built from short motives. The opening motive, which repeats several times, descends. Similarly, the melody chorus is built from brief motives, the first of which repeats several times. In contrast with the repeated motive of the verses, however, the prominent opening figure of the chorus ascends. The instrumental texture remains consistent throughout the song, although the chorus sections are somewhat louder. The relative similarity of instrumental texture throughout "Tuesday Morning"—especially compared with some Etheridge songs of the twentieth century—provides the piece with a feeling of being an integrated whole.

Unfortunately, "Tuesday Morning" suffers from a touch of the overproduction that marred some of Etheridge's other early twenty-first-century tracks in the view of some reviewers. In this case, Etheridge and coproducer Ross Hogarth include sampled spoken vocal effects that tend to stand out so completely from the prevailing texture of the song that they draw attention away from what otherwise is a heartfelt tribute to Bingham and a description of the trials that he faced as a gay man.

Study of the songwriting credits on *Lucky* reveals that it was easily Melissa Etheridge's most collaboratively written album up to that time. Arguably, though, some of the most personal-sounding expressions and strongest statements are found in the songs that are credited to Etheridge alone. In the latter category, the song "Giant" stands as a firmly stated (in its lyrics, musical arrangement, and performance style) testimony against repression and discrimination. At the time of the release of *Lucky*, some critics and commentators remarked on the strength of "Giant." For example, writing in *The Advocate*, critic Margaret Coble described "Giant" as a "gay pride anthem." Furthermore, Coble praised Etheridge for moving "out of her interpersonal tunnel vision to make some more universal political statements."[17]

Certainly, "Giant" can be understood as an autobiographical song about the relationship between and the eventual marriage of Melissa Etheridge and Tammy Lynn Michaels Etheridge. That being said, "Giant" can be read entirely outside of the context of Melissa Etheridge's personal life, outside of the context of discrimination against, persecution of, and the lack of parental and spousal rights, and so on, for homosexuals. If one takes the listener's knowledge of who Etheridge is, her difficult childhood and adolescent life, and the battles that she had fought ever since her acknowledgment of homosexuality in 1993, and the accompanying strong likelihood that it is an autobiographical statement about the repression of both homosexuality and homosexuals in the United States out of the equation, one can still hear "Giant" as a personal stand against virtually any kind of repression and discrimination. This is because—as is the case with the bulk of her work from throughout her lengthy career—a literal reading of the text of the song reveals nothing that is gender-specific, sexual orientation-specific, or specifically attributable to any other sort of minority status.

The powerful message of "Giant" is enhanced by Etheridge's musical setting and the arrangement and production by Etheridge and Ross Hogarth. Etheridge and Hogarth turn to hard rock, with touches of heavy metal, on this song. While "Giant" might not be Melissa Etheridge's most musically accessible or memorable song, the combination of lyrics and music deliver a solid blow against homophobia.

One of the challenges faced by well-known, long-established popular musicians is to balance new/contemporary sounds and styles with the kinds of styles, musical textures, and rhetorical schemes that resonate with longtime fans. In other words, how can artists win new fans and keep their music modern sounding without alienating the audience that was drawn to them for their early work? One of the peculiarities of *Lucky* is the inclusion of hip-hop references on several tracks. At times, the hip-hop references and production techniques are fully integrated into the rock/folk/singer-songwriter texture. At other times, however, the hip-hop references on *Lucky* do not fit quite so well. In fact, at times they might seem like gimmicks to some listeners. For example, on the song "Come on Out Tonight," coproducers Etheridge and David Cole precede the song proper with the sound of the scratches and pops from a record playing on a turntable. The problem with an effect such as this is that it had been done numerous times before. In fact, among singer-songwriters, genre-boundary-breaking artist Lauryn Hill had done the same thing on her song "The Mis-education of Lauryn Hill" six years earlier. And numerous other pre-*Lucky* hip-hop artists integrated the old-school sound of a scratchy record on a turntable into their productions well before the recording and release of *Lucky*.

While the high energy level and brisk tempo of "Come on Out Tonight" align with the sexual urgency of Etheridge's text, the arrangement is one of the most highly produced of Etheridge's career up to that point. With changes of tempo, abrupt changes from a live band sound to a thin, sampled sound, to the old-school turntable effects, and so on, some listeners will hear the track as fundamentally overproduced, and possibly as confusing.

In fact, the production of the entire album is noteworthy. Because Etheridge coproduced so many of the tracks with a variety of collaborators, there are few song-to-song production connections. It is not just the case of, say, the lead guitar sometimes being predominantly in one of the stereo channels or another. Rather, a track-by-track listening to *Lucky* reveals some songs that evolve subtly from the previous arrangement and production. However, at times the arrangements and productions shift abruptly in style and in such attributes as the relative prominence of the voice, the amount of reverberation, and so on. Interestingly, track-to-track continuity and sometimes unexpectedly abrupt jumps in production style that seem to be disconnected from Etheridge's rhetorical voices in the songs and from the specific situations that Etheridge and her collaborative songwriters set to music manage to coexist on *Lucky*. In other words, the production on *Lucky* provides a perhaps unintended irony: the stories and situations of the songs exhibit a near-concept-album relationship; however, the production suggests a collection of individual stand-alone tracks at times.

In the album's penultimate song, "Kiss Me," Etheridge propositions a lover with a fantasy scenario. She calls her partner on the telephone and suggests that they meet at a bar, pretend that they do not know each other, dance, and (in no uncertain terms) let one thing lead to another. The danceable rock feel of the song is appropriate for the story line and the fantasy world that Etheridge's character creates. Listeners might argue about whether or not the fact that the couple has to resort to sexual role-playing bodes well for the long-term future of the relationship. In the context of the entire album—an album that seems to explore the entire range of relationships that one might experience before meeting one's life partner—the role-playing of the characters can be interpreted as a representation of one aspect of intimate relationships that had not be explored in any of the album's earlier songs.

The lyrics alone of "Kiss Me" are suggestive of the raw sexual desire that might be played out through fantasy role-playing. However, the musical arrangement and the instrumental and vocal performance of the song take that rawness and that physical passion to an even higher level. "Kiss Me" opens with a funky accompaniment style that is performed at a moderate volume level. Etheridge begins her proposition in a somewhat coy, seductive manner. As the lyrics move into describing in more direct detail what Etheridge's character ultimately hopes to experience through role-playing, her singing and the instrumental accompaniment jump up in volume and intensity. The full, distorted electric-guitar-based triads of the harmony can only be described as visceral, which suggests the purely physical nature of the pent-up desire of Etheridge's character.

"When You Find the One" is a beautiful ballad that can be interpreted as a reflection of the Melissa Etheridge life story up to and through the early stages of her relationship with Tammy Lynn Michaels. In fact, this song, the finale of *Lucky*, serves an important structural role because it puts the rest of the album into context. In other words, because "When You Find the One" describes the highs and lows of love over a period of time and through a variety of relationships, before finally concluding that Etheridge's character finally has found "the one," the song clarifies for the listener the fact that the rest of the album represented the path along the way.

The musical setting of "When You Find the One" is notable in several regards. For one thing, the sweetness of the ballad is heightened by its placement immediately after the hard rock, visceral song "Kiss Me." The instrumental arrangement also includes the accordion, played by guest artist Rami Jaffee. Jaffee's accordion, Etheridge's restrained singing, and the largely acoustic nature of the song provide an intimacy that is missing from some of the more elaborately produced tracks on *Lucky*. In fact, the texture contrasts with the bulk of Etheridge's twentieth-century work, which generally leaned in the direction of assertive, jangling, electric guitar-based rock.

Despite the overproduction of some tracks on *Lucky*, the wide stylistic range of the production, and the references to some contemporary popular music styles that some listeners might hear as incompatible with what defines the "Melissa Etheridge sound," the best tracks on the album (e.g., "Lucky," "This Moment," "Giant," "When You Find the One," and "Tuesday Morning") easily stand up to repeated listenings. This is true even when little production idiosyncrasies (e.g., the hip-hop-ish spoken text insertions in "Tuesday Morning") draw some of the attention away from Etheridge's words and music.

In the final analysis, *Lucky* can be counted as a success for Melissa Etheridge on many levels. The album can be interpreted as a synopsis of the Etheridge's life up to time she cemented her relationship with Tammy Lynn Michaels, whom she later married. Despite the likelihood that some of Etheridge's fans continue to assess the album's significance in that light, however, there are other aspects of the album that are notable. This was the first Melissa Etheridge album that found her working in collaboration with quite so many songwriters and with so many coproducers. It clearly shows that she was expanding her stylistic range at an age at which some rock musicians might be simply willing to rest on their laurels and crank out the kind of material that made their name in the first place.

GREATEST HITS: THE ROAD LESS TRAVELED (2005)

Record companies have been releasing greatest hits packages for their pop artists for decades. Traditionally, these packages contained songs that had been the artists' most commercially successful singles. In the twenty-first century, however, the concept of the single as a separately released recording available in a physical medium might seem like a distant memory to some fans of popular music. Consequently, greatest hits packages of the digital age might include prominent album tracks. One of the highlights of Melissa Etheridge's *Greatest Hits: The Road Less Traveled*, however, was the fact that it contained much more than just her iconic hit singles and some of the more prominent cuts from earlier albums that had not been issued as singles. Sure, "Come to My Window" was there, as were "I'm the Only One," "Bring Me Some Water," "I Want to Come Over," and other well-loved songs, but the real meat of this album lies within the new songs that were included, in part because Etheridge's major hits were already so widely available, but also because the new recordings presented sides of Etheridge as a writer and as a performer that were new and that represented an expansion of her musical range.

Greatest Hits: The Road Less Traveled opens with Etheridge's version of Tom Petty's hit "Refugee." Generally, new versions of older material are known in the music industry as "cover" versions. Unfortunately, the term can suggest to some music fans a sound-alike remake of the original, or alternatively a radically different stylistic take on a song put together for commercial reasons (e.g., Pat Boone's 1950s recordings of contemporary songs by black R&B artists such as Little Richard). Melissa Etheridge takes neither of these two approaches on "Refugee." Listeners who are familiar with the 1979 Tom Petty and the Heartbreakers version may notice that Etheridge adopts Petty's parlando-style flexibility of pitch and rhythm in the verses. Although Etheridge's vocal performance sounds particularly Petty-esque, the approach is not new for Etheridge, who uses the same almost speech-like approach in performances of some of her own songs. Another link to the Heartbreakers' original recording can be heard in the unison "You don't have to live like a refugee" backing vocals in the chorus sections of the song. The Etheridge version of "Refugee" features the same kind of jangling electric guitar sound as heard in the original; however, Etheridge recordings dating back to the start of her recording career include that same tone color quite frequently and quite normally. Because the early Melissa Etheridge sound was closely aligned to the same overall aesthetic of Tom Petty and the Heartbreakers, this arrangement avoids sounding derivative. Etheridge and her band also make the arrangement of "Refugee" on *Greatest Hits: The Road Less Traveled* their own by means of abrupt texture changes, similar to those that have defined her hard-rock-style arrangements throughout her career.

Ever since the late 1990s, Etheridge's studio recordings had included stylistic references to hip-hop. In some of the recordings, the hip-hop double-time rhythms, drum loops, turntable sounds, and so on, did not integrate particularly well into the overarching style. Interestingly, the Etheridge band's performance of "Refugee" includes hip-hop-style double-time rhythms in the drums. Here, it works, in large part because it does not interfere with the rock nature of the song and the rest of the musical arrangement on this track.

Listeners should be aware that the single mixes and edits of Etheridge's biggest hits sometimes differ from the album versions. Because some fans may prefer one version over another, it is important to note that *Greatest Hits: The Road Less Traveled* generally is centered around the longer, album versions of the Etheridge's best-known and most commercially successful songs.

One of the most noticeable features of Melissa Etheridge's music that emerges from a collection such as this, which includes material from the 1980s, 1990s, and 2000s, is the extent to which it is consistent in voice. There are, to be sure, some outliers, but for the most part the Etheridge original material on *Greatest Hits: The Road Less Traveled* revolves around relationships; loss in love, lust and physical desire, common themes throughout Etheridge's career as a songwriter, are all well represented here.

Because the reissues on *Greatest Hits: The Road Less Traveled* focus on the lengthier, album versions of Etheridge's most iconic work, it should be noted that "I'm the Only One" and "Come to My Window" are single edits. That being said, in the overall context of this collection, the differences between the original album and the single versions of these two songs are relatively minor.

The fact that *Greatest Hits: The Road Less Traveled* covers so many years also means that it includes some songs that sound dated. In particular, the synthesized keyboard tone colors that play such a prominent role in the arrangements of songs such as "Similar Features" do not hold up particularly well. It should be noted, however, that this certainly is not unique to the recorded output of Melissa Etheridge. Other artists who worked throughout the 1980s also succumbed to the allure of the synthesizer. Fortunately, the bulk of this album leans heavily on the side of guitar-based rock, thus avoiding the obsolescence of electronic fads.

One of the highlights of the album is the inclusion of Etheridge's live performance of "Piece of My Heart" from the 2005 Grammy Awards show. Etheridge's vocal performance and the entire arrangement clearly are modeled on the original popular version of the song as recorded by Janis Joplin and Big

Brother and the Holding Company back in the late 1960s. It should be noted that Joplin's performance of "Piece of My Heart" was one of the most iconic recordings of a thoroughly iconic performer of what arguably was rock's heyday. No recording of "Piece of My Heart" after 1968 stood a chance of competing with the original Big Brother and the Holding Company version. Despite that, Melissa Etheridge took the song on first in the mid-1990s and made it her own. Not only did she compete with Joplin, some listeners might prefer the consistency of her take on the song to the recording that defined Joplin. Critics, too, have expressed their appreciation of Etheridge's powerful version of the song. For example, *Rolling Stone*'s Brian Hiatt referred to Etheridge's 2005 single release of "Piece of My Heart" as "the most spine-tingling performance her career."[18]

Another unexpected highlight of the album—unexpected because it was a relatively new song—was Etheridge's uplifting cancer-related anthem, "I Run for Life." Melissa Etheridge's battle against breast cancer and her reemergence was well documented in the media. After beating the dread disease, Etheridge made numerous television appearances and, of course, performed live, still bald from cancer treatment, at the 2005 Grammy Awards celebration. While it is difficult to assess to what extent Melissa Etheridge is more widely recognized as a gay rights activist or as an advocate for cancer sufferers and survivors, for a period of time after her recovery, Etheridge perhaps was the most recognizable spokesperson for cancer survivors in popular culture.

Melissa Etheridge explains the genesis of the song and the way in which she interwove her own experience with breast cancer in "I Run for Life" on her official website. According to Etheridge, "Ford asked me to write a song for their 'Race for the Cure' initiative to raise funds and awareness for breast cancer charities. I wanted to write a song that was personal; climb into people's emotions and portray a woman who has had breast cancer but is out of it. The first verse is about a survivor. The second verse is from my own experience and the last verse is for those who have not been diagnosed or don't know anyone with breast cancer yet. We are all running for answers and to make the situation better."[19]

While Etheridge acknowledges that running is part of the search for answers and for improvement of the situation, the chorus of the song delivers a more focused message. Etheridge puts a human face on the people affected by the disease (e.g., "your mother, your sister, your wife"), and then she concludes that ultimately she "run[s] for life." The ultimate focal point of the battle against breast cancer provided by the title line and Etheridge's intense vocalization has been seen as an inspiration to cancer sufferers and cancer survivors, and was recognized as such by music critics at the time of the song's initial popularity. *Billboard*'s Christa Titus, for example, wrote in her review of the single release of the song that Etheridge's performance provides "hope and determination."[20]

As inspiring as its lyrical message is, "I Run for Life" is also notable for its musical structure. Some of the melodies of Etheridge's songs from this general era of her career were built from short motives. In "I Run for Life," the main melodic motive of the verses is not repeated as it is in some of other compositions of the period. Here, Etheridge builds longer-range melodic phrases by varying the motive in its repetition and by treating it sequentially. In short, the melodic construction in "I Run for Life" is more mature and sophisticated—more compositional, if you will—than in some of Etheridge's earlier, more conventional pieces.

The theme of battling against the impossible or the near-impossible can be found in earlier songs by other composers. For example, the 1965 Broadway musical *Man of La Mancha* featured as its most popular song the Mitch Leigh and Joe Darion composition "The Impossible Dream (The Quest)." Curiously, whether by design or by accident, the opening melodic motive of the chorus of "I Run for Life" closely resembles the principal melodic motive of the chorus of the Leigh and Darion song.

Because this particular greatest hits album contains new material, previously recorded (but unreleased) live material, as well as Melissa Etheridge's earlier hit songs, it exhibits the transitional nature of Etheridge's work in the middle of the first decade of the twenty-first century. It was at this point that her work began showing greater social awareness on a wider range of issues than her music of the past. Certainly, that can be heard in "I Run for Life." In the next phase of her career, Etheridge would continue to grow in maturity and in integrating her growing social awareness into her compositions.

Maturity

By her own admission, Melissa Etheridge's battle against breast cancer made her reevaluate her life and her work. Etheridge's postcancer songs have reflected a higher degree of spirituality than her earlier work. Likewise, she has expressed concern with environmental and other social issues to a greater extent after recovering from cancer than she ever did before her diagnosis. In this phase of her career, roughly 2006 to the present, Etheridge has continued to explore the good and the bad, the lust, the passion, the regret, and the anger that all surround interpersonal relationships; however, even the relationship-based songs reflect greater maturity and contemplation. To date, this period of Etheridge's career has seen the release of four studio albums: *The Awakening*, *A New Thought for Christmas*, *Fearless Love*, and *4th Street Feeling*. In addition, Etheridge has received more recognition for her career's canon as a songwriter, including the Founders Award from the American Society of Composers, Authors, and Publishers, arguably one of the most exclusive and prestigious awards for songwriters.

Certainly, an argument can be made for marking the beginning of this phase of Melissa Etheridge's career with the her 2005 song "I Run for Life." However, despite the universal nature of the song with regard to the battle against breast cancer, "I Run for Life" is also intimately tied to Etheridge's life and her personal battle against the disease. Perhaps a stronger signal of Etheridge's maturity as a songwriter, and particularly her newfound, postcancer desire consciously to be a writer and performer with a purpose was her 2006 song "I Need to Wake Up."

Etheridge wrote "I Need to Wake Up" for former vice president Al Gore's film *An Inconvenient Truth*, a documentary about human-caused environmental and climate change and the disastrous results of that change. Ultimately, the song won the Academy Award for Best Original Song. Likewise, music critics and op-ed writers heaped praise on "I Need to Wake Up," providing Melissa Etheridge with some of her most favorable reviews in years. For example, in an op-ed piece in *National Wildlife*, Larry J. Schweiger favorably compared the song with Joni Mitchell's classic of environmentalism, "Big Yellow Taxi."[1] *Billboard* magazine critic Chuck Taylor wrote that "Etheridge sings with symbolic conviction" on the single release of the song.[2]

Listeners familiar with the continuing popularity of Joni Mitchell's "Big Yellow Taxi" (Mitchell's recording and a number of other commercially successful versions that have been issued over the years), a song that has enjoyed a far greater shelf life than the bulk of popular music of the year 1970, might consider any comparison of it and the relatively unproven "I Need to Wake Up" as hyperbole. However, Etheridge's song does deserve study, and it did make an impact, especially during the run of popularity and notoriety of *An Inconvenient Truth*. Etheridge's arrangement is largely acoustic guitar-driven. This allows the emphasis to be on her voice, something that is most appropriate for a message song. Compared with some of Melissa Etheridge's recordings of the late 1980s and early 1990s, there is not a huge dramatic dynamic contrast between the verses and the chorus. In keeping with her new almost-folk-influenced style, Etheridge allows the message of her feeling of needing to wake up to the problems that modern technology and consumerism have wrought on the environment to emerge pretty much from the lyrics alone, and from her singing of them—dramatic, crashing distorted electric guitar chords do not overwhelm the voice.

It is significant that Chuck Taylor's review in *Billboard* focuses on the "symbolic conviction" in Etheridge's singing,[3] because Etheridge avoids the tendency to overdramatize her lyrics that had elicited mixed reviews of some of her earlier recordings. Even the official video for "I Need to Wake Up" is exceptionally free of special effects and trickery that might otherwise draw attention away from the lyrics and the Al Gore film's focus on the effects of human-caused environmental degradation. The video consists solely of Etheridge playing acoustic guitar and singing in front of a screen on which scenes from *An Inconvenient Truth* are projected. It remains one of Etheridge's more highly effective music videos, principally because of its stripped-down, from-the-heart production style.

"I Need to Wake Up," as heartfelt as it might be, and as critically praised as it was, seems unlikely to compete with Joni Mitchell's "Big Yellow Taxi" as a pop song commentary on environmental degradation. For one thing, while "I Need to Wake Up" is closely tied to *An Inconvenient Truth* and the new wave of environmentalism that was emerging in the first decade of the twenty-first century, "Big Yellow Taxi" has the advantage of having been issued at the start of the environmental movement in the United States. For another, the song does not have the kind of easily remembered melodic or lyrical hook that the 1970 Mitchell song did. In fact, Etheridge's only slightly earlier issue-based song "I Run for Life" seems more intimately tied to its cause and exhibits stronger melodic, lyrical, and arrangement/production hooks.

THE AWAKENING (2007)

By all accounts, the fact that Melissa Etheridge was diagnosed with, was treated for, and recovered from cancer was a life-changing event. Etheridge discussed the effects of her battle against cancer on her view of the world and her life priorities in numerous interviews.[4] As an activist, and as an artist, Etheridge changed her foci. The songs of *The Awakening*, and the stories behind them, as presented in the uncustomarily extensive liner notes of the album, reflect Etheridge's focus on social issues and clearly explain to the listener the connection between her battle with cancer and the change in her writing style and life priorities. As a result of this change of focus in Etheridge's life and work, *The Awakening* reflects environmental awareness, a heightened sense of spirituality, clearly autobiographical references, and a thematically connected suite of three songs that combine these points of focus.

The album opens with "All There Is," a brief song[5] that includes sci-fi-ish, otherworldly electronic processing of the guitar parts. Etheridge's lyrics consist of two short lines, the gist of which is that the only thing that truly exists in the universe consists of that which consists of electrons, protons, and neutrons. She concludes that all other things that people believe to exist are illusory.

In the next song, "California," Etheridge recounts her move from her native Leavenworth, Kansas, to California. This event occurred shortly after she dropped out of the Berklee College of Music in order to pursue a career as a singer-songwriter. As Etheridge recollects this time of her life, the move resulted in her becoming "almost free." The lyrics of "California" are so vague in terms of what Etheridge's reference to being "almost free" means that it is possible to interpret the song in a variety of ways. Given the real-life story of Melissa Etheridge's life—and her struggles for full marital and full parental rights as a lesbian—the reference might most logically be understood as commentary on society's acceptance of her. In other words, despite the fact that California has been known for decades as a state in which nontraditional lifestyles are accepted, Etheridge has continued to have to battle against discrimination.

Because of the fact that Melissa Etheridge has become an increasingly more sophisticated songwriter over the years, it probably is not surprising that the music of "California" is thoroughly Californian in its style. The arrangement includes a heavy dose of acoustic guitar and a blend of country and rock that owes much to the great hits of the Eagles. The music is clear, relatively laid back, and considerably less rock oriented than many of Etheridge's recordings of the past. Etheridge's music and arrangement largely are successful; however, the backing vocals—a male ensemble, apparently provided by her band mates—do not blend with Etheridge's lead as well as they might in, say, an old-school California-based band such as the Beach Boys or the Eagles.

Weighing in at nearly seven minutes in duration, "An Unexpected Rain" is the longest song on *The Awakening*. From the standpoint of its harmonic basis, the piece might best be described as minimalistic: the verses and the guitar solo sections consist of alternations of the tonic chord (Am7) and the submediant chord (F add9). Over minimal accompaniment, Etheridge recounts an encounter with a fan who becomes a lover. For some listeners, however, the main focus of "An Unexpected Rain" might very well be the electric guitar solos of Philip Sayce. In his blues-rock-oriented licks and use of effects, Sayce seems to be channeling the ballad style of the iconic guitarist Jimi Hendrix. In particular, the Hendrix ballad "Little Wing" sounds as though it might well have been one of Sayce's inspirations.

Perhaps even more significant than the autobiographical-sounding references in the lyrics or the harmonic minimalism and focus on the guitar stylings of Philip Sayce, "An Unexpected Rain" represents a new exploration of musical space for Melissa Etheridge. Generally, Etheridge's earlier compositions consist of carefully defined verses, chorus sections, and a bridge or middle eight. Earlier pieces generally have clearly distinctive chord progressions in the different sections. These earlier works, which frequently also include electric guitar solos, generally fall within traditional pop song structure. By contrast, "An Unexpected Rain" has a more open structural feel. To be sure, the song's bridge is built on more rapidly changing and more varied harmonies than the verses. However, so much of the musical space consists of near harmonic stasis that the song feels more open-ended in structure than any previous Etheridge piece.

The open structural feel of the music of "An Unexpected Rain" and the relatively low tessitura, almost heightened speech-like melody that Etheridge sings work effectively to create a mood of contemplation. Because the song is not structured like conventional pop music, it can be interpreted as a work that comes straight from the heart. In this respect, it stands out from other, more conventionally constructed Melissa Etheridge pieces in the same way that the through-composed art songs of nineteenth-century German composer Robert Schumann stood out from the conventional strophic-form songs of his day.

Some of Melissa Etheridge and her various coproducers' experiments of the 1990s and the first decade of the twenty-first century led to mixed results. For example, the hints of hip-hop-inspired production and effects of some of the songs from the period stood out from the bulk of Etheridge's work such that they could be heard as somewhat artificial. By contrast, the electronic processing at the opening of the song "Message to Myself" is understated and clever. Coproducers Etheridge and David Cole strip the opening of the song of the lowest and highest frequencies in imitation of the audio fidelity—or lack thereof—of an inexpensive radio. Etheridge sings of writing a song "as a message to [herself]." She tells the listener that hearing the song on the radio will remind her that she is "fine."

Because "Message to Myself" references Etheridge's state of being, as well as the more specific "blackness in [her] chest," it is easy to interpret the song's inspiration and opening lyrics as her self-acknowledgment of having beaten breast cancer. However, there is much more to the song than that. The bulk of Etheridge's lyrics revolve around the basic theme of (not in her words), "What goes around comes around." Without using the world *karma*, Etheridge explores the karmic relationships between expressing love and receiving love. While this is really nothing new, particularly in popular music going back to the hippie days of the 1960s, the message is significant in Etheridge's output as a songwriter. A substantial number of her earlier works revolve around the wants, desires, and losses of her characters—not around the process of giving.

Still, because the overarching message of "Message to Myself" is not entirely new, it seems likely that it was not just the lyrics that caused *Billboard* critic Chuck Taylor to call the track Melissa Etheridge's "best song of the decade."[6] While the song's ranking among Etheridge's compositions between 2000 and 2007 is subject to debate, "Message to Myself" perhaps unquestionably is Etheridge's most thoroughly engaging pop track of the period. The song is upbeat and optimistic and contains an easily memorable melodic hook in the chorus that ranks among the best (in terms of pop accessibility) in Melissa Etheridge's career.

There is one other aspect of "Message to Myself" that makes the track so successful: the production of Etheridge and David Cole. Aside from the faux-AM-radio effect in the opening of the song, "Message to Myself" is free of any obvious studio effects. What Etheridge and Cole did was to further the track's commercial accessibility by muting some of the customary Melissa Etheridge vocal edge. The production does not represent nearly the kind of dramatic change in vocal timbre witnessed in Bob Dylan's iconic *Nashville Skyline* album (in which Dylan's voice sounds quite different than it does on any other Dylan recording); however, clearly Etheridge and Cole exhibit more attention to integrating Etheridge's vocal tone color into the overall texture of the final mix than what tends to be heard on the immediate predecessors to *The Awakening*. And, in fact, one of the hallmarks of the entire album is the feeling of structural coherence provided by the unified writing style and the consistency of the arrangements and productions. It must be remembered that the album's immediate predecessor was perhaps Melissa Etheridge's most highly collaborative album. The fact that Etheridge was the sole writer and that Etheridge and David Cole were the sole producers of all of the tracks on *The Awakening* made for a more coherent, consistent collection.

The next piece, "God Is in the People," contains the briefest lyrics of any song that Etheridge had recorded or has recorded since. The gist of the text is that although people continue to believe in a supreme being whose existence cannot be proved, the reality of life is that "God is in the people." The message contains an element of spirituality; however, Etheridge's view of the universe might best be described as secular humanistic in nature.

The music of "God Is in the People" exhibits the influence of gospel music. This is suggested by the 12/8 (compound quadruple) meter of the piece, the slow tempo, and the background, backing chorus. Despite these gospel touches, the musical arrangement retains a characteristic Etheridge touch, in the form of gritty distorted electric guitars, played by Etheridge and Philip Sayce. Although individual listeners might disagree about what Melissa Etheridge's most memorable musical arrangements and most memorable melodies are, I suspect that "God Is in the People" is not likely to top very many lists. For one thing, at one tick under two minutes in length, "God Is in the People" is one of Etheridge's shortest recordings ever. In addition, the song is highly repetitive, with a substantial amount of time devoted to repetitions of the chorus as an extended coda, or fadeout, section. On the surface, this might appear to be a deficiency in the composition and arrangement. Interestingly, the simplicity, the repetition, and the clarity of Melissa Etheridge's voice in the arrangement and recording production combine to funnel the listener's attention squarely on the text, and especially on the song's title line. And if the listener considers the song to be a secular humanistic version of what otherwise might be a religious piece, then the repetitions can be understood in the context of the choruses that are used sometimes in late twentieth-century and early twenty-first-century contemporary Christian worship and praise services. It is also possible to understand the song as a pop music version of a chanted secular humanistic mantra.

In "Map of the Stars," Etheridge explores the world of the stereotypical dream of young girls: to become a star of film and stage. As Etheridge observes the girl, apparently during the character's high school years, she sees the girl eating little and taking up smoking in an attempt to keep her weight down. When the girl becomes a young woman and finally begins to realize her dream, she continues the pattern of dieting, smoking, and anything else that she needs to do in order to keep the kind of figure that helped her to become a star. As her career finally sees less-than-stellar film roles and the personal problems that come from fame, she turns to drink and moves into a downward spiral in her personal relationships. Because the release of *The Awakening* occurred during the more apparently blissful days of her relationship with Tammy Lynn Michaels, but followed Etheridge's breakup with Julie Cypher, it is tempting to understand the song as a reference to Cypher. However, the piece is broad enough that the listener might be more likely to hear it as commentary on the unreasonable expectations that young women are fed by Madison Avenue, the fashion industry, and the entertainment industry.

Musically, "Map of the Stars" is subdued pop-rock, with minute touches of contemporary country-pop and gospel. Interestingly, even though the collection of tone colors favor Etheridge's voice and acoustic guitar, there is a backing electric guitar part (noticeable perhaps most clearly in the chorus) that uses a touch of distortion and a tremelo effect similar to what is used in "God Is in the People." Small touches such as this help lend a structural coherence to the musical settings of *The Awakening* that is missing from some of Etheridge's earlier albums. What is perhaps most interesting about this background feeling of structural coherence that some listeners might perceive is the fact that the songs of this collection exhibit the widest range of durations of any Melissa Etheridge album, and—at 16 tracks—the songs are significantly more numerous than on any other Etheridge album.

The fact that Etheridge's vocals are placed relatively far forward in the mix in "God Is in the People," "Map of the Stars," and some of the other songs cannot be overlooked. The listener might easily suspect that coproducers Etheridge and David Cole intentionally made the lyrics of these songs more prominent. And, this would be a natural assumption, because *The Awakening* is, by and large, a message-song collection.

Despite the song's titillating title, "Threesome" is not some sort of invitation to a *ménage à trois*. Quite to the contrary, the song finds Etheridge's character singing to a lover that she explicitly does not want to be involved in a relationship in which she has to share her lover with someone else: she wants a stable one-to-one relationship with her partner. It is a somewhat unusual—for a pop song—way to declare one's undying love. For that reason, its unusual imagery and turn of phrase, "Threesome" can stay in the listener's mind longer than more conventional expressions of love. What really turns this into an even more memorable album cut, though, is the contemporary country-rock hybrid style. In fact, the musical composition, rhythmic style, and arrangement would not be out of place on an album by virtually any young, contemporary female rock-influenced country star. Even though the way in which Etheridge's character declares her undying love—"I don't want to have a threesome"—is unusual, the lyrics of the song, too, would not be entirely out of place in the modern country music of the day. In short, this demonstrates Melissa Etheridge's continuing broadening of stylistic range and means of expression.

Within the Melissa Etheridge canon, *The Awakening* is unique, in part because of the incorporation of four songs that are under two minutes in length. The album's opener, "All There Is," and the album's eighth track, "All We Can Really Do," are aphoristic expressions of Etheridge's global and interpersonal philosophy. In the latter song, she presents the listener with one brief line that explains that the only possible thing that people can do to bring meaning to life is to "love one another." After a fairly substantial instrumental introduction—28 of the song's 78 seconds—Etheridge sings the song's brief, two-phrase chorus. When the chorus is repeated, a chorus of backing singers joins her, singing in unison. This texture, and the fact that the song consists only of a chorus section (there are no verses), calls to mind the way in which some contemporary Christian music is used in worship services: the chorus is sung first perhaps by the singers in the praise band, and then repeated a number of times with the congregation joining in. In sharp contrast to a contemporary Christian praise chorus, however, the message of "All We Can Really Do," noble though it might be, stands entirely within the camp of secular humanism, and likely would never find its way into a praise service.

Undoubtedly, it was risky for Etheridge as a songwriter and for Etheridge and David Cole as coproducers to include several obvious references to musical styles closely associated with various Christian worship traditions. In addition to the contemporary Christian stylistic touches in "All We Can Really Do," the reader might recall that the song "God Is in the People" clearly references black gospel music in its rhythmic and metrical style and in the lead vocal/backing chorus texture. Like the present song, "God Is in the People" represents Etheridge's secular humanistic philosophy. The challenge of references to gospel and contemporary Christian music is that one might hear Etheridge's work on *The Awakening* as gimmicky, as sacrilegious, or as mockery.

In the next song, "I've Loved You Before," Etheridge moves back to the subject of romantic love. As Etheridge's character addresses her lover, the gist of the text is that the two share such a strong, inseparable bond that Etheridge's character feels as though she has loved her partner in a former life. This, despite my description of the text, is not a song about reincarnation as the concept is believed in some religious traditions of the Indian subcontinent; it is really about the thoroughness of the bond and knowledge of and understanding the other partner in the relationship.

The acoustic guitar-focused accompaniment and restrained singing help to make "I've Loved You Before" a quite accessible song. Etheridge's melody in the verse sections, like some of her work extending all the way back to the early days of her professional career, is built from repetitions of, sequential treatment of, and slight variations of a short motive, or melodic kernel. There are, however, some unusual features to the structure of the verses, and to the structure of the entire song.

Let us begin by considering the verse sections. Each verse consists of 12 measures of quadruple-meter music. These 12 measures are divided into five, 2-measure sung phrases, which are finished off with 2 measures of instrumental music. Depending upon how closely the listener thinks that the fourth phrase resembles the first, five sung phrases exhibit a phrase structure relationship of either a-a-b-a^1-c, or a-a-b-c-d. The final one of the sung phrases contains a rhythmic effect that resembles a momentary suspension of time.

In fact, the use of five sung phrases (pop songs usually are constructed in even numbers of phrases) in the verse sections also creates something of a feeling of the suspension of measurable time. These effects mirror the text's references to an eternal love.

The overall structure of the song is also somewhat unusual. The worlds of pop and non-blues-based rock music are populated by an enormous number of songs that bear some resemblance to the old Tin Pan Alley-era AABA pop song form. In other words two verses are presented, and then a chorus, followed by another verse. There may be other sections, such as a so-called middle eight section; however, AABA forms the basis for much of the non-blues-based American popular music canon of the twentieth and early twenty-first centuries. The song "I've Loved You Before" contains three verses (e.g., AAA) before the chorus section is first heard.

Without undertaking a scientific study of listeners' perceptions of musical form and deviations from the "norm," it is difficult to speculate as to how listeners are apt to interpret or react to Etheridge's inclusion of three verses before the chorus in "I've Loved You Before." Furthermore, it is possible that some listeners might not even notice any deviation from a theoretical norm. From a personal standpoint—because I have listened to the song analytically—I hear the form as another confirmation of the distortion of human-perceived time (the concept of the eternal and the recurring) as reflected in the lyrics.

The album's next track, "A Simple Love," is another of the sub-two-minute aphoristic pieces. Perhaps as tuneful as any verse or chorus that Melissa Etheridge has written, the piece sounds more like a fragment of a never-completed song than the other short pieces on *The Awakening*. In fact, on the surface it sounds like a chorus directed at Etheridge's partner. In that respect, "A Simple Love" can be heard as a piece that takes the listener into the private, personal world of Melissa Etheridge and Tammy Lynn Michaels. In doing that, "A Simple Love" serves a worthy function. However, it is possible that some listeners will hear the piece as a structural mismatch for *The Awakening*, because the other aphoristic songs speak directly to Etheridge's philosophical/religious beliefs and this one does not.

If the listener goes beneath the surface of "A Simple Love," however, the song can be interpreted as something greater than at first it appears. Melissa Etheridge's songs of the 1980s and the 1990s frequently present the prospects for a relationship as somehow dark, perhaps even illicit. In the concluding chapter of this book, I will suggest the possibility that the nature of these relationships might be tied to a psychological phenomenon known as internalized sexual stigma, which some researchers tie to the minority status of members of the lesbian, gay, and bisexual communities. Interestingly, the instability of the relationships and the foreground and background implications of illicitness that populate Etheridge's twentieth-century canon are absent in this brief chorus/song. While this may reflect the relationship between Tammy Lynn Michaels and Etheridge, it might also be understood as reflective of a wider acceptance of members of the LGB community in American society at large in the twenty-first century.

The Awakening contains so many songs that some listeners might find it difficult fully to appreciate all of the individual tracks. Because of the relative simplicity and clarity of the arrangement—compared with some of Melissa Etheridge's more powerful hard-rock recordings—it is easy to overlook the song "Heroes and Friends." It is simply impossible fully to appreciate the song without hearing it. Etheridge takes the images of an individual's heroes and an individual's friends and mixes the images in a number of intriguing ways. The upshot of all of this is that giving serious consideration to the lyrics of the song can cause the listener seriously to consider to what extent she or he can consider her or his friends to be hero figures.

"Heroes and Friends" is one of Etheridge's more lyrics-focused compositions in that the musical setting focuses fully on Etheridge's voice. The challenge that the listener faces is that the focus of the lyrics is somewhat difficult to pin down. Part of the message is that one cannot fully understand and appreciate all of the good in life without first experiencing loss, disappointment, and sorrow. Part of the message is that one must take responsibility for one's life: if an individual wants change on a personal or global scale, one must actively work toward that change. Part of Etheridge's message, however, is that there are universal truths, and that part of what makes up a person cannot be changed. Conceivably, one could tackle each of these intertwined messages individually and provide more focus. Because "Heroes and Friends" freely moves between these messages, it is more difficult to grapple with—and less focused—than some of the best songs that Melissa Etheridge has written.

Although Etheridge does not state it directly, the next song, "The Kingdom of Heaven," sounds at the beginning as though it could have been written in direct response to the antigay protests of the Topeka, Kansas-based, Westboro Baptist Church.[7] The references that Etheridge makes, to antigay epitaphs and to statements from an unidentified religious group that espouses the belief that God hates the United States, all seem to relate to the highly controversial—and well-publicized and highly public—statements of the congregation and its leaders. In contrast to the hate-filled beliefs that Etheridge apparently sees from the more reactionary side of Christianity, she tells the listener that "[her] God is love," and further explains that love extends to everyone, without exception.

Interestingly, as "The Kingdom of Heaven" progresses, Etheridge seems also to take on radicals who use religion as a justification for hate from other countries and from other religious backgrounds. Specifically, her descriptions of believers "strapping" the expression of their beliefs on their backs is quite easy to interpret as a post-9/11 reference to Islamist suicide bombers, despite the mostly general and somewhat oblique nature of her lyrics.

Etheridge sets the text of "The Kingdom of Heaven" to thoroughly engaging music. The melody of the verses meanders somewhat and the rhyme scheme is more free than in Etheridge's more rock-oriented works, giving the song a feeling of spontaneity. The guitar tone color that she and coproducer David Cole emphasize on the track includes a touch of flanging and other effects that give it a diffuse, atmospheric feel. The thin texture allows the listener to focus fully on Etheridge's voice and, thereby, on her philosophical statement. Etheridge rarely turns to an acoustic (or nearly acoustic) confessional singer-songwriter style in her musical arrangements. When she does so, the songs tend to delve into Etheridge's philosophy of life, such as in the case of "The Kingdom of Heaven."

As one experiences *The Awakening* as a complete whole work, one might notice right around the time of "Open Your Mind" that the overall progression of tracks changes dramatically. Specifically, all four of the short, aphoristic, sub-two-minute chorus-like tracks are sequenced within the first 10 songs of the album. The final six tracks all last between three and approximately six and one-third minutes. It seems likely that different listeners will react to this structure change differently. It is possible to hear the album as settling in for the last four or five tracks. This seems especially likely to be the case if one hears the short pieces to be brief interruptions that introduce ideas that are not fully developed. However, regardless of how one interprets the four short tracks, it does seem likely that some listeners will sense the change of pacing and progression that occurs because of their segregation in the first part of the album. Perhaps more important than whether listeners react favorably or unfavorably to the structure of *The Awakening* is the fact that it is possible to hear the change in the progression of the album as fully intentional. This suggests Melissa Etheridge's increasing attention to the album as an entity.

In the song "Open Your Mind," Etheridge seems to channel the blues-rock of the late 1960s, in form, rhythmic style, and guitar tone colors. This 12/8-meter song features Etheridge's characteristically high degree of melodic contrast between the verses and the chorus. While the chorus melody is not the most easily memorable of Etheridge's career, it is suitably dramatic. The verses, by contrast, are understated and the melody stays in the bottom of Etheridge's vocal range. This contrast of style and range, the sharp contrast in volume between the verse and chorus sections, and the pseudo-late-1960s blues-rock style of the verses call to mind Janis Joplin's work with Big Brother and the Holding Company.

In the opening verse of "Open Your Mind," Etheridge asks why so many people live their lives in fear, in desperation, and in hopelessness. In the chorus, Etheridge invites the downtrodden to "open [their] mind[s]" and find meaning in the "ancient mysteries" of life. Some listeners might find the invitation to be too simple: can one truly change one's life just by changing how one views and interprets it? Other listeners might wonder if Etheridge perhaps is espousing a particular ancient belief system or philosophical system that she does not specifically name. Some of the lyrics are impressionistic enough that, while they might suggest poetic images of states of being and changes in states of being based on belief, some listeners might find them difficult to follow. Interpreted as a sort of embodiment of the musical and impressionistic lyrical styles of the late 1960s—the psychedelic blues era—the piece makes more sense.

Etheridge continues to explore a similar theme in "The Universe Listened"; however, with more focused lyrics. Here, she wonders why it is that people seem to be unable fully to live life until they are at the ends of their lives. It is this reference that seems to be tied to Etheridge's experience with cancer and the change it made in her view of life. Although she does not use the old saw, the theme here is that people need to live every day to its fullest. In this context, the meaning of the title line might not be immediately apparent. And, it is open to interpretation; however, it is easy to imagine that the message is that when one decides to live life to its fullest, to pursue real meaning in life—which for Etheridge is love—one will find that the universe provides.

Despite the thematic connections of the lyrics of "Open Your Mind" and "The Universe Listened," the latter song is actually the opening of a 3-track song cycle. Although the cardboard sleeve that contains the CD, and the song titles programmed into the physical disc list the last three songs as "The Universe Listened," "Imagine That," and "What Happens Tomorrow," the multifold album booklet gives the titles as "The Awakening: The Universe Listened," "The Awakening: What Happens Tomorrow," and so on. Taken as a short song cycle, the last 3 tracks on the album do, in fact, summarize much of what Etheridge covers over the course of the previous 13 tracks, with a special focus on social, political, and philosophical issues.

The musical setting of "The Universe Listened" moves in the direction of Etheridge's new, more acoustically based folk-rock, singer-songwriter style. Of potentially particular interest to Etheridge fans, "The Universe Listened" bears some melodic, harmonic, and arrangement resemblance to "Kansas City," the opening track on Etheridge's later *4th Street Feeling* album. "Kansas City" is a more powerful, more focused, and likely to be experienced as a more memorable song.

One of the criticisms that can be leveled at Melissa Etheridge as a musical social activist is that she is at times slow to tackle issues in her compositions and recordings. To put it another way, she seems at times to be a slightly temporally displaced topical songwriter. Such is the case with the second movement of her "Awakening" cycle, "Imagine That." The song opens with Etheridge recounting the story of a soldier's mother who mourns the loss of her son in battle. The woman—and Etheridge as observer—wonder aloud how the president could have led the soldier into war on false pretenses. Etheridge's text refers to "weapons" that were thought to exist as the pretense of the war, as well as to the fact that those "weapons" were never found once the invasion began. In the context of the post–September 11, 2001, world, especially with the frequent references to "weapons of mass destruction" that were made by the George W. Bush administration as the justification for the U.S.-led invasion of Iraq in 2003, Etheridge's somewhat vague references to a war at the beginning of the song were understood as pertaining to the Iraq War.

In the second verse of "Imagine That," Etheridge narrows the focus, and clarifies the fact that the song is indeed a direct response to the ongoing war in Iraq. She tells the story of a career military man who is on trial for refusing to serve in the Iraq War. The soldier refuses to fight because, in his view, the war is being waged solely for profits. As an antiwar protest song, "Imagine That" suffers on two counts. First, pop musicians had already been protesting public statements of U.S. President George W. Bush calling for war against the "Axis of Evil" and the subsequent U.S. military action in Iraq since 2003. For example, Natalie Maines, of the alt-country band the Dixie Chicks, had made her famous proclamation about being embarrassed that Bush was from her native Texas in 2003. Although this caused some furor among the Dixie Chicks' country audience, by 2005 the Dixie Chicks were back on the top of the alt-country charts. Here, then, was Melissa Etheridge making her musical protest two years after the Dixie Chicks had regained their popularity.

The second problem that some listeners might have with "Imagine That" is that the song's focus abruptly shifts for the third verse. Here, Etheridge returns to restating her belief that God can be found in subatomic particles and in love that is shared between people. In short, the song can be heard as losing its focal point.

That is too bad, because "Imagine That" is a melodically engaging piece. The fact that the song is not all that it might have been, particularly after the success of Etheridge's first issues-focused songs after her battle against cancer, "I Run for Life" and "I Need to Wake Up," suggests that Etheridge's best work seems to come with her individual songs. "Imagine That," for example, bears the stamp of a composition that might have been more successful, but for the possible fact that it had to conform to the constraints of an album.

The album's finale, "What Happens Tomorrow," revolves around the possibilities offered by commitment to betterment of the world. In short, Etheridge ponders—and invites her listeners to ponder—what can happen when individuals come together to work for the good of all. She frames her vision specifically around the United States of America, and envisions a time in the future when a woman can be president of the United States. She concludes the song by telling listeners that "truth is of the people; by the people; [and] for the people." Etheridge's adoption of a key line from President Abraham Lincoln's Gettysburg Address aligns with the secular humanistic sentiments that she developed in the earlier songs on *The Awakening*, perhaps most clearly in "God Is in the People." The Lincoln quote might also suggest to some listeners that the ultimate Truth—with a capital *T*—can come from the full and complete living out of the democratic ideals that are contained in the U.S. Constitution. Ultimately, the political message of the song seems somewhat blurry. For example, the listener might be confused over the exact meaning of the Lincoln quote. And, the fact that the song opens in a very general way and then abruptly changes to focus on gender-based equality within the U.S. political area seems curious. While the connections to the album's earlier secular humanistic-based lyrics allows "What Happens Tomorrow" to function as a suitable conclusion to *The Awakening*, the narrowing of the song's focus to gender-based equality runs counter to what might best sum up the album.

The Awakening signaled Melissa Etheridge's emergence as a singer-songwriter fully engaged with social and spiritual issues, although sometimes those are not always as clearly defined as they might be. Interestingly, it is Etheridge's most effusive studio album. Etheridge's early albums generally weighed in at approximately 10 songs in length. *Lucky*, the album that can be understood as Etheridge's recounting of the good and the bad of her romantic relationships up to and including her relationship with Tammy Lynn Michaels, stood out from those earlier efforts, in part because of its 13 tracks. However, the 16 tracks of *The Awakening* took Melissa Etheridge into an entirely different realm as an album artist. Again, though, it was not just the sheer size of *The Awakening* that distinguished it from its predecessors; it was also the range of the subject matter (e.g., romantic love songs; songs about the nature of God; songs about the importance of universal, platonic love; autobiographical recollections of the past; and so on). In addition, within those broad categories, Etheridge explored new ways of expressing old ideas (e.g., her character's declaration of love in "Threesome").

The general public received *The Awakening* a touch better than they had its immediate studio predecessor, as measured by chart standings: *Lucky* peaked at No. 15 on the *Billboard* 200, while *The Awakening* peaked at No. 13. However, some critics preferred *Lucky*. For example, *All Music Guide*'s editors gave *Lucky* four and one-half stars (out of five), while awarding *The Awakening* only three and one-half. That critical reaction was not necessarily universal: writing in *People*, Chuck Arnold praised Etheridge's work on *The Awakening* for being "more nuanced" than her past work.[8] Despite individual preferences—especially in musical approaches—*The Awakening* at least in part lived up to its name: Etheridge more fully integrated her own life story with her personal philosophy and her observations about the world at large to a greater extent on this album than she had up to that time. Ultimately, though, Melissa Etheridge's greatest musical contributions might be heard as her individual songs. Even though *The Awakening* is a formidable album—and an exceptionally rare concept album from Etheridge—the abrupt shifts in focus, the seriousness of the focus on difficult issues, the timing of some of the social statements, and the album's unusual pacing structure make the overall work less likely to live on as well as the best of Etheridge's individual songs from her other albums.

Not only did *The Awakening* serve as an expression of Melissa Etheridge's growing sense of social awareness and spirituality, Etheridge became increasingly vocal in her support of breast cancer sufferers and for environmental stewardship around the time of the album's recording and release. For example, Etheridge provided an op-ed piece for *Time* in support of Al Gore for the magazine's Person of the Year award. As one might expect, based on the fact that Etheridge had been a supporter of the Clinton-Gore ticket back in 1992 and had written and recorded the song "I Need to Wake Up" for Gore's documentary film about global climate change, *An Inconvenient Truth*, her endorsement of Gore is based largely on his commitment to exposing and slowing human-induced large-scale environmental change.[9] Etheridge also wrote a brief profile of breast cancer sufferer Elizabeth Edwards, whose husband John was a onetime U.S. senator and unsuccessful candidate for the U.S. vice presidency and presidency, for *Time*.[10] The fact that Etheridge provided these brief pieces for *Time* suggests the fact that by the 2006–7 period she had achieved significant name recognition as a pop culture personality. The fact that Etheridge expressed her views in *Time* also signifies that she had found a mainstream, mass-market forum for her social activism.

And not only did Melissa Etheridge gain an increasingly broad forum for her observations about society and politics than in the past, thus suggesting her iconic place in American pop culture, she also received new official recognition for her work as a singer-songwriter. ASCAP presented Etheridge with the 2007 ASCAP Founders Award. According to the Society, "The ASCAP Founders Award is our most prestigious honor and is given to songwriters and composers who have made pioneering contributions to music by inspiring and influencing their fellow music creators."[11] In receiving this award, Melissa Etheridge joined the ranks of previous winners such as Joni Mitchell, Neil Young, Bob Dylan, Emmylou Harris, and Stephen Sondheim, as well as more recent winners, such as Patti Smith and Sean "Puffy" Combs.

A New Thought for Christmas (2008)

In the liner notes for her 2008 album *A New Thought for Christmas*, Melissa Etheridge writes, "I have never been a religious person, yet Christmas has always been one of my favorite times of the year."[12] Given Etheridge's rock—as opposed to pop—style, her penchant for dramatic lyrics about relationships gone wrong, and her self-proclaimed lack of religiosity, a betting person probably would not have put down a whole lot of money on the possibility of a Christmas album coming from Melissa Etheridge. *A New Thought for Christmas* balances traditional Christmas season pop songs (e.g., "Blue Christmas," "Christmas [Baby Please Come Home]," "Have Yourself a Merry Little Christmas," and "Merry Christmas Baby") with Etheridge compositions that include musical and lyrical references to and quotes from traditional carols, but that revolve around the need for love, freedom, equality, peace, and hope. Etheridge's songs, save one, include her own lyrics and exhibit a nonreligious spirituality that is rarely found in songs that she wrote before suffering from and overcoming cancer. Musically, the songs of *A New Thought for Christmas* range from hard blues-based rock, to pop, to R&B-influenced jazz. In fact, the album fits squarely in with Etheridge's other work of the twenty-first century in which she stretches her stylistic range across a broader spectrum of American popular music styles.

The album opens with Etheridge and her band's take on "Blue Christmas," the Billy Hayes and Jay Johnson composition initially popularized by Elvis Presley, and still one of the few true rock-and-roll Christmas season classics. This is not, however, an arrangement or performance that in any way can be understood as a mere cover of the famous Presley recording. Etheridge's version exhibits a wider emotional and dynamic range than that of the famous Elvis Presley recording. This version opens as almost a gentle stroll, with Etheridge singing at a subdued dynamic in the lower tessitura of her range. The instrumental backing, too, is subdued, with a few brief electric guitar licks that suggest an R&B influence. As the track continues, however, Etheridge adds a considerable amount of passion into her presentation, and at times utilizes the upper part of her range—something sometimes missing from her performances of her own compositions. Perhaps just as notable as Etheridge's singing, though, is the searing, tortured electric guitar solo of Philip Sayce. Sayce's work on the track combines high-energy blues-rock with a touch of heavy metal-influenced shredding.

In her composition "Glorious," Etheridge turns to a gentle singer-songwriter pop style. In other words, the music, musical arrangement, vocal style, and instrumental tone colors of "Glorious" stand in stark contrast to those of "Blue Christmas." The emotional content of the piece also stands in stark contrast. Here, Etheridge deconstructs the texts of the traditional Christmas carols "Silent Night" and "Angels We Have Heard on High," and uses key phrases to reconstruct her text. The Etheridge text presents a series of images that revolve around the coming together of groups of friends and families at Christmas, and the songwriter's observation that these gatherings find the participants dispensing with the "fear" and "judgments" that might otherwise cloud or poison relationships.

It is interesting to note that both the verses and the chorus of "Glorious" share principal melodic motives, and in particular one that emphasizes scale-step five. Interestingly, this melodic emphasis on scale-step five calls to mind the opening of the carol "Silent Night," which begins on the fifth scale-step.

Next, Etheridge turns to the Jeff Barry, Ellie Greenwich, and Phil Spector composition "Christmas (Baby Please Come Home)," a song best remembered from Darlene Love's early 1960s hit recording. The arrangement, particularly in the rhythm section and the backing vocals sounds, can be understood as a twenty-first-century update of the style of Phil Spector's so-called girl group productions of the early 1960s. A continuum that connects back to the Darlene Love recording is more challenging to establish in Philip Sayce's searing guitar solo and Etheridge's vocal work. And, it is Etheridge's work that is most notable in this recording. Throughout the first part of the recording—basically that part of the song that comes before the guitar solo—Etheridge exercises restraint. Although her vocal tone color has never been that of a glitzy pop diva, her performance in the first half of "Christmas (Baby Please Come Home)" is less impassioned and less edgy than is customary, particularly in many of her up-tempo recordings of songs of heartache. As a consequence, *that* part of her performance does connect back to the recordings of the early 1960s girl groups. After Sayce's electric guitar solo, however, Etheridge turns up the vocal heat several notches. While this suggests the ongoing development and intensification of her character's desire for her relationship to return to the state it was in the previous Christmas, it is something of a double-edged sword. While this intensification suggests the direction of her character's feelings over time, some listeners might hear it as being at least somewhat overdone in this particular song.

Throughout her career, Melissa Etheridge has been characterized as a rock singer-songwriter-guitarist. While it is true that much of Etheridge's best-known work and the majority of her recordings might be characterized as "rock" in the mold of predecessors such as Janis Joplin, Bob Seger, and Bruce Springsteen, such a characterization fails to take into account Etheridge's work as a ballad singer and her R&B- and jazz-influenced work. Of all the tracks on *A New Thought for Christmas*, Etheridge's recording of the standard "Have Yourself a Merry Little Christmas" exhibits her R&B ballad style. Still, the performance includes some of Etheridge's raw vocal edginess, as well as a Philip Sayce solo that includes enough blue notes and distortion to tell the listener that this is not a conventional jazz reading of the song.

Melissa Etheridge has been the sole author of so many of the original songs that she has recorded since the 1980s that her collaborations are especially notable. The next track on *A New Thought for Christmas*, "Ring the Bells," was cowritten by Etheridge and Pakistani guitarist-singer-songwriter Salman Ahmad. The song is a call for peace and universal human unity, in the lyrical tradition of rock-era Christmas works such as John Lennon and Yoko Ono's "Happy Xmas (War Is Over)." In contrast to the Lennon-Ono song, however, "Ring the Bells" does not mention the Christian holiday of Christmas. In its almost secular humanistic lyrical message, then, perhaps "Ring the Bells" could be thought of as a descendant of Lennon's "Imagine." The Etheridge-Ahmad song is anthem-like in scope, breaking the six-minute mark. Despite the nobility of the song's message of world peace, the melody is not as instantly memorable as Etheridge's best, and the colead vocals that Etheridge and Ahmad share at times seem awkward, not being entirely independent vocals, nor being a conventionally harmonized duet.

The next track, the 1940s R&B song "Merry Christmas Baby," is more successful. Etheridge gives a somewhat understated performance, which works well. The arrangement, with blues- and jazz-influenced fills and a retro-style Hammond organ sound in the keyboards, pays tribute to the song's long-standing status as an R&B Christmas classic. In fact, the entire performance speaks to the influence of R&B on Etheridge to a greater extent than her compositions generally do. At the risk of committing rock music heresy, it might even be safe to say that this vocal performance by Melissa Etheridge shows her to be a more emotionally convincing, stylistically wider ranging, and more technically gifted blues singer than the predecessor with whom she is often compared: Janis Joplin.

As one listens to *A New Thought for Christmas*, one might be struck by the emotional range of the lyrics that run through the album. I mention this because some of Etheridge's albums of the 1980s, 1990s, and very early twenty-first century tended to focus on pain, relationships gone bad, and emotional upheaval, with the emotional content shifting dramatically on songs that expressed intense sexual desire. The combination of original material and new arrangements of Christmas standards on this album not only move Etheridge closer to R&B music but also find her expressing a wider emotional range.

Speaking of emotional range, the optimism of "Merry Christmas Baby" gives way to longing in Etheridge's composition "Christmas in America." This song first appeared on the earlier album *Greatest Hits: The Road Less Traveled*, a "greatest hits" collection that, despite its title, contained several new songs. In this song, Etheridge's character describes the routine preparations for Christmas that she is undertaking, counterpointed by her one Christmas wish, "send my baby home" "far away from harm." In the context of the U.S. involvement in wars in Iraq and Afghanistan at the time of the song's release on *Greatest Hits: The Road Less Traveled*, its reissue on *A New Thought for Christmas*, and the nation's continuing involvement in hostilities in the Middle East at the time of this writing, it is easy to understand the relationship between the person about whom Etheridge sings and her own character as soldier and the spouse/domestic partner still at home. As Etheridge customarily does in her lyrics (especially in the songs of her first several albums), she leaves the gender of her character's partner unspecified. This gives the song a universality that is fitting, especially given the twenty-first-century makeup of the American military.

"Christmas in America" also provides an example of one of the musical attributes of Melissa Etheridge's writing that makes it stand out from the ordinary and the stereotypical. Harmonically, the song is mostly grounded around diatonic triads in the key of E major. That is, the E major, F sharp minor, G sharp minor, A major, C sharp minor, and D diminished chords all continue three notes (triads), all of which are contained within the E major scale (and are therefore diatonic). Interestingly, Etheridge also uses a B minor chord in the verses and in the chorus. Because this chord contains the pitch D natural—as opposed to the D sharp that is the seventh scale-degree in the key of E major—and, therefore, is the one harmony that is not diatonic, it tends to draw the listener's attention into the song. The irony is that the sole nondiatonic chord in the song is that which is built on the fifth note of the scale, and generally the chord built on scale-step five is the *one* harmony in a key besides the tonic chord that is usually diatonic. Adding to the irony is the fact that Etheridge's musical setting employs every other possible diatonic harmony in the key of E major. Although the reason behind the use of this unusual and unexpected harmony might not be clear to the listener, and despite the fact that Etheridge has discussed the details of her musical composition very little, it is possible to imagine that the use of the minor dominant (v) chord might symbolize her character's pain and the one missing piece of the Christmas puzzle for her.

The next track, "Light a Light," returns to the milieu of John Lennon and Yoko Ono's "Happy Xmas (War Is Over)" and "Imagine." Here, Etheridge calls on the people of the world to "light a light of change this year" and to "choose only love." Lyrically, the piece is not as pointed and imagery-driven as Etheridge's best work, and musically "Light a Light" is not the most instantly memorable of Etheridge's original songs on the album.

Etheridge continues the lyrical focus on universal love and peace, but also adds a condemnation of consumerism in "It's Christmas Time." This fast-paced rock shuffle-style song is more successful than "Light a Light," in particular because of the deft way in which Etheridge integrates her original text with images and snippets of lines drawn from traditional Christmas carols. In this respect, "It's Christmas Time" reflects back to the album's second track, "Glorious." The song is also notable for its distinctive chorus hook.

A New Thought for Christmas concludes with "O Night Divine," a song that Etheridge based on the traditional Christmas hymn "O Holy Night." The piece opens with a powerful rhythm section riff, which is soon joined by Philip Sayce's heavy metal-influenced performance of the melody of Adolphe Adam's "O Holy Night." After one instrumental statement of the entire form of the song, the texture thins and the dynamic level drops dramatically. Etheridge then sings her original melody over the harmony of "O Holy Night." Throughout the newly composed stanza, the texture thickens, the dynamic level grows, and Etheridge moves from relative understatement to powerful, full-throated singing.

Etheridge's superimposition of a new tune (with new lyrics) over a preexisting accompaniment calls to mind earlier works in the European art music tradition, such as the nineteenth-century composer Charles Gounod's *Méditation sur le Premier Prélude de Piano de S. Bach*, a work in which Gounod superimposed a new melody over an eighteenth-century keyboard composition by the composer Johann Sebastian Bach. Etheridge's work here, though, is fundamentally different from the work of a composer such as

Gounod. Because of his training, Gounod likely would have been thoroughly conversant in the harmonic and formal style of Bach. However, as a rock songwriter, the vast majority of Melissa Etheridge's fully original work as a composer utilizes different harmonic patterns, different cadential patterns, and vastly different degrees of chromatic (outside of the prevailing key) harmonies than the source material over which she composed her new melody. Despite the fact that the harmonies, harmonic functions, and cadential patterns of "O Holy Night" differ so much from the norm in Etheridge's style of rock music, her melody seems natural, thereby demonstrating her range as a musician.

Etheridge's lyrics in "O Night Divine" declare the dawn of a new age of "peace on earth and good will to men." Interestingly, throughout the song, Etheridge mixes Christmas imagery with that which celebrates the winter solstice; in fact, the listener might be left wondering if the divine night of the song's title is that of December 21st or December 24–25. In spite of the deliberate vagueness of the December date, however, the lyrical focus primarily aligns with the secular humanism of her other solo compositions on the album.

As Etheridge suggested in the album's liner notes, *A New Thought for Christmas* might have been an unlikely project for the singer-songwriter. While the album and its tracks have not made the same level of commercial impact as the classic Christmas albums and individual songs of the past, *A New Thought for Christmas* is successful on several levels: "Christmas in America" has continued to resonate now for nearly a decade, and Etheridge's versions of Christmas classics stand up well to repeated listenings and demonstrate her (and her band's) stylistic range.

Although her 2008 album *A New Thought for Christmas* represented an expansion of Melissa Etheridge's stylistic range, it was by no means the only example from the first decade of the twenty-first century. On October 1, 2009, Etheridge joined Dwight Yoakam, Emmylou Harris, and Vince Gill to perform at the All for the Hall fund-raiser in Los Angeles. Etheridge had performed with musicians from the country genre in the past, for example her appearance with Dolly Parton on the *CMT Crossroads* television program in 2003. The October 2009 benefit concert for the Country Music Hall of Fame, however, perhaps was more significant because of the acoustic nature of the setting.

FEARLESS LOVE (2010)

Of all of Melissa Etheridge's albums of the twenty-first century to date, her 2010 work *Fearless Love* has fared the best from a commercial standpoint. The album solidly made it into the Top 10 on several of *Billboard* magazine's charts, the only Etheridge album since the early 1990s to do so. So, what made *Fearless Love* such a sales smash? The answer has several components.

First, *Fearless Love* sounds energetic without resorting to the sometimes awkward hip-hop references that represented a love-it-or-hate-it part of the Etheridge sound dating back to the late 1990s. In fact, some of the musical arrangements on *Fearless Love* reflect the influence of famed Irish rock band U2 to a far greater extent than in any other Etheridge album. Other rock bands, perhaps most notably the Rolling Stones, too, can be heard as direct musical ancestors to the songs of *Fearless Love*. Second, Melissa Etheridge fans can hear *Fearless Love* as a collection that includes some of Etheridge's most deeply personal, no-holds-barred lyrics.

That being said, *Fearless Love* was not a universal favorite of music critics. Writing in *Entertainment Weekly*, Chuck Arnold generally found favor with the album, but noted that "the disc loses steam toward the end."[13] A brief review in *Billboard* said of the title track, "The song's updated, high-gloss rock sound may take some getting used to ... but the strong delivery is classic Etheridge."[14] *All Music Guide*'s Stephen Thomas Erlewine gave the album two out of five stars, and complained about the "slightness" of *Fearless Love*. Erlewine wrote, that "slightness would be fine, even welcome, if Etheridge weren't compelled to produce every song as a stadium-busting anthem, an unholy combination of Springsteen, U2, and Coldplay stripped of any sense of majesty."[15] Part of the range of reactions to *Fearless Love* might be attributed to the style of the arrangements and production, which according to Etheridge herself pays tribute to some of her musical heroes, such as "Bruce Springsteen, the Who, [and] Peter Gabriel."[16] Jenny Eliscu, who conducted an interview of Melissa Etheridge for *Rolling Stone*, also noted the influences of U2 and the Rolling Stones.[17] Yes, hints—strong at times—of all of Etheridge's musical heroes of the past can be detected; therefore, it is possible to hear *Fearless Love* as not-quite-as-original sounding as some of Etheridge's albums. On the other hand, Etheridge's lyrics have a consistent, concept-album-like focus, and the arrangements are more consistent and coherent as a whole than a list consisting of U2, Peter Gabriel, Bruce Springsteen, the Who, and the Rolling Stones might suggest.

The album opens with its title track. In "Fearless Love," Etheridge reflects on her desire for a love without fear. Etheridge's expressed desire for a "fearless love" can be interpreted as an expression for a relationship that is free of the external baggage that conventional American society continues to place on lesbian and gay relationships. On the other hand, because of the fact that Etheridge had exposed significant details about the emotional brutality of her first lesbian relationship in her autobiography, part of the fear might stem from her earliest same-sex sexual and emotional-attachment experiences.

Despite the possibility that longtime Melissa Etheridge fans might focus on the lyrics of the album's opening track, "Fearless Love," the musical arrangement and production are also significant. A quick perusal of the CD booklet of *Fearless Love* reveals that the album bears a singular production statement: "Produced by John Shanks. Co-Produced by Melissa Etheridge."[18] While it is not evident until the listener has experienced several songs on the album, the opening track sets the sonic stage for the entire album. This is significant because *Fearless Love*, unlike Etheridge's most recent previous albums, had a more unified production style and overarching soundscape. Significant, too, is the fact that Etheridge is credited as the sole writer of every track on *Fearless Love*. As a result of the more focused production and more intimate songwriting, *Fearless Love* feels more like a complete, fully conceived whole than any Melissa Etheridge album in many, many years. That, despite the fact that *The Awakening* was packaged in such a way as to make it appear to have been more obviously conceived of as a concept album.

The opening song, too, feels more like a fully integrated whole than some of Etheridge's more conventional rock songs. Specifically, the instrumental introduction makes a strong motivic reference to the opening melodic figure of the song's chorus. Etheridge's lyrical structure also contributes to the feeling of "Fearless Love" being a fully integrated whole. Lyrically, the opening verse finds Etheridge taking a simple, declamatory phrase, "I am what I am," and repeating it with the addition of the words "afraid of." This transition reflects the state of mind of Etheridge's character—that she accepts who she is, yet harbors some fears about her identity—but it also shows that Etheridge was moving into more clever and intricate lyrical writing in the twenty-first century. This is especially noticeable when "Fearless Love" is compared with the more straightforward—and what some listeners might hear as the more pedestrian—style of her earlier lyrics.

Let us return briefly, though, to the musical structure of the song's verses. Melissa Etheridge's compositional style throughout her career owes much to the mainstream rock tradition. In particular, Etheridge's best-remembered popular successes have strong melodic hooks, particularly in their chorus sections. Her best-known songs also tend to exhibit a high level of contrast between the melodic material of the verses, the chorus, and the bridge sections. The general shape of the most prominent melodic motive of the memorable chorus of "Fearless Love" is anticipated in the shape of the opening melodic motive of the verse sections. In other words, even though the chorus melody is in a higher pitch range and emphasizes a higher scale-degree than the melody of the verses, the principal motivic shapes reflect the integrated feel that is reflected elsewhere in the song.

The melodic connections between verse and chorus sections in "Fearless Love" continue into the album's second track, "The Wanting of You." Interestingly, the verses of this song also open with repetitions of an ascending figure that is balanced with a melodic descent at the end of each verse. The similarity of melodic shape is not so strong as to make the first two songs seem too repetitious; however, Etheridge's use of short motives with similar shapes might be heard by some listeners as a link between the songs that suggests a conscious attempt to make *Fearless Love* a more fully conceived song cycle than some of Etheridge's previous albums.

In "The Wanting of You," Etheridge explores the theme of an unwanted relationship—one that is at the same time unavoidable, because of a dark, illicit desire that was initiated by a sexual encounter some time before. It may be the easiest Etheridge composition since "I Want to Come Over" to interpret as a possible manifestation of the kind of internalized sexual stigma that results from the minority status suffered by lesbians and other members of the LGB community, as detailed in this book's final chapter.

One of the challenges that Melissa Etheridge presented to her listeners, particularly in her work from the late 1980s and very early 1990s, was that some of her compositions sounded uncomfortably close to songs that were already in circulation—and in some cases huge hits—from other songwriters and performers. For the most part, however, this apparent near-imitation became significantly less evident from the mid-1990s to the present. That being said, Etheridge was particularly forthcoming in her own descriptions of *Fearless Love* to acknowledge the influence of her musical heroes from the rock world on the songs of the album. Therefore, it should not be too much of a surprise that some of the album's songs are reminiscent of earlier rock songs.

Interestingly, while a song such as "Fearless Love" seems to focus on one specific influence—the work of U2 on their iconic album *The Joshua Tree*—the song "Company" suggests several songs by disparate bands. The chord progression of the introduction and verses suggests both Bachman Turner Overdrive's "You Ain't Seen Nothin' Yet" and several works by the Who, including "Baba O'Riley" with perhaps a touch of "Won't Get Fooled Again." Unlike all of these songs, "Company" is a moderately slow ballad-style piece. That being said, the electric guitar tone colors would not sound at all out of place in the mainstream rock music of the 1970s. The possible influences on "Company," though, are even wider ranging than the Who and Bachman Turner Overdrive. In particular, the melodic emphasis and melodic shape of the chorus is reminiscent of Bob Seger's "You'll Accomp'ny Me."

The fact that elements of Bob Seger, the Who, Bachman Turner Overdrive, and possibly others can be heard in "Company" can be taken as evidence of Melissa Etheridge's growth as a composer since the early years of her career as a singer-songwriter. "Company" clearly demonstrates that Etheridge is inexorably tied to the mainstream rock traditions of the 1970s and is part of an evolving continuum in the genre; however, the song also demonstrates that she is not a mere imitator of any of her predecessors—she is a synthesizer of a personal style that lies within the continuum.

In the text of "Company," Etheridge's character explains to the listener that she has just ended a relationship. Although she admits that she makes every attempt to project a surface façade of calm and happiness, Etheridge's character admits that beneath the surface she is desperate for someone's "company." As is the case with the music of the song, the situation with which Etheridge deals in the lyrics is not entirely new by any means. Even in

American popular music, one can find numerous examples of songwriters creating characters who present a façade of happiness in an attempt to mask inner sadness. "The Tears of a Clown," a collaboration of Stevie Wonder, Henry Cosby, and Smoky Robinson made famous by Robinson and his group, the Miracles, is one such example. Like lyricist Robinson[19] did in "The Tears of a Clown," Etheridge takes a familiar premise and makes it sound at least somewhat novel by means of a clever turn of phrase.

The next track, "Miss California," is possibly Etheridge's most pointed, and most bitter, song of rejection. "Miss California" is also a more interesting song than "Company." It must be noted that Etheridge has written songs in which she has portrayed the wronged party in a relationship throughout her career. In some songs, her character has shouldered the blame for the failure of a relationship; however, in most it has been her partner who was responsible. In "Miss California," Etheridge reached a new level of invective. Listeners may debate whether or not Etheridge referenced the end of her relationship with Tammy Lynn Michaels Etheridge in this song. Certainly, Etheridge's soon-to-be-ex-wife was not a native of California; however, at the time of the couple's breakup, the Etheridges were living in California and Tammy Lynn Etheridge was part of the Los Angeles television establishment.

Even if one does not read "Miss California" as an entirely autobiographical song that projects invective against Tammy Lynn Michaels Etheridge, the song does play a significant role on *Fearless Love*: it shows an entirely different aspect of love—and its loss—than any of the other songs on the album. "Miss California" is also one of the hardest-edged blues-rock songs of Melissa Etheridge's career. The intensity of the blues-rock style, the intensity and aggressive tone colors of the instrumental accompaniment, and the power of Etheridge's forceful singing successfully reinforce the intensity of the accusatory sting of the lyrics.

The album's next track, "Drag Me Away," can be interpreted in a number of ways. Etheridge refers to her refusal to leave the character to whom she sings "for death," and she later tells that individual that she refuses to "be a hostage to my own disease." Listeners who search for autobiographical meanings in Etheridge's lyrics seem likely to tie the song to Etheridge's battle against cancer. However, the references are oblique enough that it seems as though it would be possible to understand the threat to the singer's character's life in a more general way. Likewise, the identity of the character to whom Etheridge sings is left vague: it could be a lover, or it could be one of Etheridge's children, even if one reads the song autobiographically. Etheridge expresses an intense love and attachment to the other character, to be sure; however, she avoids the inclusion of any specifics that could define the relationship as a sexual one, as a parental one, or in any other detailed manner.

One interesting little lyrical detail in "Drag Me Away" connects this piece to other songs that cover the entire historical range of Melissa Etheridge's career. She refers in this song to "the angels I believed in" being the ones who came to "carry [her] away" to death. Angels appear in several roles in Etheridge songs, and are included in the titles of the songs "The Angels" (*Brave and Crazy*), "Talking to My Angel" (*Yes I Am*), "Angels Would Fall" (*Breakdown*), and after *Fearless Love*, "An Unexpected Angel" (*4th Street Feeling*). However, such as in the case of "Drag Me Away," angels of various types appear in other songs as well (e.g., "It's Only Me," from *Skin*, and "This Moment," from *Lucky*). In some songs, "angel" is used as a metaphor for a romantic interest for Etheridge's character; however, this is not always the case. In "This Moment," for example, Etheridge's character battles against angels in a similar manner as her character does in "Drag Me Away." In both cases, the angels seem to represent fate, the inevitable, that which seems to be preordained. In both of these songs—and in a great many songs without angelic references—Etheridge rails against fate. In "Drag Me Away," she does not denounce the angels; however, her character does make it abundantly clear that she believes that it is not her time to die, and that she will not give in to the "disease" that threatens her.

Musically, "Drag Me Away" represents classic Melissa Etheridge style and structure. The recording is defined in part by the high degree of contrast between the vocal melodic range, rhythmic materials, instrumental arrangement, and dynamic levels of the verses and chorus. As Etheridge has done throughout her career, she sets the verses in the lower tessitura of her voice. Likewise, her singing and the instrumental accompaniment are quiet and subdued during the verses, particularly during the introduction and the opening verse. In this opening verse, her character acknowledges the fears that are felt by her counterpart: that Etheridge's character is about to leave forever, and is fated (to use an old saw to which Etheridge refers) to have her proverbial ticket punched.

Etheridge constructed the melody of the verse from repetitions and sequential statements of a brief, descending stepwise, narrow-range motive. This figure traverses the interval of a third (e.g., Mi-Re-Do). The low, almost speech-like tessitura, quiet dynamic level, and simple narrow-range melody suggest the intimacy of a conversation between lovers or between parent and child.

In contrast, the melody of the chorus utilizes the more powerful middle range of Etheridge's vocal tessitura, is sung noticeably more forcefully, and is more complex. The chorus melody includes repetitions of the same pitch, has more rhythmic variety, and concludes with disjunct figures that cover a wider pitch range than Etheridge explores in the verses. This works beautifully to dramatize her rejection of the fate of death from—if one interprets the song as an autobiographical statement—breast cancer. The listener might also note that Etheridge includes more harmonic variety in the chorus sections.

Etheridge next plays the role of observational storyteller in her song "Indiana." She sings of a girl who is rejected by a father who is suspicious that she is not his. The girl's mother raises her in an economically deprived situation in Indiana. Eventually, the girl made her way to New York City and became a television star. Ultimately, however, she abandoned stardom to return home to Indiana. Although this rare Melissa Etheridge celebration of home and roots begins in a largely acoustically based arrangement that includes orchestral strings, it eventually moves into a brasher electric guitar-based texture with a double-time feel in the rhythm section. If the song did not move into a harder-rock feel, the tale, the melodic and harmonic styles, and the arrangement at the opening of the song would not have been out of place in the singer-songwriter genre of the 1970s. In fact, the text is so universal and so thoroughly American sounding that artists from a variety of genres could adapt "Indiana" to their own unique styles. It is a rare Etheridge composition that could perhaps be equally at home in the acoustic singer-songwriter, rock, and country genres.

In her review of *Fearless Love*, *Rolling Stone* magazine's Jenny Eliscu identified the song "Nervous" as comparable to the music of the Rolling Stones.[20] While the song exhibits touches of the Rolling Stones' 1970s-era approach to blues rock (e.g., the settings on the album *Exile on Main Street*), "Nervous" could just as readily be compared with the work of any one of a number of other 1970s blues-rock bands. For example, some listeners might hear elements of the electric guitar accompaniment figures of Norman Greenbaum's "Spirit in the Sky" in "Nervous." To put it another way, Etheridge was more catholic in her tribute to the blues-rock genre than Eliscu's review might suggest.

Let us return to Jenny Eliscu's review of "Nervous" in *Rolling Stone*. Perhaps the aspect of the song that most closely betrays the influence of the Rolling Stones is the lyrical situation itself. The nervousness that Etheridge's character feels is caused by the unwanted attention of an undesired and socially undesirable would-be suitor. Of course, the hint of the sexual taboo runs through Etheridge's output; however, "Nervous" is fundamentally different from Etheridge's more significant earlier songs with suggestions of being torn between rejecting and giving in to the sexually dangerous. In the majority of her earlier songs of this type, Etheridge portrayed the pursuer; here, she is the innocent afraid of being led to the slaughter, as it were. In addition, Etheridge rarely presented her opposites in her early songs as social outsiders. By contrast, the character of the social outsider figures prominently in the work of the Rolling Stones over the decades.

Etheridge and her band turn to an acoustically based folk-oriented style for the song "Heaven on Earth." In her lyrics, Etheridge's character acknowledges that at some point in her life she was able to "lay [her] burden down," which enabled her to "find [her] power." This power enables her to offer support to the character she addresses, a character who is in need of love, support, and encouragement. Even as early as 1997, 13 years before the release of *Fearless Love*, Etheridge acknowledged that motherhood had affected her songwriting, and that she focused more on "the social" than on "the sexual."[21]

"Heaven on Earth" fits in with Etheridge's move away from an almost single-minded focus on the sexual side of relationships. In fact, there is little in her text that defines the relationship. The two characters could be parent and child, lovers, friends, and so on. In fact, some listeners might hear "Heaven on Earth" as an early twenty-first-century take on some of the platonic songs of friendship and sisterly and brotherly love such as Carole King's "You've Got a Friend" or Paul Simon's "Bridge over Troubled Water."

A pop song is much more than just the lyrics, and some listeners might be drawn to "Heaven on Earth" for Etheridge's melodic writing, which is decidedly more expansive than in her motivically based tunes. Or, some listeners might be drawn to the song for its hints at mainstream country-pop style, especially in the instrumentation, which includes Etheridge playing Mando guitar (an instrument tuned an octave higher than a traditional 12-string guitar, but that produces approximately the tone color of a traditional mandolin). In any case, "Heaven on Earth" is an example of a Melissa Etheridge composition that could function particularly well as a cover for a broad range of contemporary artists. It also demonstrates the fact that the Etheridge song catalog is significantly deeper than Etheridge's hit singles or best-known "greatest hits"-style album tracks.

The next track, "We Are the Ones," in some ways seems like something of an outlier on *Fearless Love*. For one thing, the song incorporates spoken text in the opening in several languages. English translations of the lines are included in the album's CD liner note booklet. Listeners can debate the effectiveness of Etheridge and her coproducers' use of found texts, overdubbed hip-hop-influenced studio and turntable effects, and other production techniques over the years. On "We Are the Ones," the spoken addition is so minimal that it does not intrude on the song proper, in contrast to what seems more to be the case on some of Etheridge's recordings from the 1990s and very early years of the twenty-first century.

In this song, Etheridge draws from June Jordan's work "Poem for South African Women." Specifically, the album's liner notes acknowledge that the line "We are the ones we have been waiting for" "originated" with the Jordan poem.[22] By using the line as a jumping-off point and as a focal point, Etheridge effectively changes Jordan's context. However, Etheridge suggests—as did Jordan—the dawning of a new age. Jordan's poem dealt with the beginning of a protest movement against apartheid in South Africa that was led by women and children back in the 1950s. Etheridge used the line from Jordan's poem to suggest the emergence of a generation that is accepting of the diversity of the people who constitute their own generation. The lyrics reflect back to the theme of the song "God Is in the People," from *The Awakening*. It is important to note that, while some listeners might read the text as a commentary on diversity in sexual orientation, the song does not have to be interpreted that way: Etheridge's text is so general enough in its references to diversity, freedom of expression, and so on that it can be understood as a celebration of the universal, secular humanistic sisterhood and brotherhood of all humankind.

Writing in *Entertainment Weekly*, music critic Chuck Arnold gave *Fearless Love* a generally favorable review shortly after the album was released. However, as mentioned earlier, Arnold noted that "the disc loses steam toward the end."[23] Part of the challenge that *Fearless Love* poses for the listener is that of the first eight tracks on the album, only one is greater than five minutes in length. By contrast, each of the last four songs, "We Are the Ones," "Only Love," "To Be Loved," and Gently We Row," is over five minutes long. In addition, the last three of these songs are moderately slow to moderately paced acoustically based ballads. As a result of the focus on longer, slower, gentler tracks at the end of *Fearless Love*, the album clearly relaxes from the intensity and drive of songs such as "Fearless Love" and "Nervous."

Interestingly, the sequencing of tracks on *Fearless Love* makes a great deal of sense rhetorically if one considers the album as a reflection of the progression of life. Specifically, early album tracks, such as "Fearless Love" and "Nervous," reflect some of the lust and interplay of lust and fear that populates a fair number of the songs Melissa Etheridge wrote when she was in her 20s and early 30s. The songs at the end of the album seem to reflect the postcancer, more family- and human-issues-focused Etheridge, a woman in her 40s. In fact, some listeners might hear Etheridge herself suggesting such an autobiographical life chronology as the basis for *Fearless Love* in the album track "Indiana," which includes the protagonist's turn from high-intensity pursuit of fame to a slower-paced life that emphasizes her children. That being said, it is important to note that "Indiana" is not an autobiographical song. In fact, the relationship between the song's protagonist and her father stands in sharp contrast to the relatively close relationship of Melissa Etheridge and her father.

Etheridge returns to familiar lyrical territory in the song "Only Love." To an even greater extent than "Heaven on Earth," this song reflects back to the all-encompassing secular humanistic philosophy that defined the bulk of the material on *The Awakening*. The lyrical message tends toward the general—and thus might be heard by some listeners as somewhat generic—however, the folk, acoustic singer-songwriter musical setting and Etheridge's restrained vocal approach to the text make for an engaging combination.

The album's penultimate song, "To Be Loved," opens with the sound of children playing. Etheridge's text welcomes a child into the world. While her welcome provides some degree of hope, it is largely framed around the lack of love, the brokenness, and the lack of acceptance that Etheridge's character tells the child to expect, based on her own experience. As Etheridge has done from time to time throughout her career, she constructs the melody of the verses of "To Be Loved" from repetitions and sequential treatment of a short, narrow-range motive. Interestingly, two of the other songs in which Etheridge took a similar approach to melodic construction, "Drag Me Away" and "I've Loved You Before," also deal with love. The nature of love, however, is quite different in the three songs: in "Drag Me Away," it is love that makes Etheridge's character determined to battle disease; in "I've Loved You Before," Etheridge sings of an eternal love that precedes the births of her character and the character she addresses; and in "To Be Loved," Etheridge focuses on an unfulfilled desire for love. It is worth noting that two of the motivically oriented pieces, "Drag Me Away" and "To Be Loved," involve children; the narrow range and simplicity of the motives from which the verses of the two songs are constructed seem to confirm the songs' status as lullabies.

The earlier album track "Indiana" began with a man's rejection of a baby girl out of the suspicion that he was not her biological father. The song "To Be Loved" painted a not-so-rosy picture of a child's prospects for love, based on the experience of the continuing lifelong longings of Etheridge's character. "Gently We Row" continues the theme of loss, brokenness, and loneliness. The song's title comes from Etheridge's description of life as a slow-flowing river on which each human being rows alone. So, the album's last three songs confirm that "only love is real," but then offer the very real possibility—or even the probability—that one will never find that "fearless love" for which Etheridge's character expressed such a strong yearning in the album's opening track.

Some listeners who especially are drawn to Melissa Etheridge's more lyrically direct and more musically and lyrically visceral work might prefer *Fearless Love* songs such as the title track and "Nervous" to "Gently We Row." However, the finale to the album demonstrates Etheridge's ability to write a song with autobiographical references that are oblique enough that the song has a universal quality. Specifically, the lack of full connection and lack of nurturing that the character of the mother exhibits in the song is consistent with the portrait of her own mother that Etheridge paints in her autobiography; however, Etheridge's lyrics provide no specifics that tie the mother character in the song to her own mother. Etheridge sets her lyrics of hopelessness to triple-meter music that has a folk-like, mournful quality. It seems unlikely that "Gently We Row" is destined to enjoy the lasting power of Stephen Foster's composition "Hard Times Come Again No More"; however, like Foster, Etheridge's lyrics exhibit a sense of the universal, and the melodic and harmonic style fits within the realm of folk music. The instrumentation—with its heavy emphasis on acoustic guitars—and the performance practice on "Gently We Row" also suggest that of the early 1960s folk revival and the work of folk-oriented introspective singer-songwriters of the early 1970s.

On *Fearless Love*, Melissa Etheridge presented her fans with a challenge. The album opens with a focus on the pursuit of love, a touch of the excitement of sex, and settings that capture the rock side of Etheridge's musical style. However, the last several tracks on the album are significantly more introspective and decidedly pessimistic about the prospects for deep abiding love. The CD's sleeve and booklet are in black-and-white, and Etheridge's compositions contain a bit of that mix, a touch of that dichotomy. While the lives of the characters that populate *Fearless Love* ultimately do not resolve in a very rosy manner, the music of the album's closing track, "Gently We Row," is effectively haunting, just as the album's opening track, "Fearless Love," had been exhilarating. The overall shape of *Fearless Love*, however, suggests a heavy dose of reality that dampens hope.

Icon (2011)

Compared with some artists of the past 30 years, Melissa Etheridge has produced a moderately and *only* moderately sized canon of work. Between the 2005 release of Etheridge's first greatest hits album, *Greatest Hits: The Road Less Traveled*, and the 2011 release of her second such compilation, *Icon*, Island Records had released only three new studio albums. As a result, *Icon* did not represent a compilation of Etheridge's most memorable songs of the 2005–11 period. Rather, *Icon* is a career-length compilation that is better focused than *Greatest Hits: The Road Less Traveled*.

Icon includes classic Etheridge tracks such as "I Want to Come Over," "I'm the Only One," "Bring Me Some Water," "Come to My Window," "If I Wanted To," and "Similar Features," as well as more recent songs, such as "I Need to Wake Up" and "Fearless Love." For listeners who are interested in a retrospective of the best-remembered work of Melissa Etheridge's career—at least up through the first decade of the twenty-first century—*Icon* likely is the best choice among Island's collections. That being said, the live and the other bonus tracks on Etheridge's previous collection, *Greatest Hits: The Road Less Traveled*, make it the more important and the more diverse of the two albums.

4th Street Feeling (2012)

During the twentieth-century portion of Melissa Etheridge's career, relatively lengthy periods of time elapsed between album releases. In the twenty-first century, Etheridge has been more prolific; however, her pace of releasing new material still is slower than that of some artists. Perhaps in part because of her what might be labeled "relaxed" recording schedule, Etheridge's new releases are preceded by fan anticipation. Such was the case with her most recent album to date: *4th Street Feeling*. Part of the fascination with this album came from Etheridge's acknowledgment that it was autobiographical. The title, for example, comes from the name of a prominent street in Etheridge's hometown of Leavenworth, Kansas. However, *4th Street Feeling* is perhaps Melissa Etheridge's most musically diverse album ever. That fact alone makes for particularly fascinating listening. And, *4th Street Feeling* features Etheridge's work as an instrumentalist to a greater extent than any of her previous albums. She is the sole guitarist on the album, provides prominent keyboards in some of the tracks, and also provides several powerful, roots-music-oriented harmonica solos. The more extensive use of the harmonica, numerous references to different varieties of blues music, and touches of R&B and gospel music make *4th Street Feeling* Melissa Etheridge's most roots-styled album to date. Significantly, *4th Street Feeling* plays an important role in the Etheridge canon, in that it provides color, hope, and promise in the wake of the downward emotional drift at the end of Etheridge's previous studio album, *Fearless Love*. In part, this may have been due to the fact that by the time of the writing and recording of *4th Street Feeling*, Melissa Etheridge had entered into a relationship with television producer Linda Wallem.

4th Street Feeling opens with "Kansas City." This song introduces the roots-music influence that runs throughout the entire album. "Kansas City" also introduces the theme of travel—of Etheridge's characters on a quest—that also runs throughout *4th Street Feeling*.

In "Kansas City," Etheridge portrays a character in an automobile ("my old man's Delta 88") who is on her way to the Missouri city of the song's title. Although Etheridge does not provide the listener with much detail about the character's background or the reasons behind her feelings, it is clear that she has fallen on hard times and has gone through so much emotional turmoil that she is now without hope. The character addresses the song to an undefined party, whom Etheridge's character apparently left at some point. She asks the other character—who could be a lover, a parent, or a grandparent (the other character at one time called Etheridge's character her "baby"; however, that is the extent of the detail Etheridge provides about the relationship)—if they will accept her back. Some listeners might sense a touch of the Parable of the Prodigal Son[24] in the song (e.g., Etheridge's character left in search of better life, but now returns, broken and hopeless). And, the roots-rock style of the musical setting can be heard as a descendant (albeit several generations removed) of the Rev. Robert Wilkins's "The Prodigal Son" and other early twentieth-century rural blues songs that present the prodigal narrative.

The instrumentation of "Kansas City" also suggests a connection to early twentieth-century rural blues, as well as to its direct descendant, mid-twentieth-century electric blues. This especially is evident when Etheridge provides the track's sole instrumental solo, on harmonica. Etheridge plays the instrument in such a way that demonstrates why the harmonica is also called the blues harp. In other words, her approach, in contrast to the single-line jazz-inspired style of, say, Stevie Wonder, is true to the use of the harmonica in rural and electric blues. That being said, the rock rhythms and guitar-based accompaniment of the song place "Kansas City" more in the category of roots-based rock (with harmonica) by American artists such as Bruce Springsteen and Bob Dylan. Etheridge's use of the harmonica as the solo instrumental voice in "Kansas City" is also significant because as an expressive instrument on which the artist uses her own breath, the blues harp lends a more personal feel to the proceedings, something that is entirely appropriate for such an autobiographical-sounding song.

Sometimes the past, even times when life was particularly rough, or when one was just starting out on a career and struggling financially, can bring back fond memories. The album's second song, the title track, "4th Street Feeling," finds Etheridge reflecting back on a time when all of her worldly possessions fit in her car. The theme is not entirely divorced from her 2010 song "Indiana," another exploration of the attachment to home, even in the face of early economic deprivation in that home. Significantly, Etheridge identifies the car in which she places all of her worldly possessions as a Chevrolet. The stereotype of a Chevrolet is that it is the workingman's and workingwoman's automobile. Therefore, whether or not the real-life Melissa Etheridge actually drove a Chevrolet as she began her musical career shortly after dropping out of the Berklee College of Music (she is pictured with a Chevrolet Impala in several photographs in the album booklet), the imagery fits perfectly with the way in which Etheridge paints her first-person character. Her choice of vehicle also aligns particularly well with that of her character's "old man's Delta 88" from the song "Kansas City," in that the two references to General Motors vehicles affirms the kind of familial brand loyalty that is part of American popular consciousness.

Etheridge's character in "4th Street Feeling" believes that everything that she does, she is "doing wrong," and that she was the last person in her circle to come to that realization; however, her nostalgic reflections back on the days in which she was just starting life on her own seem to provide hope. Hope, incidentally, is the one thing that was noticeably in short supply at the end of Etheridge's previous album. In this song, and throughout *4th Street Feeling*, even the more emotionally down songs offer some degree of hope. This might be tied to the events of Etheridge's life: her separation from Tammy Lynn Michaels Etheridge occurred in 2010, the year in which the album *Fearless Love* appeared; Etheridge had a new partner by 2011 and had settled her custody battle with Michaels several months before the fall 2012 release of *4th Street Feeling*.

Regardless of whether or not *Fearless Love* and *4th Street Feeling* are completely tied to contrasts in Melissa Etheridge's life and range of emotional states in 2010 and 2012, it is interesting to note the subtext that seems to lie behind the song "4th Street Feeling." Etheridge's character reflects back with nostalgia on a past in which she had little in the way of material possessions (e.g., a used car and no more possessions than those that could fit in that used car), but much in the way of hope for the future. Contrast this with her state in the present tense of the song: *possibly* much in the way of material possessions—although Etheridge does not provide information on the character's material wealth—but coupled with self-doubt and regret. The character's reflections on the past suggest the relatively high importance of emotional stability, emotional security, and hope with respect to material possessions.

Some listeners may hear the most intriguing aspect of "4th Street Feeling" as the musical style and Etheridge's singing. The musical setting is in an easy, laid-back R&B/gospel style that leans in the direction of earlier artists such as Al Green. The decidedly un-stereotypically-Etheridge-like instrumental arrangement includes only keyboards (electric piano), bass, and drums. Etheridge's electric keyboard playing and decidedly old-school, Fender Rhodes electric piano-style tone color of the keyboards suggest a touch of gospel and jazz influence. The tone colors and the musical style align particularly well with the nostalgia for the past of Etheridge's lyrics.

Etheridge's singing style in "4th Street Feeling" is not quite like anything the listener can find on any of her previous recordings. Etheridge extemporizes on the melody more than is customary, and she adopts a new vocal tone color. Whether or not future Melissa Etheridge recordings move so strongly in the direction of old-school gospel-influenced R&B and jazz remains to be seen; however, on this song Etheridge provides a taste of an expansion of her stylistic range that seems to fit the material and her voice well.

The next song on *4th Street Feeling*, "Falling Up," opens with Etheridge telling the listener of a photograph that her character "sent to [her] very best friend." The photograph was of the character and her automobile, "at another dead end." So, although Etheridge is less specific than she was in "Kansas City" (Oldsmobile Delta 88) and "4th Street Feeling" (a Chevrolet of unspecified model), an automobile plays a role in "Falling Up." The progression through these songs from the specific to the increasingly more general works well in the context of the album. The automotive references do not continue throughout the rest of *4th Street Feeling*; therefore, the move to the general at the opening of "Falling Up" provides a smooth transition into the rest of the album. The concentration of automotive references at the beginning of *4th Street Feeling* tends to emphasize the Americana aspect of the album, as well as cement in the listener's mind the idea of travel, of a journey or quest.

In fact, if one considers the concept of mobility-versus-stability, then *4th Street Feeling* exhibits a greater feeling of overall structural shape than is typical in Etheridge's albums: the entire album moves—perhaps much as Etheridge's life had—from mobility and lack of stability, to stability. This stability is defined not only in terms of location and lack of travel, but also in terms of emotional state and sense of purpose.

The music of "Falling Up" suggests not only contemporary country-pop, but also the possible influence of country-rock of the 1970s, for example the work of Poco, Gram Parsons, the Eagles, and Mike Nesmith, to name a few. The introduction and the verses are based on a brief recurring harmonic pattern that is not entirely dissimilar to that of the early Rolling Stones incorporation of American country music influences in a rock-and-roll context, "The Last Time." Although there is nothing to suggest that Melissa Etheridge meant for "Falling Up" to be taken as a deconstruction of "The Last Time," comparison of the rhetorical background of the two songs makes for interesting study. "The Last Time" is, in essence, a put-down and a warning about the possible impending end of a relationship, while "Falling Up" is a celebration of favorable possibilities for the future in the face of disappointments and "dead ends" of the past.

Adding to the country-rock flavor of "Falling Up" is the song's instrumental arrangement. The arrangement includes Etheridge playing the banjitar (essentially a combination of the banjo and the guitar that leans strongly in the direction of the banjo's distinctive tone color), as well hints of slide guitar, and a rare Melissa Etheridge guitar solo. However, it is not the optimism in the face of past defeats, nor the arrangement alone that makes "Falling Up" a successful piece. The melody is engaging, and the playfulness that Etheridge implies in her use of the apparently self-contradictory phrase "falling up" is mirrored by the deliberate, at-first-unexpected, and ultimately catchy phrase interruptions of the tune.

The next track, "Shout Now," represents electric blues in a sort of ZZ Top meets George Thoroughgood and the Destroyers mold. Musically, the piece opens with a stereotypical lick of the electric blues-rock genre, an electric guitar figure that moves from repeated statements of tonic to the lowered third scale-step to the fourth scale-step (e.g., C, E-flat, F, in the key of C). Unfortunately, although Etheridge strongly hints at 1970s blues-rock, the production on "Shout Now" by Jacquire King and Etheridge presents the listener with a fairly mild version of the genre. What is especially problematic about this is that Etheridge's lyrics speak of how her character has reached the breaking point and will no longer cover up her pain and anger at having been wronged in relationships. While she tells the listener that instead of staying silent, she is going to "shout now," the intensity of the instrumental accompaniment does not quite shout at the level of the song's blues-rock predecessors, nor at the level of Etheridge's hard-rock songs of the 1990s. An intensity mismatch or a deliberate mismatch between lyrics and musical setting can be effective, if they force the listener to ponder the "true" meaning of the song (e.g., the single version of the Beatles' "Revolution," which focuses on pacifism and evolutionary change in the lyrics, while presenting the Beatles playing some of the hardest rock of their career). In the case of "Shout Now," some listeners undoubtedly will hear the conflict of intensities as indicative of a musical setting that simply is too mild for the lyrical sentiments.

Etheridge's emphasis on country and blues—so-called roots-music styles—continues in the album's next track, "The Shadow of a Black Crow." In this song, Etheridge turns to a swampy electric blues style in the verses. In contrast to classic blues form, however, "The Shadow of a Black Crow" includes a distinctive—albeit brief—chorus section. Another aspect of the song that marks it as representing conventional rock and pop music (as opposed to textbook blues) is the inclusion of a brief interlude, which begins approximately one minute and 45 seconds into the piece. The melodic material of the interlude is based on that of the verses; however, the texture is considerably thinner than that of the verses, and the interlude consists of a short aphoristic statement about the pain of aging and dealing with unresolved personal issues.

The tone colors of "The Shadow of a Black Crow" are distinctive, both on *4th Street Feeling* and within the bulk of Melissa Etheridge's recorded output. According to music contributor to the Washington, DC-based gay publication *Metro Weekly*, Doug Rule, "Brett Simons's growling bass guitar adds visceral weight to Etheridge's lyrics about owning up to her 'wicked ways' and 'misspent youth.' "[25] While it is rare for the electric bass to play such a prominent role on an Etheridge recording, some listeners might perceive the most distinctive feature of the instrumentation and Jacquire King and Etheridge's coproduction to be the lack of prominence of guitar parts. The song, while certainly autobiographical sounding, is not necessarily the most effective piece on *4th Street Feeling*. A phrase such as "I'd rather die fast than to ever live slow" (from the chorus of "The Shadow of a Black Crow") is distinctive and apt to stay in the listener's mind, in part because of its association with a catchy melodic motive; however, the phrase also joins images such as "a six-pack of sorrow," the "shadow" of the song's title, and "a bottle of the blues" as expressions that lean too far in the direction of blues clichés to sound entirely natural and from the heart. As an album track, the piece might even have been more effective and memorable for the long term if Etheridge had added an electric blues guitar solo to the arrangement.

Listeners who are familiar with the emotional roller coasters of Melissa Etheridge's personal life might take the album's next track, "Be Real," as a commentary on Etheridge's ex-partner/ex-wife Tammy Lynn Michaels. However, the song need not be interpreted as a strictly autobiographical song. In either case, Etheridge's character addresses a former lover, and accuses her ex-partner of selling her (or his, because the antagonist's gender and sexuality are not revealed in the lyrics) soul for "fame, fame, fame"; she accuses her ex-partner of creating an unnatural manufactured image of Etheridge's character, rather than allowing her to be herself; however, in the end, Etheridge concludes that she "will be fine." So, while the relationship and the breakup between the song's characters were contentious (like the Michaels-Etheridge breakup) Etheridge's character is left with some hope for the future, unlike the characters—whether autobiographical, fictional, or a hybrid of the two—of the concluding tracks of *Fearless Love*.

The music of "Be Real" is especially notable, particularly because a song about a relationship that ended badly is certainly not anything new in the Melissa Etheridge canon. And, it is Etheridge's musical setting of the lyrics that make "Be Real" a memorable, effective song. The melody and Etheridge's funk-soul style of singing emphasize her character's focus on "doing" the "natural thing." In fact, it is relatively easy to connect "Be Real" back to soul of the 1960s and 1970s that focuses on the "natural," such as

"(You Make Me Feel Like) a Natural Woman." However, it is not just the melodic setting of one brief phrase and Etheridge's vocalizations that stand out. Coproducers Etheridge and Steve Booker—who also collaborated on the album's title track—give "Be Real" a minimalistic, stripped-out feel. Each time I hear the song, I am reminded of the striking effect of John Lennon's 1970 album *John Lennon/Plastic Ono Band*, on which the former Beatle offered brutally personal, confessional, soul-bearing lyrics in minimalist, sometimes almost non-commercial-sounding settings. Etheridge plays the multiple sparse electric guitar lines that come directly out of the funk style, as well as a blues-oriented harmonica obbligato that enters partway through the song. The sparseness of the setting is heightened by the fact that song ends with a multitracked Etheridge playing the role of soul soloist and backing chorus repeating affirmations that she "will be fine," eventually accompanied only by handclaps once the instruments fade out.

While "Be Real" offers a balance between invective and affirmation, the album's next track, "A Disaster," does not. Etheridge's character is so disgusted by the "anger" in her ex-partner's "hair," and "lies upon [her] lips" that all she is able to do is urge her (possibly him, since Etheridge does not specify the gender of the object of her character's scorn) to "move on." As Etheridge's character paints her ex-partner, she is "genocidal" in her fear and has "nuclear fingertips"; in other words, referring to the relationship as the "disaster" of the song's title sounds as though it is not an overstatement.

Despite the surface harshness of the remarks of Etheridge's character in "A Disaster," one reference in the text suggests that it was the ex-partner who considered Etheridge's character to be "the enemy." In other words, in the view of Etheridge's character, it was the attitude, distrust, paranoia, and spitefulness of the other character that precipitated her feelings. The music setting and Etheridge's singing style also lend a deeper layer of meaning to the song. The piece is performed at a moderately fast tempo of approximately 116 beats per minute. Interestingly, Etheridge does not spit out the lyrics like one might expect, given the literal reading of the text. Instead, she sings with a sense of resignation, which is confirmed by the uncharacteristically piano-based instrumentation, a lightness of the production texture, and a mournful minor-key tonality. The musical setting and Etheridge's vocal style seem greatly to soften the blow of the lyrics and help to portray Etheridge's character in a better light than the lyrics might suggest. In fact, the text alone could suggest that it is really Etheridge's character that is mean-spirited and taking out her frustrations on her former lover. The song, as composed, arranged, performed, and produced, paints Etheridge's character as the victim, who now perhaps only halfheartedly is reduced to meanness of language by her ex-partner's significantly greater evils.

It is significant to note that the deeper level of meaning that Etheridge's music and her coproduction with Jacquire King represent is a more sophisticated approach to composition than in many of her earlier songs. Instead of directly supporting a literal reading of the text with the music and singing style, here, Etheridge constructs a meaning that relies on the interplay between and the integration of music and text.

In the next song, "Sympathy," Etheridge's character addresses someone whom she would like to help through her (or his) darkest time. She expresses empathy for the other character, and asks them to have some "sympathy" for her and to allow her to help. However, the other character is caught up too fully in denial, in drugs and drinking, and in self-pity to accept Etheridge's reaching out. Etheridge turns to her more characteristic straight-ahead rock style in "Sympathy," a musical style and setting that suggests at least in part the style of the Rolling Stones. Some listeners might hear this especially in the tone colors and the minimalistic, touched-by-Keith-Richards style of Etheridge's electric guitar solo.

It is tempting to hear some of the songs on *4th Street Feeling* as forming a deeper narrative structure. For example, "Sympathy" can be understood as one way in which Etheridge's character reaches out to another in an attempt to help relieve some of the other person's pain. Perhaps it was a failed attempt, though, because the next track, "Enough Rain," revolves around the same theme. In contrast to the fuller, higher-energy, faster-paced, in-your-face rock texture and style of "Sympathy," "Enough Rain" is gentler, slower, and almost coy. The equating of "pain" with "rain" and the sparser musical setting suggest that Etheridge's character tries a different tack in her attempt to reach out to someone who is suffering with self-pity because of her losses: this time she uses the soft sell. Interestingly, although the instrumental texture thickens approximately one minute and 35 seconds into the two-minute-50-second-long song—and remains thick during the higher-pitched and more passionately sung bridge section—the text and the overall impact in "Enough Rain" is more affirming that that of "Sympathy." The 12/8 (compound quadruple) meter feel of the song suggests the mid-1960s folk influences on pop music, perhaps because the metrical feel calls to mind songs such as the Beatles' "Norwegian Wood (This Bird Has Flown)." Perhaps the most interesting feature of the first minute and a half of the song, though, is the fact that in the thin-textured part of the song, the multitracked electric guitarist Etheridge and drummer Blair Sinta—with assistance from bassist Brett Simons and keyboardist Zac Rae—hint several times at breaking into a full-throttle, 1990s *Yes I Am*-style rock dynamic; however, they never make the abrupt shift that some listeners might anticipate. This denial of listener expectations may be more striking because of the fact that "Enough Rain" follows the hard-rock-style song "Sympathy." The effect of prolonging anticipation works effectively to underscore the almost coy way in which Etheridge's character tries to appeal to her counterpart.

The songs "Sympathy" and "Enough Rain" dealt at least in part with the theme of self-doubt. It is important to note, though, that this self-doubt was associated not with Etheridge's character, but with the person with whom her character interacted. The sense of self-confidence in the Etheridge characters of those songs comes into full and complete focus in the song "A Sacred Heart." If the listener understands the song as a fully autobiographical testament, then Etheridge expresses defiance in the face of cancer, defiance in the face of homophobia, defiance in the face of society's demands for consumerism, and defiance in the face of having to live life as someone's "pawn," "puppet," or "slave." Interestingly, Etheridge refers most directly to the idea of slavery to a master, without specifying who or what that master is. Listeners with a knowledge of Etheridge's well-publicized cancer battle of the early twenty-first century, and her battle for full marital and parental rights for homosexuals, and her own earlier battles to achieve self-confidence as a gay woman, can easily read these themes into the song, despite the fact that Etheridge provides only the vaguest hints as to the nature of her defiance. This is not, however, a weakness. Rather, it allows the listener to project a broad range of possible specific themes, social ills, and the like into "A Sacred Heart." This aligns the song with Etheridge's earlier work "Giant" (from *Lucky*). The reader might recall that reviewer Margaret Coble of *The Advocate* called "Giant" a "gay pride anthem," despite the nature of the protagonist's stand against discriminatory social norms in that song.[26] In the same way, "A Sacred Heart" implies at least a partial focus on homophobia, but only within the context of the listener's familiarity with Melissa Etheridge's life story.

Etheridge sets her testament of defiance in "A Sacred Heart" in a dramatic, slow-tempo rock power-ballad style. Interestingly, she returns to her use of dramatic volume contrasts that were a more regular part of her work in the 1990s. The production also features Etheridge's fullest-throated singing of the entire album. In short, "A Sacred Heart" is the structural climax of *4th Street Feeling*. As such, it puts the entire album in context: *4th Street Feeling* began with Etheridge's reflections back on the simplicity of life when she moved away from home and began her career; as the album progressed, Etheridge encountered love, heartache, self-doubt, deceit, resistance from former and would-be partners; and now, in "A Sacred Heart" she delivers a clear, unambiguous statement about her firm sense of self-worth.

The standard digital download, CD, and vinyl versions of *4th Street Feeling* that Island Def Jam issued in 2012 included two more songs: "I Can Wait" and "Rock and Roll Me." These tracks provide relief from the sonic and emotional intensity of "A Sacred Heart," as both are far gentler ballads from a musical standpoint. Etheridge presents a logical progression of emotional recovery in these two songs. In "I Can Wait," she offers solace and emotional support to a friend who seems also to be a potential lover. As Etheridge expresses in the title line, she will wait for her friend and possible future lover to feel fully ready before the relationship goes any further. In "Rock and Roll Me," Etheridge plays the role of the party that is recovering from emotional pain. Here, however, her character has just reached the point of emotional recovery; she and her new lover begin a full-fledged physical relationship, initiated by Etheridge's request that her partner "rock and roll [her] all night long." In fact, if one goes back to songs such as "Sympathy" and "Enough Rain," one can see a logical progression from those songs of emotional and physical isolation that followed the breakup, which is so clearly documented in "Be Real" and "A Disaster," through the emotional recovery and recognition and expression of self-worth of "A Sacred Heart," all the way through to the new emotional and physical connection that is initiated in "Rock and Roll Me."

Despite the fact that "I Can Wait" and "Rock and Roll Me" can both be characterized as ballads, they present wide musical contrasts. The first song is a primarily acoustic guitar-based, folkish, singer-songwriter-style piece. Melodically, "I Can Wait" meanders, almost in musical imitation of the tentativeness that Etheridge expresses in her lyrics. Because of this, it is not likely to be one of her better-remembered individual songs; however, the combination of lyrics and music works very well within the context of the progression of a relationship that unfolds over the second half of *4th Street Feeling*. In contrast, "Rock and Roll Me," as the title implies, is an invitation to physical lovemaking. Appropriately, Etheridge set her text in a slow but sultry R&B style that is an extension of the sexy, seductive, and sometimes erotic Quiet Storm genre that was popular in the 1970s and 1980s.

The original standard release of *4th Street Feeling* concluded with "Rock and Roll Me"; however, consumers may encounter the special Deluxe Edition of the CD version of the album that Island Def Jam also issued in 2012. The Deluxe Edition CD contains three additional songs, "You Will," "The Beating of Your Heart," and "Change the World." These songs are not necessarily essential to the structure of *4th Street Feeling*; however, they extend the narrative posed by the album's principal songs and allow the listener to settle into a focus on a favorable resolution of Etheridge's characters' love lives. "Rock and Roll Me" hints that the cycle of falling in love and becoming involved in a new physical relationship is about to commence, and thusly suggests that Etheridge's character has found healing from her losses in love of the recent past. "You Will," "The Beating of Your Heart," and "Change the World," however, confirm that she (to the extent that the listener understands Etheridge's characters as different facets of the same character) has found love, and the trio of songs conclude by putting human romantic love and parental love into a broader spiritual context.

In "You Will," Etheridge turns to an easygoing contemporary country style. By using references to the transition from tricycles to bicycles and by comparing time to "a Slinky toy," Etheridge seems to aim the lyrics directly at her children; however, the references are general enough in nature that the piece takes on a more universal parent-child conversation. The gist of Etheridge's message is that, as she puts it in the song's chorus, "You are what you believe." It is possible to imagine that earlier in her career, Melissa Etheridge might have set an expression of the importance of self-acceptance and self-confidence to more powerful rock music. The relaxed nature of the contemporary country style seems much better to fit the context of the parent-child conversation and provides an example of Etheridge's growth as a songwriter who is sensitive to context. This is not to imply that "You Will" is entirely musically passive; in the verses, Etheridge uses double-time rhythm to set her text about children rushing around to get to their bicycles and other toys. While "You Will" is not likely to be a significant pop hit—particularly because of the parent-child context—it is a thoroughly engaging song musically and lyrically and deserves wider recognition than that of a "bonus track."

In "The Beating of Your Heart," Etheridge adopts a more impressionistic lyrical tone. Her overall message is that romantic love can generate intense feelings (e.g., "a living fire coursing through my veins"), and that it can sometimes leave an individual feeling powerless. In a sense, "The Beating of Your Heart" explores approximately the same theme as Etheridge's earlier song "Fearless Love." Curiously, the song includes examples of soft rhymes, rhymes that are soft to the extent that some listeners might find them to be a touch on the awkward side. Likewise, the fact that the chorus section includes asymmetrical phrase lengths might not appeal to all listeners.

Etheridge expands upon the message of "You Will" in the final bonus track on the Deluxe Edition of *4th Street Feeling*, "Change the World." Here, she expresses her supreme self-confidence, she is completely in control of her own destiny. Likewise, her character expresses the belief that she can "change the world" for the lover to whom she sings. It is a song that can be interpreted and understood on several levels. On the surface, Etheridge's character seems to be expressing a love and desire for the character to whom she sings. The power of desire and love between the two will, in the view of Etheridge's character, allow them to change their immediate worlds for the better. In the context of the ongoing debate in the United States about civil rights issues and homosexuality—and especially in light of U.S. Supreme Court's striking down of the Defense of Marriage Act and California's Proposition 8 just less than 10 months after the release of *4th Street Feeling*—the song's lyrics also can be understood as to suggest that the act of taking a stand for the legitimacy of a relationship can bring political and social change. This, despite the fact that "Change the World" is one of Melissa Etheridge's customary gender-neutral songs.

With its wide stylistic range, with its mix of generalized lyrical references and clearly autobiographical lyrical references, and with Melissa Etheridge's most complete instrumental domination of any album of her quarter-century-plus-long career, *4th Street Feeling* is one of Etheridge's widest ranging and most essential works.

Although Melissa Etheridge continues to perform live and make television appearances, *4th Street Feeling* is her last full, album-length release to date. Nevertheless, Etheridge also remains in the public eye. Within hours of the U.S. Supreme Court striking down the Defense of Marriage Act and California's Proposition 8, the entertainment press covered Etheridge's June 26, 2013, announcement that she and her partner of three years, Linda Wallem, are now engaged and plan to wed in the near future.[27]

Conclusions: Assessing Melissa Etheridge's Significance

As a "heartland rocker," a moniker sometimes applied to Melissa Etheridge, and as a proponent of "classic rock," Etheridge's work as a performer, composer, and arranger fits in at least in part with a cadre of musicians such as John Mellencamp, Bruce Springsteen, Bob Seger, and others of their approximate style. Etheridge's musical settings include references to the acoustic singer-songwriter style, occasional references to hip-hop rhythms and drum loops, touches of blues and jazz; however, the bulk of her work is as a mainstream rock artist. Her real significance as a songwriter lies in part in her craft as a composer, but even more so in her work as a lyricist. In addition, Melissa Etheridge has cultivated a singular voice, both literally and metaphorically, a voice that sets her apart from her predecessors and apart from her contemporaries, and that resonates with a particularly loyal audience.

If one were to list Melissa Etheridge's most memorable songs, it seems logical that a variety of listeners could develop radically different lists. Listeners drawn to Etheridge's work in projecting the experiences of lesbians into rock songs might logically value the songs of *Your Little Secret*—the album that includes Etheridge's most overtly lesbian-oriented lyrics—over some of the artist's other work. Other listeners might prefer Etheridge's work that deals with gender and sexuality issues in more oblique, universal ways. They would probably tend not to be drawn as fully to the songs of *Your Little Secret*.

Whatever the listener's preferences with respect to rhetorical style, it probably is safe to say that on a purely musical level, or in considering the intersection of music and lyrics, one of Etheridge's greatest strengths is in composing easy-to-remember music, with singable melodies and harmonizations that draw largely on the traditional tonic (I), subdominant (IV), and dominant (V) chords, but that frequently include motion to the minor chords within the prevailing key. Harmonically, Etheridge also tends to include added note chords in her rhythm guitar parts, particularly (but not limited to) in her slow- and medium-tempo ballads on which she plays 12-string or 6-string acoustic guitar. This particular aspect of her harmonic vocabulary and guitar arrangements aligns her work with that of the acoustic singer-songwriter style of the 1970s through the present. The chorus sections of her compositions often utilize a higher register of her vocal range than the verses, and in the best-remembered songs the chorus sections include dramatic lyrical references that are highlighted by this higher pitch range. An example is the phrase, "I'm the only one who'd walk across the fire for you," in "I'm the Only One."

Certainly, one aspect of Melissa Etheridge's importance as a singer, songwriter, and popular culture icon is her role as an example of a highly visible and highly successful member of the LGBT community. Although I believe that ultimately her principal importance is as an artist who breaks down gender boundaries, stereotypical gender roles, and sexual identity boundaries—in other words, as an artist who speaks to the universals of all of humanity—it is important to consider Etheridge's iconic status within the LGBT community, and especially within the lesbian community. This iconic status is confirmed by the extent of the coverage of Melissa Etheridge's private life and public work by *The Advocate*, arguably the leading publication of the community. While *The Advocate* has provided coverage to other celebrities, Etheridge has been covered—and featured—perhaps more than any other. In fact, in January 2008 the historically significant 1,000th issue of the magazine, a publication that had featured Melissa Etheridge's photograph on the cover nine times, included an extensive interview of her on the occasion of the release of the album *The Awakening*.[1]

Articles about Melissa Etheridge, her life, and her work as a singer-songwriter that have appeared in publications such as *The Advocate*, *Off Our Backs*, and *Lesbian News* have not entirely focused on biography and Etheridge's work as a gay rights advocate. Her musical works—her songs and albums—also are praised for their realistic and sensitive portrayal of lesbian relationships and life experiences, this despite the fact that some reviewers in these publications have not always been as consistently supportive of some of the musical settings and musical production on some of Etheridge's albums.[2] Praise for the lyrics, and for Etheridge's characters, character development, and the characters' relationships, though, is the norm in publications for the LGBT community. For example, in the July 1996 issue of *Off Our Backs*, Diane Spodarek praised Etheridge's sensitive portrayal of a lesbian relationship in the official video for the song "I Want to Come Over."[3] Similarly, in a December 1999 article in the same publication, Karla Mantilla discussed the realism and sensitivity of Etheridge's portrayal of lesbian sexuality in her songs.[4] This recognition suggests that the angst, the broken relationships, and the dark cloud that hangs over the sexuality in Etheridge's songs do not just happen to align with challenges faced by the LGBT community in some vague way. Rather, Etheridge's characters and their experiences and feelings resonate with members of the LGBT—and especially the lesbian—community.

The question might arise, then, in what specific ways do Etheridge's characters and their experiences and emotions represent shared experiences within the lesbian community? This question is made especially intriguing by the fact that such a high proportion of Etheridge's songs contain second-person characters that are completely undefined by gender or sexuality. So, what are the commonalities in the characters, their relationships, and their emotions that tie the bulk of Melissa Etheridge's songs together? Interestingly, especially in her songs from the twentieth century, Etheridge tended to cast the relationships and potential relationships of her first-person characters in a light that suggested darkness, illicitness, and perhaps even something bordering on taboo. For example, in "I Want to Come Over," Etheridge tells the object of her affections—who happens to live next door—that she wants to join her, despite of (or, in her words, "to hell with") "the consequences." The characters that are the objects of desire for Etheridge's character generally seem to be at least a bit reluctant to engage sexually and emotionally with Etheridge's character. Such is the case, for example, in "I Want to Come Over." The implication that these relationships are somehow outside of the norm or even illicit can be understood in many ways. And, these ways do not necessary rely on the listener connecting the nature of the relationships to Etheridge's self-acknowledged gay identity. However, because *Your Little Secret*, the album on which "I Want to Come Over" appears, is the sole album to date on which Etheridge focused on overtly lesbian relationships, and therefore is the Etheridge album that is by far the most fully saturated with gender-based references, "I Want to Come Over" is perhaps the easiest song to use as an example of Etheridge's account of lesbian desire. Dark, hidden desires with implications of female-female sexual relationships, however, are implied in other Melissa Etheridge songs. While this aspect of Etheridge's work is less frequently found in her twenty-first-century songs, "The Wanting of You," an album cut from the 2010 album *Fearless Love*, is one example of how the theme continues to reemerge in Etheridge's character portraits.

If the listener connects the implied illicit nature of the would-be relationships with the real-life Melissa Etheridge's identity, and if the listener also recalls that the just-ended relationships that form the rhetorical basis of a large number of Etheridge's early songs generally ended badly for Etheridge's character (the amicable splits were few and far between), then the songs of Melissa Etheridge, particularly in the 1980s and 1990s, might be understood as manifestations of what the some psychological researchers refer to as "internalized sexual stigma" or "internalized homophobia."

In her study of the work of lesbian writers Adrienne Rich and Minnie Bruce Pratt, Rachel Stein opens by tracing Western society's negative treatment of gays and lesbians to Paul's letter to the Romans from the first century CE, in which Paul wrote that some women engaged in activities that went against nature. According to Stein, Paul interpreted that the main function of sex—and hence its role in nature—was that of "seeding."[5] Stein concludes, "Thus the Pauline application of agricultural analogies to human sexual practices has undergirded centuries of social stigma, legal persecution, and cultural silencing of same-sex desire."[6] Biblical scholars debate whether or not Paul was actually referring to lesbianism in this extended passage, Romans 1:18–32. Some scholars argue that Paul referred not to sexual relations but to other activities, such as participation in the goddess religions of the first century CE, that upset the "natural" male-dominated social order of the day.[7] However, the point that Stein makes is that the passage has been *interpreted* as a comment on and condemnation of lesbian sexual relations for nearly two millennia. In fact, Stein sees it as the basis for Western, Christian society's rejection of homosexuality in general.

In her important article "Compulsory Heterosexuality and Lesbian Experience,"[8] Adrienne Rich argues against any view of lesbianism that would treat it as anything other than natural. Interestingly, Robert McRuer builds upon Rich's work of the 1980s and equates the marginalization suffered by the disabled and the marginalization suffered by homosexuals in his similarly titled 2013 article "Compulsory Able-Bodiedness and Queer/Disabled Existence."[9] The work of Rich and McRuer suggests, then, a connection between the way in which society at large perceives and treats members of the LGBT community and other minorities, particularly the "disabled."

Various psychological studies of the late twentieth century and early twenty-first century suggest that the "social stigma" and "cultural silencing" of which Rachel Stein writes and the marginalization of which Adrienne Rich and Robert McRuer write can affect members of minority communities, including the LGBT community, on a profound level. Although one can find several studies in the literature, let us focus on just two, and on how they might speak to the characters of and character development in the work of Melissa Etheridge. In their 2009 *Journal of Counseling Psychology* article "Internalized Stigma among Sexual Minority Adults: Insights from a Social Psychological Perspective," researchers Gregory M. Herek, J. Roy Gillis, and Janine C. Cogan document how socially ingrained sexual stigma becomes internalized in some members of the LGB community, leading to a lower sense of self-worth than in the population of the United States in general.[10] The question might arise as to how this lower sense of self-worth might manifest itself in affected individuals' life experiences.

In their 2009 *Journal of Counseling Psychology* article "Internalized Homophobia and Relationship Quality among Lesbians, Gay Men, and Bisexuals,"[11] David M. Frost and Ilan H. Meyer go one step further than Herek, Gillis, and Cogan. Frost and Meyer detailed the findings of a study of 396 lesbian, gay, and bisexual individuals in which they found evidence to support the view that members of the LGB community suffer stress based on the fact that they are part of a socially marginalized minority community. This, incidentally, provides a social scientific basis to the more humanities-related work of Adrienne Rich and Richard McRuer mentioned earlier. Furthermore, Frost and Meyer found that the minority-status-based stress that they identified in their subjects leads to what they and other researchers have termed internalized homophobia (what Herek, Gillis, and Cogan call internalized sexual stigma), and that this internalized homophobia within members of the LGB is correlated to difficulty in establishing and maintaining romantic relationships.

It is possible, therefore, to understand Etheridge's work that treats relationships as dangerous or illicit as a reflection of the effects of straight society's rejection of homosexuality. According to this interpretation, Etheridge's first-person characters—to the extent that the listener understands them to share Etheridge's identity as gay women—appear to suffer from the internalized sexual stigma that research studies such as those of Herek, Gillis, and Cogan, and Frost and Meyer have found. The reader might also recall that the vast majority of Etheridge's twentieth-century songs find her character wanting a relationship or having just suffered the breakup of a relationship. In other words, Etheridge's first-person character is not in, nor likely to remain in, a stable, long-term relationship. Perhaps one of the clearest album-length cases in point is Etheridge's second album, *Brave and Crazy*, in which relational dysfunction seems to rule the day. This is fully in keeping with the relationship difficulties that internalized homophobia causes, as shown by Frost and Meyer and other psychologists. So, while Etheridge's songs tend not include references to the sexuality or gender of the characters, even the gender-reference-free works can be understood as reflective of the specific challenges of members of the lesbian community.

Etheridge hints at her recognition of internalized sexual stigma in some of her lyrics. Perhaps the best example is her 2010 recording "Fearless Love," in which Etheridge writes and sings of a sense of fear that has permeated the past relationships of her first-person character. Part of the fear is external— perhaps imposed by society; perhaps imposed by a history of painful experiences—however, Etheridge's character also clearly identifies part of the fear as internal: she *is* (in part) what she is afraid of. Interestingly, this expression of self-fear followed Etheridge's 2007 recording "A Simple Love," a song in which Etheridge seemed to express a recovery from past experiences (and possibly from past internalized sexual stigma). It is interesting to note that the album on which this apparent retreat from an expression of security within a relationship appeared, *Fearless Love*, was released only approximately two weeks after *TV Guide* reported on the breakup of Melissa Etheridge and Tammy Lynn Michaels Etheridge.[12] Perhaps, then, on either a conscious or a subconscious level, the approaching end of Etheridge's marriage took her back to her earlier feelings about the viability and stability—or lack thereof—of relationships.

Although "Fearless Love" suggests the psychological phenomenon of internalized sexual stigma, the fact is that elements of the competing self-love and self-loathing can be found in Melissa Etheridge's compositions dating back to her professional recording debut in the 1980s. Because of the fact that Etheridge was so forthcoming about the childhood sexual abuse that she suffered at the hands of her sister, it is interesting to speculate as to how many of the connections that her characters seem to have to more generalized internalized sexual stigma might actually be rooted in Etheridge's individual early experiences.

Despite Melissa Etheridge's success at writing, performing, and recording distinctive songs with melodic, stylistic, and arrangement hooks that can stick with a listener for a long period of time, and that hold up under repeated listenings, and despite her success in speaking to the experiences of members of the LGBT community, perhaps her greatest lasting importance as a songwriter lies in how she constructs her characters, whether they are purely fictional, semiautobiographical, or more fully autobiographical, and what she tells—or does not tell—the listener about them. In short, by creating the characters she creates, by portraying them the way she does, Etheridge might be one of the best examples of a feminist songwriter who does not necessarily overtly appear to be one.

Aside from the bulk of the songs on *Your Little Secret*, and just a relatively few songs on her other albums, the characters with whom her character interacts in her compositions tend to be gender neutral. In fact, in making self-references, Etheridge's first-person characters also tend to be defined in such a way that they could be understood as gender neutral. In other words, a male singer could convincingly perform a large number of Etheridge's songs without having to change a word. To put it another way, aside from the bulk of *Your Little Secret* and the occasional reference in songs from other albums, the vast majority of the characters in Melissa Etheridge's songs could be female, male, gay, or straight. In short, Etheridge focuses on the universals of human beings in Western society, and she avoids any references to character traits that could in any way be interpreted as stereotypes. So, although Melissa Etheridge does not say it in so many words, the lust, the love, the loss, the passion, the anger, and virtually every other conceivable emotion associated with Western human pairings that find their way into Etheridge's songs are shared to some extent across boundaries of gender and sexual orientation.

Although Etheridge does not detail her reasons for maintaining fairly strict gender neutrality in her lyrics, it is interesting to speculate as to possible reasons why, and how these possible reasons might relate to the American society of her time. In addition, Etheridge's work might be understood as a reflection of changing attitudes toward sexual orientation and self-identity over the course of her 25-plus-year career.

On the most surface level, Etheridge's avoidance of reference to the sex or gender of her opposites in her songs can be read as a pop songwriter's attempt to appeal to the broadest possible audience. While some listeners might interpret this as an attempt to cover up her sexual orientation, it should be noted that, with the exception of *Your Little Secret* and the very occasional subsequent individual song, Melissa Etheridge has continued to define her opposites in terms of her feelings for them and not in terms of who they are, female or male, gay or straight, black or white, rich or poor, and so on. In other words, even after her public coming out in early 1993, anything that can be construed as a gender reference seems to continue to be almost studiously avoided. This suggests that obfuscation of her own identity probably was not the motivation for the universality of the characters of Etheridge's songs.

Another way to interpret Melissa Etheridge's avoidance of gender references in the vast majority of her compositions is that she follows in the lineage of confessional singer-songwriters of the 1970s, such as Jackson Browne, Joni Mitchell, Carly Simon, James Taylor, and others. Etheridge's predecessors within the singer-songwriter genre tended to focus—highly introspectively at times—on their own feelings (or those of their first-person characters). If the listener understands Melissa Etheridge and other singer-songwriters of her generation as the spiritual inheritors of the 1970s singer-songwriter tradition, then the vague nature of Etheridge's characterizations make perfect sense: the emphasis of the confessional singer-songwriters of the 1970s (and, by extension, of those who inherited their tradition) was on the feelings of the songwriter's character. To put it another way, the "I" of the song is more important than the "you." This interpretation of Melissa Etheridge's work, although plausible, suffers somewhat from the fact that, in contrast to most of her contemporaries and the singer-songwriters of the 1970s, Etheridge is primarily a rock (as opposed to a pop or folk-oriented) artist. Her musical style differentiates Melissa Etheridge from the confessional singer-songwriter camp, just as it differentiates her from many of the later confessional singer-songwriters, few of whom perform in an Etheridge-esque mainstream rock style.

Author Joan Laird devotes much space to discussion of various "difference" paradigms that have been advanced over the years to differentiate lesbians from the female population in general.[13] While there is not sufficient space here to explore all of these paradigms, or others that might exist, suffice it to say that one way in which Melissa Etheridge's tendency toward gender neutrality can be read is as a way—conscious or otherwise—to avoid the them-versus-us paradigms that separate women into straight and gay camps, or into particular stereotypical camps within the lesbian community.

Perhaps the most intriguing way to read Melissa Etheridge's avoidance of sexual identity and gender-role stereotypes, as well as even the most fleeting of references to gender in her second-person character development is that it casts her as a universalist, not only as a writer who largely minimizes the differences between women, but also as a writer who minimizes differences between genders. By leaving the identity of her characters—first-person and second-person—undefined and stereotype-free, Etheridge treats all relationships, all genders and sexual orientations, and all individuals' sexual needs, wants, and desires on an equal footing. Her characterizations, then, represent the expression of equality at the most basic level.

Interestingly, although she can be understood as a proponent of equality on the sexual level, Melissa Etheridge does not often overtly deal with gender-based discrimination in her lyrics. In fact, it could be argued that she does this so infrequently that the outliers within her list of compositions, such as "All American Girl," "Silent Legacy," and a few others, tend to stand out sharply in relief against the bulk of her output. While her song lyrics do not focus on gender-based discrimination, as a musician Melissa Etheridge lives feminism and equality, and thereby serves as a role model, rather than as a spokesperson. She is—and has been for over a quarter century—a female leader of studio and touring bands that have been largely or exclusively male. The significance is not that Etheridge happens to be a female singer who is backed by male instrumentalists; one can find numerous examples of that, even in the earliest part of the American recording industry (e.g., the early twentieth-century classic blues singer-songwriter Bessie Smith). The significance of Etheridge's work is found in the fact that in this setting—female vocalist accompanied by male instrumentalists—Etheridge also writes or cowrites the vast majority of the material, she produces or coproduces the recordings, she composes or cocomposes the arrangements, and her work as an instrumentalist—usually on rhythm guitar or keyboards—is always an integral part of every recording. So, Etheridge is much more than just the vocalist star of the sessions: she also is the leader and creator of the songs and arrangements and productions. As natural as this situation might seem to her loyal fans, it must be remembered that rock music (as opposed to folk or pop or some other genres) throughout its history has been heavily male dominated. Certainly, other women of the rock era have been the principal songwriters, lead vocalists, and important instrumental contributors to their recordings; however, generally these women have inhabited the pop world, or the acoustic singer-songwriter world, as opposed to the mainstream rock world. In this respect, Melissa Etheridge stands virtually alone. In addition, she is one of the few musicians in the world of rock—female or male—to have made significant contributions through music and social activism in the 1980s, 1990s, 2000s, and 2010s. Etheridge's recent broadening of stylist range in her compositions, lyrics, and vocal techniques suggests that she remains a vibrant, relevant, and still-evolving artist into the second quarter century of her career as a singer-songwriter.

Annotated Discography

Melissa Etheridge. Melissa Etheridge, vocals and guitar; various assisting musicians. "Similar Features" (Melissa Etheridge), "Chrome Plated Heart" (Etheridge), "Like the Way I Do" (Etheridge), "Precious Pain" (Etheridge), "Don't You Need" (Etheridge), "The Late September Dogs" (Etheridge), "Occasionally" (Etheridge), "Watching You" (Etheridge), "Bring Me Some Water" (Etheridge), "I Want You" (Etheridge). Produced by Chris Blackwell and Niko Bolas. Simultaneously released on 33⅓-rpm LP and CD, Island 842 303 (LP) 842 303-2 (CD), 1987. Etheridge's self-titled debut topped out at No. 22 on *Billboard*'s Top 200 Albums chart. The album's most successful singles, "Bring Me Some Water" and "Similar Features," made it to No. 10 and No. 6, respectively, on the Mainstream Rock charts. Etheridge was nominated for a Grammy for Best Rock Vocal Performance, Female, for "Bring Me Some Water."

Brave and Crazy. Melissa Etheridge, vocals and 12-string guitar; various accompanying musicians. "No Souvenirs" (Melissa Etheridge), "Brave and Crazy" (Etheridge), "You Used to Love to Dance" (Etheridge), "The Angels" (Etheridge), "You Can Sleep While I Drive" (Etheridge), "Testify" (Etheridge, Kevin McCormick), "Let Me Go" (Etheridge), "My Back Door" (Etheridge), "Skin Deep" (Etheridge), "Royal Station 4/16" (Etheridge). Produced by Kevin McCormick, Niko Bolas, and Melissa Etheridge. CD, Island 422 842 302-2, 1989. On the sales charts, *Brave and Crazy* performed comparably to Etheridge's debut, topping out at No. 22 on the *Billboard* album charts. The singles "No Souvenirs" and "Let Me Go" performed well on the Modern Rock charts, topping out at No. 9 and No. 13 respectively. Etheridge received a 1990 nomination for Best Rock Vocal Performance, Female, for "Brave and Crazy" and a 1991 nomination in the same category for "The Angels."

Never Enough. Melissa Etheridge, vocals, electric and acoustic guitar, and keyboards; various assisting musicians. "Ain't It Heavy" (Melissa Etheridge), "2001" (Etheridge), "Dance without Sleeping" (Etheridge, Kevin McCormick, Mauricio Fritz Lewak), "Place Your Hand" (Etheridge), "Must Be Crazy for Me" (Etheridge), "Meet Me in the Back" (Etheridge), "The Boy Feels Strange" (Etheridge), "Keep It Precious" (Etheridge), "The Letting Go" (Etheridge), "It's for You" (Etheridge, McCormick). Produced by Kevin McCormick and Melissa Etheridge. CD, Island CID 9990 512 120-2, 1992. *Never Enough* topped out at No. 21 on the *Billboard* Top 200 Albums chart. The singles drawn from the album performed similarly to those from Etheridge's first two albums; however, "Dance without Sleeping" marked Etheridge's first appearance on the Adult Contemporary charts. Etheridge won a 1993 Grammy for Best Rock Vocal Performance, Female, for the track "Ain't It Heavy."

Yes I Am. Melissa Etheridge, vocals and guitar; various assisting musicians. "I'm the Only One" (Melissa Etheridge), "If I Wanted To" (Etheridge), "Come to My Window" (Etheridge), "Silent Legacy" (Etheridge), "I Will Never Be the Same" (Etheridge), "All American Girl" (Etheridge), "Yes I Am" (Etheridge), "Resist" (Etheridge), "Ruins" (Etheridge), "Talking to My Angel" (Etheridge). Produced by Hugh Padgham and Melissa Etheridge. CD, Island 422-848 660-2, 1993. The importance of *Yes I Am* as Melissa Etheridge's breakthrough album is evidenced only in part by its chart performance; it topped out at No. 15 on the *Billboard* Top 200. The principal singles drawn from *Yes I Am*, "Come to My Window" and "I'm the Only One," established a strong Melissa Etheridge presence on the Hot 100 and Top 40 Mainstream charts. "I'm the Only One" became Etheridge's first chart topper, and Etheridge won a 1995 Grammy for Best Rock Vocal Performance, Female for "Come to My Window." Although they did not win, both "Come to My Window" and "I'm the Only One" were nominated for Grammys for Best Rock Song.

Your Little Secret. Melissa Etheridge, vocals, guitars, and keyboards; various assisting musicians. "Your Little Secret" (Melissa Etheridge), "I Really Like You" (Etheridge), "Nowhere to Go" (Etheridge), "An Unusual Kiss" (Etheridge), "I Want to Come Over" (Etheridge), "All the Way to Heaven" (Etheridge), "I Could Have Been You" (Etheridge, John Shanks), "Shriner's Park" (Etheridge), "Change" (Etheridge), "This War Is Over" (Etheridge). Produced by Hugh Padgham and Melissa Etheridge. CD, Island 314-524 154-2, 1995. *Your Little Secret* topped out at No. 6 on the *Billboard* Top 200. The singles drawn from the album, "Your Little Secret," "I Want to Come Over," and "Nowhere to Go," populated *Billboard*'s Top 40 Mainstream, Adult Top 40, and Hot 100 in 1995 and 1996, with "Nowhere to Go" appearing on the Top 40 Adult Recurrents in 1997. Despite the album's commercial success, *Your Little Secret* did not result in any Grammy nominations for Etheridge.

Breakdown. Melissa Etheridge, vocals, guitars, and keyboards; various assisting musicians. "Breakdown" (Melissa Etheridge), "Angels Would Fall" (Etheridge, John Shanks), "Stronger than Me" (Etheridge), "Into the Dark" (Etheridge), "Enough of Me" (Etheridge), "Truth of the Heart" (Etheridge, Shanks), "Mama I'm Strange" (Etheridge), "Scarecrow" (Etheridge), "How Would I Know" (Etheridge), "My Lover" (Etheridge), "Sleep" (Etheridge), "Touch and Go" (Etheridge), "Cherry Avenue" (Etheridge), "Beloved" (Etheridge). Produced by Melissa Etheridge and John Shanks. CD, Island 314-546 608-2 (enhanced edition), 1999. *Breakdown* received a Grammy nomination for Best Rock Album, and the track "Angels Would Fall" received both a Grammy nomination both for Best Rock Song and for Best Rock Vocal Performance, Female. The album was not as commercially successful as its two immediate predecessors, just failing to make it into the Top 10 on *Billboard*'s Top 200 album chart. Two songs, "Enough of Me" and the better-known "Angels Would Fall," appeared on various singles charts, but did not chart as highly as the most successful singles on *Yes I Am* and *Your Little Secret*. The enhanced version of the album includes the bonus tracks "Touch and Go," "Cherry Avenue," and "Beloved," as well as material that could be played on Windows and Macintosh computers of the time. The computer-only bonus material is incompatible with computer operating systems of the 2010s.

Skin. Melissa Etheridge, vocals, guitars, harmonica, keyboards, mandolin; various assisting musicians. "Lover Please" (Melissa Etheridge), "The Prison" (Etheridge), "Walking on Water" (Etheridge), "Down to One" (Etheridge), "Goodnight" (Etheridge), "It's Only Me" (Etheridge), "I Want to Be in Love" (Etheridge), "Please Forgive Me" (Etheridge), "The Different" (Etheridge), "Heal Me" (Etheridge). Executive producer, John Carter. Produced by Melissa Etheridge; coproduced by David Cole. CD, Island I2 48661, 2001. Etheridge's confessional breakup album marked her return to the Top 10 in *Billboard*'s Top 200 albums chart; however, it resulted in only one Top 40 single, "I Want to Be Loved."

Lucky. Melissa Etheridge, vocals, guitar, and keyboards; various accompanying musicians. "Lucky" (Melissa Etheridge), "This Moment" (Etheridge, John Shanks), "If You Want To" (Etheridge), "Breathe" (Ryan Jordan, Marc Wanninger, Andrew Dwiggins, Douglas Randall, Brandon Armstrong), "Mercy" (Etheridge, Jonathan Taylor), "Secret Agent" (Etheridge, Taylor), "Will You Still Love Me" (Etheridge), "Meet Me in the Dark" (Etheridge), "Tuesday Morning" (Etheridge, Taylor), "Giant" (Etheridge), "Come on out Tonight" (Etheridge), "Kiss Me" (Etheridge), "When You Find the One" (Etheridge). Produced by Melissa Etheridge, David N. Cole, Ross Hogarth, Rick Parashar, and John Shanks. CD, Island B00001822-02, 2004. Etheridge's cover of the song "Breathe" received a Grammy nomination for Best Rock Vocal Performance, Solo. While *Lucky* generally was more highly regarded by some critics than *Skin*, *Lucky* topped out at only No. 15 on the *Billboard* Top 200.

Greatest Hits: The Road Less Traveled. Melissa Etheridge, vocals, guitars, and keyboards; various assisting musicians. "Refugee" (Tom Petty, Mike Campbell), "Similar Features" (Melissa Etheridge), "Like the Way I Do" (Etheridge), "Bring Me Some Water" (Etheridge), "You Can Sleep While I Drive" (Etheridge), "No Souvenirs" (Etheridge), "Ain't It Heavy" (Etheridge), "I'm the Only One" (Etheridge), "Come to My Window" (Etheridge), "If I Wanted To" (Etheridge), "I Want to Come Over" (Etheridge), "Angels Would Fall" (Etheridge, John Shanks), "Lucky" (Etheridge), "Christmas in America" (Etheridge), "Piece of My Heart" (Jerry Ragovoy, Bert Berns), "This Is Not Goodbye" (Etheridge), "I Run for Life" (Etheridge). Produced by Melissa Etheridge and various coproducers. CD, Island B000ND91RM, 2005. Although this album primarily consists of previous released "greatest hits" material, the track "Piece of My Heart" was recorded live at the 2005 Grammy Awards, and "I Run for Life," "Christmas in America," "This Is Not Goodbye," and the cover of Tom Petty and the Heartbreakers' "Refugee" were new recordings. *Greatest Hits: The Road Less Traveled* reached No. 14 on the *Billboard* 200, and the single "I Run for Life" was a Top 10 hit on the Adult Contemporary charts.

The Awakening. Melissa Etheridge, vocals and guitars; various assisting musicians. "All There Is" (Melissa Etheridge), "California" (Etheridge), "An Unexpected Angel" (Etheridge), "Message to Myself" (Etheridge), "God Is in the People" (Etheridge), "Map of the Stars" (Etheridge), "Threesome" (Etheridge), "All We Can Really Do" (Etheridge), "I've Loved You Before" (Etheridge), "A Simple Love" (Etheridge), "Heroes and Friends" (Etheridge), "The Kingdom of Heaven" (Etheridge), "Open Your Mind" (Etheridge), "The Universe Listened" (Etheridge), "Imagine That" (Etheridge), "What Happens Tomorrow" (Etheridge). Produced by Melissa Etheridge and David Cole. CD, Island B0009463-02, 2007. *The Awakening* peaked at No. 13 on the *Billboard* 200.

A New Thought for Christmas. Melissa Etheridge, vocals and guitars; various assisting musicians. "Blue Christmas" (Billy Hayes, Jay Johnson), "Glorious" (Etheridge), "Christmas (Baby Please Come Home)" (Jeff Barry, Ellie Greenwich, Phil Spector), "Have Yourself a Merry Little Christmas" (Ralph Blaine, Hugh Martin), "Ring the Bells" (Etheridge, Salmad Ahmad), "Merry Christmas Baby" (Lou Baxter, Johnny Moore), "Christmas in America" (Etheridge), "Light a Light" (Etheridge), "It's Christmas Time" (Etheridge), "O Night Divine" (Etheridge). Produced by Melissa Etheridge and David Cole; "Christmas in America" produced by John Shanks. CD, Island B0011475-02, 2008. Although *A New Thought for Christmas* fared poorly on the pop charts at the time of its release, it was a successful seasonal album for several years.

Fearless Love. Melissa Etheridge, acoustic and Mando guitars and vocals; various assisting musicians. "Fearless Love" (Melissa Etheridge), "The Wanting of You" (Etheridge), "Company" (Etheridge), "Miss California" (Etheridge), "Drag Me Away" (Etheridge), "Indiana" (Etheridge), "Nervous" (Etheridge), "Heaven on Earth" (Etheridge), "We Are the Ones" (Etheridge), "Only Love" (Etheridge), "To Be Loved" (Etheridge), "Gently We Row" (Etheridge). Produced by John Shanks; coproduced by Melissa Etheridge. CD, Island B0014020-02, 2010. *Fearless Love* performed better on the various album charts than any of Etheridge's releases since the early 1990s. The album placed solidly in the Top 10 on the Top Rock Albums, *Billboard* 200, and Top Digital Albums charts.

Icon. Melissa Etheridge, vocals, guitars, and keyboards; various accompanying musicians. "I Want to Come Over" (Melissa Etheridge), "Fearless Love" (Etheridge), "I'm the Only One" (Etheridge), "I Need to Wake Up" (Etheridge), "Bring Me Some Water" (Etheridge), "Come to My Window" (Etheridge), "Ain't It Heavy" (Etheridge), "Similar Features" (Etheridge), "Like the Way I Do" (Etheridge), "No Souvenirs" (Etheridge), "If I Wanted To" (Etheridge). Produced by Melissa Etheridge and various coproducers. CD, Island B004J2FIYI, 2011. Etheridge's second "best of"-type album is more concise and focused than the earlier *Greatest Hits: The Road Less Traveled*, although *Icon* is heavily weighted toward Etheridge's work in the 1980s and 1990s.

4th Street Feeling. Melissa Etheridge, vocals, keyboards, harmonica, and all guitars; various accompanying musicians. "Kansas City" (Melissa Etheridge), "4th Street

Feeling" (Etheridge), "Falling Up" (Etheridge), "Shout Now" (Etheridge), "The Shadow of a Black Crow" (Etheridge), "Be Real" (Etheridge), "A Disaster" (Etheridge), "Sympathy" (Etheridge), "Enough Rain" (Etheridge), "A Sacred Heart" (Etheridge), "I Can't Wait" (Etheridge), "Rock and Roll Me" (Etheridge), "You Will" (Etheridge), "The Beating of Your Heart" (Etheridge), "Change the World" (Etheridge). Various tracks produced by Jacquire King, Steve Booker, and Jon Kaplan; coproduced by Melissa Etheridge. CD, Island B0017306-02 (Deluxe Edition), 2012. *4th Street Feeling* peaked at No. 18 on the *Billboard* 200 and No. 8 on the Top Rock Albums chart.

Notes

INTRODUCTION

1. Melissa Etheridge with Laura Morton, *The Truth Is ... My Life in Love and Music* (New York: Random House Trade Paperbacks, 2002), 6–10.
2. Ibid., 33–34.
3. See, for example, Karla Mantilla, "Melissa Etheridge and Lesbian Sexuality: The Hunger," *Off Our Backs* 29 (December 1999): 8–9; and Diane Spodarek, "Melissa Etheridge," *Off Our Backs* 26 (July 1996): 13.

CHAPTER 1

1. The discussion of this album is drawn heavily from my essay on *Melissa Etheridge* in James E. Perone, "Melissa Etheridge: *Melissa Etheridge*," *The Album: A Guide to Pop Music's Most Provocative, Influential, and Important Creations* (Santa Barbara, CA: Praeger, 2012), 3: 319–22.
2. Vik Iyengar, "*Melissa Etheridge*," *All Music Guide*, http://allmusic.com/album/melissa-etheridge-r6881/review (accessed October 17, 2012).
3. Melissa Etheridge with Laura Morton, *The Truth Is ... My Life in Love and Music* (New York: Random House Trade Paperbacks, 2002), 94.
4. Ibid., 97.
5. See http://shop.fanasylum.com/mein/index.php?route=product/product&product_id=182 (accessed March 22, 2013).
6. Etheridge with Morton, *The Truth Is.*
7. See, for example, David M. Frost and Ilan H. Meyer, "Internalized Homophobia and Relationship Quality among Lesbians, Gay Men, and Bisexuals," *Journal of Counseling Psychology* 56 (January 2009): 97–109.

8. See, for example, Chris Willman, "Ace of Abasement," *Entertainment Weekly*, November 17, 1995, 76–77.

9. Holly George-Warren, "Melissa Etheridge," *Rolling Stone*, October 31, 2002, 124.

10. Johnny Loftus, "*Never Enough*," *All Music Guide*, http://www.allmusic.com/album/never-enough-mw0000275946 (accessed December 28, 2012).

11. Melissa Etheridge, Liner notes for *Never Enough*, CD, Island CID 9990 512 120-2, 1992.

12. Etheridge with Morton, *The Truth Is*, 55.

CHAPTER 2

1. The discussion of Etheridge's *Yes I Am* is drawn heavily from my essay on the album that is included in James E. Perone, "Melissa Etheridge: *Yes I Am*," *The Album: A Guide to Pop Music's Most Provocative, Influential, and Important Creations* (Santa Barbara, CA: Praeger, 2012), 4: 51–56.

2. Stephen Holden, "Review: Reveling in the Agonies of Good Love Gone Bad," *New York Times*, June 11, 1990, 18.

3. Chris Willman, "Ace of Abasement," *Entertainment Weekly*, November 17, 1995, 77.

4. Melissa Etheridge with Laura Morton, *The Truth Is ... My Life in Love and Music* (New York: Random House Trade Paperbacks, 2002), 129.

5. Ibid., 55.

6. David M. Frost and Ilan H. Meyer, "Internalized Homophobia and Relationship Quality among Lesbians, Gay Men, and Bisexuals," *Journal of Counseling Psychology* 56 (January 2009): 97.

7. Stephen Thomas Erlewine, "*Breakdown*," *All Music Guide*, http://www.allmusic.com/album/breakdown-mw0000256267 (accessed January 11, 2013).

8. Joel Stein, "Q&A Melissa Etheridge," *Time*, October 25, 1999, 131.

9. Etheridge with Morton, *The Truth Is*, 181–84.

10. Through-composed song structure is most closely associated with European art music composers of the nineteenth century. In through-composed works, the poetic structure tends to dictate the musical structure, such that conventional phrase structure and the conventional use of repetition and contrast are muted or absent altogether.

11. See, for example, Larry Flick, "Etheridge Rocks Back on Island with *Breakdown*," *Billboard*, September 4, 1999, 1.

12. Etheridge with Morton, *The Truth Is*, 185.

CHAPTER 3

1. Melinda Newman, "Webb Brothers, Austin, Etheridge Serve Up New Tunes for the Summer," *Billboard*, June 23, 2001, 13.

2. Kerry L. Smith, "*Skin*," *All Music Guide*, http://www.allmusic.com/album/skin-mw0000003903 (accessed January 21, 2013).

3. Heidi Hudson, "Listen to the Music," *Lesbian News* 27 (August 2001): 39.

4. See, for example, Thom Jurek, "*4th Street Feeling*," *All Music Guide*, http://www.allmusic.com/album/4th-street-feeling-mw0002409917 (accessed January 24, 2013).

5. Liner notes to *Skin*, CD, Island I2 48661, 2001.

6. Gregory M. Herek, J. Roy Gillis, and Janine C. Cogan, "Internalized Stigma among Sexual Minority Adults: Insights from a Social Psychological Perspective," *Journal of Counseling Psychology* 56 (2009): 32–43.

7. Adrienne Rich, "Compulsory Heterosexuality and Lesbian Existence," in *Powers of Desire: The Politics of Sexuality*, ed. Ann Snitow, Christine Stansell, and Sharon Thompson (New York: Monthly Review, 1983), 177–205.

8. Rob Brunner, "Little Secrets," *Entertainment Weekly*, June 29–July 6, 2001, 135–36.

9. Laura DeHart Young, "*The Truth Is . . . My Life in Love and Music*," *Lambda Book Report* 10 (September 2001): 13.

10. Frank Zappa, with Peter Occhiogrosso, *The Real Frank Zappa Book* (New York: Poseidon Press, 1989), 188 (capitalizations and italics in the original).

11. Jeff Shannon, "*Melissa Etheridge Live . . . and Alone*," Amazon.com, http://www.amazon.com/Melissa-Etheridge-Live-Two-Disc-Edition/dp/B00006MFPL/ref=sr_1_fkmr0_1?ie=UTF8&qid=1359142270&sr=8-1-fkmr0&keywords=Melissa+Etheridge+Live%C2%85And+Alone (accessed January 25, 2013).

12. See, for example, Etheridge's description of her growing sense of environmentalism in Elysa Gardner, "*Awakening* Finds Etheridge with Eyes Open to the World," *USA Today*, October 9, 2007, 5d.

13. Bonnie J. Morris, "Melissa Etheridge: Hitched, Happy, and on Tour," *The Lesbian and Gay Review* 11 (March/April 2004): 30–31.

14. See, for example, Margaret Coble, "Happy? Go *Lucky*," *The Advocate*, March 30, 2004, 65.

15. Christa L. Titus, " 'This Moment,' " *Billboard*, June 12, 2004, 35.

16. Melissa Etheridge, Liner notes for *Lucky*, CD, Island B00001822-02, 2004.

17. Coble, "Happy? Go *Lucky*," 65.

18. Brian Hiatt, "Melissa Etheridge and Joss Stone: 'Cry Baby'/'Piece of My Heart,' " *Rolling Stone*, April 21, 2005, 119.

19. Melissa Etheridge, " 'I Run for Life,' " http://www.melissaetheridge.com/album/road-less-traveled/i-run-for-life (accessed March 22, 2013).

20. Christa L. Titus, " 'I Run for Life,' " *Billboard*, November 12, 2005, 37.

CHAPTER 4

1. Larry J. Schweiger, "I, Too, Need to Wake Up," *National Wildlife* 45 (December 2006/January 2007): 9.

2. Chuck Taylor, "I Need to Wake Up," *Billboard*, April 14, 2007, 38.

3. Ibid.

4. See, for example, Tamra Conniff, "6 Questions with Melissa Etheridge," *Billboard*, April 21, 2007, 44.

5. "All There Is" lasts for approximately one minute and four seconds.

6. Chuck Taylor, "Message to Myself," *Billboard*, August 4, 2007, 42.

7. Significantly, Melissa Etheridge hails from Leavenworth, Kansas.

8. Chuck Arnold, "Quick Cuts," *People*, October 8, 2007, 45.

9. Melissa Etheridge, "My Person of the Year," *Time*, December 11, 2006, 14.

10. Melissa Etheridge, "Elizabeth Edwards," *Time*, May 14, 2007, 102.

11. The American Society of Composers, Authors, and Publishers, "ASCAP Founders Award," http://www.ascap.com/eventsawards/awards/founders/index. aspx (accessed March 20, 2013).

12. Melissa Etheridge, Liner notes for *A New Thought for Christmas*, CD, Island B0011475-02, 2008.

13. Chuck Arnold, "*Fearless Love*," *Entertainment Weekly*, May 17, 2010, 61.

14. C. M., " 'Fearless Love,' " *Billboard*, January 30, 2010, 33.

15. Stephen Thomas Erlewine, "*Fearless Love*," *All Music Guide*, http://www. allmusic.com/album/fearless-love-mw0001960374 (accessed April 18, 2013).

16. Jenny Eliscu, "Fear and Love in Malibu: Melissa Etheridge's New LP," *Rolling Stone*, January 21, 2010, 20.

17. Ibid.

18. Liner notes for *Fearless Love*, CD, Island B0014020-02, 2010.

19. John Morthland, liner notes to *Sounds of the Seventies: 1970*, Time-Life Music SOO-01, 1989.

20. Eliscu, "Fear and Love in Malibu," 20.

21. Christina Kelly, "Melissa Etheridge," *Rolling Stone*, November 13, 1997, 159.

22. Melissa Etheridge, liner notes for *Fearless Love*, CD, Island B0014020-02, 2010.

23. Arnold, "*Fearless Love*," 61.

24. The Parable of the Prodigal Son is found in the New Testament of the Bible, Luke 15: 11–32.

25. Doug Rule, "Passionate Feeling," *Metro Weekly*, January 20, 2012, http:// www.metroweekly.com/arts_entertainment/music.php?ak=7749 (accessed June 3, 2013).

26. Margaret Coble, "Happy? Go *Lucky*," *The Advocate*, March 30, 2004, 65.

27. Sadie Gennis, "Melissa Etheridge Happily Engaged Following DOMA Ruling," *TV Guide* Online Edition, http://www.tvguide.com/News/Melissa-Etheridge-Engaged-1067211.aspx, June 26, 2013 (accessed June 27, 2013).

Conclusions: Assessing Melissa Etheridge's Significance

1. Rachel Dowd, "Sweet Melissa," *The Advocate*, January 15, 2008, 34–37.

2. See, for example, Heidi Hudson, "Listen to the Music," *Lesbian News* 27 (August 2001): 39.

3. Diane Spodarek, "Melissa Etheridge," *Off Our Backs* 26 (July 1996): 13.

4. Karla Mantilla, "Melissa Etheridge and Lesbian Sexuality: The Hunger," *Off Our Backs* 29 (December 1999): 8–9.

5. Rachel Stein, " 'The Place, Promised, That Has Not Yet Been': The Nature of Dislocation and Desire in Adrienne Rich's *Your Native Land/Your Life* and Minnie Bruce Pratt's *Crime against Nature*," in *Queer Ecologies: Sex, Nature, Politics, Desire*, ed. Catriona Mortimer-Sandilands and Bruce Erickson (Bloomington: Indiana University Press, 2010), 286.

6. Ibid., 287.

7. See, for example, Dale B. Martin, "Heterosexism and the Interpretation of Romans 1:18–32," *Biblical Interpretation* 3 (1995): 332–55; and Jeramy Townsley, "Paul, the Goddess Religions, and Queer Sects: Romans 1:23–28," *Journal of Biblical Literature* 130, no. 4 (2001): 707–28. Both Martin and Townsley argue that the passages that today's conservative Christians view as a condemnation of lesbianism were in fact meant by Paul as a condemnation of the religious practice of idolatry and was not directed exclusively to homosexuals.

8. Adrienne Rich, "Compulsory Heterosexuality and Lesbian Existence," in *Powers of Desire: The Politics of Sexuality*, ed. Ann Snitow, Christine Stansell, and Sharon Thompson (New York: Monthly Review, 1983), 177–205.

9. Robert McRuer, "Compulsory Able-Bodiedness and Queer/Disabled Existence," in *The Routledge Queer Studies Reader*, ed. Donald E. Hall, Annamarie Jagose, with Andrea Bebell and Susan Potter (London and New York: Routledge, 2013), 488–97.

10. Gregory M. Herek, J. Roy Gillis, and Janine C. Cogan, "Internalized Stigma among Sexual Minority Adults: Insights from a Social Psychological Perspective," *Journal of Counseling Psychology* 56 (2009): 32–43.

11. David M. Frost and Ilan H. Meyer, "Internalized Homophobia and Relationship Quality Among Lesbians, Gay Men, and Bisexuals," *Journal of Counseling Psychology* 56 (January 2009): 97–109.

12. Joyce Eng, "Melissa and Tammy Etheridge Separate," *TV Guide* Online Edition, http://www.tvguide.com/News/Melissa-Etheridge-Split-1017323.aspx, April 15, 2010 (accessed April 18, 2013).

13. Joan Laird, "Gender in Lesbian Relationships: Cultural, Feminists, and Constructionist Reflections," *Journal of Marital & Family Therapy* 26 (October 2000): 455–68.

Annotated Bibliography

Anderson, Kyle. "*4th Street Feeling.*" *Entertainment Weekly*, September 7, 2012, 75.
The author compares Etheridge's work on the album *4th Street Feeling* with the work of Bruce Springsteen in Etheridge's "signature chesty yelp" and the album's "bottomless bucket of Americana."

Arnold, Chuck. "*Fearless Love.*" *Entertainment Weekly*, May 17, 2010, 61.
A generally favorable review of *Fearless Love*. The reviewer notes, however, that "the disc loses steam toward the end."

Arnold, Chuck. "*Lucky.*" *People*, March 8, 2004, 35.
The author describes Etheridge's rock style on the album *Lucky* as "solid if unsurprising."

Arnold, Chuck. "Quick Cuts." *People*, October 8, 2007, 45.
Etheridge's performance on *The Awakening* is called "more nuanced" than in her past work in this brief review of the album.

Atwood, Brett. "Island's Melissa Etheridge Cracks Top 40 with Hit Set." *Billboard*, December 10, 1994, 44.
A brief profile of Etheridge and her album *Yes I Am*.

Belcher, Christina. " 'I Can't Go to an Indigo Girls Concert, I Just Can't': *Glee*'s Shameful Lesbian Musicality." *Journal of Popular Music Studies* 23 (December 2011): 412–30.
The treatment of lesbianism in the television program *Glee* is discussed, including the program's references to the Indigo Girls and the use of the Melissa Etheridge song "Come to My Window."

Bianoco, Robert. "Critic's Corner." *USA Today*, December 29, 2009, 10d.
A preview of the Kennedy Center Honors television program in which the performance of Bruce Springsteen compositions by Etheridge, John Mellencamp, and Sting is described as a highlight.

Billboard. http://www.billboard.com.
Various web pages at *Billboard* magazine's website were consulted for chart information.

Brunner, Rob. "Little Secrets." *Entertainment Weekly*, June 29–July 6, 2001, 135–36.
The author describes Etheridge's autobiography, *The Truth Is ... My Life in Love and Music* as "banal" and overly general in this negative review.

Castro, Peter, with John Griffiths. "A House in Harmony." *People*, September 5, 1994, 57–58.
A profile of the domestic life of Melissa Etheridge and Julie Cypher.

Caulfield, Keith. " 'Breathe.' " *Billboard*, January 24, 2004, 32.
A highly favorable review of the single "Breathe."

Caulfield, Keith. " 'Refugee.' " *Billboard*, July 23, 2005, 39.
According to this review of Etheridge's single cover of Tom Petty's "Refugee," Etheridge's recent "stellar Grammy Awards performance" might lead to more radio airplay for "Refugee" than that enjoyed by Etheridge's recent singles.

"Classic Rock." *Rolling Stone*, September 20, 2007, 28.
This article contains a brief review of *The Awakening*.

Coble, Margaret. "Happy? Go *Lucky*." *The Advocate*, March 30, 2004, 65.
In this generally favorable review of *Lucky*, the author describes "Giant" as a "gay pride anthem" and praises Etheridge for moving "out of her interpersonal tunnel vision to make some more universal political statements."

Coble, Margaret. "Live ... and Powerful." *The Advocate*, November 26, 2002, 56.
A favorable review of Etheridge's DVD release *Melissa Etheridge Live ... and Alone*.

Cohen, Rich. "Melissa Etheridge." *Rolling Stone*, December 29, 1994–January 12, 1995, 110ff.
A feature-length profile of Etheridge, including discussion of her latest recordings, her coming out as a lesbian, and her work as a political activist.

Conniff, Tamara. "6 Questions with Melissa Etheridge." *Billboard*, April 21, 2007, 44.
Etheridge and Conniff discuss Etheridge's Academy Award for Best Original Song for "I Need to Wake Up," her successful battle against cancer, and how those events and others have affected Etheridge's work.

Cullen, J. "Recordings." *Rolling Stone*, May 14, 1992, 103.
A brief review of *Never Enough*, in which the writer describes the album as "rather conventional ... in the Bob Seger mold of heartland rock," but more importantly, as "Etheridge's best work to date."

Dagostino, Mark, and Chris Gardner. "Melissa Rocks the Boat." *People*, August 1, 2005, 47.
A brief report on Etheridge's performance on a cruise for gay families.

DeCurtis, Anthony. "*The Awakening.*" *Rolling Stone*, October 4, 2007, 72.
According to this review of *The Awakening*, Etheridge "finds both a depth and an ease that eluded her on previous releases."

DeCurtis, Anthony. "*4th Street Feeling.*" *Rolling Stone*, September 13, 2012, 79.
A generally favorable review of *4th Street Feeling*, an album that "expands [Etheridge's] sonic palette" and an album in which the producers "deftly curb [Etheridge's] over-the-top tendencies."

D'Erasmo, Stacey. "Melissa Etheridge." *Rolling Stone*, June 2, 1994, 20.
In this brief interview, Etheridge discusses her album *Yes I Am*, her coming out as a lesbian, and the fact that because of her openness about her sexuality she can now convincingly sing the Rod Stewart song "Maggie May."

Dowd, Rachel. "Sweet Melissa." *The Advocate*, January 15, 2008, 34–37.
A profile of Etheridge on the occasion of the release of *The Awakening* and the 1,000th issue of *The Advocate*, a magazine that had featured her on the cover nine times.

Dunn, Jancee. "Melissa Etheridge Takes the Long Hard Road from the Heartland to Hollywood." *Rolling Stone*, June 1, 1995, 38ff.
An extensive interview with Etheridge and Julie Cypher.

"Election '92." *Rolling Stone*, December 10, 1992, 98.
Melissa Etheridge's support of the Clinton-Gore ticket is mentioned in this brief article about celebrity endorsements in the 1992 presidential election.

Eliscu, Jenny. "Fear and Love in Malibu: Melissa Etheridge's New LP." *Rolling Stone*, January 21, 2010, 20.
According to Etheridge, her album *Fearless Love* honors some of her musical heroes, such as "Bruce Springsteen, the Who, [and] Peter Gabriel." Eliscu compares "Fearless Love" with the music of U2 and "Nervous" with the music of the Rolling Stones.

Eliscu, Jenny. "The Tao of Etheridge." *Rolling Stone*, July 10, 2008, 20.
This article provides information on Etheridge's life since her recovery from breast cancer.

Eng, Joyce. "Melissa and Tammy Etheridge Separate." *TV Guide* Online Edition. http://www.tvguide.com/News/Melissa-Etheridge-Split-1017323.aspx, April 15, 2010. Accessed April 18, 2013.
A brief report on the breakup of the Etheridge marriage.

Erlewine, Stephen Thomas. "*Breakdown.*" *All Music Guide*. http://www.allmusic.com/album/breakdown-mw0000256267. Accessed January 11, 2013.

Erlewine, Stephen Thomas. "*Fearless Love.*" *All Music Guide*. http://www.allmusic.com/album/fearless-love-mw0001960374. Accessed April 18, 2013.

Etheridge, Melissa. "The Choice Is Ours Now." *Huffington Post*. http://www
.huffingtonpost.com/melissa-etheridge/the-choice-is-ours-now_b_152947.html,
December 22, 2008.
Etheridge touches on subjects such as the struggle for gay rights, her conversation
with evangelist Rick Warren, and her performance of the song "Ring the Bells"
for the Muslim Public Affairs Council.

Etheridge, Melissa. "*The Dark Side of the Moon*." *Rolling Stone*, December 11, 2003,
156.
Etheridge provides brief thoughts of the importance of Pink Floyd's album *The
Dark Side of the Moon*, which is listed in this issue of *Rolling Stone* as No. 43 of
the 500 Greatest Albums of All Time.

Etheridge, Melissa. "Elizabeth Edwards." *Time*, May 14, 2007, 102.
A brief profile of cancer sufferer Elizabeth Edwards.

Etheridge, Melissa. "My Person of the Year." *Time*, December 11, 2006, 14.
In this brief piece, Etheridge explains why she would like to see Al Gore receive
Time magazine's Person of the Year award.

Etheridge, Melissa. "An Open Letter from Melissa Etheridge." *Lesbian News*,
November 2004, 10.
Etheridge tells readers of her experience with recovery from breast cancer, how
her wife, Tammy Lynn, has helped with her recovery, and of her interest in the
Dr. Susan Love Research Foundation.

Etheridge, Melissa. Liner notes for *Fearless Love*. CD, Island B0014020-02, 2010.

Etheridge, Melissa. Liner notes for *Lucky*. CD, Island B00001822-02, 2004.

Etheridge, Melissa. Liner notes for *A New Thought for Christmas*. CD, Island
B0011475-02, 2008.

Etheridge, Melissa, with Laura Morton. *The Truth Is . . . My Life in Love and Music*.
New York: Random House Trade Paperbacks, 2002.
Etheridge's autobiography focuses on her childhood, her career development, her
realization of her sexual orientation, and her lengthy relationship with Julie
Cypher. Of particular interest, however, are Etheridge's explanations of the inspi-
rations behind several of her best-known songs up to 2001.

"Facing Cancer Head-On." *People*, February 28, 2005, 78.
A brief report on Etheridge's battle with cancer.

Feliciano, Kristina. "Melissa Etheridge." *Entertainment Weekly*, February 13, 2004, 72.
According to Feliciano, *Lucky* suffers from too much "sturdy purposefulness" and
rates a B–.

Filipenko, Cindy. "*The Awakening*." *Herizons*, Spring 2008, 41.
An Italian-language review of Etheridge's *The Awakening*.

Flick, Larry. "Etheridge Rocks Back on Island with *Breakdown*." *Billboard*,
September 4, 1999, 1–2.

An overview of the unusual marketing of *Breakdown* as a standard CD and limited edition, enhanced CD. The article includes brief quotes from Etheridge and Island Records executives about the album and several of the songs.

Flick, Larry. "Single Reviews: Rock Tracks." *Billboard*, September 11, 1993, 53.
Etheridge's "I'm the Only One" is among those included in this review.

Flick, Larry. "Singles Reviews: Pop." *Billboard*, January 20, 1996, 70.
A brief favorable review of "I Want to Come Over."

Frost, David M., and Ilan H. Meyer. "Internalized Homophobia and Relationship Quality among Lesbians, Gay Men, and Bisexuals." *Journal of Counseling Psychology* 56 (January 2009): 97–109.

"Fully Committed." *People*, October 6, 2003, 84.
A brief report on the commitment ceremony of Melissa Etheridge and Tammy Lynn Michaels.

Galvin, Peter. "Pop View: Boy George Crosses a New Line." *New York Times*, August 27, 1995, 26.
Melissa Etheridge is included in this profile of gay artists who have come out in the 25 years since the start of the gay rights movement.

Gardner, Elysa. "*Awakening* Finds Etheridge with Eyes Open to the World." *USA Today*, October 9, 2007, 5d.
Etheridge and the author discuss Etheridge's support of Democratic candidates, her growing sense of environmentalism, and encounters she has had with antigay activists.

Gennis, Sadie. "Melissa Etheridge Happily Engaged Following DOMA Ruling." *TV Guide* Online Edition. http://www.tvguide.com/News/Melissa-Etheridge-Engaged-1067211.aspx, June 26, 2013. Accessed June 27, 2013.
A brief report on the announcement of the engagement of partners Melissa Etheridge and Linda Wallem on the heels of the U.S. Supreme Court overturning the Defense of Marriage Act and California's Proposition 8.

George, Courtney. " 'It Wasn't God Who Made Honky-Tonk Angels': Musical Salvation in Dorothy Allison's *Bastard out of Carolina*." *Southern Literary Journal* 41 (Spring 2009): 126–47.
Etheridge's belief that her music provides her with a feeling of inner peace is discussed in this study of musical salvation in Dorothy Allison's book *Bastard Out of Carolina*.

George-Warren, Holly. "Melissa Etheridge." *Rolling Stone*, October 31, 2002, 124.
Etheridge discusses the importance of the music of Bruce Springsteen, Janis Joplin, Bonnie Raitt, and several other musicians in her life and her music.

Gliatto, Tom, and Julie Jordan. "Still Rocking." *People*, June 18, 2001, 83ff.
This article profiles Etheridge and her relationships with Julie Cypher and Tammy Lynn Michaels, her motherhood, and her selection of David Crosby as the father of her children.

Grega, Will. "Gay Alternative Music Has Sales Potential." *Billboard*, May 27, 1995, 6.
Etheridge's work is among that which is included in this article.

Halperin, Shirley. "Melissa Etheridge." *Entertainment Weekly*, October 5, 2007, 27.
A profile of and interview with Etheridge on the occasion of the release of *The Awakening*.

Healy, Patrick. "Melissa Etheridge to Join *American Idiot*." *New York Times*, January 19, 2011, 2.
A report on Etheridge's upcoming weeklong run as the character St. Jimmy in the Broadway musical version of Green Day's *American Idiot*.

Hensley, Dennis. "Melissa Rewinds." *The Advocate*, September 28, 2004, 66–67.
Etheridge provides her analysis of her recordings up to 2004 in this article. Interestingly, she states that she considers the songs on *Brave and Crazy* to be "some of my best writing."

Herek, Gregory M., J. Roy Gillis, and Janine C. Cogan. "Internalized Stigma among Sexual Minority Adults: Insights from a Social Psychological Perspective." *Journal of Counseling Psychology* 56 (2009): 32–43.

Hiatt, Brian. "Melissa Etheridge and Joss Stone: 'Cry Baby'/'Piece of My Heart.'" *Rolling Stone*, April 21, 2005, 119. Hiatt describes Etheridge's recording of "Piece of My Heart" as "the most spine-tingling performance of her career."

Holden, Stephen. "Review: Reveling in the Agonies of Good Love Gone Bad." *New York Times*, June 11, 1990, 18.
Although this review of Etheridge's concert at the Beacon Theater is largely favorable, her songs are described as "melodramatic."

Holden, Stephen. "Rock Singer's Yuppie Image." *New York Times*, December 18, 1988, 96.
According to this article, the emergence of Melissa Etheridge as a rock star symbolized a basic change in the image of the female rock musician.

Hopkins, Jim. "Media Offer New Outlets for Gay Audiences." *USA Today*, March 2, 2006.
The author discusses Etheridge's work as a singer-songwriter, as well as gay-oriented television programming on the Bravo network and the film *Brokeback Mountain*.

Hudson, Heidi. "Listen to the Music." *Lesbian News*, August 2001, 39. A largely favorable review of *Skin*, although the album is referred to as "over produced."

"The Inspiration Behind Miley's New Song '7 Things.'" *People* 70, August 6, 2008, 38.
In this article Miley Cyrus reveals that she thinks of the song "7 Things" as inspired in part by the style of Melissa Etheridge.

Intini, John. "John Intini Starts a Sentence … Melissa Etheridge Finishes It." *Maclean's*, March 1, 2004, 54.

Intini and Etheridge discuss "the culture of skin and bones that exists in Hollywood," U.S. President George W. Bush, risk taking, and other topics in this short interview.

Iyengar, Vik. "*Melissa Etheridge.*" *All Music Guide.* http://allmusic.com/album/melissa-etheridge-r6881/review. Accessed October 17, 2012.

Jones-Zimmerman, Melanie. "Our Song of Freedom." *Lesbian News,* April 2005, 27.
The author praises Etheridge for her performance at the 47th Grammy Awards, because the musician's appearance after a successful battle with breast cancer could "make a huge, huge difference in the lesbian healthcare world."

Jurek, Thom. "*4th Street Feeling.*" *All Music Guide.* http://www.allmusic.com/album/4th-street-feeling-mw0002409917. Accessed January 24, 2013.

K., M. " 'Fearless Love.' " *Rolling Stone,* March 4, 2010, 65.
A brief favorable review of the single "Fearless Love."

Katz, Dian. "Soul 2 Soul with Melissa Etheridge." *Lesbian News,* March 2006, 26–27.
The author and Etheridge discuss Etheridge's recovery from breast cancer—especially the benefits of humor—and her development as a musician and her future plans.

Kelly, Christina. "Melissa Etheridge." *Rolling Stone,* November 13, 1997, 159.
In this brief profile and interview, Etheridge mentions—among other things—that her recent songwriting has been affected by her motherhood, focusing more on "the social" than "the sexual."

Kennedy, Dana. "The Unplugged Melissa Etheridge." *Entertainment Weekly,* March 17, 1995, 42ff.
An interview with Etheridge on the occasion of her *MTV Unplugged* performance.

Keveney, Bill. "Stars Line up for 'Stand Up.' " *USA Today,* September 8, 2008, 3d.
Melissa Etheridge's scheduled performance at the Stand Up to Cancer benefit is mentioned in this article about the event.

Kizer, Jennifer Graham. "Melissa Etheridge's Green Makeover." *Health* 22 (April 2008): 180.
A report on Etheridge's growing sense of environmental awareness in the wake of her battle against cancer.

Knopper, Steve. "Etheridge Back on Track." *Rolling Stone,* November 3, 2005, 3.
A report on Etheridge's activities since being declared cancer-free. According to the article, Etheridge's greatest hits collection, *The Road Less Traveled,* debuted on the *Billboard* charts at No. 14.

Kornblum, Janet. "Etheridge Rediscovers Love." *USA Today,* September 21, 2005, 1d.
This feature article includes information on Etheridge's breakup with Julie Cypher, her new relationship with Tammy Lynn Michaels, her battle with cancer, and her first postcancer performances.

Kort, Michele. "40 Heroes." *The Advocate,* September 25, 2007, 49–71.

The author provides a brief profile of Etheridge, who was ranked at No. 5 on this list of 40 heroes of the gay, lesbian, bisexual, transgendered community.

Laird, Joan. "Gender in Lesbian Relationships: Cultural, Feminists, and Constructionist Reflections." *Journal of Marital & Family Therapy* 26, no. 4 (October 2000): 455–68.

Loftus, Johnny. "*Never Enough.*" *All Music Guide.* http://www.allmusic.com/album/never-enough-mw0000275946. Accessed December 28, 2012.

M., C. " 'Fearless Love.' " *Billboard*, January 30, 2010, 33.
According to this review of the single "Fearless Love," "the song's updated, high-gloss rock sound may take some getting used to . . . but the strong delivery is classic Etheridge."

Manning, Kara. "Election Watch." *Rolling Stone*, August 20, 1992, 23.
Etheridge's support of California congresswoman Barbara Boxer is mentioned in this article.

Mantilla, Karla. "Melissa Etheridge and Lesbian Sexuality: The Hunger." *Off Our Backs* 29 (December 1999): 8–9.
The author discusses the realism and sensitivity of Etheridge's portrayal of lesbian sexuality in her songs.

Martin, Dale B. "Heterosexism and the Interpretation of Romans 1:18–2." *Biblical Interpretation* 3 (1995): 332–55.

Marty, Martin E. "Me, My Church and I." *Christian Century* 122 (January 25, 2005): 47.
The author dissects Etheridge's views on religion and spirituality and describes Etheridge's views and beliefs as "narcissistic" and lacking in "gifts of grace."

McCormick, Moira. "Esralew's Audio, Video, Software Releases Show the Kids Count." *Billboard*, September 14, 1996, 71.
Etheridge's appearance on the television program *Sesame Street* performing a parody of her song "Like the Way I Do" is mentioned.

McKnight, Connor. " 'The Wanting of You.' " *Billboard* 122, July 17, 2010, 37.
The writer compares the single "The Wanting of You" as an "anthemic dose of full-tilt American rock," with influences of Bruce Springsteen, Rod Stewart, Meat Loaf, and Coldplay.

McRuer, Robert. "Compulsory Able-Bodiedness and Queer/Disabled Existence." In *The Routledge Queer Studies Reader*, edited by Donald E. Hall, Annamarie Jagose, with Andrea Bebell and Susan Potter, 488–97. London: Routledge, 2013.

"Melissa Etheridge." *Current Biography* 56 (May 1995): 26–29.

"Melissa Etheridge—Awards." *All Music Guide.* http://www.allmusic.com/artist/melissa-etheridge-mn0000345355/awards, 2012.

"Melissa on the Awakening." *Lesbian News*, September 2007, 17.
This article presents a favorable review of *The Awakening*.

Miles, Sara. "Mommy Melissa." *The Advocate*, June 22, 1999, 44–51.
   A feature-length profile of Etheridge, her political and social views, and her role as a gay parent.

Morris, Bonnie J. "Melissa Etheridge: Hitched, Happy, and on Tour." *The Lesbian and Gay Review* 11 (March/April 2004): 30–31.
   Morris and Etheridge discuss the latter's concern with the U.S. government's treatment of 9/11 hero Mark Bingham because of his sexual orientation, Etheridge's marriage to Tammy Lynn Michaels, and the songs on Etheridge's album *Lucky*.

Morthland, John. Liner notes to *Sounds of the Seventies: 1970.* Compact disc. Time-Life Music SOO-01, 1989.

Newman, Melinda. "The Beat." *Billboard*, September 28, 2002, 12.
   A detailed report on the marketing and distribution of Etheridge's DVD, *Melissa Etheridge Live . . . and Alone.*

Newman, Melinda. "Brooks, Lang on Bill for Human Rights Campaign Concert; Goldmark, Jive in Talks." *Billboard*, February 12, 2000, 12.
   Etheridge's participation in Equality Rocks is included in this article about the concert for the Human Rights Campaign Foundation.

Newman, Melinda. "Island Targeting Etheridge Abroad." *Billboard*, October 14, 1995, 1.
   Newman reports that Island Records has planned to market Etheridge's *Your Little Secret* internationally, a first for the singer-songwriter.

Newman, Melinda. "Melissa Etheridge to Soar with the Eagles." *Billboard*, April 16, 1994, 14.
   A brief report on the choice of Etheridge to open for the Eagles on their 1994 summer tour.

Newman, Melinda. "Survivor's Tale." *Performing Songwriter*, September/October 2007, 56–62.
   A feature article in which Etheridge discusses her songwriter styles and procedures.

Newman, Melinda. "Webb Brothers, Austin, Etheridge Serve up New Tunes for the Summer." *Billboard*, June 23, 2001, 13.
   In this brief review of *Skin*, the author concludes that the album's best songs are those "where Etheridge uses a velvet glove rather than a hammer to make her point."

Ocamb, Karen. "Melissa Etheridge: Lucky in Love." *Lesbian News*, February 2004, 24–25.
   An interview in which Etheridge discusses her legal difficulties in ending her relationship with Julie Cypher, her recent marriage to Tammy Lynn Michaels, and the story behind several of her songs, including "Tuesday Morning," her tribute to Flight 93 hero Mark Bingham.

Ocamb, Karen. "Melissa Etheridge Sheds Her Skin." *Lesbian News*, July 2001, 30–31.
   Etheridge discusses her breakup with Julie Cypher, her new relationship with Tammy Lynn Michaels, and the sexual abuse she endured as a child at the hands of her sister in this feature article on the artist's personal life.

Paoletta, Michael. "*Lucky.*" *Billboard*, February 21, 2004, 37.
   The author describes *Lucky* as the antithesis of *Skin*. According to the review, the first single release from the album, "Breathe," which was not composed by Etheridge, "fails to ignite in the same way that past hits … did."

Paoletta, Michael. "Outside The (Big) Box." *Billboard*, August 25, 2007, 11.
   This article cites Island Records' marketing of Melissa Etheridge's *The Awakening* in 1,500 Safeway supermarkets as an example of nontraditional marketing of music-related products.

Paoletta, Michael. "Spotlight." *Billboard*, July 21, 2001, 20.
   A largely favorable review of *Skin*. The reviewer wonders, however, if Etheridge's work might be more effective if her songs were more universal and less intensely autobiographical.

Pareles, Jon. "She's Pleading for Love While It's Raining Flowers." *New York Times*, August 16, 2001, 5.
   A largely favorable review of Etheridge's solo performance at New York's City Center.

Pareles, Jon. "A Strong Voice on Nuances of Love." *New York Times*, March 2, 1994, 19.
   A favorable review of a performance by Etheridge at New York's Irving Plaza.

Penn, Denise. "Melissa Etheridge: Looking Back and Forging Ahead." *Lesbian News*, August 2009, 22–25.
   Penn and Etheridge discuss Etheridge's experiences as a gay activist in the wake of her coming out in the mid-1990s, as well as Etheridge's battle with breast cancer.

Perone, James E. "Melissa Etheridge: *Melissa Etheridge*." *The Album: A Guide to Pop Music's Most Provocative, Influential, and Important Creations*. Santa Barbara, CA: Praeger, 2012, 3: 319–22.

Perone, James E. "Melissa Etheridge: *Yes I Am*." *The Album: A Guide to Pop Music's Most Provocative, Influential, and Important Creations*. Santa Barbara, CA: Praeger, 2012, 4: 51–56.

Powers, Ann. "Rock Review: Where Sensuality and Solidarity Meet." *New York Times*, October 28, 1999, 1.
   A review of an Etheridge performance at the Theater at Madison Square Garden.

Powers, Ann, and Walters, Barry. "Recordings." *Rolling Stone*, October 28, 1999, 99ff.
   This article contains a favorable review of the album *Breakdown*.

Presley, Lisa Marie. "Melissa Etheridge." *Time*, April 18, 2005, 88.
   A brief article in which Presley recounts that the first time that she ever sang in front of another person as an adult was when she "belted out" Etheridge's "Similar Features."

Price, Deborah Evans. "A Scruggs Cut-by-Cut." *Billboard*, September 1, 2001, 36.
   The author offers the observations of Louise Scruggs on the recording of the album *Earl Scruggs & Friends*. According to Louise Scruggs, Melissa Etheridge

performed a second take of the song "The Angels" on her own initiative. Her vocal performances were greeted by "a standing ovation" from the assembled musicians.

Puterbaugh, Parke. "Melissa Etheridge: *Lucky.*" *Rolling Stone*, March 4, 2004, 66.
A brief, generally favorable review of *Lucky*.

Reighley, Kurt B. "Hip Hymns." *The Advocate*, December 16, 2008, 68.
This article contains a brief review of *A New Thought for Christmas*.

Rich, Adrienne. "Compulsory Heterosexuality and Lesbian Existence." In *Powers of Desire: The Politics of Sexuality*, edited by Ed Ann Snitow, Christine Stansell, and Sharon Thompson, 177–205. New York: Monthly Review, 1983.

Rizzo, Monica. "Spotlight on … Melissa Etheridge." *People*, November 1, 1999, 53.
A brief profile of Etheridge on the occasion of the release of *Breakdown*.

"Rocker Melissa Etheridge, Who Is Both Acoustic and Electrifying." *People*, May 15, 1989, 163.
A brief profile of Etheridge in the wake of her debut album.

Rule, Doug. "Passionate Feeling." *Metro Weekly*, January 20, 2012. http://www.metroweekly.com/arts_entertainment/music.php?ak=7749. Accessed June 3, 2013.
A brief favorable review of Etheridge's *4th Street Feeling*.

Schweiger, Larry J. "I, Too, Need to Wake Up." *National Wildlife*, December 2006/January 2007, 9.
In this opinion piece, the author discusses the importance of Etheridge's song "I Need to Wake Up," comparing it with Joni Mitchell's classic of environmentalism, "Big Yellow Taxi."

Shannon, Jeff, "*Melissa Etheridge Live … and Alone.*" Amazon.com. http://www.amazon.com/Melissa-Etheridge-Live-Two-Disc-Edition/dp/B00006MFPL/ref=sr_1_fkmr0_1?ie=UTF8&qid=1359142270&sr=8-1-fkmr0&keywords=Melissa+Etheridge+Live%C2%85And+Alone. Accessed January 25, 2013.
A highly favorable review of Etheridge's live DVD.

Skaggs, Austin. "Melissa Etheridge Rocks Harder than Ever on Zep-Inspired Disc." *Rolling Stone*, May 13, 2010, 28.
A brief interview with Etheridge on the occasion of the release of *Fearless Love*.

Smith, Kerry L. "*Skin.*" *All Music Guide*. http://www.allmusic.com/album/skin-mw0000003903. Accessed January 21, 2013.
A generally favorable review of the "perfect breakup album."

Smith, Kyle. "Picks & Pans: Song." *Entertainment Weekly*, July 16, 2001, 353.
A generally favorable review of the "raw and revealing" album *Skin*.

Song, Sora. "Q&A: Melissa Etheridge." *Time*, October 10, 2005, 71.
Song and Etheridge discuss Etheridge's new greatest hits album, Etheridge's same-sex marriage, and her displeasure with the conservative politics of California governor Arnold Schwarzenegger in this brief interview.

Spodarek, Diane. "Melissa Etheridge." *Off Our Backs*, July 1996, 13.
  The author praises Etheridge's sensitive portrayal of a lesbian relationship in the video for the song "I Want to Come Over."

Steele, Bruce C. "Melissa & Tammy." *The Advocate*, January 20, 2004, 50–64.
  In this feature-length article, Etheridge and Tammy Lynn Michaels discuss their wedding, their relationship, the challenges of growing up gay, their experiences with psychotherapy, Michaels's work as an actor and author of children's books, and other topics.

Stein, Joel. "Q&A Melissa Etheridge." *Time*, October 25, 1999, 131.
  Stein and Etheridge discuss the behavior of Etheridge's fans at concerts (they throw bras at her), the paternity of her children, the high visibility of songs from the album *Breakdown* on VH1, and other topics in this brief interview.

Stein, Rachel. " 'The Place, Promised, That Has Not Yet Been': The Nature of Dislocation and Desire in Adrienne Rich's *Your Native Land/Your Life* and Minnie Bruce Pratt's *Crime against Nature*." In *Queer Ecologies: Sex, Nature, Politics, Desire*, edited by Catriona Mortimer-Sandilands and Bruce Erickson, 285–308. Bloomington: Indiana University Press, 2010.

Strauss, Neil. "The Pop Life." *New York Times*, December 14, 1994, 20.
  The author details Etheridge's concert tour.

Taylor, Chuck. "I Need to Wake Up." *Billboard*, April 14, 2007, 38.
  According to this brief review of the single "I Need to Wake Up," "Etheridge sings with symbolic conviction."

Taylor, Chuck. "Message to Myself." *Billboard*, August 4, 2007, 42.
  Taylor refers to Etheridge's "Message to Myself" as "her best song of the decade."

Taylor, Chuck. "Singles: Pop." *Billboard*, June 23, 2001, 24.
  Included is a favorable review of the "spirited" song "I Want to Be in Love."

Taylor, Chuck. "Spotlights." *Billboard*, December 15, 2001, 25.
  The author laments the fact that female singer-songwriters such as Etheridge are having difficulty making the kind of commercial impact that they made in the 1990s, particularly since Etheridge's *Skin* is "the most emotive collection of her career."

Titus, Christa L. " 'I Run for Life.' " *Billboard*, November 12, 2005, 37.
  According to this review of the single "I Run for Life," Etheridge's vocal performance provides "hope and determination."

Titus, Christa L. " 'This Moment.' " *Billboard*, June 12, 2004, 35.
  According to this favorable review of the single "This Moment," the song "is likely to become a new anthem at proms, graduation parties and wedding celebrations."

Townsley, Jeramy. "Paul, the Goddess Religions, and Queer Sects: Romans 1:23–28." *Journal of Biblical Literature* 130, no. 4 (2011): 707–28.

Verna, Paul. "Album Reviews: Pop." *Billboard*, December 2, 1995, 81.
  This article includes a brief, but highly favorable review of *Your Little Secret*.

Verna, Paul, and Chris Morris. "Album Reviews: Pop." *Billboard*, October 2, 1993, 74. Etheridge's *Yes I Am* is among those albums reviewed.

Vozick-Levinson, Simon. "*The Awakening.*" *Entertainment Weekly*, September 28, 2007, 106.
While this generally is a favorable review of *The Awakening*, the writer finds that "the first few tracks find Etheridge wasting her ... voice on bland lyrics and arrangements."

W. B. "*Fearless Love.*" *Rolling Stone*, April 29, 2010, 102. A brief, generally favorable review of *Fearless Love*, which receives three and one-half stars.
The reviewer lists the "key tracks" as "Miss California," "Fearless Love," and "Indiana."

Walters, Barry. "Tammy's Tunes." *The Advocate*, October 13, 1998, 89.
A brief review of tribute recordings of songs associated with Tammy Wynette, in which Etheridge's performance of "Apartment #9" is described as "convincing."

Watrous, Peter. "Pop Review: Singing of Love Universal." *New York Times*, June 19, 1995, 12.
A favorable review of Etheridge's June 1995 performance at the Brendan Byrne Arena, East Rutherford, New Jersey.

Whitburn, Joel. *Joel Whitburn Presents Billboard's Top Pop Singles, 1955–2010.* 13th ed. Menomonee Falls, WI: Record Research, 2011.

Whitburn, Joel. *Joel Whitburn Presents the Billboard Albums (Billboard Albums: Includes Every Album That Made the Billboard).* 6th ed. Menomonee Falls, WI: Record Research 2007.

Willman, Chris. "Ace of Abasement." *Entertainment Weekly*, November 17, 1995, 76–77.
Willman finds *Your Little Secret* to be a continuation of Etheridge's previous work of emotional upheaval. Despite an increasing touch of singer-songwriter sensitivity, the album points "in just one direction: the next meeting of Overstaters Anonymous."

Winters, Rebecca. "Not Second String." *Time*, May 6, 2002, 20.
This article on signature model guitars named for famous female artists includes information on Ovation's Melissa Etheridge six-string guitar.

Wood, Mikael. "*Fearless Love.*" *Billboard*, May 15, 2010, 59.
A generally favorable review of *Fearless Love*.

Young, Laura DeHart. "*The Truth Is ... My Life in Love and Music.*" *Lambda Book Report* 10 (September 2001): 13.
A highly favorable review of Etheridge's autobiography.

Zappa, Frank, with Peter Occhiogrosso. *The Real Frank Zappa Book.* New York: Poseidon Press, 1989, 188.
The famed rock composer-guitarist Zappa discusses the importance of orchestration, arrangement, and recording production in influencing listeners' understanding of the content of a rock song.

Index

Adam, Adolphe, 95–96
Ahmad, Salman, 93
"Ain't It Heavy," 19
"All American Girl," 30
"All There Is," 79
"All the Way to Heaven," 37, 38
"All We Can Really Do," 83–84
"Angels, The," 13–14
"Angels Would Fall," 43
Armatrading, Joan, 61
Azanoff, Kenny, 67

"Be Real," 111–12
"Beating of Your Heart, The," 116
"Beloved," 50
Berklee College of Music, 1, 2
Big Brother and the Holding Company,
   87. *See also* Joplin, Janis
Bingham, Mark, 69
Blackwell, Chris, 2, 6, 10
"Blue Christmas," 92
Booker, Steve, 112
"Boy Feels Strange, The," 22–23
"Brave and Crazy," 12, 15
"Breakdown," 42–43
"Breathe," 66

"Bring Me Some Water," 8, 10, 11
Browne, Mark, 34
Bush, George W., 89
Bushnell, Paul, 67

"California," 79–80
"Change," 34, 38
"Change the World," 116
"Cherry Avenue," 49–50
"Christmas (Baby Please Come
   Home)," 92–93
"Christmas in America," 94–95
"Chrome Plated Heart," 7
Cocker, Joe, 65–66
Cole, David, 53, 54–55, 57, 63, 71,
   81–84
"Come on Out Tonight," 71
"Come to My Window," 29–30
"Company," 99
Crosby, David, 27
Cypher, Julie, 27, 45, 51, 52, 53, 55, 58,
   82–83

"Dance without Sleeping," 19, 20–21
Difranco, Ani, 61
"Disaster, A," 112

"Don't You Need," 8
"Down to One," 55
"Drag Me Away," 100–101, 104–5
Dylan, Bob, 56

Eagles, The, 80
Edwards, Elizabeth, 91
"Enough of Me," 44–45
"Enough Rain," 113–14
Etheridge, Jennifer (sister of Melissa
    Etheridge), 1, 45
Etheridge, John (father of Melissa
    Etheridge), 25, 32
Etheridge, Melissa, approach to musical
    structure, 37, 45–46, 47, 56, 68, 76,
    80–81, 84–85, 94–95, 115, 120; as
    victim of abuse, 1, 58–59; awards
    presented to, 2, 19, 30, 41, 52, 91;
    breast cancer, 52, 61–62, 75, 77, 101,
    114; gender neutrality in the lyrics of,
    10, 16, 34, 43, 58, 124–26;
    incorporation of hip-hop style, 22, 43,
    55, 71; lyrics and internalized sexual
    stigma, 9, 14, 36, 57, 84–85, 99,
    121–24; musical similarities to other
    artists, 5, 6, 8, 10, 11, 17, 19, 21, 23,
    33–34, 43, 44, 46, 48, 49–50, 56,
    65–66, 68–69, 73–74, 76, 79–80,
    87–88, 99, 102; references to sexual
    identity in the songs of, 15, 16,
    33–34, 37–39, 46–47, 70; social
    commentary in the songs of, 20,
    29–30, 37–38, 39, 69–70, 77–79,
    82–83, 86–87, 88–89, 94–95, 114,
    116; ties to acoustic singer-songwriter
    music, 14, 21, 38, 125; ties to classic
    rock style, 17, 19, 99; ties to grunge
    music, 8, 12, 16–17, 28–29; ties to
    roots music, 7, 56, 106–7; use of
    preexisting materials in the songs of,
    13, 14, 42–43, 89–90, 92, 95–96, 103

"Falling Up," 109
"Fearless Love," 97–98, 123–24
"4th Street Feeling," 108–9

Gaines, Jim, 2, 6
"Gently We Row," 105

"Giant," 70
"Glorious," 92
"God Is in the People," 82, 103
"Goodnight," 55–56
Gore, Al, 78, 91

"Have Yourself a Merry Little
    Christmas," 93
"Heal Me," 57–58
"Heaven on Earth," 102–3
"Heroes and Friends," 86
Hogarth, Ross, 69–70
"How Would I Know," 48

"I Can Wait," 114–15
"I Could Have Been You," 34, 37–38
"If I Wanted To," 29
"If You Want To," 66
"Imagine That," 88–89
"I'm the Only One," 28–29
Inconvenient Truth, An, 2, 3, 78
"Indiana," 101–2, 105
"I Need to Wake Up," 77–78
"Into the Dark," 44
"I Really Like You," 34
"I Run for Life," 75–76, 77
Island/Def Jam Records, 2, 5
"It's Only Me," 56
"I've Loved You Before," 84–85
"I Want to Be in Love," 56–57
"I Want to Come Over," 34–36, 121
"I Want You," 10
"I Will Never Be the Same," 30–31

Jaffee, Rami, 72
Joplin, Janis, 5, 9–10, 40–41, 74–75, 87
Jordan, June, 103

"Kansas City," 107–8
"Keep It Precious," 23
King, Jacquire, 110, 111
"Kingdom of Heaven, The," 86–87
"Kiss Me," 71–72

"Late September Dogs, The," 8
Lennon, John, 48
Leopold, Bill, 2
"Let Me Go," 14–15

"Letting Go, The," 24
Lewak, Mauricio Fritz, 20, 23, 24
Lewis, Juliette, 29–30
"Light a Light," 95
"Like the Way I Do," 7–8, 41
"Lover Please," 53–54
"Lucky," 63–64, 65

Maines, Natalie, 89
"Mama I'm Strange," 46
"Map of the Stars," 82–83
McCormick, Kevin, 19, 20, 23, 24, 42
"Meet Me in the Back," 22
"Meet Me in the Dark," 68–69
Mellencamp, John, 6
"Merry Christmas Baby," 94
"Message to Myself," 81
Michaels, Tammy Lynn, 62, 65, 66–67,
    72, 85–86, 90, 100, 111, 124
"Miss California," 100
Muhoberac, Jamie, 67
Mulroney, Dermot, 21
"Must Be Crazy for Me," 21–22
"My Back Door," 15–16
"My Lover," 48

"Nervous," 102
"No Souvenirs, 11–12
"Nowhere to Go," 34, 35

"Occasionally," 8–9
"O Holy Night," 95–96
"O Night Divine," 95–96
"Only Love," 104
"Open Your Mind," 87–88

Padgham, Hugh, 28, 37, 42
Petty, Tom, and the Heartbreakers,
    73–74
"Piece of My Heart," 40–41, 74–75
"Place Your Heart," 21
"Please Forgive Me," 57
"Precious Pain," 8
Prince, 20, 49–50
"Prison, The," 54

Rae, Zac, 113
Raitt, Bonnie, 17

"Refugee," 73–74
"Resist," 31
"Ring the Bells," 93
"Rock and Roll Me," 114–15
Rolling Stones, The, 19, 102
"Royal Station 4/16," 17
"Ruins," 31

"Sacred Heart, A," 114
Sayce, Philip, 80, 92, 93, 95
"Scarecrow," 46–47
"Secret Agent," 67–68
Seger, Bob, 6
"Shadow of a Black Crow, The," 110–11
Shanks, John, 34, 42, 46, 64, 66, 67, 97
Shepard, Matthew, 46–47
"Shout Now," 110
"Shriner's Park," 34, 38
"Silent Legacy," 30
"Similar Features," 6–7, 11, 74
Simon, Paul, 49
Simons, Brett, 111, 113
"Simple Love, A," 85–86
Sinta, Blair, 113
"Skin Deep," 17
"Sleep," 48
Springsteen, Bruce, 6, 11
"Stronger than Me," 44
"Sympathy," 113–14

"Talking to My Angel," 32
Taylor, James, 21
Taylor, Jonathan, 67, 69
"Testify," 14, 16
"This Moment," 64–66, 101
"This War Is Over," 39, 40
"Threesome," 83
Thurston, Scott, 23
"To Be Loved," 104–5
"Touch and Go," 49
Truth Is . . . My Life in Love and Music,
    The, 58–59
"Truth of the Heart," 45–46
"Tuesday Morning," 69–70
"2001," 19–20

"Unexpected Rain, An," 80
"Universe Listened, The," 88

"Unusual Kiss, An," 34, 35, 36, 38
U2, 23, 49, 65, 97

"Walking on Water," 54–55
Wallem, Linda, 107, 117
"Wanting of You, The," 98–99
"Watching You," 9
"We Are the Ones," 103
"Weakness in Me, The," 61
Weeds, 5
"What Happens Tomorrow," 89–90

"When You Find the One," 72
"Will You Still Love Me," 68
"With a Little Help from My Friends,"
   65–66

"Yes I Am," 31, 53
"You Can Sleep While I Drive," 14
"You Used to Love to Dance,"
   12–13, 21
"You Will," 115–16
"Your Little Secret," 33–34

About the Author

JAMES E. PERONE, PhD, is the Margaret Morgan Ramsey Professor in Music at the University of Mount Union, Alliance, Ohio. He earned his BM in music education from Capital University, and he earned his MFA in clarinet performance, MA in music theory, and PhD in music theory from the State University of New York at Buffalo. Jim is the author of several other titles for Praeger Publishers, including *The Words and Music of Prince*, *Music of the Counterculture Era*, and *The Words and Music of Carole King*.